TO

the Men and Women of Goodwill

in Management and Labor

Whose Cooperative, Constructive Work

Built the Meat Industry

CONTENTS

ILLUSTRATIONS

PREFACE

THIS BOOK originated in a suggestion made to me in the fall of 1945 by Patrick E. Gorman, secretary-treasurer of the Amalgamated Meat Cutters and Butcher Workmen, AFL. He asked me, after I had given a course on economic problems at the Amalgamated Institute of the School for Workers, University of Wisconsin, if I would do a book on unionism in the meat industry. I answered yes, but proposed that the work should be a study of the whole industry and where unionism played a part in it. Mr. Gorman agreed.

Many books have been written on the economics of various American industries, with, however, little if any mention of unionism. And in recent years many books on specific unions have appeared, but they make only incidental references to the industry, its economic organization and policy, and its management. I know of no book which covers an industry in all its interrelated aspects: economics, management, and unionism within the larger framework of their social performance, significance, and problems.

That is the kind of book I have tried to write in *Meat and Man.* It is, in one sense, an experimental work. My aims, which will become clear in the book itself, may be summed up thus: To study the meat industry, within the complex of general economic organization and its relation to other food industries, with special emphasis on monopoly, unionism, and food policy. Few industries offer as much opportunity for this kind of approach as does the production and distribution of meat products, because of its long history and social importance as a major food industry.

In carrying out those aims I have tried to be objective, with no special pleading and no disregard of facts, but with a conscious regard for the values that promote human welfare. Those values include recognition of the social functions that industry must perform, the contribution that both management and unionism have made to its performance, the need for union-management cooperation for industrial peace and progress in a dynamic liberal democracy, and the urgency of a food policy designed to make the fullest use of available scientific-economic resources for the liberation of mankind from hunger, disease, and sloth.

I have criticized management and unionism where I believe the material calls for criticism. But I have tried to avoid muckraking and one-sided criticism. I have concentrated on the evidence of constructive progress and the need for further progress, whether provided by unionism or management. Finally, I have stressed union-management cooperation because it is so necessary to avoid a knockdown fight in industry and consequent creation of the social turmoil upon which Left and Right totalitarian reaction feeds.

I wish to express my deep appreciation of the aid given me by the Amalgamated Meat Cutters, especially President Earl Jimerson and Secretary-Treasurer Patrick Gorman. Without their cooperation this book would not have been written. The analyses and conclusions are exclusively my own, however, and I alone am responsible for them.

October 13, 1949   LEWIS COREY

MEAT AND MAN

CHAPTER I

INTRODUCTORY:
FOOD, MEAT, AND POLICY

1. SCOPE OF THE FOOD INDUSTRIES

THE MEAT industry and the food industries of which it is a part operate within a larger economic setup. While the economics of the meat industry are a specific operation, and so have their own special problems, they cannot be understood without reference to the larger complex of the food industries as a whole.

All manufactured foods had a value in 1939 of more than $10,-600,000,000. Their value in 1947 was around $20,000,000,000; most of the increase, however, came from inflationary prices. A more accurate measure of expansion is provided by the number of employees in the food industries, which rose from 1,212,000 to 1,440,000.

The production and distribution of food in the United States employs upward of 7,500,000 people, counting those engaged in farming, manufacturing, and selling.

In terms of the value of its output, the meat-packing industry is the most important of the food industries, upon which depend the health and well-being of our people. While packing stands first in value of output, it ranks lower in "value added by manufacture" and in number of employees. This is because around two-thirds of the value of meat products is contributed by the cost of animals supplied by livestock producers. The value of the packing industry's output rose from $3,002,000,000 in 1939 to $8,635,000,000 in 1947, and the number of employees from 229,265 in 1940 to 252,748 in 1947.

BREAKDOWN OF FOOD MANUFACTURES, U.S.A., 1947

Product	Total Value of Product	Value Added by Manufacture	Number of Employees
Meat	$8,860,715,000	$1,045,155,000	230,062
Dairy	5,364,749,000	1,225,575,000	207,669
Canned foods	2,469,424,000	916,621,000	201,627
Grain-mill	5,226,736,000	1,001,692,000	113,217
Bakery	2,416,891,000	1,100,836,000	233,310
All foods	(not available)	9,022,000,000	1,440,000

EMPLOYMENT COMPARISON, THREE LARGEST INDUSTRIES

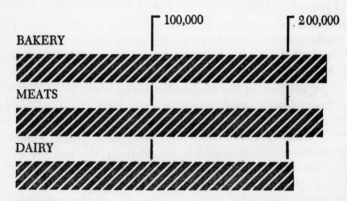

Source: U.S. Department of Commerce, Bureau of the Census. These figures are from the preliminary reports of the 1947 Census of Manufactures. The relative ranking of the food industries did not change from that of 1939.

"Canned foods" includes preserved foods. The grand total of "All Foods" includes sugar, confectionary and related products, beverages, and miscellaneous food products. "Total Value" means the wholesale prices of foods as sold by manufacturers to distributors.

The various divisions of the food industries have been merging. Integration is a continuous process. Meat packers, for example, produce a number of staple grocery products; manufacturers of packaged foods process increasing amounts of meats; grocery stores sell more and more meat products. Large-scale corporate organizations, including chain stores, have come to play a dominant part in the production and distribution of foods. At the same time cooperatives are emerging as a serious factor, especially in marketing.

These economic changes have been paralleled by changes in food consumption. A writer in 1930 said:

The average diet today includes more milk and dairy products, more sugar, more vegetables, more fruits generally, but fewer apples and fewer breadstuffs than in the 1900's. An estimated decline of 10 per cent in the per capita calorie value of the food consumed has been attributed . . . more particularly to a greater knowledge of food values, which has led to care in the selection of diet.[1]

These consumption changes, expressed in more diversified and nutritional diets, slowed down the production of meat, whose per capita consumption dropped from 160 pounds yearly in the 1900's to 131 pounds in 1929 and 133 pounds in 1939. World War II, which brought a greater output of meat products, ended with a yearly per capita consumption of around 150 pounds. Over the years the consumption of beef fell from an average 74 pounds per capita for 1907–1910 to 55 pounds in 1940; pork consumption increased while that of veal remained stationary, and there was a shift from mutton to lamb.

The changes in meat consumption were neither a result of consumers' whims nor limited to meat and dairy products. They were symptomatic of a revolution in food habits which is still going on, whose further development will influence profoundly the economics of food production and distribution, including that of meat.

Food consumption began to change in the 1880's. Earlier Americans usually had plenty to eat, but their meals were "ill-balanced, ill-cooked, and hastily devoured," [2] with not enough variety. In the fifty years that followed considerable progress was made, especially in the number of foods available and in their purity. By the 1930's so much knowledge had been accumulated by plant physiologists, soil chemists, plant breeders, nutritionists, geneticists, food technicians, and other scientists, research workers, and experts, that in

[1] Inez Pollak, "Food Industries—Introduction," *Encyclopedia of the Social Sciences,* vol. 6 (1931), p. 302.

[2] For an interesting discussion see the chapter, "Foods in the Making of America," in A. M. Schlesinger's *Paths to the Present* (1949).

the next ten years nutritional understanding made amazing progress, ranging from improvements in livestock to greater acre-crop yields and the production of synthetic foods. These developments are bound together by an increasing understanding of the nutritional value of foods—to keep man in good health, to prevent or cure disease, to make old age more satisfyingly alive. Today's food problems are set within a synthesis which provides creative potentials for man's welfare and freedom. Let me sum it up thus:

Available scientific knowledge and technical-economic resources make it possible, for the first time in history, to provide every man, woman, and child with the foods necessary for physical and mental well-being in a health-giving environment of convenience, beauty, and joy.

It is true that, precisely at this moment, danger looms from wastage of soil resources. The danger is all the more serious because, in a majority of nations, social-economic progress (especially in medicine) has increased the number of people faster than it has increased the food supply through modernization of agriculture. Still worse, depleted soils have become more depleted, in most of the world's areas, as population has grown. In the United States millions of acres have been ruined—farm lands for crops, range lands for livestock; and other millions of acres are being ruined. The conservation program, great as are its scope and results, is still striving to catch up with the destruction. And great as is the American problem of renewing the soil's fertility, it is vastly greater in other nations, where teeming populations press pitifully upon diminishing food resources.

Yet despite these dangers, the decisive fact is that they can be overcome. There is no call for the neo-Malthusian gloom that conjures up a world unable to feed all its people. We know how to refertilize depleted soils. We know how to grow more food on an acre of land. We are beginning to make foods in the factory—among them food-yeast, which supplies low-cost meatlike protein. And this factory production of food may become a primary means to end the world's hunger.

The need is world action for soil replenishment, for a speed-up in scientific research to provide new sources of foods or "factory" foods in order to insure an adequate diet for every human being, for a rational population policy. The stakes are greater than the end of malnutrition and starvation, infinitely desirable as this objective is. For our new understanding of food can become a major force to build a world of greater prosperity, happiness, and peace.

2. PROBLEMS OF POLICY: I—MONOPOLY AND PROFITS

In terms of output the American meat industry did a splendid job during World War II. In the four war years 1942–45 the livestock and meat industry produced 5,000,000 carloads of meat and lard. Canned meat output rose from around 400,000,000 pounds yearly to 2,000,000,000 pounds for some of the war years. Great scientific and economic progress was made in dehydrated foods and frozen and pre-packaged foods, among them frozen boneless beef.

Yet the record has some black spots. The meat industry (along with other industries) pursued pretty much of a "sky's the limit" price policy. Its war profits were large, but the packers justified them and explained them away as "an *exceedingly modest return of 1 per cent on sales.*" Wesley Hardenbergh, president of the American Meat Institute, trade association of the packing industry, said:

Misunderstanding arises over the industry's profits. Ours is a large industry, with a tremendous output of $6,000,000,000. On that volume of business even a modest rate of return yields a profit that seems large in the aggregate—and our rate of return is exceedingly modest; too small for the best interests of those whom the industry serves. . . . This small return may be shown by comparison with the profits earned by a retailer or a farmer or anybody else doing a business of $50,000 annually, who would earn, at the same rate of return, a profit for the entire year of only $500.[3]

The comparison limps. Farmers and retailers are direct workers, not absentee stockholders who get dividends out of profits. The "rate of return on sales" for the retailer and farmer must include payments for their work as well as profit; and such payments (in the form of wages and salaries) are excluded in the meat industry's "exceedingly modest return of 1 per cent on sales."

As a matter of fact, the rate of return on sales rose during the war years. In the case of the Big Four and the ten larger Independent packers, the return (after taxes) rose from around one cent on the dollar to an average of around two cents in 1945–47.

[3] Proceedings, 40th Annual Convention, American Meat Institute, *The National Provisioner*, November 10, 1945, p. 118.

Nor is the rate on sales a proper measure of the profitability of an industry. It is part of capitalist economics, one of the progressive aspects, that unit profit and price *should go down.* At the same time the total profit may go up from larger sales—*profit measured as a percentage of return on capital investment or net worth.* This rate of profit may be high with a low rate of return on sales. I shall discuss this subject more fully later on; meanwhile, let me point to one crucial fact: by 1945 *the rate of profit on net worth (investment)* of the Big Four and the ten Independents had risen to 5.7 per cent, *and it doubled in 1946* to a high of 10.8 per cent. This was net profit after the payment of taxes.[4]

The public's stake in the packing industry is not the profits, which go to a small number of stockholders. That stake is in the quality and price of meat products, in the wages paid to wage workers and the salaries paid to lower-salaried employees, in continuous full-capacity production and full employment.

These conclusions flow clearly from the facts in the case. In 1947 an advertisement of Swift & Company said:

It is not the investment of a few rich people that has built Swift & Company, but the pooled savings of 63,365 people. Among them you'll find farmers, ranchers, lawyers, doctors, mechanics, business people— folks from every walk of life. . . . The return for their thriftiness comes to them as dividends paid out of the company's profit. In 1946 that dividend amounted to $1.90 a share.

But the Swift family owned (as of 1937) 5 per cent of the company's shares; their total dividends in 1946 must have been around $600,000. And consider the distribution of the ownership of all Swift shares: 2.5 per cent of the stockholders (individual ownership of 500 shares up) owned 41.5 per cent of the shares; 13.5 per cent of the stockholders owned 31 per cent of the shares; 37.7 per cent of the stockholders owned 21.9 per cent of the shares; and 46.2 per cent, or nearly half of the stockholders, owned only 5.6 per cent of the shares. This group of stockholders owned an average 20 shares of Swift stock, with an average dividend in 1946 of $47.50 —certainly no great stake in Swift profits!

Concentration of stock ownership is not limited to Swift. In the case of Armour & Company, 3 per cent of the stockholders owned

[4] Securities and Exchange Commission (SEC), *Survey of Listed Corporations, Data on Profits and Operations Including Surplus,* 1945–46, Part I, pp. 155-66.

33 per cent of the shares, while 84 per cent owned only 2 per cent of the shares.[5]

Nor is concentration of stock ownership evident in meat packing alone. It is characteristic of American corporate industry. The total number of individual stockholders is, according to a 1948 Federal Reserve Board survey, 5,500,000, no more (out of 60,000,000 Americans gainfully employed). Of these stockholders around 300,000 own upward of 70 per cent of all corporate stock, which means that 5,000,000 or more stockholders receive annual dividends of $200 *down*.

Profits are necessary. They contribute to the capital investment with which to expand the forces of production. But there must be a balance in the relation of profits to wages and salaries, to investment, production, and consumption. If the balance is upset, production and employment, profits and wages, all go down as unused productive capacity mounts, with an eventual crash into cyclical depression.

This problem of profits is connected with that of monopoly. The meat-packing industry is dominated by four giant packers, as similar corporate giants operate in other industrial areas. The whole of industry is dominated by a handful of 1500 monopoly corporations, which, year in and year out, receive 70 per cent of all profits made by all American corporations. I am using "monopoly" to designate an unbalancing concentration of economic power.

Four giants—Armour, Swift, Wilson, and Cudahy—produce and sell more than half the packing industry's output. They have for two generations occupied a dominant position in their industry. The government tried in the 1900's, with several anti-trust actions, to break their power, and failed. It tried again in 1918–20, and failed again. And in 1948 the government brought still another anti-trust suit to break the Big Four packers into smaller competing organizations.

One aspect of the monopoly-and-profit drive is the packing industry's advertising pressure to sell more meat products regardless of other foods needed for nutritious meals. This attitude was criticized by a speaker at the first postwar convention of the American Meat Institute:

[5] Stock ownership figures from TNEC Monograph No. 29, *Distribution of Stock Ownership in 200 Largest Non-Financial Corporations* (1940), pp. 242, 1503.

You, generally speaking, promote meat and meat products. I think that is fine. It is very desirable. I sometimes feel, however, that it would be a little more subtle and a little more effective if the particular interests engaged in handling and marketing animal products were willing *to put more stress on the optimum diet and on the kind of meals the American people ought to eat, and less stress on their particular contribution to those meals.* . . . I believe the milk and poultry and egg and the meat groups in this country should give some rather careful thought to the idea of all of them supporting the kind of meal which people ought to eat, and relying on that concept to pull their products, rather than to put out some advertising copy which I have read, and which a woman doesn't believe anyway, where the point is made that if she doesn't have so many quarts of milk or so many pounds of meat, her family is going to hell. She knows it isn't so.[6]

The advertising emphasis of all food industries, not only of meat packers, is to sell more of their particular foods regardless of where they fit into balanced meals. This attitude is obviously not the best for consumer welfare, despite the work manufacturers are doing to improve the nutritional quality of foods and to develop new foods. It sets cramping limitations on the development of the revolution in nutrition, and it raises important issues of economic organization and policy.

3.   PROBLEMS OF POLICY: II—UNIONISM

Labor unions are as much a part of the economics and policy of industry as are technical-economic organization and management, prices, wages, profits, and markets.

Industrial management, on the whole, has stubbornly fought to stop American workers from organizing into unions. This has been true of the meat industry, especially among the big packers, whose labor relations have been marred by savage industrial disputes. To be sure, understanding and cooperation have increased in recent years. Nevertheless, many elements in management still refuse to recognize union labor as a necessary institutional element in the industry of a truly democratic society, and as a cooperative partner.

A number of speakers at the first postwar convention of the American Meat Institute indulged in undiscriminating criticism of

[6] Proceedings, 40th Annual Convention, American Meat Institute, *The National Provisioner*, November 10, 1945, p. 155.

unions. One speaker blamed high prices on high wages, ignoring the fact that war wages, by and large, rose under pressure of rising prices. The same speaker went on to attack labor unions:

Events of recent years (including "class legislation") have conspired to reduce productive efficiency. Since the enactment of the National Recovery Act in 1933 the organizing efforts of union leaders have been effectively aided and abetted by our government, and organized labor has traditionally and consistently *opposed increased productive efficiency.* . . . The restrictive practices of many labor unions are matters of common knowledge. . . . The great spread of restrictive practices under labor union auspices has been concealed to a large extent. Their effect upon the postwar economy may be profoundly disturbing.[7]

The facts in the case are that restrictive practices are limited to a few unions. The restrictive practices of industry's rulers have a much larger scope and are more effective. In the prosperity years 1923–29 an *unused* productive capacity of 20 per cent existed in American industry. And what can compare with industry's restriction of output in the ten-year depression of the 1930's (it was not union labor that made the economic policy responsible for depression), when more than $250,000,000,000 *more* of goods and services could have been produced if not for depression unemployment? Restrictive practices, whether by management or unions, should meet with equal condemnation.

Moreover, productivity in the meat industry went up during the war, except for a drop in 1942–43 when large numbers of trained workers left the industry to go into the Armed Forces. Using 1939 as the base year, the United States Bureau of Labor Statistics found that productivity in packing (measured in output per man-hour) was around 11 per cent higher in 1945 and 14 per cent higher in 1946.

Today it can be said that union-management cooperation is growing in the meat industry, especially in those areas where the Amalgamated Meat Cutters and Butcher Workmen operate. Howard Greer, for nine years vice-president and general manager of Kingan & Company, independent meat packers, said in an address to a conference of Amalgamated organizers in Chicago, August 29, 1947: "Labor unions are in industry to stay. I challenge the responsibility

[7] Proceedings, 40th Annual Convention, American Meat Institute, *The National Provisioner,* November 10, 1945, pp. 171, 175.

of management as well as the responsibility of labor unions. With both groups working together their mutual problems can be solved much easier." [8]

The Amalgamated works for union-management cooperation, on an equal partner basis, as one functional economic requirement for democratic self-government in industry. This broadens into creative recognition of the larger social framework within which unionism operates. The Amalgamated's director of research and education wrote in 1948:

Intelligent collective bargaining requires a detailed knowledge of the economic, financial, and technological facts of the industry. And because our industry is such a crucial element in the whole economy, very little that we do does not have its repercussions for every nook and cranny of our society. . . . Just as we cannot be intelligent citizens of our community without knowing something of its background and its people, we cannot be intelligent citizens of the union without having some idea of its struggles and achievements, of its structure and philosophy. . . . In a very real sense we are members of our communities—part and parcel of the general public. We know what hurts the community hurts us. [9]

Progressive unionism can make a contribution to management, production, and economic policy. This conclusion is as pertinent for the meat-packing industry as it is for all industry. The interplay of policy, management, and unionism should operate freely and fully to call forth the creative forces in all useful functional groups for the realization of greater economic progress and human welfare. In no industrial area is the need for this cooperation greater than in the food industries.

4. PROBLEMS OF POLICY: III—INTERNATIONAL

The American diet is the most diversified and nutritious in the world. Yet there is still need for greater American understanding of nutritional values and, above all, for more equal consumption of food. In nearly all other nations the food-and-nutrition problem is acute. In normal times at least one-half the world's people are

[8] From a report in *The Butcher Workman,* October 1947, p. 3.

[9] Jack Barbash, "Research and Education in the Amalgamated," *The Butcher Workman,* May 1948, p. 12.

underfed and eat little, if any, meat; unbalanced diets are responsible for disastrous chronic malnutrition and disease.

Americans provided food in generous abundance to relieve postwar starvation in Europe and Asia. American industry—including the packing industry, its management and its unions—supported this policy. Professor A. R. Upgren, economist of the University of Michigan, told the packers in 1945: "We know that peace is not divisible. We know peace requires economic health. . . . Economic progress and strength, therefore, must be promoted everywhere." [10]

And the attitude of the Amalgamated Meat Cutters and Butcher Workmen was thus expressed by its director of research and education: "The union and its members must play an effective role in the labor movement as a whole, in the nation and the world. On the international front the Marshall Plan and its administration will mean much to us as unionists and as citizens." [11]

Peace is not divisible, nor can it be separated from economic progress. World economic cooperation is needed. And food can be a major instrument of policy to promote world peace.

Food can promote peace, however, only if all the elements of world cooperation come alive. American food cannot feed the world, nor can we draw special foods from the world when its agriculture is insufficient to feed its people. The world must multiply food production. This can be done only if a great world effort (in which the United States, through the United Nations, can play a major part) is carried through on an unprecedented scale.

Nor is that all. In specific terms of the meat industry, there is not enough livestock in the world today to provide its people with an American standard of meat consumption, nor is there likely to be. This means the world will have to work hard to increase the meat supply and to find adequate substitutes for meat, whose protein is indispensable for adequate nutrition. In the years ahead, moreover, the United States cannot depend upon imports to offset any deficiency in American meat production. Hence constructive American policy must work to conserve and replenish livestock to insure the future meat supply and to produce any necessary substitutes for it.

[10] Proceedings, 40th Annual Convention, American Meat Institute, *The National Provisioner*, November 10, 1945, p. 112.

[11] Barbash, "Research and Education," *The Butcher Workman*, May 1948, p. 12.

One aspect of the international problem is the imbalance between agriculture and industry. In most of Europe the imbalance comes from an overdevelopment of industry in relation to agriculture (especially in England), so that these European countries depend upon food imports, including meat. The imports may not always be forthcoming. In Asia and Latin America the imbalance is worse: while agriculture is overdeveloped in relation to industry, it is underdeveloped in its productive efficiency and output (especially meat), with resultant surplus populations, low living standards, and malnutrition. The answer is, of course, agricultural modernization and a more intensive development of industry.

Agricultural modernization is complicated, however, by a number of factors. There is, first of all, the persistence of feudal relations in agriculture and feudal capitalism in society. In addition, population in most regions presses upon diminishing land resources for the production of crop-and-livestock foods. The problem is twofold: to bring new lands into cultivation and, especially, to increase the productivity of cultivated lands whose soils have been terribly depleted.

The United Nations recognizes the importance of these problems. Its Food and Agriculture Organization (FAO) was organized to keep the world food and agriculture situation under constant review and to recommend national and international action. An official source puts it thus:

FAO's policy is based on the conviction that consumers can be assured of adequate supplies of food and other farm products, and producers of steady markets at fair prices, only if there is a balanced expansion of the whole world economy. Greater farm production and greater industrial production, especially in the less developed countries, are the two great aims. . . . Governments working through the United Nations and its economic agencies [should] bring about parallel development of industry and trade, and through the Economic and Social Council secure effective integration of all efforts directed toward expansion of the world economy.[12]

The dangers and complexities of the situation can be met, it is clear, only by world understanding, cooperation, and action. This depends on the kind of economic policy that is pursued *within each*

[12] "The Geneva Conference," *FAO Information Service Bulletin,* October 20, 1947, pp. 2-8.

nation—on whether that policy works for or against world cooperation. Of decisive importance in this connection is the United States,
because of its dominant economic position. And national economic
policy in a democratic society is made by the decisions of all useful
functional groups, including farmers, industrial management, and
unions.

* * *

The nature and problems of the meat-packing industry are interrelated with those of other food industries and with society as a
whole. These, in turn, are what they are because of the history that
shaped economic organization and policy, management and unionism, the agricultural setup. In addition, there is a new dimension of
technical-scientific knowledge whose revolutionary influence is now
only in its first phase. Without an understanding of the interplay of
all these factors, we can understand neither packing as an industry
nor its relation to the world in which we live and its future.

CHAPTER II

MEAT HISTORY:
A GLANCE BACKWARD

1. IN ANCIENT TIMES

MEAT has been an important part of civilization since man became man. The development of agriculture and animal husbandry marked decisive advances in civilization. Domestication of cattle, swine, sheep, and goats for food—their flesh and milk—and for skins, began before animals were used to draw plows and chariots and to operate machines. With the appearance of villages and towns and division of labor, the need arose for industrial production and sale of foods. As urban civilizations grew, a "foreign" trade in meat products began, man having learned early how to cure meats by smoking and salting them.

Primitive man ate more meat, in the form of game, than the majority of men after they became civilized. In all ancient civilizations the consumption of meat was limited almost exclusively to an upper-class minority—the top warriors and priests, the rich and the rulers: the aristocracy.

As important as the meat trade was the trade in spices. The people of antiquity knew little about breeding livestock to produce choice cuts of meat; moreover, since their preserving methods were crude, meats consumed in the towns were generally in a bad state. Hence the need for flavory spices to disguise the meat's taste; and the culinary arts were concerned largely with sauces and spices.

These spices were a major import, from Africa and Asia, of the Mediterranean countries.

Meat production and meat consumption among the Romans were typical of conditions in the ancient world. Pork was the most popular Roman meat, especially among the middle class, with salted pork and fish the main imports. Game birds were extensively cultivated as a luxury for the aristocracy, who also loved sturgeon, mullet, and pike.

The Roman aristocrats were enormous eaters, and made a gross ritual of dining. They lay on couches around the banquet table, feasting on one delicacy after another, with swarms of slaves to serve them. After having gorged to the filling-point these charming men and women would retire to the *vomitorium* (required equipment in the more aristocratic houses), where they would gag themselves to throw up their meal, get rid of the fumes of wine, and return to the banquet to start eating all over again.

What Romans wrote about their aristocratic eating habits is revealing. I quote from *The Satyricon* of Petronius Arbiter, who lived in the times of Nero, the description of Trimalchio's feast:

Well! at last we take our places, Alexandrian slave-boys pouring snow water over our hands, and others succeeding them to wash our feet and cleanse our toenails. . . . An attendant at my side poured out wine. . . . Among the hors d'oeuvres stood a little ass of Corinthian bronze with a packsaddle holding olives. . . . On arches built up in the form of miniature bridges were dormice seasoned with honey and poppy-seed. There were sausages, too, smoking hot on a silver grill. . . . Meantime, whilst we are still at the hors d'oeuvres, a dish was brought in with a basket on it, in which lay a wooden hen, her wings outspread as if she were sitting. Instantly a couple of slaves came up and to the sound of lively music began to search the straw, and pulling out a lot of peafowl's eggs one after the other, handed them round to the company. . . . We take our silver spoons, which weighed at least half a pound each, and break the eggs, which were made of paste . . . and found a very fine fat beccafico swimming on yolk of egg flavored with pepper. . . . Suddenly at a signal from the band, the hors d'oeuvres are whisked away by a troupe of slaves, all singing too. . . . Our host ordered a separate table to be assigned to each guest. "In this way," Trimalchio said, "by preventing any crowding, the stinking servants won't make us so hot." Simultaneously there were brought in a number of wine-jars of glass carefully stoppered with plaster. "Well, bumpers then!" said our host.

. . . The oddity of the second course drew the eyes of all. An immense circular tray bore the twelve signs of the zodiac displayed round the circumference, on each of which the arranger had placed a dish of suitable and appropriate viands: on the Ram's-head pease, on the Bull a piece of beef, on the twins fried testicles and kidneys, on the Lion African figs, on the Virgin a sow's haslet, on Libra a balance with a tart in one scale and a cheese-cake in the other, on Scorpio a small sea-fish, on Sagittarius an eye-seeker, on Capricornus a lobster, on Aquarius a wild goose, on Pisces two mullets. In the middle was a sod of green turf cut to shape and supporting a honeycomb. . . . Four fellows ran prancing in, keeping time to the music, and whipped off the top part of the tray. This done, we beheld underneath, on a second tray in fact, stuffed capons, a sow's paps, and as a centerpiece a hare fitted with wings to represent Pegasus. . . . Trimalchio, as pleased as anybody, cried, "Cut!" Instantly the carver advanced, and posturing in time to the music, sliced up the joint with such antics you might have thought him a jockey struggling to pull off a chariot-race to the thunder of the organ. . . . The second course had now been removed . . . succeeded by another huge tray, on which lay a wild boar of the largest size, with a cap on its head, while from the tusks hung two little baskets of woven palm leaves, one full of Syrian dates, the other of Theban. Round it were little piglets of baked sweetmeat. A great bearded fellow drew his hunting knife, made a furious lunge and gashed open the boar's flank, from which there flew out a number of blackbirds. Fowlers with their rods caught the birds. Slaves ran to the baskets that were suspended from the animal's tusks and divided the two kinds of dates in equal proportions among the diners. . . . At the end of this course Trimalchio left the table to relieve himself. . . . Trimalchio re-entered, wiping his brow and scenting his hands. . . . We thank our host for his generous indulgence. But we were only halfway through the elaboration of the meal. With the flourish of music . . . a tray supporting an enormous hog was set on the table. The cook slashed open the animal's belly—out tumbled a lot of sausages and black-puddings. . . . A slave dropped a cup. Trimalchio looked at him and said, "Go at once and kill yourself; you are a careless fellow." . . . A boiled calf was borne in on a silver dish weighing two hundred pounds. A slave carried around a goblet of wine. . . . By this time the lights seemed to burn double, and I thought the whole room looked changed. . . . A fatted hen was set before each guest and goose-eggs. . . . Trimalchio next ordered the dessert to be served—thrushes of pastry, stuffed with raisins and walnuts . . . oysters and scallops, snails on a little gridiron. . . . "Well," said Trimalchio, "let's jump into the bath." . . . After dissipating the fumes of wine by these means, we were next conducted to another dining hall, where Fortunata [Trimalchio's wife] had laid out a dainty banquet of her own, with wine pouring from a wine-skin before our eyes. Trimalchio said, "Let's be jovial, friends, and keep it up till the daylight appears." [1]

Meanwhile the great majority of Romans, the plebeians and the slaves, lived mainly on polenta, a porridge made up of ground corn. Vegetables, usually beans and onions, were sometimes added to the polenta, with now and then a bit of pork.

Governments early were forced, as a matter of public health, to regulate meat production. Animal slaughterhouses were located helter-skelter in crowded city streets, and the blood, offal, and stench that issued from them became a public nuisance. In Rome, by Nero's time, the slaughterhouses had been grouped together in one of the city's most imposing market structures.

The imperial state owned much of Roman industry, including the meat industry. Lands in more remote parts of the Empire were devoted to the raising of livestock and fowl, and to the production of olive oil and wine for transportation to Rome. The majority of workers were slaves. Free craftsmen organized into corporations, or guilds; from free associations these corporations became, in the

[1] I have quoted from the translation used in the Hogarth Press edition of *The Satyricon* (1932). In an introduction to the Modern Library edition, C. K. Scott Moncrieff suggests that Trimalchios are not exactly unknown in the modern age, and recalls "the favorite of James VI, of whom the historian tells us that 'his first favor arose from a most strange and costly feast which he gave the king.' With every fresh advance his magnificence increased, and the sumptuousness of his repasts seemed in the eyes of the world to prove him a man made for the highest fortunes and fit for any rank. As an example of his prodigality and extravagance, Osborne tells us that he cannot forget one of the attendants of the king, who, at a feast made by this monster in excess, 'eat to his single share a whole pye reckoned to my lord at £ 10, being composed of Ambergris, magisterial of pearl, musk,' etc. . . . The company was ushered in to a table covered with the most elegant art in the greatest profusion. While the company was examining and admiring this delicate display, the viands of course grew cold, and unfit for such choice palates. The whole, therefore, called the ante-supper, was suddenly removed, and another supper, quite hot, and forming the exact duplicate of the former, was served in its place. So, in those days as in these, your Trimalchio was ennobled." I might add: during World War II a "Trimalchio" feast given by a money-aristocrat in Washington, and severely criticized by American Communists, was more than matched by a Stalin feast in Moscow, where for five hours rare viands and wines, and plenty of them, moved down the gullets of Russian Communists and foreign diplomats.

later Empire, compulsory organizations formed, approved, and managed by the imperial state, with final control vested in Caesar. The corporations refused membership to slaves, although they might own slaves. Most important were corporations in the imperial mints, mines, and factories, and in the food industries—including that of meat.

The state corporations served not only as a means for the operation, regulation, and control of imperial industries, but also as the mechanism for control over the people. The Empire was a tyrant state to which the "corporate state" of the imitation Caesar, Mussolini, was to bear strong resemblance.

2. BUTCHERS AND THE GUILD ORDER

With the breakdown of the Roman Empire around the fifth century came a collapse of industry and trade. The towns and cities of Western Europe shriveled up, and the self-contained agricultural economy of feudalism rose to dominance.

In the later medieval period trade began to revive and with it came a new growth of towns and cities. By the tenth century the "merchant adventurers," who penetrated into all parts of Europe and Asia to trade, were well on the way to development of a new capitalism and a new class, the bourgeoisie. The Crusades brought Europe into contact with Byzantium, where industry, trade, and the arts still flourished. The exchange was especially influential in developing the trade and wealth of the mercantile city-states of Italy. Venetian, Genoese, and Florentine merchants sent their agents to Byzantium and as far east as China. Spices were a major commodity of trade: "The Italians brought back the spices—cinnamon, ginger, pepper, cardamon, cloves, nutmeg—with which the European had learned to tickle his palate and—more important—to disguise the taste and smell of his stale meat." [2]

As trade and the towns grew so did the crafts, craftsmen, and artisans necessary for the production of goods. The towns needed a growing amount of manufactured goods to sustain their populations, while the merchants needed more goods to carry on their inter-city and international trade.

[2] J. W. Thompson and E. N. Johnson, *An Introduction to Medieval Europe* (1937), p. 565.

As early as the tenth century the merchant guilds were in existence, followed somewhat later by craft guilds. These guilds were free associations, unlike the corporations of the Roman Empire and the surviving corporate organizations in Byzantium, where the "guilds" had become exclusive state instruments for monopoly subjection and control of industry and labor, a kind of "corporate" state. (The church, too, was a Byzantine department of state.) The new European guilds were, on the contrary, free associations that made a considerable contribution to the break-up of feudal tyranny and the development of democracy.

By the thirteenth century the guilds were ascendant in Western Europe, although by no means universal. The Italian city-state of Florence provides one illustration of the guilds' organization and significance. Here merchants and craftsmen were all organized into guilds: merchants and professional people into seven Greater Guilds (*Arti Maggiori*), while fourteen Lesser Guilds (*Arti Minori*) constituted organizations of craftsmen and artisans. The Lesser Guilds were headed by the guild of butchers and cattle dealers (*L'Arte de' Beccai*). The distinction was maintained all through Florentine guild history.

The fact that butchers led the Lesser Guilds testifies to the importance of the meat industry in Florence. It was a profitable business: in 1321 the Butchers' Guild stood fourth in the order of taxes paid by guilds, and in 1472 Florence, a not over-large city, had seventy butcher shops as well as eight large shops where fowl and game were sold. These shops, in addition, sold *mischiasto*, a highly prized delicacy which consisted of dried beef powder imported from Barbary.

The guild regulations were strict. Retail butchers were not allowed to go into partnership with cattle dealers; cattle driven into the city, whether for slaughter or not, underwent strict regulation, which was true also of meat slaughtering and dressing. Heavy fines were imposed on unskillful and untidy workmen, particularly for carelessness in disposing of offal, fish bones, and other wastes.

A "poet of the markets" (today he might be a highly paid composer of advertising jingles) wrote:

And look where'er you will, in spite of jeer and jest,
Are open butchers' stalls with joints quite of the best.

On one side poulterers with many luring words
Sell hares and boars and kids—prey of sportive shepherds,
And pheasants, starlings, pigeons, and all kinds of birds.[3]

In relation to feudal aristocracy the guilds were a progressive democratic force. While a new mercantile aristocracy early arose out of the merchant guilds, the craft guilds remained democratic for some time, foremost among them the butchers' guilds. One writer reports: "In every country in Europe in the Middle Ages 'butchers' played a leading role, not only in the arena of commercial enterprise but in that too of political activity. This pre-eminence was in part due to hereditary antecedents and traits, and in part to effective physical culture." [4]

The limitations of guild democracy were manifest in Florence. The *Popolani,* or merchants, defeated the *Grandi,* or nobles (some of whom became merchants), and excluded them from the city government. Three classes emerged: the *Popolo Potente,* who were the rulers, the *Popolo Grasso* or middle class, and the *Popolo Minuto,* the "little people," composed of members of the Lesser Guilds who had secured the franchise. But below these classes were a majority of the people, the unskilled operatives and laborers who had no civil or economic rights.

The *Potente* oligarchy dominated the Florentine government. The Lesser Guilds struggled for more power and they slowly got it. Most of this new power went to the five intermediate guilds, led by the butchers, whose chief officers began to be invited to deliberations of the officers of the seven Greater Guilds. In 1342 one podesta (chief magistrate), in order to get popular support, placed a butcher at the head of the governing priors and, with him, three merchants and three artisans.

The merchants, craftsmen, and artisans, who struggled for power among themselves, ignored the mass of laborers and oppressed them. These workers were derisively called *Ciompi,* from the wooden shoes they wore while doing carding, washing, and other unskilled tasks. The *Ciompi* worked hard and long for low wages; the masters, they complained, were able to "fix the price of work at their pleasure" and often withheld payments of wages for years. The *Ciompi*

[3] Edgcumbe Staley, *The Guilds of Florence* (1906), p. 449.
[4] Staley, *Guilds of Florence,* p. 297.

were on the side of progressive forces in the great struggles out of which a democratic England later was to emerge.[6]

In England, as in Europe, the butcher guilds were among the foremost in economic and political activity. Nor did butchers despise earthly goods. The records of Colchester give an inventory, at the end of the thirteenth century, of a butcher, one of the town's wealthiest citizens. In addition to instruments of his trade—pickling tubs, meat, fat, corn, barrels, and a cart—this butcher had a trestle table, two silver spoons, a cup, a tablecloth and two towels, a brass cauldron, a brass dish, washing basin and ewer, trivet, an iron candlestick, two beds, two gowns and a mantle, and some cloth and wool. (Butcher workmen today, although not among "the wealthiest," do much better in worldly goods!) And listen to a market cry:

> Cooks to their knaves cried "Hot pies, hot!
> Good pork and geese—go, dine, go!"
> Taverners unto them told the same tale—
> White wine of Oseye, and red wine of Gascoyne,
> Of the Rhine, and of Rochelle, the roast meat to digest.[7]

It is interesting to note that, in medieval and early modern England, the preparation and sale of meat were not an exclusive busi-

---

[6] Wherever guilds operated in Europe they were at first a progressive force. Their decline into reaction came unevenly, in time and country, in accord with the uneven development of capitalism. As late as the 1650's the guilds in Poland, among them the butchers, were still an economic and progressive force. When Sweden invaded Poland, and the Polish nobles betrayed their country for personal place and power, the guildsmen resisted; they expressed a national consciousness that Poland needed for survival and further advance. In his historical novel, *The Deluge* (American edition, 1891, vol. 1, p. 526), Henryk Sienkiewicz writes: "From the townspeople of Warsaw, Kmita [a renegade noble who had repented and determined to organize resistance to the Swedes] heard that they regretted past times, and the good king of the fallen country. The Swedes persecuted them savagely, seized their houses, exacted contributions, imprisoned them. *They said also that the guilds had arms secreted, especially the linen-weavers, the butchers, the furriers, and the powerful guild of tailors;* that they were looking continually for the return of Yan Kazimir, the king, did not lose hope, and with assistance from the outside were ready to attack the Swedes. Hearing this, Kmita did not believe his own ears. It could not find place in his head that men of mean station and rank should exhibit more love for the country and loyalty to their lawful king than nobles, who ought to bring these sentiments into the world with their birth. But it was just the nobles who stood by the Swedes, and the common people who for the greater part wished to resist."

[7] G. G. Coulton, *Medieval Panorama* (1944), pp. 308-310.

had no right of free association and hence no right to organize in guilds. Masters could dismiss laborers, but the laborers could no give notice and quit. Low wages and rising prices finally drove the *Ciompi* to revolt in 1378. Their rebellion was something of a strike but more of an uprising. (Similar uprisings took place in Paris and Ghent in the early 1380's.)

The rebels of Florence swung into action with cries of: "Long live the people! Close the shops and follow us! No more tolls and taxes! Down with the despots!" A new government was set up which granted reduction of taxes, higher state interest on workers' savings, repeal of laws against small debtors, recall of exiled workers, extension of the franchise. In addition, the unskilled operatives and laborers secured the right to organize into guilds. They formed three guilds of operatives. The new guilds had three representatives among the priors in the new municipal government, along with six who represented the Greater and Lesser Guilds. These developments marked the high point of democratic ascendancy in Florence.

Reaction came swiftly. In 1382 the new operatives' guilds were suppressed, and political power was centralized in the Greater Guilds. Early in the fifteenth century a new guild of unskilled operatives and laborers was formed, *L'Arte de' Lavori*, but it was meaningless; the age of the guilds was over. The tyranny of the Medici, who first appeared at the time of the *Ciompi* uprising as supporters of the popular party, subordinated the guilds and the people to oligarchical power.[5]

As the guilds became stronger throughout Europe, the struggle between merchant guilds and craft guilds kept on. The merchants, becoming capitalists, tried to establish a monopoly of political power. But craft guilds frequently secured the right of representation in municipal government; in one case at least, in Liége in 1384, the craft guilds came into complete control of government, with not too happy results.

In England the guilds were not always dominant in municipal politics, although they were a potent force for self-government. Guilds existed in London and other English towns as early as the year 1100. They were limited, harassed, suppressed. After Magna Charta they flourished. The guilds, including craft guilds, grew stronger, as did their influence in town politics; in general the towns

[5] Staley, *Guilds of Florence*, pp. 17-19, 49, 54-56, 165.

ness of guild butchers. Much of the meat supply, except for that of the larger towns, came from baronial estates and monasteries. These lay and religious lords often carried on what might be called "unfair competition" against ordinary butchers.

3. CHANGES IN ECONOMIC POLICY

Though the guilds were progressive when they began to develop under feudalism and for some time after, they finally became a barrier to economic progress because of their restrictive practices.

The guilds' major objectives were: (1) to organize all members of a particular trade, determining conditions of admission and policy; (2) to secure guild control of a trade against "foreigners," that is, people from any other town; this in effect meant a town monopoly for the guild; (3) to maintain "equality" among guild members by regulating trade practices to restrain the more enterprising members; (4) to set up and enforce standards of quality and price for goods and so protect the consumer; (5) to carry on training through an apprentice system.

These practices coalesced to do the preparatory job of building up the modern economic system. They were, however, restrictive almost from the beginning, and abuses kept on growing.

At first the guilds were open to new members. Then restrictions on admission grew increasingly severe; in some cases the guilds tried to make membership hereditary. These monopoly abuses were especially evident in the merchant guilds, whose members became capitalists; but they spread to include craft guilds. The craft guilds excluded from membership the mass of unskilled operatives and laborers; soon they were converted into masters' organizations and, with ruthless government support, journeymen were denied representation in guild assemblies and finally excluded from membership. Journeymen became a class of permanent wage workers, who formed their own journeymen's societies (earliest prototype of the later trade union) and often went on strike.

Price regulation by the guilds did protect the consumer at first, but not for long. In Florence, as early as the thirteenth century, guild prices favored the masters, not the purchasers. As the guilds established their monopoly of the market they set prices at a point to yield the highest profits in a closed market without price competition. This high-price policy was especially adopted by the merchant guilds.

So, too, with guild standards of quality. The rules and the original intentions were good. Records of the German town of Haguenau, for the year 1164, show a guild regulation which provided that a butcher who sold unwholesome meat must be expelled from the guild. And a London chronicle of the early fourteenth century tells of one John Russell, a butcher, who

. . . exposed 37 pigeons for sale, putrid, rotten, stinking, and abominable to the human race, to the scandal, contempt and disgrace of all the City. And the said John Russell says that the pigeons are good and proper for sale to mankind, and he offers to prove the same, etc. And hereupon, two pie-bakers, being sworn to inspect and examine whether the said pigeons are good and proper or not, say upon their oath that the said pigeons are not good or wholesome for mankind, but rather to the corruption of man. Therefore John Russell is to have judgement of the pillory, and the said pigeons are to be burnt beneath the pillory, and the cause of his punishment is to be there proclaimed.[8]

Despite such efforts at punishment, abuses of quality increased until they became almost universal.

The guilds began to stifle the economic progress they had set in motion. They repressed individual initiative, opposed technological improvements, considered doing work faster and with lower costs as injurious to fellow members of the guild, and, in the midst of commercial revolution, insisted on the customary way of doing business.

Then the big merchant capitalists and the state combined to break guild power. The end result of these efforts, however, although they brought considerable progress, was not economic freedom or free enterprise but the still harsher restrictions of the mercantilist state and its big-merchant allies. Chartered companies, for example, were given inclusive monopoly powers. Where the objectives of guild restrictions had been to make work and profit for guildsmen, the restrictive monopoly policy of mercantilism served to build state power for military aggression, as well as to make money for courtiers, the king's favorites, and capitalist merchants.

[8] Coulton, *Medieval Panorama*, pp. 303-304.

It brought centralization of economic and political power in a new absolute statism.[9]

In the 1640's the Puritan revolution in England under Cromwell (many of whose officers and men were butchers) aimed to destroy absolute monarchy and the mercantilist restrictions on free economic enterprise. This revolution did much to prepare the way for economic freedom and democracy. It did not, however, wholly up-root mercantilism, and it did not set up popular democratic government, since the Puritans believed in government by the elect of God.

It was John Lilburne, outstanding spokesman of the Levellers, who set forth a liberal-democratic program in economics and politics. He formulated the political principles later embodied in the American Revolution. He "took the initiative in organizing popular demand for economic relief and, to that end, the reform of government . . . to incorporate the principle of free speech to clear the way for free enterprise."

Lilburne called for implementation of the declaration that "Monopolies of all kinds are against the Fundamental Laws of the Land, and all such restrictions of Trade, do in the consequence destroy not only Liberty but property." He demanded immediate abolition of "all Monopolies whatsoever, and in particular that oppressive Company of Merchant Adventurers, and a free trade restored . . . by which thousands of poor people might be set to work, that are not ready to starve."

Lilburne cited his own experience, his inability to get into business, as evidence of the curbs on free enterprise:

For a Trade, I must either follow it in London, or in some other Corporation [town]: and in another Corporation . . . can I not with industry be suffered to follow a Trade or Merchandizing to get me bread, unless I be a Free man thereof [that is, already established in it]. . . .

So being for the foregoing reasons block'd off from following a Trade any where else but in or about London [I decided] to set up a shop in the City; which I was staved off from, for these Reasons: Because the Court of Aldermen are so oppressive in their government of the City,

[9] There are some interesting parallels, which I shall discuss later, between the mercantilist statism that came after the breakdown of guild restrictive practices and the dangers in the restrictive practices today of monopoly corporations and trade associations.

setting up their own wills, humours, and irrational ridiculous customs above the Law, Reason and their own Charters. . . .

I had thoughts of the Cities Freedom to turn Soap-boyler, being a good trade and most vendible for ready mony, and in it I met with these discouragements; viz. First, That there are new Monopolies upon some of the principall materials that makes them double priced to what they used to be . . . and scarce anything free from Excise that belongs to it, or to the backs and bellies of the men that work it, but the very water. . . .

And therefore last of all I had thoughts . . . to lay out my mony in some adventure for Holland. [But] I found First, A strict Monopoly that none whatsoever shall ship any white cloth for that place but the monopolisers themselves, and Secondly a general monopoly upon woolen commodities whatsoever . . . yea and thereby break the back of new beginners.[10]

It took another hundred and fifty years after Cromwell and Lilburne for mercantilism to give up the ghost in England. The emergence of free enterprise, together with the Industrial Revolution, gave a tremendous stimulus to the development of industry, including meat packing.

4. THE MEAT INDUSTRY GROWS

From the breakdown of the guilds to the Industrial Revolution, which began toward the end of the eighteenth century, there was considerable progress in the meat industry. In particular, improved preservation methods made more general the consumption of cured meats. A minor element in increasing consumption was the easing of religious restrictions on meat eating.

The most significant progress came in the improvement of livestock breeding, especially in England. From the fourteenth century on the English sheep industry (primarily for wool) was outstanding. Many improvements culminated in the early 1800's when Robert Bakewell, a yeoman farmer, changed the coarse, large-boned and slow-maturity sheep into the well-fleshed animal which he called the New Leicester, the ancestor of many of today's famous sheep breeds. About the same time another yeoman farmer, Benjamin Tomkins, began the breeding work which eventually resulted

[10] William Haller and Godfrey Davies, editors, *The Leveller Tracts* (1944), pp. 48, 111, 159, 436-37, 438-40.

in the Hereford, a breed of cattle which thrives on the rangelands of Australia and Texas as well as on the pastures of its native land. Then came the Shorthorn cattle, now found in more climes than any other breed. During these same years a pig was reared which became the forerunner of the Large White, the world's most renowned breed of pig.

Of twenty breeds of cattle of outstanding reputation today, all but three originated in Britain. Hence that country, although a large importer of meat, is the world's leading livestock exporter.

More understanding of feeding developed. It was in the nineteenth century, for example, that breeders and scientists began to study the bad effect on livestock of mineral deficiency in the pastures of practically every agricultural region in the world. This deficiency lowered both the fertility of livestock and the nutritional quality of its meat. The final significance of this mineral deficiency was understood in the twentieth century; today the finest livestock get a sufficiency of minerals in their diet.

Other forms of progress lagged, however. Thus in Paris, up to the year 1818, when the city built model abattoirs, or slaughterhouses, the abattoirs stood forth near the principal streets and avenues; the gutters ran with blood and offal that poisoned the air as they flowed on to the River Seine; while footsore, lamenting, bellowing animals stopped the traffic.

So, too, as late as the 1830's-40's livestock fouled most American cities, including New York, which did not have the excuse of being a frontier town. In addition:

Pigs roamed the streets of New York, feeding on offal, their proletarian owners having notched their ears or branded their hindquarters for purposes of identification. When New York passed an ordinance outlawing this practice, destitute proletarian housewives fought the enforcing officers with brooms, battledores and fingernails. The great depression of 1837 paralyzed even the frontier trading towns of the Mississippi, but struck hardest at the cities of the Eastern seaboard. During these years, which seemingly were blacker than the "trough" years of the 1930 depression, Horace Greeley saw children burrowing in a cellar, "a prey to famine on the one hand and to vermin and cutaneous maladies on the other." [11]

[11] James Rorty and N. Philip Norman, *Tomorrow's Food: The Coming Revolution in Nutrition* (1947), p. 33.

Conditions were not much better in London. The French artist Gustave Doré has left us a searing picture of "the hopelessness of the general aspect" of a street market in Drury Lane, where "the mark of misery seems to be upon every man, woman and child." A visitor is astonished:

"What! You have no district markets in London? People buy their meat and vegetables in these horrible little shops? And, pray, why are the police hustling these wretched fellows who are trying to sell a few more oranges, or another knife, or comb? Remark that tottering old woman with the laces—driven into the road! Look at the customers of that hard-faced street butcher!" [12]

Nor did progress mean provision of more meat for the masses of the people. Adam Smith wrote in the 1770's:

Butcher's-meat, except in the most thriving countries, or where labor is most highly rewarded, makes but an insignificant part of [the worker's] subsistence; poultry makes a still smaller part of it, and game no part of it. In France, and even in Scotland, where labor is somewhat better rewarded than in France, the laboring poor seldom eat butcher's-meat except upon holidays, and other extraordinary occasions.[13]

The great development of the meat industry came after the Industrial Revolution, the spread of the factory system, and the liberating influence of free enterprise. Cities, growing constantly more numerous and larger, called for more and more commercial foods, including meat. The process was speeded up by mechanical inventions, especially by the development of railroads and refrigeration, and by a rapidly growing livestock industry in the rangelands of the United States, Canada, Argentina, and Australia, and on farms, where great improvements in animal husbandry were taking place. Rising standards of living, among workers as well as more prosperous groups, multiplied the amount and variety of foods that people were able to buy. These factors, along with a growing population, increased the demand for meats and gave rise to a larger industry.

[12] Gustave Doré and Blanchard Jerrold, "London: A Pilgrimage," *Harper's Weekly* (Supplement), February 22, 1873.

[13] Adam Smith, *The Wealth of Nations* (Modern Library edition), p. 18.

PER CAPITA CONSUMPTION OF MEAT
(*in pounds*)

Country	1912	1931
Argentina	302	265
Australia	264	188
United States	153	147
Canada	136	148
England	124	138
Germany	116	118
France	106	101
Belgium	86	89

Source: Compiled from statistics of the U.S. Department of Agriculture. The 1912 figures for Argentina and Australia may include waste.

The figures show an uneven development in the world's per capita consumption of meat. Most nations are not represented in the table, for their people consume an almost negligible amount of meat products. Among the industrial nations, too, there is inequality, with the lowest consumption in Belgium and the highest in the United States. These variations represent differences in national prosperity and living standards. In the cases of Argentina and Australia the exceptionally high meat consumption represents eating more meat, because of a plentiful cheap supply, than is needed for balanced diets. This condition is characteristic of "new" nations with great spaces for livestock production but relatively small populations and underdeveloped industry:

Consumption of meats tends to vary with conditions of production and transportation. It is distinctly heaviest in pioneer countries where cattle and sheep are extensively raised for export, as in Argentina, New Zealand and Australia. As new countries pass out of the frontier stage in which grazing is a leading industry, the cattle and sheep industries decline in relative importance, their meats tend to become relatively expensive, and per capita consumption of beef and veal, mutton and lamb tends to decline. This has been true in the United States. On the other hand, pork consumption is commonly light in new countries; and as agriculture becomes more intensive the proportion of pork in the diet tends to rise while other meats tend to decline.[14]

[14] National Bureau of Economic Research, *Recent Economic Changes* (1929), vol. 1, ch. 1, "Consumption and Standards of Living," pp. 34-35. Beef consumption per capita in the United States fell from around seventy pounds in the 1900's to sixty pounds in 1929.

The decline of per capita meat consumption in Australia represented a higher standard of living. So did the Canadian increase, which came from additions of pork to more diversified diets. Argentine meat consumption remained excessively high, due to the prevention of industrial progress by the dominant cattle barons, who opposed industrialization as a threat to their economic and *political* power (as American slave owners did in the South up to the 1860's). Economic diversification is as much a condition for national prosperity as diversified diets are for human health.

It must be remembered that the increase in meat consumption was limited to highly industrial nations and to new nations with great uninhabited spaces like Argentina, Australia, and Canada. For most of Europe (except the Western and Scandinavian nations) the consumption of meat was not much greater than in Adam Smith's century. This was truer, in general, of Latin America (except Argentina) and Asia. For most of the world's people the traditional condition still prevails: meat, as well as many another wholesome food, is not for them but for their masters.

The consumption of meat has grown as capitalism has grown. But a majority of the world's people still live under what are primarily pre-capitalist conditions. They have neither the industry and management nor the unions to develop a large meat industry and to distribute its products among increasingly large numbers of people.

5. A GLIMPSE OF LABOR UNIONS

One of the most important aspects of the meat industry (and of all industry) is the interplay of ownership and management, the workers and unionism.

When journeymen butchers became wage workers they were thrown out of the guilds. The masters, predominantly wealthy capitalists, increased the number of apprentices and the time of their indenture, in order to save on wages. In addition, they further depressed working conditions by the employment of low-paid laborers in preference to craftsmen. A class of "free" workers arose: free in the sense that they worked for themselves in their homes and in petty one-man shops, and sold their products directly to consumers, or they worked for other free craftsmen as skilled workers (e.g., masons, carpenters). They were an independent class, these free workers, and they fought back when the guilds sought to stifle their competition.

The guilds now had become barriers to free enterprise, the free market, *and free labor,* to economic and political progress; while "free" labor became a major support of religious, economic, and political freedom.[15]

Journeymen organized themselves into protective societies, frequently secret organizations; from Germany to France and England these societies bargained for wages and working conditions. Thus it was not the guilds but the journeymen's societies which were the "ancestors" of trade unions. The societies disappeared, but their traditions, if not their actual organizations, survived. They reappeared in the earliest trade unions, many of which were styled "Journeymen's Society of ——," whatever the particular craft might be. Such societies still exist as craft unions in Europe, where meat packing remains predominantly a small-scale industry. The connection between journeymen's societies and trade unions is clearly evident in English labor history:

It was by means of their journeymen's societies that the feltmakers organized a successful strike, or rather a series of strikes, in 1698–99. In 1720 the master tailors obtained an act of Parliament with a view to resisting the collective demands of their journeymen, who to the number of 7,000 and upwards were said to possess an organization. In 1714 the journeymen wheelwrights established a club, and between 1718 and 1734 struck three times for higher wages and shorter hours. . . . By the end of the century the interests of the manual workers had passed with few exceptions to the trade unions.[16]

In the United States, almost from the beginnings of industrial packing in the 1870's, butcher unions made their appearance. At first these unions were local craft or "journeymen" groups, with no

[15] Ralph Roeder, *Catherine de' Medici and the Lost Revolution* (1937), p. 350, writes: "Among the small artisans the Reformation recruited its earliest support. It satisfied, and it organized, their need for dissent; and by a process of sympathetic adaptation the religious was assimilated to the economic revolt. The doctrine of free labor and moral independence went hand in hand. . . . Fraternizing in one faith, associated in professional [craft] solidarity, they were doubly obnoxious to the guilds, and heresy served to focus the jealousy of capital and labor, and to mask it."

[16] George Unwin, *The Guilds and Companies of London* (1908), pp. 348-50.

national organization, contacts, or policy. In 1897 they set up a national organization, the Amalgamated Meat Cutters and Butcher Workmen of North America, chartered by the American Federation of Labor as an industrial union to organize *all* meat workers, from packinghouses to retail stores.

Older literature on the meat-packing industry rarely mentions the Amalgamated union, except perhaps to attack it. And even today the struggle of meat workers to unionize—a long, heartbreaking struggle—is seldom written about. There is much about livestock as the industry's raw material; much about corporate organization, technology and trade associations, prices and profits. The workers appear as "labor force," that is, as the human raw material of industry, and there is discussion of jobs, mechanization, and labor costs. But the meat workers rarely appear *as people* with human needs, sufferings, and aspirations.

When in 1905 Upton Sinclair published a novel, *The Jungle,* it created an international sensation. Sinclair wrote to call attention to the misery of packinghouse workers—their starvation wages; the stinking, hazardous conditions under which they worked, scourged by industrial diseases and accidents; and the obscene slums where they lived. The public was alarmed but for different reasons—it was the revelation of the conditions under which the meats he ate were produced that frightened the consumer and made him speak up about the hazards to his health. Public pressure caused Congress to enact an inspection law to insure the production of pure meat products. That was important and good. But nothing was done about the workers' low wages, the abominable conditions under which they worked and lived; nor about the brass-knuckle tactics used by monopoly packers to crush the Amalgamated union and beat its strikes. The public's stomach responded, not its heart.

Still the packinghouse workers kept on trying to organize and improve conditions. Their strikes were beaten down, their union shrank almost into nothingness. Yet the packinghouse "labor force" *as workers* needed a union to protect and promote their economic interests. They tried again and again, desperately, hopelessly it seemed. Forty years after it began to organize, the Amalgamated became an established, strong union. And around 1940 another union appeared, the United Packinghouse Workers, CIO. Now unionism is as much an institutional element of the packing industry as management.

During the long years between, the union meant disappointment and heartbreak most of the time. But it also meant a human aspiration for freedom, human dignity, and solidarity, expressed in the labor song "Hold the Fort." This song's original, called "hymn from an abattoir" by Lloyd Lewis in his book, *It Takes All Kinds,* was a revivalist song inspired by the signal, "Hold the fort; I am coming," flashed by General Sherman to beleaguered soldiers in a small but bloody Civil War battle. The workers, among them packinghouse workers, picked up the song, gave it new words and meaning, and sent it singing forth in union halls and in strikes (often small but bloody battles). Its upsurging spirit is part of the American worker's heritage:

> *Hold the fort for we are coming,*
> *Union men be strong!*

CHAPTER III

AMERICAN MEAT PACKING:
FROM ECONOMIC DWARFS TO GIANTS

1. FROM PRE-INDUSTRIAL TO INDUSTRIAL PACKING

FROM earliest colonial times the American settlers ate much more meat—and other foods—than most people did in Europe. This was, of course, largely a result of the abundance of land and animals. A contributing factor, however, was the comparative freedom in a new world where the rigid class structures of England, France, and Holland were relaxed. And from earliest colonial times meat packing flourished as an industry.

Packing began in New England early in the 1600's, shortly after the Pilgrims came. Packed meats, primarily cured and smoked pork products, were prepared for consumption by the growing local population.[1] Still more pork was packed in barrels for export: for

[1] An interesting description of early colonial packing appears in *Of the Earth Earthy*, by Marion Nicholl Rawson (1937), pp. 18-20: "The smoke-house was the early butcher shop. . . . 'Be sure your smoke-house is airtight, then make a fire in the pit or in an iron vessel, of good hickory wood. Let it smoke away like I tell you until the ham is sure smoked through and then you'll taste that special flavor that only old hickory can give.' Virginia has spoken. 'You better put your killing in brine for about six weeks; the shoulders and hind quarters for ham, the fat pieces alongside for bacon. The rest you can use for sausage and spareribs and pork chops. You'll have been eating so much beef up to killing time that they'll taste uncommon good if you do 'em right. After they come out of the brine you hang 'em in the smoke-house for about ten days. Each morning you start a fire in the ash kettle down in one corner, cover it well to make a smudge-fire of corn cobs. You got to be sure you build a good smoke, though.' So New England. Naturally these smoke-houses were built

the increasing numbers of ships that plied back and forth from New England ports, for trade with the Southern plantation colonies, and for the important trade with the West Indies. Meat exports to the West Indies paid for the imports of sugar to use in manufacturing rum. New England was noted for this product, which made the fortune of many a merchant capitalist.

Meat packing also spread along the colonial seaboard, mainly for local consumption. And, as a part of the industry, the tanning of hides and the working of leather became a common colonial occupation. All these industrial pursuits were carried on as domestic work or in small shops.

After the American Revolution, and formation of the Federal Union, rapid urbanization made necessary increasing amounts of packed meats for city inhabitants. A new supply came from greater numbers of settlements in the Middle West, where it was cheap to raise hogs and cattle. Cincinnati, whose first packinghouse was established in 1818, became the great packing center, until supplanted by Chicago in the 1860's and after. The biggest packing enterprises were organized by industrial capitalists, among them Samuel Kingan, who operated plants primarily for exports to Europe.

Up to the 1860's meat packing was a small-scale enterprise, not yet industrial. The merchant, not the industrial, capitalist dominated the business. Meat "packers" included commission merchants, provision dealers, commercial farmers, stock raisers, and drovers. A number of packing centers were in existence, including Cincinnati, St. Louis, and Chicago, but a considerable part of meat slaughtering and packing was done in small rural, often temporary, plants by country butchers. In the 1850's and 1860's there were hundreds of "packers" operating in Middle Western states, who carried on business through commission merchants. These merchants bought animals, arranged for slaughtering and packing, and moved the products into trade.

---

of stone or brick as a safeguard against fire. They followed the earlier smoke-closets which were built into many of the houses of the first century, and were connected with the great chimney, and generally on the second floor where they caught the escaping smoke from the hearth below and used it to cure the meats hanging from iron rod and hook. Certainly these must be allowed room among the important industrial structures of the past."

In this pre-industrial packing business the chief product was pork, which remained dominant until the 1870's, when beef began its rapid expansion. Much of the urban meat supply up to the 1870's still came from livestock driven to the cities for slaughter; the animals arrived in pitiful condition—scrawny, terrified, often diseased —from the long, arduous tramp to the city abattoirs.

A series of technical inventions laid the basis for the industrialization of packing. Railroads brought off-season vegetables and fruits to city markets, and regular milk delivery began. Refrigeration came into increasing use with the invention of the ice-cutter in the 1840's and the cold-storage plant some years later. The earlier invention of the tin can for preserving foods got a tremendous boost during the Civil War, and by the 1870's canned foods, including meat, made an increasing contribution to the food supply of city consumers.

The technical basis for the production of canned foods came in the 1840's with the invention of means for the mechanical, largely automatic stamping of tin cans and for shaping their tops and bottoms. Canning foods began with fish, vegetables, and fruits. Meats were first canned on a large scale for Civil War soldiers.

The great expansion of canned foods for civilian use began in 1872, when Libby, McNeill & Libby put canned corned beef on the market. Some six years later Gustavus F. Swift's company started to produce an increasing variety of canned meats—sixty-three different varieties by the time of Swift's death in 1900. Mechanical improvements (among them automatic soldering of cans and rotary pressure cookers) cheapened the cost of canned foods. Lower prices and intensive advertising made the use of "tins" an American habit. Much of the advertising used weird and wonderful methods its wonders to perform. Says one writer:

One of the Libby advertising series, for example, brought Shakespeare up to date. Here is the Libby production of the balcony scene from *Romeo and Juliet*:

Juliet (from the balcony): "How come'st thou hither, Romeo, and wherefore? If any of my kinsmen find thee, they'll murder thee." Romeo (below): "I have night's cloak to hide me from their sight, and I would adventure much to bring thee, Love, such merchandise as Libby, McNeill & Libby's cooked corned beef."

Some of Libby's Shakespearean productions were out-and-out blood and gore. Witness Act 3, Scene 4 from *Macbeth*. It presents the Scottish king trembling before the vengeful ghost of Banquo, once foully murdered by the dagger of Macbeth himself. Macbeth: "Hence, horrible shadow! Unreal mockery, hence! It will have blood; they say, blood will have blood! Nay, nay, offer it a can of Libby, McNeill & Libby's cooked corned beef!" [2]

What made the food revolution complete in its technical-economic aspects was the use of refrigerator cars and cold-storage warehouses. Without them, fresh meats could not have been made available to the millions of people in cities.

Refrigeration and the refrigerator car provided the basis for intensive industrialization of packing. The packers were responsible for neither development. "Most of the patents were taken out by scientists and professional inventors having no connection with the meat-packing industry. Usually they were assigned to manufacturers of refrigerating equipment. One of the few meat packers to hold patents relating to refrigeration was T. D. Kingan. His patents, however, were of little consequence." [3] The big packers seized upon these inventions and, through their control of refrigerator cars and cold-storage distribution plants, began to stifle competition while they built monopoly.

The first shipments of refrigerated meat were made in the summer of 1869 by George H. Hammond, who began to ship fresh meat in refrigerator cars from a plant in the Chicago area to Boston. By 1877 Gustavus F. Swift had established a refrigerated-meat business at his Chicago Union Stockyards, and by 1890 the refrigerator car was in general use. This practice came about despite public prejudice, railroad opposition, and restrictive legislation. Refrigeration not only transformed meat packing and distribution from a petty seasonal industry into a highly organized all-year one; it also made possible the increasing export of American meats (primarily beef) that began in the 1870's.

The sale of refrigerated meats moved slowly, but by the 1880's the business was zooming upward. New York City got its first cold-storage warehouse in 1882; I quote from a contemporary description of it:

[2] David S. Burt, "Men, Meat and the Tin Can," *The National Provisioner*, May 22, 1948, p. 19.

[3] R. F. Clemen, *The American Livestock and Meat Industry* (1923), p. 216.

An adequate and cheap supply of wholesome food is one of the most important items in the economy of a great city. . . . Other cities, in all directions, have benefitted by a lively competition between dealers in dressed beef brought from the West in the refrigerating cars and that brought on the hoof to be killed and dressed at the point of delivery, and at last this era of cheap beef has begun for New York.

Home consumers will no longer be compelled to suffer from the swindled feeling with which they have listened to statements that dressed beef shipped from here to England sells for less there than here, for the same system which for three years has supplied American beef for the roasts of Old England has been put in operation to supply New York with the beef of Western prairies.

This system is simply the shipment of dressed beef from Chicago to the East in refrigerating cars, and its storage until delivery in refrigerating buildings. Only last week the first of these buildings, located on Devoe Avenue in West Washington Market, and bearing the sign of G. F. & E. C. Swift, was opened for the new business. Most of its ground floor is divided into two large rooms, in which, by means of triple walls, and 300 tons of ice stored in rooms of similar size above them, a temperature of 38° to 40° is constantly maintained. Along the walls apertures connect the upper and lower rooms, and through these the warm air from the lower ascends on one side, while the cold air descends on the other. These refrigerators will contain 200 head of dressed beef cattle, hung from little one-wheeled iron trucks that run on railways from the ceiling.

Similar railways are attached to the ceilings of the cars in which the beef travels from Chicago; and when a car reaches Jersey City it is run upon a barge, towed across the river until its door is opposite that of the storage building, the railways of the two are connected, and the meat is easily transferred to the storage-room, which is of the same temperature as the car, without loss of time, and without being removed from the hook on which it was hung when killed.

By this method the cost of transporting the rough offal of all kinds, including hide, tallow, horns, hoofs, hair, etc. is saved, as is also the cost of feeding the cattle *en route*, and the shrinkage in weight incident upon the long journey.[4]

These were the great technical improvements which, combined with general economic and social changes, provided enterprising capitalists with the opportunity and the means for industrialization of packing on a large scale.

[4] "Cheaper Beef," *Harper's Weekly*, October 21, 1882, p. 663.

2. MEAT PACKING BECOMES A LARGE-SCALE INDUSTRY

The Union Army's enormous demand for packed meats during the Civil War gave industrial packing its real economic start. Government contracts provided the money with which enterprising packers for the export trade, like Kingan, and country butchers and merchants—among them Philip Armour, Gustavus Swift, and Nelson Morris—began to bring together and integrate the different phases of meat slaughtering and packing. Among the more enterprising merchants was Philip Armour, who made money both from packing and from speculation in pork. He sold pork "short" on the eve of Union victory and cleaned up big profits.[5]

Meat packing became an industry when packers provided cash markets for livestock and, a bit later, stockyards where animals were sold; then they built large industrial plants for slaughtering and packing and for transformation of animal waste into many by-products.

The capital for the big packing corporations came largely from the profits made during the Civil War and after (as later it came from profits plowed back into the business as surplus). Armour & Company, for example, made an average yearly profit of 42 per cent on investment from 1869 to 1873. Pretty much the same was true of Swift and of Morris. These three packers, together with Michael Cudahy (who began with Armour, then became independent), later emerged as the industry's Big Four.

What happened to meat packing after the Civil War parallels the development of industrial capitalism into monopoly capitalism. Independent small-scale production, with a relative multitude of small packers producing for a free competitive market where there was a free play of prices, profits, and wages, and only a few wage workers were organized into unions, gave way first to large-scale industry and, later, to unionism. Labor organized in spite of opposition from the packers, who invoked against unionism the theory of a

[5] Henry Clews, *Forty Years in Wall Street* (1908), p. 664. J. Ogden Armour, who inherited his father's business, also tried speculative manipulation in World War I. He tied up $150,000,000 in inventories in 1917 and after, in anticipation of great postwar demand and profit. The price deflation of 1920–21 left him $56,000,000 in debt and the Armour Company $38,000,000 in debt. J. Ogden resigned as president.

"free market" which large-scale monopoly packing worked to destroy.

Not only packinghouse workers found organization difficult to achieve. Cattle growers, and especially farmers, were also for a long time unable to organize. This disorganization placed them at the mercy of the big packers in the sale of livestock—one source (in addition to low wages) of high packing profits. Millions of livestock producers and sellers were at a disadvantage when confronted by a small number of big packers who were organized in highly compact buying units, especially when farmers had to sell in stockyards that were under packer ownership and control.

Bitter struggles went on between farmers and packers, producers and consumers, owner-managers and workers; bitter struggles with government when it swung into action to protect the public against packer malpractices. But within this turbulence there were constructive technical-economic factors at work, whose benefits were shared, although unequally, among all the people.

A summary of the dynamic factors in the expansion and industrialization of the meat-packing industry will illustrate the situation:

1. *The expansion and industrialization of production in general,* with its rapid mechanization of industry and the large-scale organization of production and distribution.

2. *The mechanization of slaughtering and packing in the meat industry,* which raised the volume of packed meats while lowering costs and prices, thus increasing the consumption of meat products of all kinds.

3. *A growing network of railroad transportation,* in particular the completion and expansion of the great transcontinental railroads. This development made it possible to ship more animals and animal products more cheaply, to and from the packing centers to markets of cities whose number and population kept on growing.

4. *The invention and increasing use of refrigeration, especially the refrigerator car,* without which the development of railroads would not, in itself, have been enough for transportation of large shipments of meats to far-flung cities. Refrigeration through chilling the carcass is indispensable for long-distance shipment of fresh meat.

5. *A complex network of national and international facilities for*

the distribution of meat products. These facilities eventually included refrigerator cars and trucks; refrigerated warehouses for the storage of beef quarters and smaller animal stock; distributing branch houses, with coolers and storerooms for perishable and non-perishable supplies of meat, poultry, and dairy products, to serve large communities; refrigerator-car routes to serve smaller communities (usually direct from the packing plant), and refrigerated ships for the export trade.

6. *The establishment of stockyards at central points,* which assured a regular market for livestock producers and a regular supply of livestock for the packers. By 1890 around seven-tenths of all cattle (other animals in proportion) were slaughtered by packing plants in and around five cities—Chicago, Kansas City, Omaha, St. Joseph, and St. Louis.

7. *A constant growth of the livestock industry, accompanied by scientific advances in animal husbandry.* The industry grew not only on the cattle ranches of the Western grazing lands but on Middle Western farms. These farms became great producers of swine. Improved livestock breeding and feeding helped to increase the number of animals and resulted in larger amounts of choice, nutritious meats.

8. *An increasing diversification of output, including increasing production of by-products from waste.* The processing of fresh and canned meats was quickly followed by the processing of poultry and dairy products. Utilization of waste for the manufacture of by-products added more savings and economies to those achieved by large-scale production and full utilization of plant capacity. "By-products constitute a third distinct source of economy, arising where different joint products result from a single process and the economy depends on turning them out in *proper proportions*—selling all the hides resulting from a given number of cattle slaughtered, and also all the meat, all the suet and other by-products." [6]

An astonishing variety of by-products, as a result of increasing chemical control, became a major part of the packing industry's output. These included not only edible products (hearts, livers, oils, lard, oleomargarine, etc.) but inedible products that ranged from skins, hides, pulled wool, and strings to soap, commercial fertilizers,

[6] John M. Clark, *Studies in the Economics of Overhead Costs* (1923), p. 59.

pharmaceuticals, and animal and poultry feeds. No parts of the animal are wasted, whether skin, bones, sinews, blood, glands, viscera, or fat.

Philip Armour made a particular point of promoting the development of by-products, and employed technologists to study livestock for that purpose. (He early recognized the importance of scientific and technical skills, and founded the Armour Institute in Chicago, which became a center of industrial research and teaching.) In the 1900's there was a popular saying: "The packers make money out of everything except the pig's squeal." In time the packers' "receipts from by-products alone largely offset the total cost of slaughter and distribution." [7]

9. *The growing export of American meats,* which by the second decade of the twentieth century provided one-third of the world's trade in meat. Then exports slowly but markedly declined until today the normal American problem is one of meat imports. But from the 1870's to the 1900's, growing meat exports provided bigger markets which, by increasing output, promoted large-scale mass production, lower costs, and higher profits. Meat exports, moreover, strengthened domination of the industry by a few corporate giants, since they handled most of the exports.

10. *Constantly more efficient industrial organization, equipment, and management.* The technical-managerial employees of the meat-packing industry did an outstanding job of organization and direction. Machines alone do not create the marvels of productive efficiency; directive skills also are needed. Basic were more efficient plant layout of machines and more efficient handling of materials and products by means of mechanical equipment. Labor was more effectively organized and used (the record was marred, however, by speed-up and low wages). Development of new products and constant, if at times slow and with lapses, improvement of quality also characterized packing management. It all added up to a job of producing more and better meats at lower costs to sell at lower prices. Greater popular consumption of meat products was one result.

Technological improvement moved rapidly in the packing industry, with Gustavus Swift and Philip Armour especially always pressing for more mechanization. The overhead conveyor, or "endless

[7] L. R. Edminster, "Meat Packing—History and American Developments," *Encyclopedia of the Social Sciences* (1933), p. 248.

chain" was already in general use by the 1870's. On this chain hooked carcasses move through automatic processes of scalding and scraping, and then whirl off to the chill rooms after being disassembled. Meat packing developed conveyor-line production before the automobile industry, with this difference: *disassembly* of carcass parts in meat packing becomes the *assembly* of parts to make a car in the automobile industry.

Around the "endless chain" developed an ever-growing variety of machines and equipment (all of it labor-saving, time-saving, and, usually, quality-improving) for hoisting, conveying, loading, and storing; for slaughtering, rendering, and cutting; for dehairing, for cooking and smoking, for sterilizing, packaging, etc. In by-products, too, the amount of machinery and equipment kept increasing. And it all moved toward greater automatic production.

This mechanization multiplied capital investment on bigger, more mechanized and efficient plants. Earlier packing "plants" (which were not much more than general merchandise warehouses, with slaughtering a separate operation) needed little investment in capital goods. Their equipment was limited almost exclusively to vats which kept the pickle, while workers used simple tools which they themselves usually provided. Not only did those packers require little investment on equipment but, since they served a local market, they needed little if any capital for distribution facilities. These primitive conditions disappeared with industrialization.

Average plant investment, according to Census figures, rose from $4000 in 1869 to $70,000 in 1909; the rise is indicative of the industrial transformation of packing. And capital investment kept on growing, with a consequent increase in large-scale industry and in the productivity of labor as mechanical efficiency advanced. One result was a decline in labor costs as a proportion of the total value of output—from 4.3 per cent in 1889 to 3.7 per cent in 1909 and 3.8 per cent in 1914. Lower labor costs resulted not only from the progress in labor-saving efficiency but also from the growing use of low-wage laborers.

3. THE ASCENDANCY OF MONOPOLY

All these economic changes brought a tremendous increase in meat output, together with concentration of production and control. While the industry's output rose from $75,000,000 in 1869 to $1,652,000,000 in 1914, an increase of over twenty times, the number of packer establishments rose only from 768 to 1279.

Refrigeration made packing an all-year business instead of a business that operated principally in the cold-weather season. But what made it a large-scale industry, carried on in larger, more efficient plants, was increasing mechanization and the growth of complex marketing facilities. Large-scale operations called constantly for more capital investment, which limited the number of small independent enterprisers who could go into the packing business.

GROWTH OF MEAT PACKING, U.S.A., 1869–1914

Year	Number of Establish- ments	Total Value of Products	Value Added by Manufacture
1869	768	$ 75,000,000	$14,000,000
1879	872	303,000,000	35,000,000
1899	882	783,000,000	101,000,000
1904	929	913,000,000	108,000,000
1909	1221	1,355,000,000	164,000,000
1914	1279	1,652,000,000	210,000,000

Source: U.S. Census of Manufactures for the respective years. Table includes establishments with a value output below $5000; 1869 and 1879 are not strictly comparable with later years because of classification changes.

The concentration of meat packing in larger and larger plants became the starting point of a drive toward monopoly, out of which four giant corporations have emerged as dominant powers to control more than half the industry's output.

Large-scale industry and monopoly are not synonymous. To be sure, wherever monopoly prevails there is usually industrial concentration, with its large producing units. But monopoly goes beyond the size of such units. It combines them by means of corporate financial and organizational power under a centralized control. Technical-economic factors alone are not enough for monopoly. For *monopoly does not necessarily arise out of industrial efficiency*; it builds on practices that beat down competitors, secure control of crucial inventions or economic areas, and absorb competitors. Monopoly is essentially a centralization of financial control.

These aspects of monopoly were clearly evident in the packing industry. What gave five (later four) big corporations their predominant monopoly position was the interplay of the following factors:

1. *Ownership and control of stockyards by packers with large financial resources.* Control of the stockyards, where livestock producers had to sell their animals, gave the big packers an assured raw material supply. It also gave them predominance over markets and prices, and decisive competitive advantages. Independent commission merchants were allowed to buy, but they had to "go along" with the "boss" packers. Small businessmen who wanted to start in the packing business were at a disadvantage because they had to buy livestock in stockyards under big-packer control. And all stockyard operations—stock-pen assignments, switching and handling of stock, grading rules, etc.—were used, often deviously, to benefit the packer owner, who was the principal buyer and who was able (within limits) to set prices that worked to the disadvantage of his competitors and the farmers.

2. *Private ownership and control of refrigerator cars and refrigerated storage warehouses,* which gave the big packers a dominant strategic position in the distribution of meat products. Both facilities involved heavy capital investment. This was particularly true of the construction and operation of refrigerator cars, because their economical use called for a great number of cars serving widespread, diversified markets. Railroads could have operated them on a freight-car basis, so they would be usable by all packers. Instead the railroads worked with the big packers (as they did with Standard Oil and other monopoly corporations). In addition, the packers received preferential concessions and discriminatory rates and rebates, often through secret agreements. This was a general practice: within three years after Congress in 1903 gave the Interstate Commerce Commission the power to do it, the ICC collected $586,-000 from fines on rebating. The activities of railroads and packers worked against free enterprise, for the combination made successful operation difficult, if not impossible, for newcomers or small concerns in the meat industry.[8]

[8] "The Big Five own 91 per cent of all refrigerator cars properly equipped for the shipment of fresh meat that are operated upon the railroads of the United States. The railroads have almost no equipment suitable for shipping

3. *Interlocking directorships in banking, railroad, and other cor-porations.* Armour, Cudahy, Morris, and Swift and their associates held directorships (as well as stock) in banks, which gave them financial advantages over competitors, and in railroads, which gave them transportation advantages. Add to this a social factor: inter-marriage of the monopolists' children in a growing, powerful money aristocracy that worked together and stuck together in business and in "society." J. Pierpont Morgan gave words to the arrogance of the new aristocracy of monopoly capitalism when he said, "Men own-ing property should do what they like with it. I owe the public nothing." [9]

Without control of stockyards, refrigerator cars, and cold-storage distribution facilities, without the massive might of centralized finan-cial resources, there could have been no monopoly. If the stock-yards and refrigerator cars, for example, had from the beginning been either independent or "public utility" enterprises under gov-ernment regulation and control, and had served the whole meat industry, the packer monopoly might have been limited in its scope.[10]

Nor must we forget the personal motives of the men who became big packers. A crucial factor in monopoly was (and is) *the deliber-ate effort, using any and all means, to build monopoly power.* The urge for power—an economic and psychological mixture—drove on the packers who became the Big Five. Their drive for money was not a miser-lust but a lust for power.

---

dressed meat, and, consequently, unless an independent packing company is large enough to afford to make a heavy outlay for refrigerator cars, it is practi-cally impossible for it to attempt to ship fresh meat out of the locality in which it is produced. The smaller independents, therefore, confine themselves either to pork packing or to cattle slaughter for local consumption." Federal Trade Commission, *Summary of the Report . . . on the Meat Packing Industry* (1918), p. 17.

[9] Lewis Corey, *The House of Morgan* (1930), pp. 301, 303. Morgan's state-ment on property was made when he testified in a law suit against the Northern Securities Company in 1902.

[10] Social policy comes into the picture. In Argentina, as in the United States, a high degree of monopoly developed in the packing industry (including American corporations). But in Australia and New Zealand the packing indus-try developed primarily as small-scale independent enterprises, not monopoly; yet technical-economic changes were substantially the same as in the United States. The reason for the difference was a social one—intervention by the governments, which formulated policy and set up public boards to prevent monopoly.

By the early 1900's five dominant meat-packing giants had emerged: Swift & Company, Armour & Company, Nelson Morris & Company (later Morris & Company), Cudahy Packing Company, and Schwarzschild & Sulzberger (which ended up Wilson & Company).

The monopoly drive began early. In most industries the bigger corporations formed trusts and pools to regulate output, markets, and prices. Among the food industries, however, meat slaughtering and packing was (with the exception of sugar) alone in the monopoly drive of this period. Consolidation and monopoly began in other food industries after World War I, and by the 1930's they had caught up. By 1940 it could be said: "There is scarcely one of the food industries in which there are not to be found at least three or four organizations operating on a national scale and controlling a substantial part of the business in which they are engaged." [11]

In 1888 Swift, Armour, Morris, and Hammond (Armour absorbed the Hammond company in 1902) formed the "Allerton pool" to "regulate" the meat industry. An investigating committee of the United States Senate stigmatized the pool as "an agreement to refrain from competition," and charged the member firms with collusion to fix prices and to divide and control livestock purchases and sales territories. This packers' pool was partly responsible for adoption of the Sherman Anti-Trust Act in 1890, which made illegal any combination in restraint of trade.

But anti-trust laws did not frighten the packers. In 1893 Armour, Cudahy, Swift, Hammond, and Morris formed the "Veeder pool" to divide markets among themselves, to apportion livestock purchases and meat sales on a quota basis, and to fix the prices of livestock and meat products. Weekly meetings were held in Henry Veeder's law office to agree on livestock purchases and meat sales, on territory and prices.

These meetings were secret; letters or code numbers were used to designate the participating corporations and their officers, and fines were levied on members who violated the agreements made. Prices for beef were set on an arbitrary computation of costs. The formula used was "test cost"—a measure of the net cost of the dressed car-

[11] TNEC Monograph 35, *Investigation of the Concentration of Economic Power,* "Large-Scale Organization in the Food Industries," by A. C. Hoffman (1940), p. 51.

cass, determined by adding to the live-cattle price arbitrary high charges for killing and cutting costs, and deducting from this total arbitrary low allowances for the value of by-products (hides, offal, etc.). This procedure made test cost higher than the actual net cost, which yielded the conspiratorial packers a high margin of profit.

After three years the packers gave up the Veeder pool, but they formed a similar pool in 1898, with the addition of Schwarzschild & Sulzberger.[12]

Meanwhile the federal government swung into action. After an investigation of the "pool" packers, the government filed suit against them in 1902. The defendants demurred, were overruled, and made no answer. In 1903 the court issued a final injunction which permanently enjoined the big packers from operating under the 1898 pool to manipulate livestock and dressed-beef markets to fix prices in violation of the anti-trust law, and from receiving discriminatory railroad rates. Swift appealed the injunction, but the United States Supreme Court sustained it in 1905.

Monopoly builders in all fields found that pools were not only illegal but inefficient, subject to disagreements and break-ups and to anti-trust "conspiracy" suits. Hence a great consolidation and merger movement began in 1898; by 1904 there were already in the United States 440 great trustified corporations with a capitalization of $20,379,000,000. If pools were illegal, mergers into bigger corporations were not, and consolidated corporate power was more effective in building monopoly than mere agreements for common action.[13]

Packing joined the merger procession. In 1902 Armour agreed to a merger with Swift and Morris. The three companies had tangible assets of $182,000,000; they decided to apportion ownership of the new corporation's stock as follows: Swift 46.7 per cent, Armour 40.11 per cent, and Morris 13.19 per cent. The plan included an agreement for each of the three to buy up independents and add them to the merger, with Schwarzschild & Sulzberger and Cudahy to come in too.

The objective was to create in meat packing what J. Pierpont Morgan had created in steel in 1902; that is, a giant corporation in control of most of the industry's output. The United States Steel

[12] Federal Trade Commission, *Summary of the Report*, pp. 22-23.
[13] John Moody, *Truth About the Trusts* (1905), p. ix.

Corporation combined in one organization enough companies to control upward of 60 per cent of the American industry's output. If the Swift-Armour-Morris plans had gone through, the new packing giant would have controlled at least half, if not more, of meat slaughtering and packing: a solid basis for dominant monopoly. These merger plans failed when the investment bankers refused to grant a $60,000,000 loan, because signs of a financial panic were evident.

Armour, Swift, and Morris went ahead with another plan. In 1903 they incorporated the National Packing Company, to which they transferred ownership of concerns they had bought or contracted to buy in preparation for the merger. The concerns included eleven packing, stockyard, and refrigerator-car companies; one manufacturing company; and one Canadian company. National stock was distributed on the basis of the percentages agreed upon for the merger. For nine years representatives of Armour, Swift, and Morris met weekly as National Packing directors to regulate and control margins, livestock purchases, and meat shipments in accordance with the interests of National's three corporate owners.[14]

The spotlight of public criticism was played upon the packers as anti-trust agitation grew. A criminal suit was instituted by the Department of Justice in 1905 against sixteen packers, among them the officers and directors of National Packing. The suit charged restraint and monopoly in livestock purchases and the sale of fresh meat. But the packers escaped through a legal loophole. They pleaded immunity from penalty under the Fifth Amendment to the Constitution, which provides that no person "shall be compelled in any criminal case to be a witness against himself." They backed up the plea with the claim that, under legal compulsion, they had given evidence to the Commissioner of the United States Bureau of Corporations, and that this evidence was part of the prosecution. The Attorney General scornfully answered: "The plea for immunity is absurd. If it prevails, Washington will become a health resort for all sorts of corporation magnates pursuing devious ways. I can imagine them meeting and saying: 'Good morning, good morning, Mr. Rockefeller, have you had your immunity bath this morning?' Look at the absurdity of the thing!"

But the judge presiding over the United States District Court at

[14] Federal Trade Commission, *Summary of the Report*, pp. 23-24.

Chicago did not consider the plea absurd. He ruled that, since the packers under criminal indictment had not volunteered information but given it under legal compulsion, "I am of the opinion they were entitled to immunity." This immunity did not, however, it was carefully explained, extend to the *corporation* but only to the *individuals* who directed its policies. "Whereat," according to one journal, "a harsh and bitter laugh has been heard throughout the land, for a corporation cannot be imprisoned." Even the conservative New York *Journal of Commerce* declared that "The more the ruling is considered the more extraordinary it appears," while President Theodore Roosevelt said: "Such interpretation of the law comes measurably near making the law a farce." [15]

The "immunity" decision ended the criminal prosecution but did not legalize the status of National Packing, whose officers in 1911 decided, under threat of a civil anti-trust suit, to dissolve the company. Its plants and other assets were turned over to Armour, Swift, and Morris in accordance with the percentages of stock they owned in National Packing. (In 1916 Thomas E. Wilson, an officer of the Morris concern and a National director, took over control of Schwarzschild & Sulzberger, changing its name to Wilson & Company. Control of this corporation was vested in a voting trust, four of whose five members were bankers—Wilson being their Man Friday.)

In all, six anti-trust suits were filed against Swift, Armour, Cudahy, and Morris, and against a number of their associates, in the nine years from 1902 to 1910. Most of them were either dismissed or nol-prossed, or the defendants were acquitted. In packing, as in other areas of monopoly activity, the anti-trust prosecutions did not get far, although they did limit monopoly power.

In the midst of charges of monopoly conspiracy, public criticism, and court actions, proof of restrictive practices piled up. The years 1900 to 1910 were marked by a public rebellion against monopoly, including the Big Five packers. Farmers, who had led an earlier revolt against the railroads which caused Congress in 1887 to establish the Interstate Commerce Commission, were among the most aggressive rebels, since they suffered most from stockyard abuses. In 1905 the Bureau of Corporations, Department of the Interior,

[15] Article, "Meat Packers and Immunity Baths," *Current Literature*, May 1906, pp. 462-63.

made a report which proved the livestock producers' case against the packer stockyards. But no reforms were made.

It is indicative of the limitations of anti-trust action that all through twenty-five years of legislation and government lawsuits the Big Five (Swift, Armour, Morris, Sulzberger-Wilson, and Cudahy) kept on consolidating their dominant power. By 1916 they had raised their proportion of the meat industry's sales to more than 65 per cent. Their one major defeat was the failure to merge in one giant monopoly corporation, the National Packing Company. But their power expanded, and so did their profits.

Meanwhile, agitation against the Big Five grew, fed from an increasing number of sources. It was part of a rising struggle against monopoly power. Theodore Roosevelt, Robert M. La Follette, and Woodrow Wilson gave political expression to the agitation. It became, moreover, social criticism of the shortcomings of monopoly policy and practices. The criticism was pressed by the "Muckrakers," social reformers, Socialists, and the labor unions.

For economic activity cannot be separated from its larger social relations and meaning. The packing industry aroused a storm of criticism that centered around significant questions of social policy and values.

CHAPTER IV

SOCIAL ASPECTS:
THE WORKERS AND CONSUMERS

1. WHAT OF THESE, O LORD?

ECONOMIC activity includes the use of natural resources, technical equipment, and organization to produce goods and services. Under organization, in modern industry, are included the owner-capitalist, who is organizer and manager of the enterprise he owns, or, as is the case today in most industrial enterprises, the hired salaried personnel who perform managerial functions for absentee owner-stockholders; and, in addition, the wage workers who are necessary to carry on economic activity, and the consumers who buy the products of that activity.

It is a truism, perhaps, to add the workers and consumers. But they have been largely ignored throughout the ages by the masters of economic (and political) power. Workers and consumers were usually overlooked—they still are, in large measure—by orthodox economics. They appeared as "market" categories: labor as a "commodity," consumers as "distribution." They appeared as "factors of production," not as human beings who were overworked and underfed, for whom insufficiency of food and food of bad quality resulted in malnutrition, illness, and death.

It is an extraordinary commenta*v* on earlier industrial civilization that, from the period of the 1850's to the 1900's and even after, the worst labor conditions, by and large, prevailed in three basic industries: the production of meat products, of iron and steel, and of coal. The blood, sinews, and bones of many workers became part of the meats, the steel, and the coal that went to market.

Industry lived up to orthodox economics. Labor was a "factor of production" like machines and a "commodity" like pigs, coal, and steel. The consumer was "the market." All consumers were alike: the rich and the poor, the individual consumer who bought food-stuffs on which to live, the corporate consumer who bought raw materials for machines to devour.

"If a worker raises his head," said one steel magnate, "hit it."

"Let the consumer beware," said a sugar magnate; this meant, sometimes in actual fact, "It's his funeral."

"God in his infinite wisdom," a coal magnate insisted, "has en-trusted the guidance and welfare of the workers to us, not to the unions."

Such attitudes prevailed in the meat-packing industry, as in many another. It took generations of struggle by unions, consumers, and reformers to correct the worst exploitation of workers and consum-ers by the monopoly meat magnates.

2. HUMAN CONDITIONS IN PACKING

The butchers in retail trade enjoyed, by and large, better work-ing conditions—more independence, higher wages, earlier unions—than other labor groups in the meat industry. A number of great packinghouse strikes were mercilessly beaten down; management rejected collective bargaining. Revolting conditions prevailed among packinghouse workers, and management did little to improve them. Immigrant and Negro workers were mercilessly exploited; most of the workers were unskilled and insecure in their jobs; living con-ditions, especially in Chicago, were abominable. Although the situa-tion of the workers is improved today, it is important to recall the old conditions, and to remember that the initiative for improvement did not come from ownership or management, but from social re-formers and labor unions.

A striking description of work in "packingtown," in a Chicago plant employing 20,000 workers, appears in *The Jungle*, by Upton Sinclair. He begins with the hog department:

One by one the workers hooked up the hogs, and one by one with a swift stroke they slit their throats. There was a long line of hogs, with squeals and life-blood ebbing away together, until at last each vanished with a splash into a huge vat of boiling water. . . .

The carcass was scooped out of the vat by machinery, and then it fell to the second floor, passing on the way through a wonderful machine with numerous scrapers, which adjusted themselves to the size and shape of the animal, and sent it out at the other end with nearly all of its bristles removed. It was then again strung up by machinery, and sent upon another trolley ride; this time passing between two lines of men, who sat upon a raised platform, each doing a single thing to the carcass as it came to him. One scraped the outside of a leg; another scraped the inside of the same leg. One with a swift stroke cut the throat; another with two swift strokes severed the head, which fell to the floor and vanished through a hole. Another made a slit down the body; a second opened the body wider; a third with a saw cut the breast-bone; a fourth loosened the entrails; a fifth pulled them out—and they also slid through a hole in the floor. There were men to scrape each side and men to scrape the back; there were men to clean the carcass inside, to trim it and wash it. Looking down this room, one saw, creeping slowly, a line of dangling hogs a hundred yards in length; and for every yard there was a man, working as if a demon were after him. At the end of this hog's progress every inch of the carcass had been gone over several times; and then it was rolled into the chilling-room where it stayed for twenty-four hours, and where a stranger might lose himself in a forest of freezing hogs. . . .

On the next floor the various waste materials were treated. Here came the entrails, to be scraped and washed clean for sausage-casings; men and women worked together here in the midst of a sickening stench. To another room came all the scraps to be "tanked," which meant boiling and pumping off the grease to make soap and lard; below they took out the refuse.

In still other places men were engaged in cutting up the carcasses that had been through the chilling-rooms. First there were the "splitters," the most expert workmen in the plant, who earned as high as fifty cents an hour, and did not a thing all day except chop hogs down the middle. Then there were "cleaver men," great giants with muscles of iron; each had two men to attend him—to slide the half carcass in front of him on the table, and hold it while he chopped it, and then turn each piece so that he might chop it once more. So through various yawning holes there slipped to the floor below—to one room hams, to another forequarters, to another sides of pork. . . .

Across the street they did the killing of beef—where every hour they turned four or five hundred cattle into meat. Here all the work was done on one floor; and instead of there being one line of carcasses which moved to the workmen, there were fifteen or twenty lines and the men moved from one to another of these. . . .

Along one side of the room ran a narrow gallery, a few feet from the floor; into which gallery the cattle were driven with goads which gave them electric shocks. While they stood bellowing and plunging, over the top of the pen there leaned one of the "knockers," armed with a sledge-hammer, and watching for a chance to deal a blow. The room echoed with the thuds in quick succession and the stamping and kicking of the steers. The instant the animal had fallen, the "knocker" passed on to another; while a second man raised a lever, and the side of the pen was raised, and the animal, still kicking and struggling, slid out to the "killing-bed." Here a man put shackles about one leg, and pressed another lever, and the body was jerked up into the air. There were fifteen or twenty such pens, and it was a matter of only a couple of minutes to knock fifteen or twenty cattle and roll them out.

The men worked with furious intensity, literally upon the run—at a pace with which there was nothing to be compared except a football game. It was highly specialized labor, each man having his task to do; generally this would consist of only two or three specific cuts, and he would pass down the line of fifteen or twenty carcasses, making these cuts upon each. First there came the "butcher," to bleed them; this meant one swift stroke, so swift that you could not see it—only the flash of the knife; and before you could realize it, the man had darted on to the next line, and the stream of bright red was pouring out upon the floor. This floor was half an inch deep with blood, in spite of the best efforts of men who kept shovelling it through holes.

The carcass hung for a few minutes to bleed; there was no time lost, however, for there were several hanging in each line, and one was always ready. It was let down to the ground, and there came the "headsman," whose task it was to sever the head, with two or three swift strokes. Then came the "floorsman," to make the first cut in the skin; and then another to finish ripping the skin down the centre; and then half a dozen more in swift succession to finish the skinning. After they were through the carcass was again swung up; and while a man with a stock examined the skin, to make sure that it had not been cut, and another rolled it up and tumbled it through one of the inevitable holes in the floor, the beef proceeded on its journey. There were men to cut it, and men to split it, and men to gut it and scrape it clean inside. There were some with hose which threw jets of boiling water upon it, and others who removed the feet and added the final touches. In the end, as with hogs, the finished beef was run into the chilling-room, to hang its appointed time. In other parts of the building were the pickling-rooms, and the salting-rooms, the canning-rooms, and the packing-rooms where choice meat was prepared for shipping in refrigerator cars, destined to be eaten in all four corners of civilization.

Sinclair then proceeds to describe the manufacture of by-products:

There was a building to which the grease was piped, and made into soap and lard; and then there was a factory for making lard cans, and another for making soap boxes. There was a building in which the bristles were cleaned and dried, for the making of hair cushions and such things; there was a building where the skins were dried and tanned, there was another where heads and feet were made into glue, and another where bones were made into fertilizer. No tiniest particle of organic matter was wasted. Out of the horns of the cattle they made combs, buttons, hair-pins and imitation ivory; out of the shin bones and other big bones they cut knife and toothbrush handles, and mouthpieces for pipes; out of the hoofs they cut hair-pins and buttons before they made the rest into glue. From such things as feet, knuckles, hide clippings, and sinews came such strange and unlikely products as gelatin, isinglass, and phosphorus, bone-black, shoe-blacking and bone-oil. They had curled-hair works for the cattle tails, and a "wool pullery" for the sheep skins; they made pepsin from the stomachs of the pigs, and albumen from the blood, and violin strings from the ill-smelling entrails. When there was nothing else to be done with a thing, they first put it into a tank and got out of it all the tallow and grease, and then they made it into fertilizer.

There is already, within the description of intensive specialization and division of labor, a glimpse of the oppressive conditions of work in packing plants. Sinclair makes it vividly specific:

Most of the men *hated* their work. They hated the bosses, they hated the owners; they hated the whole place, the whole neighborhood—even the whole city, with an all-inclusive hatred, bitter and fierce. Women and little children would fall to cursing about it. . . . The pace set for work was one that called for every faculty of a man—from the instant the first steer fell till the sounding of the noon whistle, and again from half-past twelve till heaven only knew what hour in the late afternoon or evening, there was never one instant's rest for a man, for his hand or his eye or his brain. There were portions of the work which determined the pace of the rest, and for these they had picked men whom they paid high, and whom they changed frequently. This was called "speeding up the gang." . . . The main thing the men wanted was to put a stop to the habit of "speeding up," for there were some, they said, who could not keep up with it, whom it was killing. . . .

Now the dreadful winter was come upon them. Packingtown braced itself for the struggle that was an agony, and those whose time was come died off in hordes. . . . Sooner or later came the day when the unfit did not report for work; and then, with no time lost in waiting, and no inquiries or regrets, there was a chance for a new hand. The new hands were here by the thousands. All day long the gates of the packinghouses were besieged. Blizzards and cold made no difference to them, they were always on hand. Sometimes their faces froze, sometimes their feet and their hands; sometimes they froze all together—but still they came, for they had no other place to go. . . .

The workers in each of the plant's industries had their own peculiar diseases. . . . Let a man so much as scrape his finger pushing a truck in the pickle-rooms, and he might have a sore that would put him out of the world; all the joints in his finger might be eaten by the acid, one by one. Of the butchers and floorsmen, the beef-boners and trimmers, and all those who used knives, you could scarcely find a person who had the use of his thumb. The hands of these men would be crisscrossed with cuts. They would have no nails—they had worn them off pulling hides; their knuckles were swollen so that their fingers spread out like a fan. In the cooking-rooms, in the midst of steam and sickening odors, by artificial light, the germs of tuberculosis might live for two years, but the supply was renewed every hour. . . . There were those who worked in the chilling-rooms, and whose special disease was rheumatism; their time-limit for work was five years. There were the wool-pluckers, whose hands went to pieces even sooner than the hands of pickle-men; for the pelts of sheep had to be painted with acid to loosen the wool, and then the pluckers had to pull out this wool with their bare hands, till the acid had eaten their fingers off. Some worked at the stamping machines, and might have a part of a hand chopped off. . . . Worst of any, however, were the fertilizer-men and those who served in the cooking-rooms. These people could not be shown to the visitor—for the odor of a fertilizer-man would scare any ordinary visitor at a hundred yards, and as for the other men who worked in tank-rooms full of steam, and in some of which there were open vats near the level of the floor, their peculiar trouble was that they fell into the vats; and when they were fished out, there was never enough of them left to be worth exhibiting—sometimes they would be overlooked for days, till all but the bones of them had gone out to the world as Pure Leaf Lard!

And here is Sinclair's description of living conditions in the Packingtown slums where the workers lived:

They were on a street which seemed to run on forever, mile after mile—thirty-four of them, if they had known it—and on each side of it one uninterrupted row of wretched little two-story frame buildings. Always the same endless vista of ugly and dirty little wooden buildings. Here and there would be a bridge crossing a filthy creek, with hard-baked mud shores and dingy sheds and docks along it; here and there would be a railroad crossing, with a tangle of switches, and locomotives puffing, and rattling freight cars filing by; here and there would be a great factory, a dingy building with innumerable windows in it, and immense volumes of smoke puffing from the chimneys, darkening the air above and making filthy the earth beneath. . . . The smoke, thick, oily, black as night, was inexhaustible; one stared, waiting to see it stop, but still the great streams rolled out. They spread in vast clouds overhead, writhing, curling; then, uniting in one giant river, they streamed away down the sky, stretching a black pall as far as the eye could reach. . . . Another strange thing, like the odor of a thing elemental—murmurings, whisperings, rumblings: the lowing of ten thousand cattle, the grunting of ten thousand swine. . . .

In back of the yards the dreary two-story frame houses were scattered farther apart, and there were great spaces bare—that seemingly had been overlooked by the great sore of a city as it spread itself over the surface of the prairie. . . . There were no pavements—there were mountains and valleys and rivers, gullies and ditches, and a great hollow full of stinking green water. One wondered about the swarms of flies which hung about the scene, literally blackening the air, and the strange fetid odor which assailed one's nostrils, a ghastly odor, of all the dead things of the universe. . . . This dumping ground for the city garbage was sprinkled over with children, who raked it from dawn to dark. Sometimes visitors from the packinghouses would wander out to see this "dump," and they would stand by and debate as to whether the children were eating the food they got, or merely collecting it for the chickens at home.[1]

These were the facts that turned the American stomach. The public revolted at the idea of human flesh going into the lard they used, but gave little thought to the human beings, the workers, to whom the flesh belonged, and to the slums in which those workers lived. An outcry went up for cleansing the stockyards and their meat products, and reforms were made. But the workers were not included; they had to depend upon their own efforts and their union for relief.

[1] Upton Sinclair, *The Jungle* (New York: 1905), pp. 27-39, 40, 41-47, 67-68, 70, 73, 92-93, 116-17.

3. LABOR UPHEAVAL—THE AMALGAMATED STRIKE
OF 1904 AND AFTER

For thirty years, since the year 1886 when they struck for an
eight-hour day in Chicago, won it, and then lost it in a packer
counter-offensive, the packinghouse workers had tried to organize
into unions. These unions broke apart, re-formed, and broke apart
again. While the big packers built up their organizations, they denied the right of organization to their employees. Strike after strike
met with ruthless opposition and defeat. What made it more difficult to form permanent unions was the multi-national variety of the
immigrants—Poles, Lithuanians, Bohemians, Slovaks—that increasingly made up the labor force as part of a deliberate policy of the
packers. These immigrant workers knew little, if anything, about
unions.

The packers used all the anti-union tricks—discrimination, yellow-
dog contracts, and blacklists, among others—to prevent union organization. In addition, they kept spies in the union. "The packers
every week," wrote Upton Sinclair, "received reports of what
was going on, and often they knew things before the members
did."

A strike takes place in *The Jungle*. The account is based on the
1904 strike in Chicago, which was led by the Amalgamated Meat
Cutters and Butcher Workmen. By this time the Amalgamated,
chartered by the AFL in 1897, had, according to T. W. Glocker,
*The Unit of Government in the Meat Cutters and Butcher Work-
men's Union* (1905), twenty-eight locals with 75,000 members.
Higher wages, a ten-hour day, and seniority were secured.

Under its dynamic president, Michael Donnelly (1898–1905), the
Amalgamated pushed the drive for union recognition from the packers. On the packers' refusal, the Amalgamated in 1904 called its
first general strike. The workers had been waiting for this; 60,000 of
them went on strike, 25,000 in Chicago. The union's demands, in
addition to recognition, included a raise in the hourly rate for laborers from eighteen cents to twenty cents. The packers countered with
an offer of sixteen cents, a two-cent reduction from the existing rate.
Strikers finished all work and left plants in "ship-shape order."

The big packers imported immigrant and Negro strikebreakers.

Many of these did not know where they were going, or why; a few of them refused to play the scab after they learned about the strike. The Negroes presented a problem to which President Donnelly responded in terms of Amalgamated policy, expressed in its pledge since 1897, against any discrimination for reasons of race or color: "Michael Donnelly realized that, despite its strength, his organization faced a serious task. 'We must,' he said, 'get everybody into the organization, including the women and Negroes.'" [2]

Victory came to the Amalgamated workers after eight days of a strike that never faltered. The big packers granted union recognition on a national scale and also arbitration of the strikers' demands.

But inexperience, misunderstanding, and bickering among the Amalgamated leaders deprived the workers of their victory. The strike settlement called for re-employment of all strikers, at their regular jobs, within forty-five days. The national strike committee had agreed that this much time, at least, was needed for management, operating in a disrupted industry, to rehire all strikers. Many of the active strike leaders in Chicago were not among the first to be rehired. The packers insisted that they had not violated the strike settlement—and they were right. But, according to R. F. Clemen, *The American Livestock and Meat Industry* (1923), page 702, the workers' "mistake was a natural one. It followed a history of grievances on both sides, and a conviction on the part of the workmen that the packers were determined to destroy their union."

Meanwhile, pressure for a strike became so great that President Donnelly reluctantly and, as some old-timers recall it, sorrowfully, yielded to the clamor. His apprehensions came true: the strikers this time had a bad moral case. The packers resisted, violence flared; some people were killed and scores injured, including Michael Donnelly, who was severely beaten in a street ambuscade. Fifteen years later an Amalgamated official said:

After the 1904 strike was over we found ourselves with a remnant of an organization, with no money and with little membership. We maintained the organization through the years, but with little change in conditions until the past two years [1918–19], when a wave of organiza-

[2] Sterling D. Spero and Abram L. Harris, *The Black Worker: The Negro and the Labor Movement* (1931), p. 266.

tion swept the country and the butcher workmen, with other workers, profited by it.[3]

A large part of the blame for this wrecking of the union must be put upon inexperienced, incompetent, and irresponsible leaders, though many of them cannot be included in this indictment, notably Michael Donnelly. He must have been an extraordinary personality. His final service to the union came in the 1905 Cudahy strike in Louisville, a long-fought struggle which he directed to victory. Forty years later his union still responded to the influence of his personality. In 1944 *The Butcher Workman* wrote of him:

If a blind man is helped across the street by a stranger, even this easily performed good deed lives in the mind of the man without eyes. Every man employed by a labor union should conduct himself in a manner so sincerely in behalf of those he represents that even when he makes way for the fellow that takes his place, his good deeds and his accomplishments will live after him.

Michael Donnelly, the never-to-be-forgotten former president of the Amalgamated, just before his retirement in 1905 personally conducted the bitterly fought strike against the John Cudahy Packing Company at Louisville, Kentucky. At the end of seventeen weeks of sacrificing on the part of the strikers, Donnelly finally forced the company to sign a closed shop agreement with wage rates being almost doubled.

The next night Thomas Love, secretary of the local union, was at the hotel while President Donnelly was packing his belongings to return to Chicago. As Donnelly closed his bag he said to Love, "Well, I think I have packed everything."

Tom Love said, "No, Mike, there are two things you cannot pack or take with you. You cannot pack the influence of your presence here, nor can you pack the glad hearts you have made." [4]

Michael Donnelly disappeared sometime after the 1905 strike. The beating up he got in Chicago, where he was left for dead on the streets, seems to have done things to his mind. He became a cook in work camps in the Southwest, among other occupations. Early in 1916 he wrote to Homer D. Call, Amalgamated secretary since 1897, asking to be made an organizer: "I am in excellent

[3] Amalgamated Meat Cutters and Butcher Workmen of North America, AFL, *Proceedings, 10th General Convention,* 1920, pp. 33-34.

[4] Editorial, "The Influence of Our Presence," *The Butcher Workman,* September 1944, p. 4.

health and fine shape to again do some good work for the trade that I still love and yearn to put in better shape once more." The union made Donnelly an organizer "because of the fact he had proved his worth as an organizer and at the same time there was a feeling in the Missouri River Valley among butcher workmen that he had not been treated fairly." The old man began, and did good work, and then—let Homer Call complete the story:

> Brother Donnelly succeeded in organizing a local union in Fort Worth, and visited some other points in the State of Texas, meeting with fairly good results. In the meantime, the organized labor movement in Chicago had requested Secretary Morrison of the AFL to commission Brother Donnelly as an AFL organizer and assign him to Chicago. But before that could be accomplished his old malady developed and Brother Donnelly disappeared, and we have been unable to locate him since, much to our regret.[5]

After the 1904 defeat the most active Amalgamated workers were blacklisted. For some years the union was pretty much an underground movement, with organizing work carried on by what were called "Boomer Butchers," union men who moved from plant to plant and region to region, using assumed names to evade the blacklists and sworn to deny they were members of the union. From 1905 to 1909 the union just kept going.

Packinghouse wages remained at the same low level for twelve years, until in 1916 the pressure of wartime living costs led to a small increase. But living costs kept on rising. After America's entry into the war, in 1917, the Amalgamated Union seized the opportunity to ask for higher wages and improved conditions. The packing magnates refused, the government stepped in, and the dispute went to arbitration. Two of the owner-employers were called to testify. They revealed little knowledge of wages and working conditions in their plants and even less sympathy for union labor. The first was J. Ogden Armour. Cross-examined by Frank P. Walsh, the union counsel, Armour testified that workers got twenty minutes for lunch, without pay:

> WALSH: How much time do office employees have for lunch?
> ARMOUR: Thirty minutes. . . .
> WALSH: Do you know that the average wage earned was $692 for 1916?

[5] Amalgamated Meat Cutters, *Report of Proceedings, 9th General Convention,* 1917, pp. 58-59.

ARMOUR: No, I do not know that.

WALSH: Do you know that the average wage of $2.75 a day made at your plant is more than $365 below the life line set by government investigators?

ARMOUR: No, I do not. . . .

WALSH: There is one man—a butcher—who formerly handled fifteen or sixteen cows in an hour; this was gradually increased to twenty-five an hour without anything being said to the man about whatever additional fatigue he might feel under the extra work. Do you feel that someone else ought to arbitrarily fix the rates for this work without consulting the man himself?

ARMOUR: They could complain to the superintendent of the plant.

The next witness was Nelson Morris. Both Armour and Morris conceded that equal pay for equal work to both men and women was fair, and that extra pay was fair, but not for overtime work in general. The Amalgamated organ, *The Butcher Workman*, commented on the testimony: "They had heard of the 33 per cent increase in the cost of living, but nevertheless had to admit that wages were not increased correspondingly. They claimed that $2.75 a day is enough for a family to live on."

Morris was more incisive in his testimony and a bit more belligerent than Armour:

WALSH: About "guaranteed time"—suppose men are laid off, do they get paid for the rest of the week?

MORRIS: Men are laid off during the slack season, but the workers so laid off are notified two or three days ahead.

ARBITRATOR: Do you notify these men when you want them again?

MORRIS: We naturally give preference to these men when we are hiring again. But we have been able to devise no system for notifying such men when they are wanted.

WALSH: If the men are laid off, on—say, Tuesday evening—would they get guaranteed time for forty hours for that week?

MORRIS: We would probably regard those men as laid off permanently and they would get no pay. . . .

WALSH: In fixing wages, don't you consider what it costs your employees to live?

MORRIS: We go principally by the wages paid in other places.

WALSH: Don't you know there was no change in wages from 1904 to 1916?

MORRIS: That was before my time. . . .

Walsh and Morris got into a discussion about "comparative comfort," in which Walsh included a worker's going to the theater three times a year:

Morris: The theater part might easily be overdone.
Walsh: How many times do you go to the theater in a year?
Morris: About twenty times.
Walsh: Do you think it would be reasonable for the worker to go to the theater three times a year?
Morris: Yes.
Walsh: Then, not knowing how much it takes for a man to support a family, you arbitrarily fix his wages?
Morris: We don't arbitrarily fix wages. If we did, and anybody else was paying more, he'd go there.
Walsh: You absolutely fix his wages, that is, he can take it or leave it?
Morris: That is correct.[6]

While the wage arbitration proceedings were going on the arbitrator visited several packing plants in Chicago. According to a news report:

Odors and changes in temperature in passing from one plant to another at the stockyards forced Judge Alschuler, arbitrator in the wage controversy between the packers and their 100,000 employees, to cut short his investigations yesterday. After being twice overcome while hundreds were at work around him, he said he could stand it no longer. . . . At the Hammond plant the first evidence was found to corroborate the union charges that superintendents speeded up machinery to get a greater output, but did not increase wages accordingly. . . . In the canning department of Libby, McNeill & Libby they learned that women employees were paid 20 cents an hour, while men who do the same work are paid 27½ cents.[7]

Public opinion in most walks of life actively sympathized with the packinghouse workers and supported their demands. One newspaper editorial said:

The wage inquiry at the stockyards will not give much satisfaction to Americans willing to think. A few years ago Upton Sinclair wrote a book about them, but they weren't greatly altered as a result of the sensation made by his exposé. If we recollect rightly, there were some

[6] News reports, *Chicago Daily Tribune*, February 19, 20, 1918; *The Butcher Workman*, February 1918, p. 2.
[7] News report, *Chicago Examiner*, February 16, 1918.

improvements in the sanitary conditions in some of the plants, but that was good business.

The wage inquiry is disclosing conditions which ought not to exist in any great and prosperous industry. They are conditions for which not merely the immediate victims but the whole community pays a heavy price. If an industry cannot prosper and pay men and women enough to keep them on a level of decent human existence the industry should cease. In the case of the packing industry we know that enormous fortunes have been made in it. . . . The existence in the midst of our comfortable household of thousands of our fellow men who cannot contrive to feed and clothe themselves and their children even at the price of the hardest toil is a confession of social incompetency.[8]

4. LET THE CONSUMER BEWARE!

The need for protection of consumers is an old story. It was urgent in the civilizations of antiquity, although little was done about it. The guilds, as we have seen, made regulations to protect consumers; later came laws to regulate the quality of meat and bread, of wine and beer, but they were largely ineffective. Consumer protection, in the modern sense, began in Europe early in the nineteenth century with the development of microscopic and analytical chemistry to detect adulteration and disease. Demands for consumer protection became stronger with the growth of manufactured foods, of scientific knowledge, and of consumer consciousness.

In the early 1900's the protection afforded American consumers of foods and drugs was insufficient. Big businessmen opposed protective and regulatory legislation. Henry O. Havemeyer, president of the American Sugar Refining Company (sugar trust), expressed the general attitude in testimony before a federal commission: "That is my theory. *Let the buyer beware: that covers the whole business.* You cannot wet-nurse people from the time they are born until the time they die. . . . I say, hands off." [9]

Some efforts were made to legislate for consumer protection. Con-

[8] Editorial, "Social Incompetency," *Chicago Daily Tribune,* February 15, 1918.
[9] U.S. Industrial Commission, *Report and Proceedings* (1900–1902), vol. 1, pp. 122-23. The sugar trust practiced all the monopoly abuses of the 1890's and after. It was accused of adulteration. Of the $586,000 in fines for illegal railroad rebates collected by the Interstate Commerce Commission within the three years after it got the power to levy fines, one-half came from the American Sugar Refining Company. In addition, although a beneficiary of tariff

gress in 1886 passed an anti-adulteration oleomargarine act. In 1890–91 and in 1895 federal legislation provided for certification of the wholesomeness of meats for export, and also for protection of domestic consumers against diseased meats. In 1898 an act placed a heavy tax on flour mixed with other ingredients; and an act in 1903 authorized the Secretary of Agriculture to establish standards for food products, but did not provide means of enforcement.

Legislation authorized the Secretary of Agriculture to set up inspection of all live cattle and of carcasses intended for export, and to establish mandatory post-mortem inspection of animals whose carcasses or products entered into interstate commerce. Since the inspection laws said nothing about rejection of meats which on post-mortem examination were found unfit to eat, these went into intrastate commerce. Moreover, annual appropriations up to 1906 were never enough to provide an adequate number of inspectors.

The consumer attack began on dangerous drugs, especially patent medicines. Then, in 1905, came Upton Sinclair's *The Jungle*, with its description of the filthy conditions in packinghouses, which aroused a storm of public apprehension and protest. President Theodore Roosevelt denounced people "who poison for profit," and appointed two special commissioners to investigate. They reported that the stockyards were filthy and unsanitary; the packinghouse atmosphere was noisome and the drainage worse; inspection, limited to the time of killing, was insufficient to detect all diseased animals; only pork intended for export to Germany received microscopic examination; meats were processed with little regard for cleanliness and wholesomeness, with little regard for the health of consumers.

The packers denied the charges and began to clean up their plants. A pure food bill, with an amendment providing for meat inspection, met stubborn opposition in Congress. It was enacted (in emasculated form, however) because of public pressure and President Roosevelt's insistence.

Inspection improved over the years. Since it operated under an interstate commerce law, federal inspection did not cover all meat output. State legislation for inspection developed slowly; it now ranges from very comprehensive and effective laws, as in California,

protection, the sugar company carried on a long-continued system of customs manipulations; the government compelled it to make restitution in the sum of $2,134,000. Eliot Jones, *The Trust Problem* (1922), pp. 111-13.

to optional inspection or none at all. As of the first quarter of 1944, federal inspection covered 98.5 pounds of meat per capita (annual rate), or 68.2 per cent of the total; the balance received no federal inspection or was farm slaughter.[10]

A unified comprehensive system of universal inspection is needed. Yet Congress in 1945 cut the appropriation for inspection by around $11,000,000 and provided that federal meat inspectors be paid by the packers. (Congress in 1892 decided on government payment of inspectors; it so continued until 1945.) The Congressional action not only endangered consumers, it weakened the competitive position of small independent packers, for whom inspection added thousands of dollars to the payroll. If these small packers paid inspection costs they lost money; if they gave up inspection they might lose business, for consumers would buy the inspected meat of big packers who could afford to pay for inspection.

From any angle the action of Congress made no sense. It went back to the old attitude: Let the consumer beware! Only this time it was the people's representatives in Congress, not the monopoly oligarchs, who disregarded the public health. Congress restored federal inspection in July 1948, under pressure from the meat-packing industry, the unions, and the public.

Union and management representatives, including those of the American Meat Institute, expressed their opposition to the 1945 action at Congressional hearings. Oscar Mayer, president of one of the larger meat-packing independents, Oscar Mayer & Company, testified on June 20, 1947, before the Senate Subcommittee on Agricultural Appropriations:

I have long been an advocate of expanded federal inspection in our industry. Though pleased over the substantial increase in the number of plants now under federal inspection, I still feel that for one pound out of every four of our commercial meat supply to be without benefit of thorough inspection is a serious reflection on what we Americans consider adequate protection of the public health. I am sure that in transferring the cost of federal meat inspection to the federally inspected packer, Congress will be directly responsible for a substantial reversal in the recent important trend toward increased federal inspection, thus defeating the basic purpose of Congress in enacting the law.

[10] Office of Price Administration, Economic Data Series No. 1, *Civilian Meat Distribution*, January-March 1944, p. 8.

Both unions in the packing industry—the Amalgamated Meat Cutters and Butcher Workmen, AFL, and the United Packinghouse Workers, CIO—supported the bill to restore to the federal government the whole cost of federal meat inspection. Said the Amalgamated spokesman at a Senate hearing:

We should do nothing to undermine the prestige of the meat inspection service which is so essential a public service. We should do everything to make meat inspection attractive to those slaughtering and meat processing companies that are presently not required to assume the obligation of inspection in their plants. . . . Congress should study ways and means which would voluntarily attract more companies to accept meat inspection rather than to impose additional restrictions which will unquestionably drive many companies not engaged in interstate commerce to give up federal inspection.

One problem of policy is evident: should not the public authority function to safeguard the consumers' welfare when it alone can do the job? Another problem is whether or not to provide the opportunity of free enterprise for small independent enterprisers. The shifting of inspection costs onto the industry threatened the small packers with limited financial resources. A spokesman for these packers, W. G. Mueller, president of the American Packing Company, said: "The inspection service is not voluntary but mandatory for packers who ship in interstate commerce. The proposal would force many small meat packers to abandon federal inspection and would place a premium on such abandonment." [11] The Congressional action that restored federal inspection should be supplemented by comprehensive legislation in states where inspection laws are inadequate.

The meat-packing industry has made substantial improvements in the sanitary conditions under which its products are processed. These improvements are rather unevenly spread from plant to plant. An address by Dr. D. H. Nelson, chief chemist of Oscar Mayer & Company, gives an interesting picture of what is being done and what can be done to protect the people's health:

We need not concern ourselves with the stockyards, where livestock are assembled, further than to say that the animals should be at all times

[11] "Livestock and Meat Industry Representatives Strike Hard at Packer-Pay Inspection," *The National Provisioner,* June 28, 1947, p. 11.

kept clean, dry and as comfortable as possible. Plenty of fresh air and clean water is an absolute necessity for all packinghouse operations.

The modern killing floor is constructed of hard surface materials. The walls are of glazed tile, glass or other similar hard, smooth, water-resistant material. The pens for handling animals should be cleaned frequently and kept reasonably dry. . . . It is the best practice, following the brilliant piece of work done by our Australian friends, to wet cattle and calves before slaughter to reduce contamination of the carcass from the innumerable bacteria on the hair and skin.

Hogs go directly to the sticking pen and after a few minutes on the bleeding rail, drop to the scalding tub. The carcass is in contact with large numbers of bacteria of many kinds but the temperature of 140 degrees Fahrenheit and the concentration of soda ash and lime maintained tend to reduce the micro population materially. . . . The dehairing machine continues the work of the scalding tub and by its manipulation of the carcass might increase or aggravate the invasion of the tissues by organisms from the intestinal tract. The use of a rosin bath at 260 degrees to 290 degrees Fahrenheit tends to reduce the flora of the skin and can be considered as one of the newer sanitary measures.

It is important that in some places gross contamination results from punctures of the gut, especially the bung. This was reduced to practically zero in a packinghouse where the inspector in charge required all parts of a carcass soiled from this cause to be trimmed off. He said that simple washing was not enough. . . . When hog carcasses are dropped onto the floor or in cases where they are railed out for additional examination or inspection, the foreman should see to it that they are handled immediately and not allowed to lie around for several hours in a warm room.

So far as possible all product-handling devices—chutes, troughs—should be made of alloys such as Monel metal and stainless steel [whose] surfaces are easily cleaned. . . . Product should flow continuously and where such items as glands or other small pieces are collected, small metal containers supplied with ice should be provided so that they can be removed frequently to offal coolers.

Chill rooms should be adequate and provided with sufficient refrigeration so that crowding may be avoided. Also sufficient overhead space is necessary to allow air circulation, to prevent condensate forming and dropping on the hogs. Unit spray coolers have proved satisfactory where managed properly. . . . Under no condition should fresh pork be held for a few days and then sent to the freezer. The quicker the meat is completely frozen, the better.

The work of the curing cellars has been increasingly mechanized in the last few years. More and more metal boxes are used for curing bacon.

Defrosting tanks are now largely of metal, also grading tables, pumping tables and equipment. All of these things must be kept scrupulously clean, and curing vats require not only scrubbing but should be steamed after each use.

The speaker then lashed out at "unsound" practices in sausage manufacture and at overdependence on the use of antiseptics to solve all sanitation problems:

No matter how sanitary the sausage department is maintained, if the meats and/or meat by-products are unsound, the manufactured product is likely to be unsound too. It is true that sausage makers have been able under some circumstances to get away with murder in using questionable materials; but in the long run they are playing with strings attached to booby traps. Green rings are much less common now than formerly, but there is a decided predisposition to this kind of spoilage when beef or bull meat has an extra high bacterial population. It is well, too, to check on the water, spice, ice, milk, flour and all other things which are to enter into or come in contact with the sausage. . . .

There is a feeling among certain people, usually the poorly informed or the exploiters, that the use of some antiseptic or other can solve all their sanitation problems. Antiseptic preparations are a very fine addition to our list of weapons for war on bacterial contamination; but they are neither the last and final word, nor, I may say, the first and most important word in most cases. They are not a short cut to cleanliness. The meat inspection division has wisely limited the use of antiseptics to a very few substances and to quite restricted conditions in the packing-house, in strict accordance with specifications.

The lethal violet rays have been found valuable in some walk-in coolers and to help disinfect the air and hold down surface contamination. They are not by any means a general cure for the many ills of contamination in the packinghouse. . . . I believe we may confidently expect the intensive research programs of this and other industries to give us the help we need to maintain satisfactory operating conditions in the packinghouse—*if we have the wisdom to learn the new methods and the will to adopt them.*[12]

Another area where consumers need protection is standards of quality. Many food products, including meat, are graded for quality according to standards of the United States Department of Agriculture. This grading service is not mandatory, however; it is accepta-

[12] Proceedings, 42nd Annual Convention of the American Meat Institute, *The National Provisioner,* September 13, 1947, pp. 126-32.

ble because of its sales appeal, but an industry can give it up if it becomes inconvenient, or for any other reason. Because of what a spokesman of the National Independent Meat Packers Association called "the government's refusal to make needed corrections" in definitions of standards, a large part of the packing industry gave up grading in 1947; the amount of graded meats dropped two-thirds—from 9,279,000,000 pounds in 1946 to 3,526,000,000 pounds in 1947. The industry assumed that, because it was united in the demand for "needed corrections," its demand was right. But that is not necessarily true. And, in any event, the consumers were denied the protection they need.

The Amalgamated, too, does a job of consumer protection. What the union did from 1947 to 1949 may serve as illustration: (1) It exposed "the filthy and inhuman conditions under which poultry is slaughtered and eggs are processed." (2) It exposed what the Amalgamated called "the pork sausage racket"—"*pure* pork sausage, with mostly a lard content, is a swindle [with] sausage from the Big Four plant sold as a pound of pure pork sausage having only five ounces of edible sausage; it might be well for Congress to consider a law that would compel sausage manufacturers to label their products." (3) Union campaigns in Oregon have protected consumers against being sold horse meat for beef and, in eleven Western states, have achieved more effective state and city inspection.[13]

To return to the 1900's situation: The hazards for consumers came from a threefold source: insufficient scientific knowledge, ignorance of existing knowledge, and packers' willful indifference. Scientific knowledge is constantly growing; by now it can insure adequate protection for the consumer. There are packinghouses where virtually everything that is known to protect consumers is standard practice. The remnants of willful indifference—it has declined, but still exists—are a danger for both the industry and the public; management can eliminate the indifference if it wants to.

[13] Editorials and article, *The Butcher Workman*, February 1944, p. 3; May 1949, p. 12; October 1949, p. 8.

CHAPTER V

PUBLIC REVOLT:
CRACKDOWN ON MONOPOLY

1. MONOPOLY PROFITS AND ARROGANCE

SOCIAL antagonism toward the Big Five multiplied rapidly in the 1900's. Consumers, not altogether satisfied with the meat inspection law and its results, kept up their attacks, although agitation diminished as improvements were made. The American Federation of Labor, understanding that the Big Five's feudal opposition to collective bargaining meant a challenge to all union labor, made it an important part of its unfinished business to organize the meatpacking industry, and cooperated with the Amalgamated union. In addition, small independent packers became more antagonistic to the monopoly giants. And progressivism, notably in its expression by Robert La Follette and Woodrow Wilson, called for more effective anti-trust action to "restore economic freedom."

Nevertheless, the Big Five became more arrogant despite legal action. Known to everyone was the expansion of the Big Five into related food lines, such as poultry, milk products, cheese, grains, etc., and into retail selling. These incursions threatened increasingly many small businessmen, who sprang into action against the big packers.

The packing industry received a tremendous impetus from the war's demand for canned and cured beef and pork products to feed the soldiers of the Allies and, in 1917–19, American soldiers in Europe.

PACKER RATE OF PROFIT, 1912–18

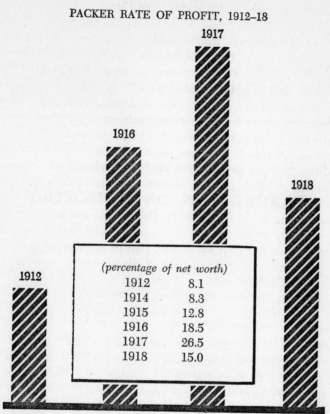

(percentage of net worth)	
1912	8.1
1914	8.3
1915	12.8
1916	18.5
1917	26.5
1918	15.0

Source: Federal Trade Commission, *Report on the Meat Packing Industry* (1920), Part V.

A glance at Big Five profits is revealing. Net profits (excluding interest payments) of these corporations up to 1918, counting from the years in which they began to do business as corporations (1868, 1877, 1894, 1896, 1899, respectively) aggregated a total of $504,298,-000. Of this sum $163,000,000 was paid out in dividends, the balance of over $341,000,000 kept in the business for reinvestment. In this period the total of outside investment, by the packer families and the general public, amounted to $126,600,000. In other words, *almost three times as much capital used in Big Five expansion came from reinvested profits as came from the money of stockholders.* Swift & Company, for example, began operation in 1868 with $160,-

000, and incorporated in 1885 with capital stock of $300,000; by 1918 its capitalization had grown to $173,000,000. Such expansion primarily out of profits was true of all the corporations moving toward monopoly from the 1870's and 1880's on. The Standard Oil Company of John D. Rockefeller is illustrative: in twenty-four years of operation, up to 1906, it paid out $548,000,000 in dividends, an average yearly rate of 39 per cent on capitalization; in addition, an even larger sum of profits was kept in the business as "surplus." [1]

In the war years 1914–18 packer profits rose, and so did the rate of profit on investment. This rate went up from around 8 per cent in 1912–14 to 26.5 per cent in 1917, and then tapered off because the government stepped into the picture to control prices and profits.

For the three war years 1915–17 the net profits of four of the five big packers were $178,000,000. In 1917, while the money value of sales was only twice the pre-war average, the profits were more than four times as much. Of course, part of the rise in profits came from price inflation. Nevertheless, it also meant a substantial increase in real profits, evident in one fact alone: the Big Five kept a large amount of war profits in the business as surplus, as liquid assets whose purchasing power went up after the postwar price deflation.

Both the profits and the arrogance of the big packers were typical of the capitalists who transformed industrial capitalism into monopoly capitalism. To the great profits arising from the expansion of new industries into all-inclusive mass-production enterprises were added the profits that came from monopoly control of competition and prices. The arrogance came from the dizzy inflow of profits and the power they gave to the packers. It was power over men, politics, and society in an age which had not learned how to direct technical-economic progress into the service of human welfare.

2. INVESTIGATION OF THE BIG FIVE PACKERS

The public, angered by high meat prices and profits, called for action against the Big Five. In 1917 President Woodrow Wilson ordered the Federal Trade Commission to investigate. After eighteen months of investigation the FTC reported, in July 1918: "We have found conclusive evidence that warrants an *unqualified* affirma-

[1] Eliot Jones, *The Trust Problem* (1920), p. 89.

tive to your question as to whether or not there exist 'monopolies, controls, trusts, combinations, conspiracies or restraints of trade out of harmony with the law and the public interest.' "

The FTC found that the Big Five were and had been in possession of monopoly power:

The menace of this concentrated control of a nation's food is increased by the fact that these five corporations and their five hundred and odd subsidiary, controlled and affiliated companies are bound together by joint ownership, agreements, understandings, communities of interest and family relationships. The combination is not a casual agreement, but a definite and positive conspiracy.

The FTC report specified a wide range of monopoly practices and abuses:

The Big Five *"are in agreement for the division of livestock purchases* throughout the United States according to fixed percentages." The commission gave evidence that these percentages were virtually stationary in the five years 1913–17: around 33-35 per cent for Swift, 24-27 per cent for Armour, 17-18 per cent for Morris, 10-11 per cent for Wilson, and 9 per cent for Cudahy. "Only one independent packer, Kingan & Company, slaughters as much as 1 per cent of the interstate total of cattle, and only nine independents slaughter as much as 1 per cent of the interstate total of hogs."

The Big Five *"exchange confidential information which is used to control and manipulate* livestock markets and to keep the actual prices of livestock as near as practical to the level which yields them the maximum profit. . . . Ownership, partial or complete, of the stockyards is not only a source of great profit, but affords a fundamental business advantage."

The Big Five *"are in ownership control of 91 per cent of all refrigerator cars and 93 per cent of all kinds of cars* owned by interstate slaughterers." They used this power to beat down competition and promote one another's interests. "The big packers have an added advantage which indicates the unity and cooperation under which they operate . . . their cars are pooled, and when one or another is in particular need of equipment, they lend them back and forth."

The Big Five make and receive *"secret and unfair" rebates from railroads,* despite the law to the contrary: an added competitive advantage in addition to their ownership of private refrigerator cars.

The Big Five *"are in control of a system of wholesale distribution* (in addition to ownership-control of stockyards, cold storage plants and refrigerator cars) through 1093 branch houses in the large towns and cities, and a system of 1297 refrigerator 'peddler car' routes which reach the smaller communities. This system of distribution through branch houses and 'peddler cars' is the bulwark of monopoly." In addition the monopolists were expanding their retail outlets.

The Big Five *browbeat and discourage competitors* by telling them that "they could not maintain themselves if they should attract unfavorable attention by aggressively trying to increase their volume of business. . . . Among other well-known methods of unfair competition used by the big packers are: bogus independents, local price discriminations, short-weighting, acquiring stock of competing concerns, and shutting competitors out of livestock markets. In addition, the Big Five employ a vicious system of rotations in price cutting. . . . Prices are cut a day at a time or a week at a time, so that the burden, distributed among the big packers, will seem light, but will fall with crushing weight on the independent competitor."

The Big Five *"act collusively in the sale of fresh meat"* by agreements to "share" markets and fix prices. This, of course, was their final purpose: to get the biggest price from the consumer, to make the biggest profit.

The Big Five *"are not only in monopolistic control of the meat industry* (ranging from 61 per cent to 86 per cent in the principal lines), but have secured control, similar in purpose if not yet in extent, over the principal substitutes for meat, such as eggs, cheese and vegetable-oil products, and are rapidly extending their power to cover fish and nearly every kind of foodstuff, including grain and breakfast foods. . . . Recently the big packers began dealing in various staple groceries and vegetables, such as rice, sugar, potatoes, beans and coffee, and increased their sales at such a great rate that in certain of these lines they have become dominant factors."

The Big Five are *"in direct control by ownership of market papers and other trade periodicals.* This was definitely established by the Commission in the case of six papers, and there are a number of others controlled by various indirect and effective methods. Control of market papers is important, both for their actual and potential influence over shipments and by the character of statements published and put on the wires as well as for protection against criticism. How important this may be is shown by a letter written by the editor of a Texas paper to Henry Veeder [Swift counsel], referring to the marked change in the policy of his papers, as he expressed it, 'before and after taking' two loans of $5,000 each from Armour and Swift. An editor of the 'National Provisioner' for years received a joint annual subsidy of $5,000 from Armour, Swift and Morris. . . . This and other correspondence from the packers' files indicates that direct ownership is not necessary for control of these publications."

The Big Five "are closely linked with a large number of banks, trust companies and railroads, which connections are utilized, often unfairly if not illegally, for the promotion of the packers' interests in the food industry." The FTC gave a list of sixty banks in fifteen cities, from Boston and New York to Chicago and San Francisco, on whose boards of directors the Big Five were represented "through members of the individual families, or through officers, directors or confidential employees of the packing companies." This system of interlocking directors was typical of developing monopoly capitalism in the early twentieth century; designated as "community of interest," it represented a combination of corporate industry and finance to work together to promote their power.

The Big Five are in conspiracy to protect themselves from punishment for their practices. "Further evidence of the existence of this conspiracy among the Big Five was found in the vault of Henry Veeder, in the form of documents relating to funds maintained by the big packers and oleomargarine manufacturers. These joint funds were used: To employ lobbyists and pay their unaudited expenses; to influence legislative bodies; to elect candidates who would wink at violations of law, and defeat those pledged to fair enforcement; to control tax officials and thereby evade just taxation; to secure modifications of governmental rules and regulations by devious and improper methods; to bias public opinion by control of editorial policy through advertising, loans and subsidies, and by the publication and distribution at large expense of false and misleading statements." [2]

[2] Federal Trade Commission, *Summary of the Report . . . on the Meat Packing Industry* (1918), pp. 3, 7, 15-19, 37, 40; also Part I, pp. 28-45, 52, 114.

In a public defense, through Swift & Company, the Big Five argued that the fixed percentages of livestock purchases merely indicated that the companies had reached a constant, more or less stationary stage in their business and that "the packers are in such active competition with each other that not one of them is willing to lose ground to another in volume of business handled, and accordingly they watch each other so closely that no single packer is able to increase his business inordinately." [3]

This argument breaks to pieces against the granite statistical facts of constant percentages, for these would tend to vary if competition were active. In addition, it was argued that the growth of independent packers would limit the Big Five's policy of monopoly prices and profit. Of course. But monopoly is seldom absolute; there are business ups-and-downs, the purchasing power and preferences of consumers, cyclical depression, and (save in rare cases) at least some competition. Nevertheless, the FTC facts proved existence of the pressure for monopoly prices.

The packers insisted they were in competition with one another. J. Ogden Armour in his testimony before the commission categorically denied any practices to restrict competition. He said: "Armour & Company are not now and have not been for many years a party in the remotest degree to any pool, arrangement, agreement or combination of any kind whatever for the control, regulation, or limitation or restriction of the purchase of livestock or the sale of any of the products thereof." The FTC found ample evidence to indicate pressure for limitation of competition.

The big packers engaged in a sort of "negative competition," that is, they watched one another to prevent the breaking of agreements, which might lower prices and profits. Larger profits were to come from high prices, not from each packer trying to secure a larger share of the market. They all "competed" to make as much money as they could from existing arrangements and from lowering of costs to make bigger profits out of established prices. In actual fact, their net profits *were* unequal. But this was not competition as it is understood in theory and practice.

The Big Five were like merchant-capitalists in the later guilds: they used restrictive practices to keep out competitors and promote

[3] Swift & Company, *Analysis and Criticism of Part II of the Federal Trade Commission's Report on the Meat Packing Industry* (1919), p. 27.

their joint interests, while they still competed to come up top-dog. Said the FTC:

There are certainly rivalries in certain lines among the five corporations. Their agreements do not cover every phase of their manifold activities. Nor is each of the five corporations a party to all agreements and understandings which exist. Each of the companies is free to secure advantages and profits for itself as long as it does not disturb the basic compact. Elaborate steps have been taken to disguise their real relations by maintaining a show of intense competition at the most conspicuous points of contact. . . . There is the natural rivalry of officials and departments, and this is made much of as indicating real competition. It is not real. Some independent packers exist by sufferance of the Five, and a few hardy ones have survived in real competition. Around such few of these as remain the lines are drawing in.[4]

Undoubtedly the Big Five represented, in addition to their monopoly practices, a force for technical-economic efficiency. This was part of their dominance and a contribution to progress. But their monopoly power grew not out of the instruments of efficiency but primarily out of control and abuse of these instruments. Consider three of them:

1. The stockyards promoted expansion of the meat industry, an expression of efficiency and progress (disregarding undesirable geographical concentration and filthy stockyard conditions). But stockyards alone would not have built the packers' monopoly power if their ownership and control had not been concentrated in the Big Five, if the yards had been independent competitive enterprises or (as they now are) public utilities not under packer ownership and control.

2. Another technical-economic instrument of efficiency, the most basic, was the refrigerator car. But here, too, the contribution to monopoly came from packer ownership and control, and from the discriminatory "favors" the packers received from railroads with whom they were allied in "community of interest." The railroads could have made more profit from the operation of refrigerator cars on an independent competitive basis, with the cars freely available to all packers, as ordinary freight cars are. Under such conditions the new instrument of efficiency might have favored independent packers as much as the Swifts, the Armours, and their associates.

[4] Federal Trade Commission, *Summary of the Report*, pp. 6, 10.

3. The cold-storage warehouses and branch houses were a decisive technical-economic instrument of efficiency for distribution of meat products. But here, too, it was centralization of ownership and control that gave the big packers their monopoly advantage. Cooperative or public ownership of the distributive network would have made monopoly difficult, if not impossible.

The FTC hearings aroused tremendous public indignation and there was a growing clamor for reform. The big packers, with their frantic efforts to conceal evidence and their unconvincing denials of its plain meaning, added to the fires of public protest.

"Records of the companies," reported the FTC, "particularly as regards stockholders' lists and other evidences of ownership, were constructed to conceal rather than reveal facts; important documents had been removed from their proper places in the files, and the reports of some of the most important corporations and statements of their officials could not be accepted. . . . Among other falsifications, the vice-president of Armour & Company omitted the company's interest in the Chicago Stock Yards, amounting to $1,-552,000, although the treasurer of the company testified that the transfer of this property from J. Ogden Armour to the company had been made prior to the time the report was prepared. . . . A committee of their confidential employees reported on April 10, 1916, that 'as matters now stand criminal prosecutions are sure to follow.' . . . We had to meet schools for witnesses where employees were coached in anticipation of being called to testify." [5]

The FTC investigators seized the files of Henry Veeder, general counsel of Swift & Company, which revealed many damaging facts. (Since the Veeder pools of the 1890's, of which he had served as secretary, Veeder had been involved in all the machinations of the Big Five.) On appeal to the courts, Federal Judge K. M. Landis upheld the FTC action and said: "The United States Constitution does not extend to granting immunity to outlaw property. . . . Henry Veeder claims that a corporation cannot be imprisoned. Then can a man, by incorporating himself, take himself away from under the search warrant law or keep himself out of jail?" [6]

All the Big Five's efforts to stop or play down the investigation merely aroused greater public indignation against them. Their

[5] Federal Trade Commission, *Summary of the Report*, pp. 8-9.
[6] News report, *Chicago Daily Tribune*, February 12, 1918.

refusal early in 1918 to grant the workers higher wages and improved conditions, although most of the demands of the Amalgamated union were consented to by an arbitrator, strengthened the clamor for remedial legislation. And Francis J. Heney, who directed the FTC investigation, was as pressing in his demands for legislation as he was in prying loose the packers' secret activities.

After America's entry into the war the government worked out a system of licensing to conserve meat supplies and to hold prices down. In October 1917 a convention of the American Meat Packers Association (now the American Meat Institute) agreed on a plan to save millions of pounds of food from going into inedible products, to eliminate waste of feeds at stockyards from overfeeding of cattle by shippers to increase their weight just before sale, and to foster more efficient utilization of the labor force. On this matter of efficiency *The Butcher Workman* commented: "The packers will find needed cooperation among the butcher workmen, meat cutters and allied trades. Economy of labor can be greatly enhanced by the cooperation and good-will of employees, adequate living wages and fair working conditions." [7]

In March 1918 Food Administrator Herbert Hoover urged on President Wilson a "reconsideration of policy" in connection with the meat industry. "This change of policy," he said, "may take the form of more definite and systematic direction of the large packers, or may even take the form of operation of the packinghouse establishments by the government." [8]

Demands for legislation to break the Big Five monopoly grew stronger in all social groups. The Amalgamated Meat Cutters and Butcher Workmen, now an organization with nearly 100,000 members, joined in the demands. The union was instrumental in causing the adoption, by the American Federation of Labor, of a resolution which said:

Mindful of the revelations made on control of the food interests of the country, a control of great danger to the country's future welfare, . . . the American Federation of Labor supports the Federal Trade Commission in its efforts to secure remedial legislation in the meat-packing industry. The AFL calls special attention to expansion of the control of the meat

[7] Editorial, "Convention of the American Meat Packers Association," *The Butcher Workman*, November 1917, p. 8.

[8] News report, *Chicago Daily Tribune*, April 1, 1918.

packers over preparation and sale of unrelated food products, which has proceeded so rapidly in recent years that absolute control of the food of the nation is passing into the hands of the five packers while the legitimate manufacturers and distributors of food products other than meat are in danger of destruction.[9]

The AFL's emphasis on Big Five invasion of the field of "unrelated products" indicates the extent to which independent businessmen in those fields were afraid of that invasion. The unions worked to rally the forces of free independent enterprise against monopoly. And the independents joined in the fight, in which all progressive Americans were engaged.

3. REFORM AND THE AFTERMATH

In its report the Federal Trade Commission recommended legislation for government ownership of stockyards, of refrigerator cars and rolling stock for transporting livestock, and of cold-storage distribution facilities. The FTC's specific proposals were:

1. *That the government acquire, through the Railroad Administration, all rolling stock used for the transportation of meat animals and that such ownership be declared a government monopoly.*

In the transportation of all other kinds of freights the transportation companies provide proper and suitable freight depots. The proper and suitable freight depot for livestock is a stockyard with its equipment of exchange buildings, terminal railways, and means of distributing full, unbiased, helpful market information, etc. We therefore recommend:

2. *That the government acquire, through the Railroad Administration, the principal and necessary stockyards of the country, to be treated as freight depots and to be operated under such conditions as will insure open, competitive markets, with uniform scale of charges for all services performed, and the acquisition or establishment of such additional yards from time to time as the future development of livestock production in the United States may require. This to include customary adjuncts of stockyards.*

A requisite for the proper transportation of fresh meat and dairy products is that type of rolling stock known as refrigerator cars. The railroads supply proper, special types of cars for other classes of freight, but the beef refrigerator cars and icing facilities, which are absolutely necessary for the transportation and distribution of fresh meats, are in private

[9] Report, "The AFL Convention," *The Butcher Workman*, June 1919, p. 1.

ownership. This ownership furnishes these five great packing companies one of their most powerful means for controls, manipulations, and restraints. Lacking access on equal terms to these facilities, competitors of the five great packers are at their mercy, and, competition being stifled, the consumer similarly is helpless. We therefore recommend:

3. *That the government acquire, through the Railroad Administration, all privately owned refrigerator cars and all necessary equipment for their proper operation and that such ownership be declared a government monopoly.*

Proper freight houses are provided by common carriers for the various sorts of freight except meat and perishable products. The indicated freight depot for such commodities is a cold-storage house. Such a depot used as distributing station, if free of access to all, would constitute an agency for fair and free competition. Such a depot, in private hands, as now, constitutes an invincible weapon for monopoly and control and manipulation. We therefore recommend:

4. *That the government acquire such of the branch houses, cold-storage plants, and warehouses as are necessary to provide facilities for the competitive marketing and storage of food products in the principal centers of distribution and consumption. The same to be operated by the government as public markets and storage places under such conditions as will afford an outlet for all manufacturers and handlers of food products on equal terms. Supplementing the marketing and storage facilities thus acquired, the Federal Government establish, through the Railroad Administration, at the terminals of all principal points of distribution and consumption, central wholesale markets and storage plants, with facilities open to all upon payment of just and fair charges. . . .*

Acquisition of the stockyards and car lines alone will not secure the fundamental improvements which we are seeking. Figuratively speaking, we will have opened only two of the doors by which the big packers have obstructed the channels of food commerce, while the third remains closed. An independent packer may with government-owned yards and cars find it possible to secure and ship his products upon terms of equality with the big packers, but unless he has an opportunity to dispose of them under fair conditions, his competition will not be effective and the consumer will not be benefited.[10]

The FTC proposals were a comprehensive program to liberate enterprise in the packing industry. Its proposals for government ownership of stockyards and of distribution facilities—rolling stock,

[10] Federal Trade Commission, *Summary of the Report,* pp. 4-5, 48-49. All italics in the original.

refrigerator cars, and cold-storage warehouses—did not mean
socialism. It meant public ownership only of the strategic factors
whose control gave the Big Five their monopoly power. Under conditions of public ownership and regulation, enterprise would have
been left free to compete freely without any competitors having
monopoly power to destroy the freedom of independent enterprisers
to compete.

What is significant, from the angle of social-economic policy,
about these proposals is this: *the FTC had to recommend government ownership in order to promote free private enterprise,* which
monopoly ownership moved to restrict and destroy. This is important, for it shows how conditions had changed since the time,
a hundred years earlier, of unrestricted free enterprise and competition.

Nevertheless, the FTC proposals were altogether in accord with
the philosophy of liberal proponents of free enterprise, from the
Levellers to Adam Smith and after. These liberals urged free private
enterprise as economic freedom against mercantilist (and guild)
monopoly restrictions on freedom. It was the "free" in free private
enterprise that the liberals stressed, not the "private." Private ownership constituted a means for the promotion of economic freedom.
The FTC proposed to limit *private* enterprise wherever monopoly
restricted or destroyed *free* enterprise.

Public opinion inclined toward acceptance of the FTC recommendations. One newspaper thus summed up the general expectations: "Government ownership and operation of stockyards and
refrigerator cars are foreshadowed as the probable results of the
investigation of the Chicago packers." [11]

But the general expectations were not realized. The FTC program
was mercilessly whittled down, and none of its government ownership proposals was accepted by Congress. Rather than risk trial and
judgment for anti-trust violations, the Big Five agreed in 1920 to
a compromise known as the Packers' Consent Decree, which provided that the monopoly packers agree: to give up their holdings
in public stockyards and railroad terminals; to give up their public
cold-storage warehouses for products other than meats; to discon-
tinue their retail meat stores and wholesale distribution of products
other than meat products, notably groceries (they were permitted to

[11] News report, *Chicago Daily Tribune,* February 13, 1919.

continue handling poultry and dairy products, cottonseed oil, and oleomargarine); to give up their holdings in market newspapers.

Undoubtedly these changes, especially separation from the stockyards, struck a serious blow at the Big Five. The blow was far from mortal, however. Discontinuation of cold-storage warehousing and wholesale distribution of products unrelated to meat products helped independent enterprisers in those areas, but it did not disturb the meat-packing monopoly. This was true also of discontinuation of the Big Five's retail meat markets. Separation of the big packers from stockyards and railroad terminals did undermine one prop of monopoly power, but other props were not affected because the Consent Decree allowed the Big Five to keep their refrigerator cars and distribution network, major elements in their power.

Moreover, Congress did not accept the FTC proposal for public ownership of the stockyards. The Packers and Stockyards Act, passed in 1922, converted the stockyards into a "public utility" with an agency of the Department of Agriculture to set up and administer regulations, but at the same time the yards were allowed to remain under private ownership, although independent of the packers.

A number of factors combined to bring about this serious whittling down, in fact virtual rejection, of the FTC program for restoration of economic freedom in the packing industry.

The Big Five put on an intensive campaign against legislative adoption of the FTC proposals. Louis F. Swift and Thomas E. Wilson appeared before the Senate Committee on Agriculture to testify in the name of "free enterprise" and defend their practices. The American Meat Packers Association used all its resources to denounce "radical" legislation. Support came from other monopoly oligarchs, who were afraid that any public ownership in the packing industry might spread to other economic areas.

Still more important, however, was a change in the public mood. The crusading spirit of the war years began to evaporate. Postwar indifference and disillusionment sabotaged the struggle against monopoly interests. The dominant public temper, a mixture of cynicism and apathy, found personal expression in the amorality of the bootleg-and-flapper era of the 1920's. On the world scene the postwar reaction led to a disastrous rejection of American participation in the League of Nations and withdrawal into a self-defeating isolationism. And, in this atmosphere, monopoly had nothing to worry about.

4. MONOPOLY IN THE 1920'S AND AFTER

Union labor, including the Amalgamated Meat Cutters and Butcher Workmen, backed up the FTC proposals. The sentiment for public ownership was growing; in 1920 the Railway Brotherhood unions, for example, proposed the "Plumb plan" to make the railroads public enterprises under the joint administration of management, the unions, and government.

But organized labor threw neither its full nor an effective weight for reform. Moreover, with the war's end the unions were put on the defensive by owner-management, which in 1919 began an aggressive campaign against labor that came to a climax during the depression of 1920–21. As a result the unions lost most of their war gains in membership and were too weakened to exert effective influence on legislation.

So in 1920 the Packers' Consent Decree allowed the Big Five to get off in comparatively easy fashion. But they were not satisfied, and a few years later they tried legal means to upset the provisions of the decree, which they had accepted to avoid trial and judgment. The Big Five had stipulated that their acceptance did not constitute an adjudication that the defendants had violated any law. Now the packers appealed to the United States Supreme Court on the ground that, since the decree was neither a trial nor a judgment of guilt, its provisions deprived them of property "without due process of law." It was precisely to avoid trial and judgment that the packers had accepted the decree, and they now used their own action to upset it! The Supreme Court decided against the Big Five. This litigation suspended the decree's operation for the five years 1925–29.

Yet the Packers' Consent Decree expressed neither good economic sense nor good anti-trust policy when it forced the packers to give up "unrelated lines" but allowed them to keep those bastions of monopoly, the refrigerator cars and cold-storage distribution facilities. For to make the Big Five give up food lines other than meat meant that their distribution network was used at a lower level of efficiency. And to leave them the major means, privileges, and power meant their continued monopoly domination of the meat industry.

Evidence appeared quickly that the crackdown on the Big Five had not ended their dominant position. In the midst of the Consent Decree proceedings the meat-packing industry experienced a post-war recession in prices and profits. This, together with the changes imposed on the Big Five, brought about financial reorganization and consolidation in the industry. The outstanding expression of consolidation was the merger of Nelson Morris & Company (whose assets were $95,000,000) with Armour in 1923.

In 1931 a plea for modification of the "unrelated lines" provision was rejected by the Supreme Court. The monopoly packers fought most bitterly against giving up these lines of food products. The Amalgamated joined with small business to fight the packers on this issue, and the packers lost.

When independent interior plants began to cut into sales of the packers, now the Big Four, they bought up scores of these plants (some of which were closed down) and built plants of their own in different regions of the country. Continued Big Four dominance is shown in the proportion of all livestock (under federal inspection) slaughtered by them in the years 1937–46, according to Federal Trade Commission figures:

Sheep	79%
Calves	68%
Cattle	58%
Hogs	54%

But this is significant: although the Big Four maintained their domination, *they were unable to increase their power.* Their proportion of total packing sales dropped from 64 per cent in 1921 to 55 per cent in 1929, rose again to more than 60 per cent in the 1930's, and stayed around that point.[12] Economic and legal barriers prevented further expansion, although the 1920's were an era of mergers, consolidations, and combinations greater than in any earlier period.

In the ten years 1919–28 total corporate mergers (in manufac-

[12] TNEC Monograph No. 35, *Concentration of Economic Power* (1940), pp. 18-19.

tures and mining) numbered 1268, which involved the disappearance of 5991 independent concerns.[13] In three months of 1929 alone (just before "prosperity everlasting" crashed into the most disastrous depression in American history) forty-two giant mergers took place affecting $12,000,000,000 of corporate assets.[14] The enormous scope of the centralization of corporate control may be seen from these figures: around 1000 giant corporations received 47.9 per cent of all corporate net profits in 1923 and 60.1 per cent of the profits in 1929.[15]

While only one merger took place in meat packing, there were many in other food industries, which, as already noted, had lagged behind the monopoly procession. They now made up for lost time. Mergers of food corporations, in the ten years from 1919 to 1928, numbered 128, causing the disappearance of 835 independent concerns. Several corporate giants came forth. One of them, Standard Brands, organized by the House of Morgan (which got two directors on the board), merged Royal Baking, Fleischmann Yeast, and other corporations; total assets amounted to $67,500,000. Another combination was General Foods, organized with assets worth $70,000,000.[16]

By the late 1930's concentration in all food industries had become a dominant fact. Three corporations did 43 per cent of the business in meat packing, with one concern alone doing 20 per cent. In dairy products three corporations did 21 per cent of the business in butter, three 63 per cent in cheese, and three 44 per cent in condensed milk. In flour milling three corporations did 38 per cent of the business; another three 17 per cent of bread baking. In the canning of vegetables three corporations did 13 per cent of the business; another three 30 per cent of the canned fruit business. The sales of three grocery chains were equal to 22 per cent of the retail sales of groceries, with one corporation accounting for 14 per cent of the sales.[17]

---

[13] National Bureau of Economic Research, *Recent Economic Changes* (1929), vol. 1, p. 184.

[14] News report, New York *Journal of Commerce,* May 23, 1929.

[15] Compiled from U.S. Bureau of Internal Revenue, *Statistics of Income* for the respective years.

[16] News reports, *New York Times,* June 21, 1929; August 25, 1929.

[17] TNEC Monograph No. 35, p. 90.

Typical of growing concentration in food was the flour-milling industry, which in the 1920's went through a period of mergers and consolidation comparable to those of meat packing from 1890 to 1910. The number of flour mills shrank from 11,690 in 1909 to 4000 in 1929, with average output per mill rising from 10,528 to 29,859 tons, and three corporations in control of up to two-fifths of the industry's production.

As in meat packing, technical-economic advance provided a basis for concentration in the food industries, but financial corporate power was the main factor in the growth of monopoly.

And in 1948 came another government anti-trust suit to dissolve the monopoly packers.

5. CRACKDOWN AGAIN—1948

In 1918 the Federal Trade Commission, ordered to investigate the Big Five, recommended action to destroy their monopoly power. Exactly thirty years later, on September 15, 1948, the Department of Justice filed another anti-trust action against these packers, now the Big Four, to break them up into fourteen separate "competing" enterprises.

The 1948 action emphasized the failure of the provisions of the Packers' Consent Decree of 1920. For the new complaint charged

. . . a continuing agreement and concept of action among the defendants . . .
. . . to refrain from competing with one another in the purchase of live-stock and in the sale of meat and meat products.
. . . to restrain competition from independents by formulating, and urging independents to follow, policies and practices identical to those followed by defendants in buying livestock, determining prices to be paid for livestock, ascertaining costs, distributing and selling meat and meat products, and determining selling prices of meat and meat products.
. . . to exclude independents from the meat-packing industry.

These were precisely the charges made against the monopoly packers in 1918. Thirty years later the government thought that the situation, apparently, was not changed.

The 1948 suit against the packers was, according to Attorney General Tom C. Clark, "a link in the drive to free production and sale of food and food products from monopolistic restraints. No avenue must be overlooked to prevent the basic necessities of life such as food from falling into the hands of monopoly groups. The channels of distribution between the farmer and the consumer must be kept free from all artificial restraints and all artificial blockades. When other methods fail the only alternative left is to separate the few dominant concerns into a number of competing companies."

The packers reserved formal answer to the suit, but their spokesmen stigmatized the charges as "false" and the suit as "politics." The chairman of Armour's board of directors, George Eastwood, said: "Similar charges have been made from time to time, and they have always failed when taken to court." Part of this statement is true, but the government had no opportunity to prove the 1918 charges in court because the big packers avoided trial by agreeing to the Consent Decree. The decree contains "no findings of fact," and the defendants consented to its entry "upon condition that their consents shall not constitute or be considered an admission . . . or be considered an adjudication that [they] have in fact violated any law of the United States." In their argument to the court for dismissal of the 1948 anti-trust suit the attorneys for the Big Four conclude: "The 1920 Consent Decree is a bar to any attempt by the government to relitigate any of the issues in that proceeding."

The American Meat Institute branded the charges "nonsense" and said:

With respect to what causes meat prices to be up or down, there is no mystery whatsoever—and the Department of Justice should know it. It is recognized by everyone who knows anything about meat . . . that prices are established by the over-all demand of consumers as a group for the available supply of meat. Demand is and has been great; the supply of meat is and has been limited.

There is a measure of truth in the AMI's argument, although supply and demand are not the only factors in price determination. Postwar meat prices were caught in the general inflationary pressure. But the AMI (along with most businessmen and, it must be added, some labor unions) opposed continuation of price controls after the war. The AMI insisted in 1945 that meat prices would fall if OPA controls were scrapped, but they went up instead, and the Institute in 1948 blamed "demand" for the rise. Moreover, inflationary pressures do not operate in a vacuum; they are not independent of the price-and-profit policies pursued by corporations. The tremendous rise in corporate profits after 1945 is indicative of the fact that business enterprises, including the meat packers, used an inflationary situation to make bigger profits.

The "answers" that the big packers dared not press for final court decision in 1919–20 are the "answers" they make today (in the public prints) against charges of monopoly conspiracy to prevent competition. I quote a summary of the government's complaint to indicate its belief in the prevalence of the old practices:

In furtherance of their market sharing, each defendant has kept constantly informed of the number of head of livestock purchased by each of the other defendants. . . . Each defendant has purchased, or merged with, a number of competing companies for the purpose of destroying competition. . . . Defendants have shared and controlled their direct purchases of cattle and hogs so that each will sell quantities of meat products in relatively stable proportions with respect to each other. . . . They used, and conspired with, the principal trade association of the packing industry, the American Meat Institute, in furtherance of their conspiracy. The defendants sell the major portion of the meat and meat products sold by member companies of the Institute; and each has been represented on the Institute's Board of Directors, Executive Committee, and other principal committees. . . . Development of uniform basic accounting principles and general practices was undertaken in 1921 by the Institute's Committee on Accounting, . . . including use of the "test cost" formulas to determine killing and cutting costs, paying prices for livestock, and selling prices of meat. These "test cost" formulas were refinements of those used by defendants under the 1898 Agreement. Armour, Swift, Wilson, and Cudahy used, and still use, these uniform principles and formulas to carry out identical buying and selling practices. . . . They determine in the morning of each market day the price at which to buy livestock. The prices are then checked against one another so that prices paid by the defendants will be held down and all will be kept in line. . . . If an independent becomes too aggressive in his buying, defendants compete with him and outbid him until he ceases his aggressive activities. . . . In their sales of meat and meat products, the defendants have refrained from price competition with one another [by means of] substantially identical selling prices. . . . When differences are found in prices, the salesmen telephone this information to the branch house managers, who then revise their own selling prices so as substantially to conform them to the level of prices being charged by other defendants. . . . The Executive Committee of the American Meat

Institute, in September 1929, authorized the development and publication of hog and cattle "cutting tests" similar to the "test costs" used by defendants, to suggest to all member packing companies the "charge which must be made on products going into cure if fresh pork operations be figured on a break-even basis." . . . The Institute has made repeated efforts to cause its members to require their salesmen to sell at the prices set out in published price lists. . . . At the present time, defendants no longer require numerous meetings and mechanisms, such as existed under the 1898 Agreement, in order to operate their combination and conspiracy. . . . By about 1920 the executives of each concern had become so habituated to the use of identical methods and policies, that they were expert in conducting the operations of their respective companies along parallel non-competitive lines. The operations of all defendants are alike. The public has been deprived of the benefits of competition among defendants, *just as if they had been merged into a single corporation.*

The complaint is comprehensive. It raises, however, a number of questions of economic organization and policy. Among them, in addition to some failure of anti-trust policy, is the question of whether competition can be restored; and, if it can be, whether competition is capable of making the most constructive response to our new understanding of natural resources and of the technical-scientific revolution in agriculture, nutrition, and foods.

Monopoly is undesirable and competition is desirable. But what kind of competition and for what? Competition on what level, within what framework of policy, and for what values?

CHAPTER VI

LIVESTOCK GROWERS:
ESPECIALLY THE FARMERS

1. CHANGES AND IMPROVEMENTS IN LIVESTOCK

MEAT packing and livestock breeding are interdependent. They
have developed as both cause and effect of the expansion in
food production and consumption.

Livestock breeding and its relation to economic progress began
almost as soon as man learned to domesticate and breed animals.
In ancient civilizations cattle, sheep, and swine not only provided
man with food, but were a part of his religion and his culture.
Cattle were invested with particular mythological significance. For
example, in one of the "mystery" religions that helped to shape
Christian mysticism, devotees were "washed" in a stream of blood
that poured over them from a butchered bull, from which they
"absorbed" the life and spirit of the god. In the refined symbolism
of mystical Christianity, this was transformed into being "washed
in the blood of the Lamb."

Livestock breeding, primarily a nomadic and pastoral occupation,
developed slowly and insufficiently. The number of breed animals
was small, and breeders knew little of animal husbandry. Animals
in general were thin, for feeding methods and supplies were inadequate to fatten them. And meat animals came to maturity late.

For the urban peoples of ancient times, therefore, there was a
comparatively small supply of meat. Moreover, meats were neither
highly nutritious nor well flavored. In most of medieval Europe the

95

breeders did little winter feeding; instead they slaughtered the animals and thus kept herds small. In England as late as the fifteenth century, for example, animals were slaughtered in the autumn and put into brine to supply salt-meat for the winter months.

There have been five major factors in the expansion of the modern livestock industry:

1. *The development of urban civilization* after the breakdown of feudalism and the growth of towns.

2. *The Industrial Revolution,* which not only created modern industry and greater urbanization but began an economic-scientific revolution in animal husbandry as part of general agricultural progress.

3. *The overseas expansion of Europe* into new regions such as the United States, Argentina and Canada, Australia, New Zealand and South Africa, where immense grasslands provided abundant pasture for breeding cattle and sheep.

4. *The growth of population,* primarily in rapidly growing industrial nations, which called for a greater commercial food supply, including meat products.

5. *The increasing production of livestock by farmers,* so that animal breeding became an integral part of farming.

These five factors combined to bring expansion in the packing industry. The tremendous development of livestock production and packing would have been impossible, however, were it not for technical-economic progress in meat processing itself, particularly the refrigeration and canning of meats that allowed all-year farflung distribution over a growing transportation network. These developments, in turn, depended upon improved breeding to provide more and better animals for meat products. And the most typical expression of this progress appeared in the American industry.

Packed pork was the chief meat product of Colonial America. In addition, both cattle and sheep were cultivated. Sheep, introduced early in the Colonies, were grown largely for their wool until about 1850. They supplied wool for New England textile mills throughout the nineteenth century, until a growing demand for mutton by industrial populations stimulated production of sheep for food purposes as well. Cattle, introduced by Spanish, Dutch, and English

Colonial settlers in North America, was an important agricultural product in the Southern states until cotton became the dominant crop.

After the Civil War, with the opening of the great Western lands and construction of the transcontinental railroads, cattle breeding experienced a rapid growth as beef became a major item of diet. Production of beef cattle reached its peak around 1900, and then began a decline that reversed itself during World War II. The total of 46,680,000 beef cattle in 1916 had dropped to 43,270,000 by 1940. These cattle losses were both absolute and relative, as other varieties of livestock, especially dairy cows and sheep, kept on increasing. In 1945 the number of beef cattle rose to 53,000,000, but it is not clear whether the gain will be maintained.

CHANGES IN LIVESTOCK PRODUCTION, U.S.A., 1916–45
(in millions)

Year	Beef Cattle	Dairy Cows	Sheep	Swine
1916	46,680	20,750	36,260	60,590
1920	48,940	21,450	37,320	60,150
1930	37,970	23,030	45,577	55,800
1935	42,760	26,080	46,130	39,060
1940	43,270	24,920	46,550	61,110
1945	53,000	26,780	37,510	62,340

Source: Compiled from statistics of the U.S. Department of Agriculture.

Note: Swine output rose to 62,127,000 in 1933; the tremendous drop in 1935 to 39,060,000 came from the "kill pigs" campaign to reduce supplies and raise prices.

As for sheep, their number grew substantially in the 1920's, and slightly thereafter to 1940; then came a drop during the war years. These reasons were given for the drop:

Unprofitable conditions and a constant market for meat at high prices have tempted wool growers to liquidate their flocks. J. H. Oppenheim, President of the Farm Equipment Institute, estimates that the United States will have to find the equivalent of 50,000,000 acres of high-yielding crop land in the next twenty-five years. "This is necessary if our present standard of nutrition is to keep pace with our estimated growth in population. This prediction of our needs doesn't take into account the added burden of tiding over the have-not nations abroad until better days." [1]

Cattle herds, too, needed replenishment. In July 1948 the Department of Agriculture, pointing to the decrease in cattle herds during the previous four years, recommended a beef slaughter 7 per cent lower than in 1947–48. It added: "However, feeding to heavier weights, now that more grain will be available, may partially offset the decrease." A larger permanent measure of replenishment may come from increased cattle breeding in the Southern states.

One final change needs mention. The proportion of meat animals slaughtered in packinghouses went up from two-thirds in 1899 to around four-fifths in recent years, with a resulting decline in farm and retail slaughter (mainly retail). The greatest change occurred in calves, the packinghouse slaughter of which rose from 28 per cent in 1899 to 77 per cent in 1937. Greater industrialization of slaughter brought no significant changes in per capita meat consumption except for a 100-per-cent increase in veal. Although industrial packing's proportional share of animal slaughter has risen, total meat output has not grown as much as population; and this fact expresses a per capita decline in the consumption of meat products.

CHANGES IN PACKINGHOUSE PERCENTAGES
OF ANIMAL SLAUGHTER, U.S.A., 1899–1937

	1899	1937
Cattle	61	83
Calves	28	77
Sheep, lambs	87	91
Hogs	67	69
Total	64	77

"Total" is an average weighted by live weight, in pounds.

Source: Solomon Fabricant, *The Output of Manufacturing Industries, 1899–1937* (1940), p. 131.

The American livestock industry has made truly great improvements in animal husbandry: in feeding, in prevention and control of disease (especially cholera, tuberculosis, and tick fever), in cross-breeding. These improvements have resulted in greater pro-

[1] News story, *New York Times,* July 17, 1948.

ductive efficiency, a larger yield of high-quality meat per unit of breeding stock, more satisfaction of consumer preferences. Still greater improvements are coming, however, as science, the livestock breeders, and industry work for more improvements. The most significant recent developments are:

1. *Greater understanding of the relation between soils and good livestock.* Soil fertility determines the amount and quality of animal foods as well as crop foods. Especially important are the soil's minerals, particularly phosphate. TVA's campaign for increasing use of mineral fertilizers has brought amazing improvements in livestock—in both the quantity and quality of animals and in the nutritional value of their meat for consumers.

2. *More efficient methods for disease prevention and control,* especially for the control of Bang's disease, internal parasites, insects injurious to livestock, and cyanide poisoning. This progress includes improved sanitation. The results may open up new regions for livestock production, such as the Southeast, as feed supplies become available.

3. *Feeding of animals for correction of nutritional deficiencies, with emphasis on vitamins and minerals.* A number of production difficulties in many areas have been overcome by the development of feeding to correct deficiencies of iodine, calcium, iron, cobalt, phosphorus, and copper. Methods for identification of nutritional deficiencies are being improved and made available to breeders. These developments may result, especially for poultry, in an increase of standardized commercial feeds that supply the necessary minerals, proteins, vitamins, and other growth factors needed to overcome nutritional deficiencies.

4. *Cross-breeding for greater productive efficiency, lower costs, and higher quality.* This has proved most successful in beef cattle; 20 per cent of cattle in the Gulf Coast region are cross-bred with Brahmans. Cross-breeding of swine is still experimental, yet the number of cross-bred hogs is already large, and is growing; such hogs need less feed, reach maturity earlier, and produce better carcasses than standard hogs. About 10 per cent of range sheep are a cross of mutton-lambs and wool-type ewes, bred for a high yield of mutton. Poultry is being cross-bred to improve broiler production.

5. *Progeny testing, for dairy cows and poultry, to locate sires capable of transmitting high producing ability to their offspring.* Selection and transmission of producing ability is a slow, gradual process, but the final result is a definite increase in the productivity of dairy animals. The same principles can be used to improve meat animals.

6. *The development of artificial insemination, to consolidate and distribute the advantages of progeny testing.* This reduces the number of males and eliminates them as a factor in the spread of disease. It also improves the genetic make-up of herds. The number of breeding associations that practice artificial insemination is growing.[2]

Of many other improvements, several may be cited as illustrations of the trend. A new method of dehorning animals, at once more efficient and more humane, uses a caustic in collodin solution which, upon application, gradually destroys the horn tissues. Dehydrated alfalfa hay fed to animals makes them gain weight faster on less feed; a small portable dehydrator is available which enables farmers to produce their own dehydrated hay. Shorthorn cattle, a favorite of small farmers (in earlier years they were known as "mortgage lifters"), are being improved for cross-breeding with all types of cattle. Cross-bred Brahman cattle are able to thrive in the hot tropical climate. A network of dairy herd improvement associations has grown up throughout the dairy regions to serve the small farmer. These associations provide their members with information and service on breeding, selection of best producers, and selective mating; licensed milk testers travel from farm to farm to test milk, make feed nutritional-and-cost analyses, help the farmer to improve his breeding work.

There are still more revolutionary developments ahead. The range of radioactive research is being stepped up by progress on atomic energy. One of the first acts of the Atomic Energy Commission was to make a grant to the Bureau of Plant Industry, Department of Agriculture, for work on development of radioactive fertilizer. The results will be better crop plants and better feeds for meat animals. Another possibility is direct radioactive improvement of livestock through changes in genetic make-up.

[2] U.S. Department of Agriculture, *Yearbook of Agriculture: Farmers in a Changing World* (1940), pp. 521-24.

2. STOCKMEN, FARMERS, AND RANGE LANDS

Expansion of beef production, it will be recalled, took place from 1870 to the early 1900's. Great ranches appeared in the West and Southwest. It was the age of feudal cattle barons in Texas, Oklahoma, Kansas, Nebraska, Wyoming, Montana, the Dakotas, Colorado, and New Mexico. As many as 18,000 head of cattle were on some of these ranches. The cattle barons were tough—a general characteristic of the West at the time; they frequently took the law into their own hands and waged guerrilla warfare with one another. They used all means, some of them pretty savage, to prevent the great open spaces from being fenced in by homestead farmers. Their theme song could have been "Don't Fence Me In!"

An interesting survival of one of these feudal domains is the King Ranch in Texas, whose boss, Robert J. Kleberg, Jr., is related by marriage to the financial-corporate aristocracy, including members of the Celanese Corporation. The ranch's holdings of 900,000 acres make it bigger than the state of Rhode Island. In 1947 King sold from $3,000,000 to $4,000,000 worth of beef and netted around $1,000,000 profit (before income taxes) from all operations. Of one aspect of King Ranch *Time* has written:

To make money on cattle Bob Kleberg runs his feudal domain with the hard fist of a feudal lord. But he has hundreds of miles of fence to mend and mind—and everything within those fences. To outsiders the feudal fist sometimes seems too hard. There were unpleasant rumbles against the ranch in 1936 when two poachers supposedly disappeared within it. (The Klebergs think that if they really did disappear on their ranch they might well have got lost and starved to death.) Now, as a goodwill gesture, forty hunters a week are permitted on the ranch during the hunting season but they are carefully circumscribed. . . .

The King Ranch cowboys' pay is low, it amounts to about $150 a month, but the ranch takes care of them in sickness and in old age and they have a feudal loyalty to the ranch. Total payroll for the 500 employees is over $400,000, a yearly average of only $800. To outsiders the ranch is a curious mixture of the new Texas of scientific big-business-minded cattlemen and the old gun-fighting days.[3]

[3] Article in *Time,* December 15, 1947, pp. 89-92. The King Ranch is a feudal-capitalist setup in which, however, science operates to improve animal breeding. *Time* writes: "A geneticist once wrote of Kleberg: 'He works in the medium of animal heredity with the steady hand and eye of a man at a lathe turning out

The King Ranch, however, seems to be kept going more by the will of its master than by economic necessity, for the production of beef is becoming more closely linked with general farming and with dairying, where, by and large, closer observation and more individual attention can be given to the job. In 1946, only 15,000,000 of 80,000,000 cattle and only one-half of 37,900,000 sheep were on the Western range lands. Independent farming is not only, in final analysis, more efficient; it is also more democratic than the feudal cattle barony. Cooperative enterprise would appear to be the democratic answer where cattle raising, as on the Western range lands, may have to be on a large-scale basis.

The production of hogs is exclusively a part of farming because they can be easily raised by every farmer. They require small capital; they multiply rapidly and mature early, and they consume foods unfit for man. The hog requires less grain per pound of meat produced than any other animal, and most of its carcass can be used as cured meat.

While hog raising in some nations, including Germany and Poland, is identified with potato cultivation, in the United States it is part of corn growing and dairy farming. In the Corn Belt around 40 per cent of the corn grown is fed to hogs and marketed as pork, particularly when the crop yields more profit as hog feed than as food for human consumption. Hybrid corn has stepped up acre-yields by 25 per cent or more, and so increased capacity to produce hogs. In dairy farming the hogs are fed on by-products such as skim-milk, buttermilk, and whey, in conjunction with small grains.

---

a part of a machine.' His first great feat was the breeding of the King Ranch's Santa Gertrudis cattle, the only new breed of U.S. cattle that has had any commercial value. Back in 1917 the ranch's cattle—English Shorthorns and Herefords—were doing poorly. They sickened in the blazing Texas sun. Kleberg decided to try Brahman bulls, which thrive on grass feeding and India's killing heat. Other cattlemen shook their heads. Brahmans had not worked out too well for other breeders. But Kleberg bred the Brahmans and Shorthorns together till he evolved what he wanted, a cross-bred bull who performed so well at siring a new breed that now all the cattle on the ranch are descended from him. The Santa Gertrudis breed, which is now widely sought wherever there is a year-round grass feeding, has one great virtue; it is hardier and grows heavier on grass feeding than any other. . . . Kleberg then turned his hand to grass. His father had brought in South African grass. Bob took seed from the best plants and perfected the strain. Later he developed a fine strain of yellow-beard grass. As one cattleman put it: 'Bob developed a breed of cattle to grow fat on grass, then developed the grass to make them fat.' "

SOURCES OF FARMERS' CASH INCOME

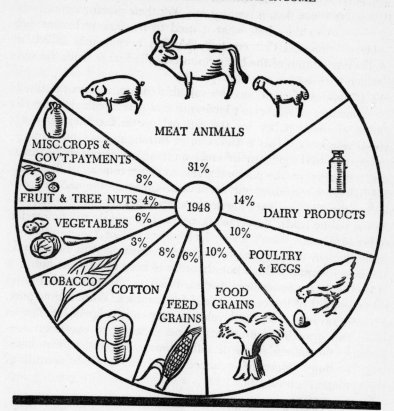

MISC.CROPS & GOV'T.PAYMENTS

MEAT ANIMALS

31%

8%

1948

14%

FRUIT & TREE NUTS 4%

DAIRY PRODUCTS

VEGETABLES 6%

10%

3%

8% 6% 10%

POULTRY & EGGS

TOBACCO

COTTON

FOOD GRAINS

FEED GRAINS

Around 30 per cent of gross farm income comes from the sale of cattle and hogs. Animal husbandry on farms, in addition, is a most effective means of soil conservation and enrichment. Grass-legume pastures improve the yields of other crops in rotation, such as corn and small grains; they prevent erosion, and add nitrogen and humus to the soil.

Although farmers now raise more cattle than they did fifty years ago, Western cattle ranches are still important producers. While these ranches are now, in general, smaller than they were in the years 1870–1910, and not so feudal in organization and attitude, they still raise an old problem of social-economic policy—the conservation of range lands. These lands constitute 40 per cent of the continental area of the United States: 728,000,000 acres, only 119,000,000 fewer than a century ago. Yet their grazing capacity is not much more than half what it used to be, largely because of stockmen's practices that created what has been gently called "a run-down condition of the basic resources—the forage, with the soil on which it grows."

This "run-down" condition of a valuable natural resource resulted from a mixture of stockmen's ignorance and greed with slow development of social policy for the rational use and conservation of natural resources. (This is true also of forests, mines, and farms.) Stockmen grazed too many livestock on their lands and, at the same time, trespassed on the public domain and ruined many of its acres. The federal government set up several agencies—the U.S. Forest Service, the National Park Service, and the Grazing Service—to protect the public lands. Nevertheless, trespassing and destruction went on because, until recent years, lack of control of the unreserved public domain tempted many stockmen to overuse this range and their own intermingled holdings in order to keep newcomers out.

Conditions are being improved on these range lands, which produce one-third of the country's feed for livestock. Work is going on to restore ravaged areas; to develop greater knowledge of the forage values and growth requirements of range lands; to encourage research in the interrelations of soils, climate, vegetation, and livestock breeding. Stockmen's practices are improving too, according to government sources:

Many stockmen, alone or in cooperation with the federal government, have reduced their herds to a safe number to maintain the grazing capacity of their ranges, are already handling the grazing on their lands closely in accordance with the best-known range practices, or are interested in gaining greater knowledge of sound management. . . . This calls for stocking year after year with the number of animals each range unit will support without injury to the range, to the tree growth or to the watershed, and without unwarranted interference with game, recreation or other land services. . . . On ranches where improved practices and other results of research have been applied, they have hastened restoration of depleted ranges, facilitated livestock production and helped to stabilize ranch operation.[4]

[4] *Yearbook of Agriculture: Farmers in a Changing World*, pp. 441-42, 446-48.

Unfortunately, not all stockmen are improving their practices. Many of them still believe that "free enterprise" means freedom to pile up bigger profits regardless of natural resources and of the population and its future. These stockmen want the public domain (a large part of the range lands west of the Rocky Mountains) turned over to them for unrestricted exploitation. They do not say so openly; what they want, they say, is to transfer the public lands from federal to state ownership. All in the name of states' rights! What these stockmen actually mean is this, in the words of Bernard De Voto in a *Harper's* article: "The plan is to get rid of public lands altogether, turning them over to the states, which can be coerced as the federal government cannot be."

Farmers have a stake in the rational use and maintenance of range lands in the West and Southwest. The stake is specific, as well as general. Range lands are a source of feeder cattle and lambs which farmers, especially in the Corn Belt areas, buy to fatten for the market, while many Western ranches grow pure-bred cattle for sale to farmers to improve their herds.

One of the more important developments in stock breeding is the emergence of the Southern states as increasing producers of cattle, both for meat and for dairy purposes. It is part of a social-economic and cultural revolution.

The South's excessive emphasis on cotton created an acute problem of soil depletion, because cotton is a monstrous devourer of soil fertility. Even before the Civil War this depletion, together with the inefficiency of slave labor, drove cotton barons to seek new virgin lands on which slave-cultivated cotton might thrive. One result was an imperialism that, in addition to being primarily responsible for the 1848 war with Mexico, developed plans for the conquest of Mexico itself and of Cuba. After the Civil War the South continued as an essentially one-crop region, with cotton depleting soils from which came decreasing returns—a major cause of Southern poverty. Cotton farming gave little if any chance for livestock, especially cattle. A number of far-seeing Southerners urged their people to switch from cotton to grass and livestock, but with little success. In any event, considerable livestock production was not altogether possible because of the limiting factors of depleted soils and cattle tick fever. Now, however, the South is becoming an outstanding producer of cattle; its beef cattle population (exclusive of Texas) in 1941 was 6,200,000 head, or about one-sixth of the country's total.

The change to cattle production truly began in the early 1930's with final elimination of tick fever. This achievement paralleled increasing Southern recognition of the pressing need to rebuild the soil's fertility with grass, diversified farming, and livestock; and, in addition, increased use of fertilizer, especially minerals. The number of cattle and calves in the seven Tennessee Valley states, for example, increased 14 per cent in the years 1935–45; while in 1940–48, 1448 new manufacturing and processing plants were established in the valley and in areas supplied by TVA power. These developments are encouraged and strengthened by TVA.[5] Its chairman, Gordon R. Clapp, said in an address to a convention of the National Fertilizer Association on November 17, 1948:

In the fifteen years the TVA has been at work with the agricultural agencies and farmers of the Tennessee Valley, 1,000,000 acres have been shifted from open cultivated crops to grass and cover crops. The acreage of pasture has increased 14 per cent. The application of phosphate and lime to grass and pasture lands is becoming an established and expanding practice. . . . With fewer acres in row crops there has been a more intensive cultivation and a greater use of fertilizers to increase the total yields of corn, cotton, and tobacco on less land, thereby helping the farmer to finance his new crop rotation systems, his new emphasis upon phosphate, pastures, and livestock.

The growing emphasis on pasture for livestock, especially for cattle, is evident throughout the Southern states. Pastures are being enriched, and depleted or abandoned lands restored for livestock grazing,[6] by the application of phosphorus and lime. For the hotter parts of the South the new Brahmans, cross-bred with range cattle, are proving their superiority to other breeds. They are finer and

[5] TVA Publications, *Regional Economic Data No. 2*, June 30, 1948, p. 1.

[6] "There are about 25,000,000 acres of Texas and Oklahoma land that need to be seeded to perennial grass. Some of these acres are grazing lands that have lost their useful perennial plants. Some are abandoned farms, and others are acres so steep that it's risky to farm them. With proper foresight in planting, the seeding of these lands can help provide cool-season grasses for grazing in the winter. That is the time when the leaves of the warm-season species, which now dominate on the bulk of our grazing land, are dormant and lowest in food nutrients. Livestock make greatest gains on green forage." B. W. Allred, "Evergreen Grazing Under Conservation Ranching," *The Cattleman*, May 1948, p. 19.

heavier animals, more resistant to parasites and disease, and mature more quickly. Above all, the Brahman crossbreeds can withstand any adverse climatic and ranch conditions of subtropical and tropical regions, such as Florida, Cuba, and Central America. All-year pasture with mild weather that eliminates the need for shelter are factors that, especially in Florida, where Brahmans thrive, encourage rapid development of a low-cost livestock industry.

The implications of these changes are more important than their influence on livestock growing. They mean not only more breeding of meat and dairy animals, in which the South has been traditionally deficient, but more production of a larger variety of foodstuffs for the improvement of dietary standards and the abolition of malnutrition.

3. FROM PRIVATE TO "PUBLIC" STOCKYARDS

As a result of the Packers' Consent Decree of 1920 the dominant packers were separated from ownership and control of stockyards. In 1922 Congress enacted the Packers and Stockyards Act, which recognized stockyards as a public utility and set up public regulation of them. A major objective of the Stockyards Act was to end packer manipulations of livestock markets and the resulting violent and unreasonable fluctuations in day-to-day prices; and, at the same time, to end collusion among the packers to apportion livestock purchases and to fix prices with downward pressure.

The big packers denied that they fixed or were able to fix the price of livestock, and this argument has been advanced frequently in their defense. They maintained that sameness of livestock prices indicated that there was competition, since competition tends to bring about one price. On this score an outstanding American economist has answered:

Economists are accustomed to assume that under competition there can be but one price at one time in one market. This assumption is partly the result of observation, for markets do show a tendency to iron out inequalities in prices, and partly an *a priori* premise, growing out of the fact that the economist's study of the laws of price have been cast in the mold of a search for the natural level of prices; thus assuming that there is some natural level toward which the different prices in a market gravitate. We have recently witnessed an interesting practical commentary on this assumption, when the Federal Trade Commission, attempting to prove that restraint of trade exists in the meat-packing industry, cited as evidence the fact that the different packinghouses all pay the same prices for live cattle, and the representatives of the packers replied that this is the traditional symptom of a perfectly competitive market and only goes to prove how keen the competition in these markets is. Both sides, it may be remarked, employ professional economists. Which is right?

On the general question the truth appears to be that the regular operation of a competitive market implies that some take the lead and others follow, and unless there is an appreciable interval during which prices differ it is difficult or impossible for those who take the lead to gain any advantage by the typical competitive tactics of raising their prices for things they wish to buy or lowering them on things they wish to sell. The gain consists typically in selling more goods at the lower price. This is something a monopoly could also do, but competing concerns are supposed to have more of an incentive to cut prices than monopolies have. If all the competitors followed suit instantly the moment any cut was made, each would gain his quota of the resulting increase in output, and no one would gain any larger proportion of his previous business than a monopoly would gain by a similar cut in prices. . . . The distinctively competitive type of gain comes from getting *more* than one's former quota of the business: getting all the new business which the reduced price brings forth, or getting business away from one's competitors. This gain takes place chiefly in the interval after the customers know of the reduction of prices and before they become aware that competitors have followed suit. . . . Thus the retarded action of the market which permits different prices to prevail at the same time is not really an "imperfection," as theoretical economics has been inclined to regard it. On the contrary it is an essential requirement.[7]

The Stockyards Act provides that no packer shall (a) "engage in or use any unfair, unjustly discriminatory or deceptive practice or device in commerce, or (b) make or give any undue or unreasonable preference or advantage to any particular person or locality in any respect whatsoever, or subject any particular person or locality to any undue or unreasonable prejudice or disadvantage in any respect whatsoever," or (c) carry on any practices "for the purpose or with the effect of apportioning the supply in commerce between any such packers if such apportionment has a tendency or an

---

[7] John M. Clark, *Studies in the Economics of Overhead Costs* (1923), pp. 417-18.

effect of restraining commerce or of creating a monopoly." In addition, the Act (d) prohibits practices for "the purpose or with the effect of manipulating or controlling prices and commerce or of creating a monopoly in the acquisition of, buying, selling or dealing with any article of commerce, or restraining commerce." And finally, the packers shall not "conspire, combine, agree or arrange with any other persons (1) to apportion territory for carrying on business, or (2) to apportion purchases or sales of any articles in commerce, or (3) to manipulate or control prices." The Act was to be enforced by the Secretary of Agriculture through the Packers and Stockyards Division of the Agricultural Marketing Service. This public agency, under final authority of the Secretary, has the power to set up procedures for licensing, bonding, and accounting; to regulate stockyard rates and commission fees; and to set up and enforce standardized accounting procedures and rules for periodic reports.[8] (In 1935 the trade in live poultry was brought under regulation, with most of the Act's provisions and the Secretary's powers extended to it.)

It will be recalled that the Federal Trade Commission recommended public ownership of the stockyards. It backed up the recommendation with these arguments:

The stockyards and their essential adjuncts, such as exchange buildings and terminal railroads, must be acquired and operated by the government under such conditions that the producer will be assured of a fair market, reasonable charges, open bidding, full and helpful market information, the limitation of violent fluctuations in price, and the elimination of unnatural market influences. Moreover, the measure authorizing acquisition of the stockyards should provide for the acquirement by right of eminent domain of such sites adjacent to the yards as may be necessary for their proper expansion and for the location of such independent, municipal, or cooperative abattoirs or packinghouses as may be established. This will open the way for the independent packers and butchers, big and little, to establish their plants and secure their livestock under such conditions as will enable them to compete actively with the big packers.

[8] Monograph No. 11, U.S. Senate, *Administrative Procedures in Government Agencies,* "Administration of the Packers and Stockyards Act, U.S. Department of Agriculture" (1940), pp. 1-2. This monograph is an excellent study of experience and problems in administration, by the Stockyards Division of the Agricultural Marketing Service, of the Packers and Stockyards Act.

This interesting proposal for a balanced combination of federal, municipal, and cooperative enterprise to promote *free* private enterprise against monopoly might have led to constructive changes in the meat industry. But Congress rejected the proposal. The changes that were made, while in many respects beneficial, did not altogether end big packer malpractices. The importance of this problem for livestock growers is clear, as most meat animals offered for sale (over 80 per cent) are sold through the stockyards, and three-quarters are sold in nine major stockyards.[9] And the practices in these yards, while superior to what they were in the 1890's and after, are still subject to criticism from a number of sources.[10]

Although stockyards are now a "public utility" under control of the federal government, they are still private property. Several corporations, including the Chicago Union Stockyards and Transit Company and the United Stockyards Corporation, own the nine major stockyards. Their stock, it appears, is closely held. It is a strange situation, to say the least, for stockyards to be a public utility yet keep private ownership. Perhaps it would be more consistent, and certainly more advantageous for livestock growers and consumers, for stockyards to become public enterprises or cooperatives.

These criticisms and suggestions are supported by the 1948 antitrust suit for dissolution of the Big Four packers. The government complaint charges that these packers pursued much the same practices in their purchases of livestock after the Act's adoption as before. They still, the complaint says, "cooperate" in livestock purchases and "share markets" to control and depress prices. To prove this, the complaint cites the defendants' constant percentages of purchases, as illustrated in one table of purchases in the Chicago stockyards:

[9] Office of Price Administration, Economic Data Series, *Civilian Meat Distribution*, January-March 1944, p. 4.

[10] One illustration of this criticism follows: "Despite the large number of important or complex proceedings which were instituted under the Act, no rules of practice were adopted until September 14, 1936. . . . The tentative rules and regulations were submitted to stockyards owners, commission merchants and others engaged in the trade, as well as to their trade associations. Public hearings were held. . . . Since that time the general regulations have undergone general revision three times, but public hearings have been held in only one instance: the regulation requiring market agencies and dealers to execute bonds." Monograph No. 11, pp. 6-7.

BIG THREE CATTLE PURCHASES, CHICAGO, 1934–45

Year	Defendants' Purchases as Per Cent of Net Supply for Sale	Armour Purchases as Per Cent of Defendants' Total Purchases	Swift Purchases as Per Cent of Defendants' Total Purchases	Wilson Purchases as Per Cent of Defendants' Total Purchases
1934	54.76	42.15	35.78	22.07
1935	57.61	37.13	35.78	27.09
1936	56.04	35.79	34.79	29.42
1937	53.33	33.40	35.75	30.84
1938	57.09	34.89	34.38	30.73
1939	58.26	33.91	35.88	30.21
1940	53.67	37.63	31.51	30.87
1941	59.25	35.62	33.00	31.37
1942	54.31	36.93	33.53	29.54
1943	44.36	36.09	34.69	29.22
1944	42.70	38.30	36.33	25.37
1945	35.98	43.33	32.22	24.45

Source: U.S. Department of Justice, Anti-Trust Division, Complaint in the suit to dissolve the Big Four. Only purchases of Armour, Swift, and Wilson are included.

If conditions have not substantially changed after government action and in the course of a quarter-century, one may conclude that this kind of anti-trust action is not effective. Perhaps the Federal Trade Commission was right when in 1918 it urged public ownership of stockyards.

4. LIVESTOCK AND THE REVOLUTION IN NUTRITION

Changes in livestock production reflect changes in the dietary habits of Americans. Their per capita consumption of meat products declined as more varied, balanced diets became customary. The losses were in beef, with a substantial increase in veal consumption and a small one in pork, while lamb and mutton about held their own. (There is still room, however, for a greater amount of meat consumption to balance the diets of millions of Americans in Southern states and in Northern urban slums.)

MEAT CONSUMPTION CHANGES

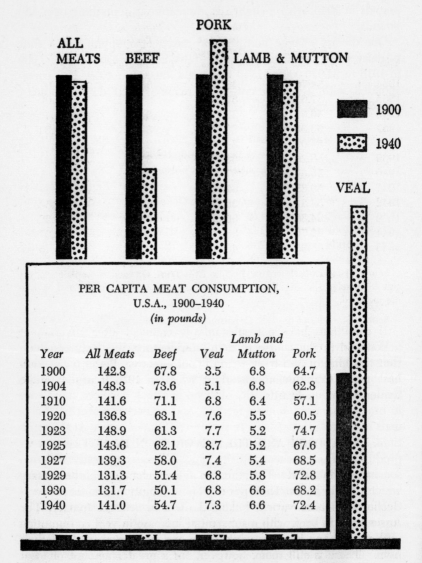

PER CAPITA MEAT CONSUMPTION, U.S.A., 1900–1940 (in pounds)				
Year	All Meats	Beef	Veal	Lamb and Mutton	Pork
1900	142.8	67.8	3.5	6.8	64.7
1904	148.3	73.6	5.1	6.8	62.8
1910	141.6	71.1	6.8	6.4	57.1
1920	136.8	63.1	7.6	5.5	60.5
1923	148.9	61.3	7.7	5.2	74.7
1925	143.6	62.1	8.7	5.2	67.6
1927	139.3	58.0	7.4	5.4	68.5
1929	131.3	51.4	6.8	5.8	72.8
1930	131.7	50.1	6.8	6.6	68.2
1940	141.0	54.7	7.3	6.6	72.4

Source: Statistics of the U.S. Department of Agriculture. Comparisons in the bars are based on percentage changes (1900 = 100%).

During the war years per capita meat consumption rose to a new high of 168.2 pounds in 1944 and then dropped to around 147 pounds in 1946, with a slight rise thereafter to something over 150 pounds.

One dietary change that affected meat consumption was a shift to dairy products. The number of dairy cows rose from 20,750,000 in 1916 to 24,920,000 in 1940 and to 26,780,000 in 1946. This corresponded with a rise in output of manufactured dairy products, especially evaporated milk and cheese.

MANUFACTURED DAIRY PRODUCTS, U.S.A.,
1924–29, 1937–40, 1945
(*in millions of pounds*)

Year	Butter	Cheese	Evaporated Milk
1924 *	2126	477	1277
1937	2132	649	1903
1938	2286	725	2104
1939	2268	709	2171
1940	2240	786	2465
1945	1699	1016	3776

* Average for 1924–29.
Source: Statistics of the U.S. Department of Agriculture.

Within meat consumption itself, in addition to the decline in beef, the substantial increase in veal and the slight increase in pork, there has been a shift from roasts and other large cuts to smaller, more tender cuts. One effect of this shift on livestock has been more care in breeding, more intensive feeding, and an earlier maturity of animals to obtain juicier meats to satisfy consumers' tastes. At the same time, and as a result, there has been greater turnover of herds, and production from earlier maturity, since animals are ready so much sooner for the market. The maturity age of beef cattle, for example, which used to be five to six years, is now usually two to three years. Cattle breeders are working with the United States Department of Agriculture to lower the maturity age still more.

Dietary changes are one expression of a revolution now going on in the understanding and practice of nutrition. The changes are not only a question of more balanced meals. They broaden to include the growing and processing of more nutritional foods, including meats, which demand a combination of sound agricultural policy and sound nutritional policy. I quote from an authoritative work on the subject:

Already, by the middle 1930's, the need for synthesis of the nutritional, agricultural, technological and economic dimensions of the food problem had become apparent to specialists in all these fields. . . . The result was a kind of revolution in progress. Leaders of the revolution are plant physiologists, agronomists, geologists, nutritionists, food technicians, soil chemists, plant breeders and geneticists—not to mention a dozen other more abstruse specialists. . . . Dehydration, the frozen food locker, the airplane, the synthesizing of new foods and food converters, and the fortification of nutritionally impoverished old foods with synthetic vitamins—each of these developments represents in itself a major revolutionary potential. Combine the best in them and cross-fertilize them with the actual and prospective success of the soil chemist and the plant breeder in stepping up the *nutritional content* of the crops the farmer delivers to the processor or the distributor, and what you get is an increment of quantity and quality from which we may expect not only a substantial improvement in the nutritional status of all classes of the American people, but in addition some highly significant economic and social emancipations affecting both the farmer and the urban housewife. . . . The average nutritional quality of quick-frozen foods has been advanced by the selection of superior, high-vitamin varieties, grown under optimum conditions of soil and climate, and by the improvement of quick-freezing technology. . . . Starting with fish, the quick freezers have learned how to process successfully nearly every food in the vegetable and animal kingdoms. . . . Pre-cooked meals are being developed and sold. . . . The yeast plant has a prodigious feeding potential. As soon as we regularly salvage, dry, and debitter all of the 200,000,000 pounds of brewers' yeast that ordinarily has gone down the drainpipe every year, the price should drop to perhaps 23 cents a pound. And once we begin making primary yeast out of molasses, as the British started to do in Jamaica, or out of hydrolyzed trash wood, the retail price of yeast should drop even further. Yeast is not only our cheapest source of B-vitamins; it is also our cheapest complete protein. . . . Nor does the taste offer serious difficulties. By adding suitable quantities of food yeast to such dishes as pork goulash, curry of veal, meat loaf, and beef-and-kidney stew, it was possible to increase substantially the workers' daily intake of vitamins and proteins—without their knowing anything about it! . . . Agricultural science has placed in our hands tools for building the national health of infinitely greater value and dependability than those provided by the manufacturer of synthetic vitamins. . . . Perhaps a third of the average household's food will come from greater distances than now, with higher speed and better preservation of nutritive value, while perhaps two-thirds will be locally grown and stored in individual or community food lockers. Nutritive value will be conserved by unit food carriers held at low temperatures, from the moment the food leaves the farmer's field or the processor's factory up to the moment it is placed in the home locker or refrigerator. . . . The city planning of the future will provide for the swift and economical delivery of food, as well as other commodities, from central warehouses to neighborhood warehouses, and from these to neighborhood groceries.[11]

This vision of things to come is inspiring. We already know enough not only to end starvation and malnutrition—although this alone would be a magnificent achievement—but to make food a means with which to create finer human beings.

Meat is caught up in the food revolution, not only in relation to the place of meat in balanced nutritional diets, but also in relation to new processes and outlets. Among the new outlets are cold-storage lockers, a side aspect of the frozen-foods trend which grew during the war. These developments are especially evident in rural areas, and locker storage may come to be used extensively in cities.

An expansion of community locker plants and of home-freezing and storage units is likely. As of the end of 1947 there were 9528 locker plants with more than 4,500,000 lockers in the United States; six months later the plants numbered 10,617 (compared with only 1300 in 1938).[12] The home freezer has grown tremendously in popularity. It presented a competitive problem to the locker industry, which decided to meet it in two ways: (1) by offering more processing service to owners of home freezers; (2) by selling home-freezer equipment and branching out into related lines. According to a 1947 report of the Farm Credit Administration, 22 per cent of locker plants provided slaughtering:

This central slaughtering produces better meat, enables the operator and farmer to spread slaughter over the year and also enables the plant to use many of the by-products largely wasted if the job is done on the

[11] James Rorty and N. Philip Norman, *Tomorrow's Food* (1947), pp. 127-28, 136, 150-51, 154-56, 158-62, 169, 172-73.
[12] Research Department, Federal Reserve Bank of Chicago, *Financial and Economic Survey of the Meat Packing Industry, 1948 Supplement*, p. 6.

farm. A few locker plants are building rendering plants to make better use of by-products.

Of all the plants reporting, 87 per cent now chill, cut, wrap, grind and freeze meat for patrons—a substantial increase over 1943. Curing pork increased from 39 per cent in 1943 to 42 per cent in 1946. Increasing numbers of plants are now rendering lard. A service comparatively new to the industry, poultry dressing, now is done by 17 per cent of the plants.

The locker plant industry is moving toward complete food processing for the community. Locker plants are doing this by expanding into more services, by increasing the number and size of plants, and by having more plants operate independently rather than simply as a side-line activity for a local grocery store, ice house, or meat market. Of an average amount of 353 pounds of food stored in lockers, 163 pounds was beef.

An increasing number of new plants are in smaller rural towns. Of all plants opened in 1945, 83 per cent were in towns under 5000 population while in 1943 only 62 per cent of the new plants were in the smaller communities. Farmers make up 73 per cent of all patrons. Besides handling the farmer's product for his own use, locker plants in rural areas are beginning to help growers dispose of their surplus meat, poultry, and fruits and vegetables.[13]

If the use of lockers spreads, and farmers and residents of small towns use their own meat animals or draw upon local supply, both meat packing and retailing will be seriously affected. Already in rural areas a shift back to local slaughter has developed from locker-storage activity. This local slaughter has been crude in many cases, and it raises the problem of inspection for sanitary conditions and quality; but improvements are taking place. If local processing continues a coordination of local disposal with outside outlets may arise to absorb products whose local use is not advantageous. This coordination may help to supplement local supplies with some from outside sources. Commercial opportunities will arise for preparing and packaging frozen meats to store in central or home lockers in urban areas, with operators making truck delivery direct to consumers.

Opportunity beckons to farmer livestock cooperatives. These cooperatives, in addition to marketing products and purchasing supplies, include processing plants of many kinds, from meat packing

[13] "FCA Survey Shows More Locker Plants Doing Meat Processing," *The National Provisioner,* March 22, 1947, p. 29.

and by-product plants to feed mills and fertilizer factories. They have begun to operate locker and frozen-foods plants. Local co-operative processing can broaden from packaging frozen meats for rural or urban locker storage to the general field of high-quality frozen meats. The quality market, a result of constantly improving consumer taste, seems a natural for livestock cooperatives. By emphasis on quality and high nutritional specifications in quick-frozen foods, the marketing and consumer cooperatives might make a constructive contribution to the food revolution.

All these changes will have a profound effect on agriculture in general, on the varieties and quality of livestock that farmers produce for market, and on the processing and distribution of meat products. The expansion in use of dairy products, the shift from beef to other meats and to poultry and fish, the improvements in animal breeding, the frozen-foods development, and the new sources and kinds of food—they all challenge the farmers, packers, and unions to understand and to master the changes now going on.

5. CONSERVATION AND THE FOOD SUPPLY

One basic American problem is the pressing need for conservation and enrichment of farm and range lands. What I have already said about the stockmen's abuse of Western grazing lands (where millions of acres have been and are still being impoverished) applies to farmers too. In the past hundred years, according to H. H. Bennett, Chief of the United States Soil Conservation Service, one-fifth of our tillable soils have been destroyed, one-third of the remainder is badly damaged, and destruction is still going on at the rate of 500,000 acres a year out of 460,000,000 acres of good crop land left in the United States.

It is true that the productivity of American farming has kept on increasing, with larger acre-yields and larger total output (including livestock) from a smaller number of farm workers. This increased efficiency has been accompanied, moreover, by improved farm practices and by conservation.

The United States Soil Conservation Service, although its appropriations are small, has excellent accomplishments to its credit. Farmers generally are becoming more conservation-conscious. The Tennessee Valley Authority has pioneered in a land policy of ecological synthesis that treats men, farm and forest lands, and water resources as one harmonious whole.

In 1948 Congress enacted a law which provides for a five-year program of research, investigation, and certain remedial projects (in cooperation with federal, state, and local governments), under general supervision of the National Public Health Service, to prevent and correct the stream pollution which is a menace to fish, wildlife, and vegetation as well as human health. Congress also provided for the expenditure, within five years, of $61,000,000 on a broad research program for wider and more efficient uses of farm products, with one-tenth of the expenditure earmarked for special research projects by non-governmental institutions or persons. And suggestions are being pressed that the federal government set up an Agricultural Resources Administration to unify the work and policy of the various agencies which deal with the conservation and promotion of natural resources.

Danger still threatens, however, for progress is uneven and it is accompanied by retrogression. Despite all conservation efforts, millions of acres of farm lands are in a condition of serious erosion, marginal and submarginal in their fertility, while other millions of acres are being eroded.

Only a handful of farmers are signed up with the Soil Conservation Service. Experts estimate that not as much as 10 per cent of our farmers are "good farmers" in the conservation sense. Western cattle-and-sheep growers, whose occupational ancestors plundered a large part of the range lands, are now trying to upset the Taylor Grazing Act policy of conservation in order to plunder the remaining lands for "quick big" profits—nor is the meat-packing industry joining with progressive forces to fight back these plunderers. Stream pollution is getting worse; industrial plants are doing little about it. Opposition prevents Congressional adoption of the plan for a series of TVA's from the Missouri Valley to the Columbia River Basin. Finally, much scientific progress in agriculture has been offset, in terms of larger crop yields, by continuing soil depletion.

These are all serious dangers which cannot be dismissed. But they can be overcome. It is undeniable that man has ruined and is ruining much of the earth's topsoil. But modern man, especially in the United States, has the understanding and has formulated the means to prevent destruction of soils into desert land and to rebuild the soils. The productivity of soils—their "biotic potential"—has no absolute limits. These limits are, by and large, relative; they are not set by nature but by man's technical-scientific knowledge and his use of it.

Soils under cultivation respond to what man does with them; they may become deserts, or they may become enriched and more fertile from proper fertilization and farming practices. Nor is topsoil irreplaceable. For man has become a creator of topsoil: he stops erosion and refertilizes, and he restores topsoil even after complete erosion has taken place. One government experiment stripped an acre of virgin land of its topsoil, after which seed corn failed to grow. But within six years, with scientific fertilization and crop rotations, the renewed topsoil yielded eighty-five bushels of corn, twice the national average.

And the fertility of millions of eroded acres has already been restored, including cotton-devoured acres that now bloom again. Moreover, not only is the soil's productivity being enriched, but plants are so improved that more of them grow on an acre without overtaxing the soil, as in the case of hybrid corn, which has raised acre-crop yields from 25 per cent up. The same is true of livestock: while stockmen have ravaged the range lands, American producers have learned to get more meat from livestock through improved breeding and feeding methods and earlier maturity of animals.

These constructive developments, however, do not offset the need for conserving and enriching American soil resources, and much is already being done. According to Department of Agriculture reports, the United States started large-scale reforestation in the 1930's; ten years later, 18,000 miles of tree belts ran from Canada to Mexico on 30,000 American farms—96 per cent of the trees alive. There are now 416,000,000 forest acres of cutting size; in 1947 alone 172,000 acres were planted. For irrigation, manufacture of electric power, and to help keep up a high ground-water level, 680,000 reservoirs have been built since 1936.

To improve grass and crop rotation systems, American farmers have done the following things: They have terraced 14,117,378 acres; and improved grazing methods are being used on 95,000,000 privately owned acres, compared with only 12,000 acres in 1935. Since 1936 fertilizer and better grass seed have been put on 36,-762,000 acres of pasture; almost nothing was being done in 1935.

In the crop year of 1947, "green manure" was planted on 18,531,867 acres (that is, crops were planted only to be turned over to enrich the soil); this was done by very few farmers in 1935. And, in addition, some 10,400,000 acres have been planted on contour. In some instances more than one of these programs has been used on the same acreage, with a resulting multiple influence on the improvement of soil fertility.

Another achievement is the comparatively new idea of grass farming, which, according to the 1947 *Yearbook* of the U. S. Department of Agriculture, "has swept the world." Livestock thrives on grass. But grass also can refertilize the soil if it is grown for a few seasons and then plowed under. In the United States the major possibilities for grass farming are in the Great Plains country, where millions of acres of short grass that grew there were plowed under by pioneer farmers and their descendants. Then came drought, and devastating winds carried away the topsoil. With the dust bowls of the 1930's came government scientific research on the problem, with this conclusion: Millions of ruined acres can be reclaimed for livestock grazing by growing grasses of the buffalo grass variety; they will not only grow again, they will grow better. The *Yearbook* reports: "Every reseeded pasture on the United States southern plains experimental range near Woodward, Oklahoma, has supported many more cattle and produced much greater total live-weight gains than the native range." The soil experts urge that 80,000,000 acres should be reseeded. They estimate it may take the natural grass from two or three to thirty years to recover. It can be done if we want to do it.

While American achievements are great, and their potential is still greater, what is being done is far from enough to solve the problem of soil depletion. This conclusion is neither scare-mongering nor defeatism, it is a sober statement of simple fact. Here is one authority's summary of the situation:

In actual accomplishment—in terms of acres under control or of farms placed under conservation management—we have only made a beginning. . . . The disconcerting fact is that crop yields have not increased in accordance with scientific progress. In Ohio, for example, the average yields of corn per acre for the state were about the same in 1920–29 as they were in the decade 1870–79. Yet the average use of fertilizer per acre on Ohio farms increased 340 per cent. This and similar illustrations point to the conclusion that the steady depletion of soil fertility has often, and perhaps generally, offset advances in the science of agricultural production. Where crop yields have been maintained in the face of declining soil fertility, it has meant increasing costs of production for a large proportion of the farmers. . . . Of the 300,000,000 acres of cropland in the United States that are affected by soil erosion, only a small part [48,269,000 acres in 1940] has been effectively placed under conservation management.[14]

The problems of soil depletion and rising production costs of crops and livestock require joint action by the farmers themselves and by government. Neither alone can or should do the job.

Much larger Congressional appropriations for broader and deeper conservation work are needed. This work should include not only control of soil erosion, which is merely one cause of depletion, but measures to prevent soil washing and blowing, to encourage terracing, contour cultivation, and crop rotation in a unified policy of most efficient land use. All the protective measures of agronomy, engineering, and management are needed, within the framework of flood control, reforestation, and control of stream pollution. And part of the appropriations is needed to speed up research on soils, crops, and livestock.

A system of incentive payments can stimulate farmers to work for more effective utilization of conservation plans, with a clear understanding of where the costs of replenishing depleted lands should be a public charge. But, in addition, the farmers should recognize more fully their individual share of the job.

Along with present reliance on local farmer committees to carry on conservation work, there can be increasing reliance on cooperatives where the task calls for a large measure of group action. Farmer and livestock organizations should develop (where they may not yet have done so) more understanding of and action on the principles of rational land use. Legal punishment and public opprobrium are necessary for organizations, such as the cattle and sheep associations, that willfully try to break down conservation measures and practices. The policy of promoting the welfare of their individual members must coincide with promotion of the general welfare. The two objectives are not necessarily contradictory; they can complement one another.

[14] *Yearbook of Agriculture: Farmers in a Changing World*, pp. 432-33, 439.

Within this conservation policy and action we need more projects like the TVA—in the Missouri Valley and the Columbia River Basin, for example. For TVA has made a substantial contribution to the conservation and development of American resources. Its idea is being discussed for adoption throughout the world. The TVA policy makes an ecological approach to resources in terms of the quality of soils and how soils of high productivity can be built and maintained; the quality of crops and of livestock in a balanced system of farming; the quality of people and the quality of their lives in country, town, and city.

In this approach, the past, present, and future stage a creative meeting: to develop the element of foresight which calls for ecological planning. There is no other approach that can deal with the increasingly complicated nature of the problems of food and their promise for the liberation of mankind from hunger and disease. Let me quote what TVA says: "Nature herself is the first planner. Hers is the first word in respect to planning—and the last. . . . Increasingly we turn to the natural scientists—to biologists, soil scientists and geographers especially—to define the terms of man's permitted and profitable collaboration with nature."

Its work on soil minerals is one illustration of TVA's unified approach to soil and food problems:

In the early years of TVA, when the first products of the phosphate plant at the Shoals were being tried out on test-demonstration farms in the Valley, amazed farmers kept reporting the curious behavior of their domestic animals. Pigs loose in the cornfield would walk right through the untreated section of the field and concentrate their eating on the part that had been limed and phosphated. What these animals were after was the critical 5 per cent of minerals needed to satisfy their highly selective hunger, and to assure proper nutrition to their bodies. . . . Lacking a sufficiency or more of these minerals, especially calcium and phosphorus, plants exhibit hunger signs that are as familiar to the plant physiologist as are the symptoms of human deficiency diseases—rickets, scurvy or pellagra—to the physician. . . . Animals, too, show unmistakable signs of mineral hunger.

Over a century ago pioneer observers and experimenters established the critical role of soil minerals with respect to the nutritive value of pasture herbage and the health, fertility and growth of domestic animals. But this knowledge entered slowly into the specialized scientific disciplines concerned with agricultural production and animal nutrition. . . .

Modern and improved breeds of animals almost without exception have been developed in mineral-rich areas of the world. The lime-rich hills of Southern Scotland and Eastern and Southern England give us the big Shorthorn, Hereford and Devon cattle, and several large breeds of sheep. Holstein cattle come from a limestone belt of soils across Northern Europe. Our main breeds of animals in the United States—cattle, hogs and sheep—have all arisen in regions where the soils are relatively high in lime and other minerals. . . . Animals will recognize soil treatment effects too small to be recorded as weight differences, as well as improvements in the crop quality lasting long after the soil treatment may have been forgotten. . . . More land in good pasture is needed in this country and all over the world, both to prevent soil losses through erosion and to increase the production of meat and dairy products.

TVA put this knowledge of improved stock breeding to work through its test-demonstration farms. This was one result:

In 1922 Doeckle Terpstra bought an old farm in the upper valley of the Powell near Big Stone Gap, in Virginia. . . . The run-down pastures grew mostly broom sedge; his ten cows produced less than 40,000 pounds of milk that year. By 1938, when Terpstra's neighbors elected him one of the test-demonstrators of Wise County, he was producing 250,000 pounds of milk a year from forty cows. Seven years later he had doubled his milk production without increasing the size of his herd. In 1940 over half his land was in corn and small grains. By 1946 only 4 per cent was in corn and 64 per cent in permanent pasture. He uses about fifty pounds of P_2O_5 per acre a year—considerably more than the TVA allotment. All told, Terpstra spends about $6.50 per acre a year for fertilizer. . . . Breeding and feeding on Terpstra's heavily fertilized pastures have increased the weight of the daughters of his original stock by an average of nearly 200 pounds. In 1946 his forty-one Holsteins and Guernseys averaged 420 pounds of butter-fat. They're healthier, too; he has had little disease in his herd since 1941. . . . Nature's limiting factor is replaceable. Given minerals, in an adjusted farming system with proper crops, livestock, machinery and farming practices, many farmers in the South are today making rainfall and warmth as constructive of fertility as they have been destructive in the past.

The TVA study enumerates "five steps of the ladder on which 58,000 demonstrators, along with their neighbors in greater or less degree, have been climbing during the past decade." They are: 1. Soil, water, and crop management (physical, chemical, botanical). 2. Livestock management (biological). 3. Development of adequate improvements, power, and machinery (engineering). 4. Development of the farm family's skills, knowledge, and judgment (sociological). 5. Development of cooperative community action, which includes not only study of the methods and results on test-demonstration farms, but combination of individual farmers in cooperative use of more expensive farm machinery and equipment along with storage and marketing facilities.

On livestock the TVA report has this to say: "Based on the larger and more nutritious feed supply, together with improved management practices, production of livestock products is increased in both quantity and quality. The livestock system is brought into proper balance with the adjusted cropping system, the labor supply and market demand."

The TVA report concludes: "If the strength and security of America is to be assured, we must look to the fertility of soils. . . . We can no longer rely upon unrational exploitation of nature to insure our survival, much less our growth. We must act upon what we know and make a constructive peace with nature's power to replenish or destroy. To do this is to use our social and political freedom, while failure to do this may lose it." [15]

One failure, of course, is the farmer himself, for most farmers are not cooperating with the soil-conservation program. Where this failure is because adequate conservation practices mean greater labor costs, the farmer should be reimbursed by government as a social obligation. But where failure is the result of a refusal to recognize the social responsibility of land ownership, appropriate measures should be taken. For farm lands belong not only to their present owners but to future generations of humanity.

One cannot understand where and why the farmers have failed without reference to their social-economic position. American agriculture suffers from what is both overpopulation and underpopulation: the first in terms of insufficient economic opportunity in rural areas, which drives farmers' children to the cities; the second in terms of a drain on population, which depletes the rural areas of their human and cultural resources. A depressed economic condition prevailed for a majority of farmers after World War I, leaving them

[15] Tennessee Valley Authority, Department of Agricultural Relations, *Food at the Grass Roots, the Nation's Stake in Soil Minerals,* by James Rorty (1947), pp. 6, 25-26, 29-30, 32, 59-60, 64, 99-100.

with neither the money nor the will for conservation practices. And, finally, one-third of the farmers are tenants or sharecroppers, insecure and (many of them) moving from one farm to another, under pressure to get all they can out of the land, with no stake in its conservation. The tenants and the land they cultivate both suffer.

Among the biggest human problems are subsistence farmers. The human crop is a factor that cannot be disregarded. When 3000 families were displaced by TVA construction of Norris Reservoir, most of them relocated on the periphery of the flooded area in rural communities similar to their old ones. Industry was not able to provide employment for these people. Experience has shown, says TVA, that "their scraps and fragments of infertile and eroded land, bad as they are, provide, on the whole, more real security than anything else they have been able to lay hold of," and that "in most cases these subsistence farmers can and do climb at least part way up the test-demonstration ladder when they are given a chance, thereby improving the net security and health of their families, of their communities, and of the nation at large." [16]

There is pressing need that two principles, until now largely ignored, should be built into the national, regional, and local programs of conservation. The principles depend on the fact that men are creatures of the land; an organic relationship exists between men and the natural world of soil, plants, and other animals—a relationship which can be neither disregarded nor violated.

The first principle is that citizens, especially the landowner, be educated to a responsibility to manage and use the land in the community interest as well as in the individual interest. It is a fallacy to assume that government must subsidize all conservation not immediately profitable for the private landowner. This doctrine can bankrupt the land and further diminish intelligent understanding of the land and of its potentialities and needs.

The second principle is that the health of the land as a whole, not merely the supply of its constituent "resources," needs conserving. Land, like other things, has the capacity for self-renewal (that is, for permanent productivity) only when its natural parts are present and functional. It is dangerous to assume that we are free to discard or change any part of the land we do not find useful to immediate economic gain (such as flood plains, marshes, and wild

[16] TVA, *Food at the Grass Roots*, pp. 69-70.

flora and fauna). Unintelligent and violent modification of the natural order has repeatedly disorganized the land's capacity for self-renewal.

Conservation policy does not, as yet, deal fully with these basic principles of harmony between land-use and land-health. It must do so if we are to achieve a rational land-economy to promote economic prosperity and satisfying human relations within a flourishing civilization.

One basic point needs emphasis: *No conservation program can work fully which does not consider the human factor in farming.* Wrapped up in conservation is the need for advancement, in agriculture, of human living, for a deep-going improvement in community and cultural relations. This calls for decentralization of industry for regional economic balance to promote economic, cultural, and recreational opportunity. It calls for a policy that supports and strengthens the family farmer as a *free* farmer, with adequate land resources, equipment, and skills; with the economic independence and the moral will to make farming a satisfying way of life.

Finally, the farmers cannot be inspired to carry out a progressive social-economic policy if industrial management, especially in the food industries, is indifferent to the problems of conservation and food supply. In this situation the meat-packing industry has a major responsibility. It has not, by and large, measured up to the responsibility. The problem of conservation is simply one aspect of the complex interrelationships of food-for-human-welfare that demand cooperative action.

CHAPTER VII

LIVESTOCK ORGANIZATIONS:
TOWARD FARMER-LABOR COOPERATION

1. SOME ANTISOCIAL PRACTICES OF STOCKMEN

As DISTINGUISHED from the farmers, the ranch producers of live-stock, concentrated on the Western range lands, are represented by two outstanding organizations: the National Livestock Association and the National Wool Growers Association. These organizations emphasize lobbying for "favorable legislation" more than any other activity.

The associations are dominated by stockmen who are not particular, to say the least, about the rational use and conservation of what remains of the Western range lands. Like trade associations in general, the National Livestock and Wool Growers Associations combine constructive activities with antisocial policies destructive of American resources and welfare. In this respect they recall the restrictive antisocial practices that ended in the downfall of the guilds.

I have already mentioned the campaign of Western stockmen to have the remaining public lands turned over to private ownership. The most recent specific developments are these:

The attack on public grazing lands has been shaping up for several years. On August 17, 1946, representatives of the National Livestock and National Wool Growers Associations met in Salt Lake City, formed a committee of four sheepmen, four cattlemen and two operators owning both of these classes of livestock and named it the Joint Livestock Committee on Public Lands. . . . The demands were clearly stated: 1. Individuals currently holding permits to graze stock on Taylor Grazing allotments would be allowed to purchase those lands. 2. Only those stockmen would enjoy the monopoly privilege. 3. Purchase price would be based entirely on grazing values of the land, *no other values* would be considered. Investigation showed that the price would range from 9 cents per acre to a top of $2.80. 4. The privileged few were to have fifteen years to make up their minds as to whether or not to make the purchases. 5. A down payment of only 10 per cent of total price would be required at the time of contracting the purchase. It would cost from one cent to a little more than a quarter of a dollar to cinch control of the lands. And there would be a period of thirty years over which the balance due the government could be paid, with 1½ per cent interest on any unpaid balance. [The committee's vice-chairman] revealed that the ultimate objective was to secure possession of *all* the present public lands in the West on which grazing might be found. . . .

After public indignation flamed in the wake of this statement, various denials were made, [but] they scarcely stand up in the light of other assertions on record. . . . A recent confirmation of that fact is found in the resolution adopted by the National Wool Growers Association at Salt Lake City, January 28, 1948, which declares:

"Embraced in many of our national parks and monuments are huge areas upon which animal growth of forage is now being allowed to remain unused. Large portions of these areas are undeveloped for recreational purposes and can be used by livestock without any conflict with their present special privilege use. We, therefore, request national parks and monuments to be opened for reasonable livestock grazing."

Sparks of anger roused by the Joint Committee's plans became a fire of protest. Grocers' associations, labor unions, civic organizations, including women's clubs—all damned the scheme. Nor was this all:

Most significant, within a few weeks twenty-six local livestock associations in the one state of Colorado repudiated the extremist leadership, its platform and plans. These and many other livestock organizations condemned the proposals by resolutions. Many individual ranchers who are in thorough accord with the conservation practices and policies now applying on our public lands protested the Joint Committee's schemes outspokenly. This was clear evidence that the Joint Committee, which has repeatedly claimed to represent the livestock industry, does no such thing. *It does not represent the industry as a whole, nor in the Western states. It does not represent even that small segment of the industry*

which utilizes forage on public lands under the present permit system. . . .
If the livestock industry were fully aware how this grasping group, which
is such a small part of the whole, is leading all to disrepute and con-
demnation, the industry might make certain it has leadership that really
represents it.[1]

The stockmen's attack, it will be noted, is concentrated on the
Taylor Grazing Act, whose provisions are a belated effort to undo
the past's destructive work and to rebuild and protect the grazing
lands.

In 1890 Congress first adopted legislation to conserve the Western
lands. It gave the President power to establish, from the remaining
public domain, forest reserves that were "wholly or in part covered
with timber or undergrowth, whether of commercial value or not."
This problem of protecting the Western lands became an important
part of the progressive conservation movement of the 1900's and
after. Legislation recognized the need to protect, in addition to
timber and watersheds, the public range against overgrazing by
livestock that trespassed upon it. Congress in a number of laws gave
the Secretary of the Interior power to permit and regulate grazing
on the public lands where and if such grazing would not harm the
conservation program.

Districts are set up under management of the United States Grazing Service, provided for by the Taylor Act. The Service regulates
and controls the amount of grazing where it is permitted, and has
power to adjust the number and size of livestock to stop overgrazing, thus preventing soil and forest depletion and the danger of
floods and erosion.

Yet it is these desirable conservation measures that "extremist"
stockmen are working to undermine and destroy. In 1946 many
Western stockmen pressured Congress to cut appropriations for the
Grazing Service, and forced disastrous reduction in a personnel
already too small to do a truly effective job against disregard of
grazing regulations. And in 1947 the New Mexico Wool Growers
Association called on Congress to make drastic reductions in appropriations for the Forest Service, enough, it said, "to cause the removal of all officials connected with the Service who defy the will
and dictates of Congress." The Association spoke of "the will and

[1] Arthur H. Carhart, "Who Gets Our Public Lands," *Atlantic Monthly,* July
1948, pp. 57-60.

dictates of Congress." Actually what it meant was removal of officials who defy "the will and dictates" of those stockmen who openly or deviously try to get the Grazing and Forest Services to allow violations of the law and of conservation practices.

While the people, through their government, have spent billions of dollars and will spend billions more on a conservation program for reforestation, for water and flood control, and for restoration of the fertility of depleted soils, many cattle and sheep raisers work to break down conservation where it stops them from greedy exploitation of the land.

Let it be said again, however, that extremists do "not represent the [livestock] industry as a whole, nor in the Western states." Yet they work their evil, while the conscientious stockmen do not work hard enough to stop them.

2. FARMER ORGANIZATIONS AND POLICY

One disadvantage of farmers, including livestock producers, has been their disorganization as against organized corporate industry. No "natural economic laws" are able to help them overcome this institutional disadvantage.

The economic nature of agriculture, which encompasses millions of independent competitive producers, moves farmers toward full-capacity production. This condition is their great disadvantage from a business angle: again and again it has brought agricultural prices down to unprofitable levels. The farmers' economic welfare depends upon marketing and sale of their output. Organized industry can curtail production when times are bad, but the farmers keep on producing. They do so not only in response to economic pressure but because their philosophy is one of production: The good God has given us the earth to use; let's use it. Hence the farmer tries to raise bigger and bigger crops, whether grains and vegetables or cattle and pigs, even though he may increase supply beyond profitable effective demand, and so depress prices.

Back in the 1870's the farmers felt a need for organization to promote their interests. The National Grange, founded in 1867, had units in nearly every state of the Union; it fought railroad abuses and stressed the formation of marketing and processing cooperatives. Through political action the farmers tried to improve their economic situation. They were responsible for a good deal of regulatory economic legislation, notably adoption in 1887 of the Interstate Commerce Act, which set up the Interstate Commerce Commission to regulate railroad freight and warehouse rates. In the 1880's and 1890's farmers were militant promoters of populism, a movement in the American radical tradition which made a public issue of monopoly; it pressed for many reforms that were later adopted (including the income tax, popular election of senators, woman suffrage). It called for economic freedom for farmers, small businessmen, and workers against monopoly capitalism. More radical Populists adopted the slogan: "Let the nation own the trusts!"

After the breakdown of populism in 1896 the farmers gave up independent political action, but not their pressure for favorable legislation. No other class has as many federal agencies working for it as the farmers have.

From the institution of federal land banks to the parity-price program the government's work for the farmer has steadily grown. Millions of livestock producers, for example, yearly receive millions of dollars in the form of livestock loans and discounts from three federal agencies—intermediate credit banks, banks for cooperatives, and regional agricultural credit corporations; all are federal institutions to provide low-cost credit for farmers. And TVA, especially, is pioneering in an agricultural revolution in the South (greater livestock production is an important part of the program) and opening new vistas for farmers' welfare.

While demanding government aid, the farmers have insisted that it fit into their democratic individualism. They have given important evidence that national planning can combine with grass-roots participation, initiative, and independence. At the same time the farmers have placed increasing reliance on their own economic organizations, primarily cooperatives.

The outstanding organization of farmer-producers of livestock is the National Livestock Marketing Association. It has more than 300,000 members in twenty-two constituent associations, and is a federation of cooperative livestock sales agencies operating on the local level. Marketing and processing cooperatives, among them meat-butchering and processing enterprises, help to stabilize marketing and prices, open new markets for farm products, including livestock, and new outlets through the quality products of cooperative processing plants.

In addition, farmers, most of whom produce some livestock, are organized into the National Grange, the American Farm Bureau Federation, and the National Farmers Union.

These three organizations represent different emphases on particular kinds of farmers and on policy. Farmers are not a unified class; they differ in their economic positions. Among the 6,000,000 farmers an upper layer of around 1,000,000 secures 60 per cent of all farm income. One-third are tenants, not independent owners; many, both tenants and owners, get a poor living from subsistence farming. These economic class differences naturally express themselves in differences of organization and policy.

There are, of course, issues on which all farmers and their organizations unite and work together for a common policy. They all, for example, were lukewarm on wartime price control of agricultural commodities; they worked, in general, for higher prices. The American Farm Bureau and Farmers Union backed up federal legislation which would empower the government to set aside remaining American reserves of phosphate and potassic minerals, located mainly in Florida, Montana, Utah, New Mexico, and the state of Washington, as a perpetual public trust. In addition, they urge that TVA and the Department of the Interior build plants for manufacture of phosphate and potassic fertilizers from public deposits, the plants later to be turned over to the farmers as cooperatives, with national and state commissions to regulate distribution of the fertilizers in a campaign to multiply by two or three times the use of mineral plant nutrients to enrich the nation's soils. The idea is to improve the fertility of soils for crop and livestock production.

The National Grange, with 8000 local Granges and 800,000 members, often mars its progressive policy with reactionary proposals. Among these are its absolute insistence on limitation of imports, its opposition to the liberal economic policy embodied in reciprocal trade agreements, and its declamations against "restrictions on business enterprise." Obviously parity-price support for farmers by the government is a "restriction" on enterprise and the "free" market. Grange farmers (and businessmen in general) accept government intervention in economic activity when they approve it; when they disapprove, the intervention is "restriction on business enterprise."

The same mixed policy prevails in the American Farm Bureau Federation, a national organization of farm bureaus in every state of the Union. Many state organizations, including the Ohio Farm Bureau, with Murray Lincoln at its head, are among the most progressive of farm groups. This is not always true, however, of the national Federation, which emphasizes "making big commercial farmers bigger and more commercial." The Federation demands legislation for livestock and poultry feed control. But it campaigns and lobbies for "modification" of the reciprocal trade agreement policy. Many farm bureaus—not all by any means—have abandoned or modified an earlier emphasis on cooperatives; the Federation places much more reliance on marketing agreements and production controls, which may move in the direction of "trade-association" restrictive practices for limitation of output.

Among the Federation's constructive proposals is its call for a new, thorough study of livestock marketing to be made in cooperation with other farm organizations. Yet the same Federation fought the payment of farm subsidies during the war to keep prices down; subsidies meant more help for smaller farmers and little for the bigger farmers. An alliance of farm bureaus with the Agricultural Extension Service, which in the 1920's practically merged the Service with the bureaus, was fought by both the Grange and the Farmers Union: they broke the alliance.

The Farm Bureau Federation, moreover, bitterly opposed the Farm Security Administration (FSA), a federal agency set up to encourage land ownership, improved agricultural practices, and cooperatives among tenant and subsistence farmers.

Both Grange and Federation have joined in attacks on "family-type" farmers as lacking in "ambition, energy, and managerial ability." The limited experience of FSA, however, proved that these "family farmers" can, when given the opportunity, perform a job of production greater, in some respects, than the job big farmers do. Nor is this all. The family farm raises the issue of whether American agriculture is to move in the direction of large-scale farming, including corporation farming, or whether we can fashion a national policy to promote independent farm ownership.

Small farmers are demonstrating clearly that they *can* produce. Their multiplying self-help activities provide the benefits of large-scale services (e.g., marketing and processing, improved farm management, professional milk and cow testing) through cooperatives and associations without making them dependent on corporate centralization of ownership and control.[2]

On this crucial point the National Farmers Union differs from other farm organizations. The Union policy accepts and promotes the family farm. Its 150,000 family-members in twenty-one states are farmers in the low- and middle-income groups. The Union cooperates closely with the National Catholic Life Conference and similar organizations for cultural improvement of rural living. Emphasis on the family farm is matched by an insistence on marketing and processing cooperatives, to include livestock slaughtering and the processing of meats:

Many changes have been taking place in the marketing of livestock. Instead of shipping by slow freight, most of the stock is hauled by

[2] Arthur Moore, *The Farmer and the Rest of Us* (1945), pp. 167-74, states the case for family-farm agriculture: "Extremists of the left and extremists of the right, often brothers under the invective, have argued alike that huge combinations are as efficient on the land as in the factory and make the family farmer as unnecessary as the cottage loom. . . . The farming enterprises of Funk Brothers, Inc. comprise about 3,000 acres. In the fall of 1943, when most corn belt farmers were wondering whether there would be any profit in feeding corn to cattle, Funk Brothers bought more than a thousand head of Texas steers. . . . But with the best of equipment, with the most skilled advice, Funk Brothers has no idea of gobbling up southern McLean County into one vast corn and cattle factory. Just as important, the family farmers in the neighborhood have no such idea. After a recent drive through Funk land I stopped at a farm where a windbreak was being planted. A man and his seventeen-year-old boy operate this 170-acre place. They raise corn and feed it to cattle. They go on making lifetime plans almost within sight of a great corporation farm. . . . Industrial farming had its greatest promotion toward the end of World War I and in the years immediately following. Thomas D. Campbell was the world's greatest wheat farmer and the world's most famous corporation farmer. He leased 120,000 acres of Indian land at extremely favorable terms, bought $500,000 of equipment, sold stock to leading financiers of the day, and boasted of J. P. Morgan on his board of directors. . . . But by 1929 the man who was going to revolutionize agriculture did not grow a spear of wheat. . . . In 1900 there were 59,085 farms operated by managers, the classification under which all corporation farms are put by the Census Bureau. In 1940 there were 36,315; they included 6.3 per cent of the nation's farm lands. . . . To sum up: Factory-type farming has had many chances over the years to prove itself. It has not shown any progress at all in the form of corporations and the high production areas show stubborn resistance to factory farms of any type of management. The family farm is still dominant in the corn belt where most of the nation's food is produced. The nation should affirm its traditional confidence in the family farmer and then act boldly and consistently to strengthen him."

trucks. That means a farmer doesn't need to wait for his neighbors to ship, because he usually ships a truck-load himself. So some of the shipping associations have been disbanded. Others have been progressive and changed to meet changed conditions; they have purchased trucks to haul to market, thus saving the farmer on transportation costs, as well as sending his animals through his own marketing organization.

In many communities cooperative cold-storage locker plants have carried the marketing of livestock a step further—to the processing of meats on a small scale. These frozen-food lockers are often operated as a department of another cooperative, since the locker rentals are scarcely enough to operate a separate business.

The farmers who rent the lockers can butcher their own hogs or cattle and have the meat frozen and stored, but very often the locker plant employs a butcher, or two, who takes care of the complete job for a small charge per pound. Some of these locker plants have developed into small packing plants, selling direct to the consumer. The development of quick-freezing makes it possible that methods of marketing livestock in the form of juicy steaks and rich pork chops will undergo marked changes in the years to come. These new trends offer opportunity for Farmers Union cooperatives to go further in controlling the marketing of livestock.

Five million chickens are being raised for broilers by members of one cooperative in Montana, the Dakotas, and Minnesota. Farmers in this "wheat area" began raising chickens and turkeys on a larger scale—and better poultry too. At the end of two years, the middleman's margin on turkeys and chickens had been reduced to such an extent that farmers in the area served were receiving at least $200,000 additional income a year. And that was approximately what the Farm Security Administration loaned to the Farmers Union Cooperative Association in the first place.[3]

Farmer cooperatives are an old story. They were given a tremendous impetus after the 1920 depression had sharply deflated farm prices and values, since prices still moved against farmers in the prosperous years to 1929. By 1927, for example, one-third of all hogs were marketed through cooperative selling agencies direct to packer plants or their local representatives. And by 1938 there were 926 livestock shipping and marketing cooperatives with a membership of 600,000 and sales of $312,000,000. One type of livestock cooperative operates primarily in the country, engaged in assembling and shipping animals. Most of them consign their shipments to

[3] Harold V. Knight, *The Farmers Union Highroad* (1944), pp. 21-24.

terminal cooperative commission associations, which now handle more than one-fifth of livestock sold in public stockyards.[4]

Cooperatives are among the more effective means to offset "natural economic laws" that bring destructive production-and-price fluctuations in agriculture. Their scope grows with technological improvements—notably, today, the opportunity for livestock cooperatives to go into production and distribution of frozen meats. But cooperatives alone cannot assure to farmers regularly expanding markets at profitable prices.

3.   CHANGES IN PRICE POLICY

Already in the 1920's the limitations of cooperatives in the crucial areas of supply, demand, and price were recognized. Marketing cooperatives may be helpful in stabilizing prices, but they cannot affect the larger interplay of supplies and prices.

Millions of independent agricultural producers find it impossible to adjust supply to demand. Farm output does not fall, or declines only slightly, while demand for farm products falls, as in the depression of the 1930's, with disastrous effects on price. Compare the industrial producers: their depression output moved down much more than their prices (output of farm machinery, e.g., fell 80 per cent, but prices fell only 6 per cent), while agricultural output moved down 6 per cent and prices about 60 per cent. The supply-and-price equation favors industrial producers against farmers, including producers of livestock and its final product, meat. On this point the economists are agreed:

The demand for meat is quite elastic: when meat prices are relatively low or times are prosperous, consumption tends to be high; when prices rise or purchasing power diminishes, consumption declines. In hard times much greater economy is practiced in utilizing meats and especially their fats. The yield of grease from garbage is said to afford a fair index of the state of employment. Changes in relative prices of different cuts also afford some indication of the purchasing power of the mass of consumers. On the whole, meats constitute one of the most flexible elements in the diet.[5]

[4] *Yearbook of Agriculture: Farmers in a Changing World* (1940), p. 700.
[5] National Bureau of Economic Research, *Recent Economic Changes* (1929), vol. 1, pp. 33-34.

In the late 1920's, farmers worked for government price aid. This campaign first took the form of agitation for federal subsidies to encourage export of "surplus" crops. But of various bills proposed— "equalization fee," "domestic allotment" plan, and "export debenture"—none received any real support from livestock growers. Congress did not enact the necessary legislation; moreover, the realistic representatives of farmers recognized that foreign markets alone, in normal times, are incapable of bringing about farm prosperity.

Then came the depression of the 1930's, with another catastrophic deflation. Income from livestock alone declined 54 per cent in the four worst depression years—from $6,805,000,000 in 1929 to $2,841,000,000 in 1933. By 1940 income from livestock had risen to $4,873,000,000, but it was still 20 per cent below that of 1929. In the years between, the government had come to the farmers' aid with the Agricultural Adjustment Administration (Triple A) and the parity-price program.

The original Triple A Act of 1933 designated hogs and corn as "basic commodities" within the Act because of their close relation (expressed in the corn-hog ratio). Cattlemen opposed the inclusion of cattle; they feared that the processing tax would make beef prices unfavorably high in relation to the prices of meat substitutes—eggs, poultry, and fish. Cattlemen placed their reliance on a pressure campaign for higher tariffs on beef, "competing" fats and oils, and hides.

One year later, under the prod of increasing numbers of breeding stock and, especially, of an increasing beef-cattle supply in a depressed market, the cattlemen decided to join up with the Triple A program. In the specific case of cattle, Congress appropriated $200,000,000 to finance surplus reductions and adjustments in production and to support and balance cattle markets, with $50,000,000 more to purchase surplus beef and dairy products for relief and for elimination of diseased beef and dairy cattle. Along with the hog reduction program (6,000,000 pigs purchased and slaughtered in 1933, and the pork used for relief), 8,300,000 cattle and calves were purchased, of which two-thirds were slaughtered for relief and one-fifth shipped to Eastern and Southern states to graze as a conservation measure; the balance were condemned.[6]

[3] D. A. Fitzgerald, *Livestock Under the AAA* (1935), pp. 174-76, 183.

The new Triple A Act which succeeded the earlier one (declared unconstitutional) made some changes (none basic) in its program and meshed in with the parity-price policy. Both were intended to offset the downward production-and-market pressure on farm prices.

Let me make this analysis more specific in relation to livestock. Technological improvements, and many others, in the production of livestock increase both the number of animals and the capital investment in buildings, equipment, etc. They therefore add to overhead costs and, in addition, to current operating costs. Hence the need for full production and sale of all livestock at profitable prices. Staggering losses are incurred if output and prices fall below a definite point.

Livestock producers cannot store their product against a time of better prices, any more than farmers in general can. It is unprofitable to feed livestock after they reach maturity (from six months for hogs to three years or less for cattle), except, of course, for brief periods. As the maturity age becomes lower, moreover, the problem becomes more acute. Nor can farmers afford to feed meat animals after they have reached maximum weight. Hence the need for regularly expanding livestock markets.

The meat industry, for its part, cannot store much of its product, or for an appreciable time period: more than 70 per cent of packing output must go into immediate consumption. When prosperity nosedives into depression, when employment falls off and purchasing power dwindles, livestock prices too begin to tumble.

The need for expanding markets for livestock at stable prices is all the greater because when

. . . crops are not sold for cash but are fed and thus converted into livestock and livestock products, the fluctuations in crop yields translate themselves into fluctuations in livestock production—unless extra grain in years of better than average crops is carried forward and used as feed in years when crops are below average. . . . Thus wide swings characterize the volume of livestock production. (That there is a hog cycle is evidence of what happens to output of pork when thousands of farmers respond simultaneously to a change in the relative prices of feed and hogs.) The inability of the farm family to finance itself over a period sufficiently long to cover the swings from bad to good weather in the Plains states is still another example of the limitations of unassisted private enterprise in agriculture. . . . At the same time, experience forces the conclusion that government cannot successfully determine the production program of individual farmers. The intricacy of the resources employed on most farms, with each farm a unique set of resources, indicates that the management decisions required from day to day and from season to season can be made only by someone in constant and close contact with the farm.[7]

Among commodities added by the Steagall Amendment to the postwar price-support program were hogs, chickens, turkeys, and eggs. Support for these products was set at comparable or parity prices, in the form of loans, to continue two years after the war's end. Beef and lamb had no price support, while poultry and hogs sold above their support levels.

Price movements in the war were favorable to the farmers. Livestock income rose from $4,511,000,000 in 1939 to $6,439,000,000 in 1942, and averaged around $11,500,000,000 for the three years 1943–45; then went to $13,668,000,000 in 1946, after removal of price controls. Not all the increase came from wartime inflated prices; a substantial part of it came from greater livestock output; it was more than one-third larger than the 1935–39 average (larger, in fact, than the output increase for agriculture as a whole). This was accomplished with 1,000,000 fewer people (a decline of around 15 per cent) working on farms than in the prewar years. The farmers were able to cut down their mortgage debt from $6,770,000,000 in 1939 to $4,777,000,000 in 1947 (the high point of this debt was $10,665,000,000 in 1924).

Farmers came out of World War II in an infinitely sounder economic position than they had held after World War I. Nevertheless, the inflation spiral, with its inevitable deflation to come, may hit the farmers hard. Their organizations were ill-advised to fight wartime price controls, to press for continuously higher prices and for immediate postwar abandonment of all controls. In this, however, they were no different from the nation's other class-economic groups,

---

[7] Theodore W. Schultz, *Agriculture in an Unstable Economy* (1945), pp. 164-65, 218. The writer, who is Professor of Agricultural Economics at the University of Chicago, adds: "Storage of feed grains (including wheat for feed) on public account is one of the more promising governmental techniques for bringing much-needed stability to the several hundred thousand farmers in areas where feed production fluctuates considerably from year to year. Here, again, one must take cognizance of the limitations of public administration, caused by the existing state of political 'irresponsibility' of pressure groups."

including business and labor. Already, in 1948, there was a reduction in agricultural income, despite the general inflationary rise in national income, with non-farm prices falling less than farm prices.

The inflationary spiral will end and prices move downward. The problem is whether this will happen in the midst of catastrophic deflation and depression, as in 1920–21, from which farmers suffered most; or whether prices will come down through a constructive cooperative effort of government working with farmers, businessmen, and unions to restore and strengthen economic balance. As of 1948–49 the economic trends favored the avoidance of disastrous price deflation and depression.

The parity policy is no final solution for production and price fluctuations in crops and livestock. Moreover, the policy introduces an element of rigidity in agricultural relations. The basis of parity prices (the average of farm prices for 1909–1914) is forty years old. It does not allow for changes in demand for food products, nor for lower costs resulting from greater efficiency. Finally, parity policy fails to respond to current and prospective supply and demand in agricultural products, and to the need for selectivity in the best use of farm resources.

Agricultural economists are moving toward agreement on a system of "forward prices"—that is, a system under which a federal agency would establish prices for commodities, based upon demand for them, to guarantee the farmer a specific price for a definite period, say, one year. Prices would be announced far enough in advance to give farmers the opportunity to develop their production plans in accordance with the prices set. If prices fell below those levels, the government would not support prices in the market but make up the difference through direct subsidy payments to farmers. Hence prices would be left to move freely in the market. The "forward prices" would be changed from year to year if and when demand for various commodities called for such changes. Price changes would be used to keep production in line with demand, allow for shifts from one commodity to another in accordance with consumer needs, and clear the market while giving protection to farmers.

In final analysis, however, the problem of marketing the whole output of agriculture, including livestock, at profitable prices can be solved neither by government price policy nor by cooperatives alone. This output is a constantly growing aggregate. It can be marketed only if there is enough purchasing power among urban consumers to buy the farmers' output. A speaker at the first postwar convention of the American Meat Institute recognized this need for purchasing power:

No government program is a satisfactory replacement for a high level of productive activity and employment in non-agricultural lines. This is an essential for agricultural welfare for which there is no substitute. Consequently, the farmer is particularly interested in policies which will aid in maintaining the employment situation and activities. . . . Professions of belief in the benefits of private enterprise are heard on every hand. It may not be out of place to recall that "faith without works is dead." The farmer has demonstrated his belief in full production. He wants the rest of the economy to join in that belief by developing full production of goods and services generally.[8]

These sentiments are wholly acceptable to labor unions. They want continuous full production and employment. Agreement on what is needed should move toward agreement and cooperation for action on how to achieve "full production of goods and services."

4. FARMER-LABOR COOPERATION

Agreement on how to implement the aim of "full production of goods and services" is the problem. There is always full agricultural production; already there are signs that surpluses may again torment the farmers as productivity and output move up. Unless full industrial employment prevails with increasing earnings for wage-and-salary employees, consumer purchasing power will not be enough to buy the farmers' output at profitable prices.

On this issue of industrial activity the interests of farmers and workers are one. Let me be more specific.

Livestock production and shipments determine the supply of meat. But demand for meat varies with the amount of money consumers are able to spend on this item in their diets. Hence the money spent on meats varies with consumer purchasing power. This means primarily, of course, the purchasing power of wage workers

[8] Proceedings, 40th Annual Convention, American Meat Institute, *The National Provisioner*, November 10, 1945, p. 140.

and low-salaried employees, for variations in food expenditures among the more well-to-do classes are unimportant. *When payrolls slump the farmers' income slumps too.* As the chart shows, a close unchanging relation exists between the income received by non-farmers and their expenditures for meat and dairy products.

FARMER STAKE IN URBAN INCOME

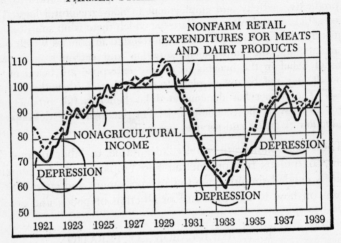

This is not the whole story, however. Farmers may not share in industrial prosperity, as they did not in the 1920's. Nor does prosperity give an automatic answer to the need for a more equal farmer share in the national income and more equal distribution of income among farmers. Nevertheless, there is no chance to solve these problems unless industrial prosperity provides profitable markets for crop-foods and livestock. Professor Theodore W. Schultz, in a study sponsored by the Committee for Economic Development, writes:

When industrial output is large relative to agricultural production, farm prices are high relative to the prices of the products that farmers buy; conversely, when industry produces little, agricultural prices are low relative to industrial prices. There is a close connection between the year-to-year changes in agriculture's terms of exchange and the changes in the relative output of agriculture and industry. . . . Several inferences may be drawn:

1. If farmers want a more favorable "parity price" in any given year, they may attain this objective by curtailing farm output.

2. If industry and labor want to keep prices and wages high relative to the prices of food and fiber, they may accomplish this in the short run by producing little while agriculture produces plentifully.

Both courses of action outlined above are, however, in conflict with the general interest and in addition give only temporary advantages to the group pursuing such a negative policy. *It is necessary for each group to produce more and not less, for to do otherwise is to curtail the wealth of the nation.*

Farm people stand to gain very considerably from a high rate of industrial output, and non-farm people gain appreciably from a large, steady volume of agricultural output.[9]

The economic situation points to the need for farmers and workers to cooperate for mutual welfare. If farm organizations and labor unions misunderstand and fight one another, they undermine their economic and democratic interests.

Yet the facts are clear: farmers and workers do not always work together. It is useless and dangerous to blame either "side." For there are no "sides" when interests are identical, only particular wrong-headed people and wrong practices. When some farmers go against strikers, or sympathize with the idea that it is good to pay low wages, or their representatives vote for anti-union laws in state legislatures (nearly a score of legislatures have done so), they aggravate a dangerous misunderstanding between farmers and workers. When some unions indulge in violence, or union teamsters get into the farmers' hair, or a union tries to blackjack dairy farmers into "joining up," they intensify the cleavage between workers and farmers.

It is worse when some farm cooperatives fight unions among their employees. One liberal, who wants workers and farmers to cooperate, writes:

The record of the National Council of Farmer Cooperatives is persistently and excitedly anti-labor. When Ezra T. Benson was its executive secretary, he expressed the Council's determination to protect agriculture from the "detrimental effects of such labor practices as the secret ballot." . . . "Union labor has become our greatest menace; to my mind, a close second to the Germans and the Japs," said a speaker at the 1943 Convention of the American Farm Bureau Federation. "An

[9] Schultz, *Agriculture in an Unstable Economy*, pp. 133-36.

enemy declares himself," said the Alabama *Farm Bureau News*, commenting on a CIO argument for lower food prices. . . . Dr. Henry C. Taylor, director of the Farm Foundation, told the National Farm Institute in Des Moines, "If economic warfare between the groups continues to intensify in this country one group may take over the dictatorship. A balance of power among warring groups cannot be maintained." He described the conflict as born of selfishness, fear, prejudice and ignorance.[10]

In most cooperatives, however, management and unions work together. One of these, the Washington Cooperative Farmers Association, employs 1500 members of the Amalgamated Meat Cutters. A writer in *The Butcher Workman* says:

Employer-employee relationships and union relationships have been most harmonious, with all differences being settled amicably in final analysis. The Amalgamated has had agreements covering all inside workers since 1935. . . . By cooperatives applying democratic principles to business, the cost to consumers is greatly reduced and better wages can be paid to the employees.[11]

Another writer in *The Butcher Workman* criticized the anti-labor attitudes of some farm organizations but insisted that unions must cooperate with farm organizations:

In far too many instances farm groups have been used to spearhead anti-labor drives. Note the anti-labor activities of the organization originally known as the Associated Farmers. On the other hand, the record of the National Farmers Union in cooperating with labor is especially notable. . . . A couple of weeks on a midwest farm at haying or threshing time is enough to convince anyone of the soundness of the claim that the farm is the backbone of American life. The friendly interest of the Amalgamated in the farmers' welfare and in farm cooperatives is general among organized workers.[12]

Every day economic and political issues arise on which cooperation is feasible and necessary between organized workers and farmers.

[10] Moore, *The Farmer and the Rest of Us,* pp. 108-111.
[11] Article, "Washington Cooperative," *The Butcher Workman,* May 1948, p. 18.
[12] Hilton E. Hanna, "Friend Farmer," *The Butcher Workman,* September 1946, p. 4.

The Amalgamated during World War II gave a practical illustration of cooperation. Its Research Division in Washington joined with progressive farm organizations to work for a program of price ceilings, rationing, and allocation that would promote the war effort as well as the interests of farmers, workers, and consumers. Specifically, the Amalgamated worked for an over-all program of regulation of the meat industry which should include equitable ceilings on livestock.[13]

Nor is this feeling for cooperation limited to the Amalgamated or to unions which have members in agricultural fields. Organized labor supports farm appropriations by Congress, soil conservation payments, and the parity-price program. The interest and cooperation move on all levels. The American Federation of Labor, in addition to working with farm organizations for progressive federal legislation, has set up a department to promote cooperatives of all kinds, including farm cooperatives. In 1948 the United Automobile Workers, CIO, of which Walter Reuther is president, adopted the following seven-point program for union-farmer cooperation:

1. Promote investment of the union's funds in farm cooperative enterprises.

2. Encourage the purchase of group insurance from farmer-built cooperative insurance companies.

3. Foster joint farmer-labor health programs.

4. Foster cooperative housing and join with the farmers in cooperative ownership of sawmills and other productive facilities.

5. Foster an examination of legislative farmer and labor organizations with a view to mutual assistance in obtaining passage of desirable laws.

6. Foster farmer-labor recreational and educational projects.

7. Publicize matters of joint interest in the farm and labor press.

This is building farmer-labor cooperation from the ground up. It is practical cooperation that at the same time promotes action for desirable social values.

Farmers' organizations, too, move toward cooperation with unions. Nor is farmer-labor cooperation feasible only if there is agreement on everything. Workers and farmers cannot, they need not always, see eye to eye. But their basic identity of interest over-

[13] Amalgamated Meat Cutters and Butcher Workmen, AFL, *Reports of Officers, International Organizers and Auditors, 16th General Convention,* 1944, p. 92.

rides all minor differences, which can be settled on a friendly give-and-take basis.

Farmers need continuing full employment in industry, the purchasing power that high wages give to worker-consumers. If industrial activity moves downward, the workers and farmers suffer together. *Reaction will crack down on the two of them if they get into a fight with one another for a larger slice from a shrinking economic pie.* They should cooperate to make the pie bigger. James G. Patton, president of the National Farmers Union, says:

It seems to me that we are often too prone to believe that farmers and working people have been on two sides of the fence in America. Much of the history has been the other way. I firmly believe that trade unions and farm organizations are now reaching the place where they will work together again. We are working together *now* in many states and localities. Each group must be organized in modern society. We must be for a good high wage in industry because the workingman is the farmer's best customer.

Nor is Patton's voice merely a lone cry in the wilderness. Of Murray Lincoln, who is head of the Ohio Farm Bureau, it has been said: "His successful work as a farm spokesman and co-op leader is a reminder that farmers and labor do have common ground where they can stand to mutual advantage." Moreover, spokesmen for farm organizations do not necessarily and always represent the membership when they talk anti-labor. The voices that ask for farmer-labor cooperation multiply among farmers:

The national leadership of the American Farm Bureau Federation has been challenged in the pages of its own publication to give farmers better leadership in relation to labor. The writer was Carleton I. Pickett, executive secretary of the Plymouth County Farm Bureau in Massachusetts. "The farmer in the northeast is more conscious of labor than any other farmers," wrote Pickett in May 1944. "Organized labor is his neighbor and his customer. The farmer here is well aware that he can ill afford to fight labor. . . . If there is ever to be unity there must be understanding on the national front, and the farmer is looking today to his national organization for better collaboration with the various people in position to sit around a common conference table." [14]

[14] Moore, *The Farmer and the Rest of Us*, pp. 183-84.

Farmers and workers must also get together, on policy and action, with progressive functional groups in the urban middle class. For great changes have taken place in class relations since the period 1820–40, when farmers and workers got together for cooperation in Jacksonian democracy. These changes have wrought what amounts to a social revolution since the 1870's.

CLASS DIVISIONS IN THE U.S.A., 1870–1940

	1870	1940
Farmers	3,100,000	5,700,000
Wage workers	6,035,000	29,500,000
Industrial	3,225,000	16,100,000
Farm laborers	1,500,000	2,300,000
All others	1,310,000	11,100,000
Middle class	2,190,000	16,630,000
Businessmen	1,300,000	3,380,000
Salaried employees	760,000	12,770,000
Professional	130,000	480,000

Source: Compiled and computed from material in *Population: Comparative Occupation Statistics for the United States, 1870–1940,* published by the U.S. Bureau of the Census.

"Farm laborers" includes hired hands only; "professional" includes only professional people working for themselves; a larger number are included among salaried employees.

In the Jacksonian age the farmers were overwhelmingly greater in numbers than all other class groups combined. The first great change was the emergence of wage workers as a result of increasing industrialization and the economic shift from agriculture to industry; this shift was already clearly apparent in the 1870 figures. As part of this change came a slowdown in the growth of the farmers, and then a decline. From a peak of 6,300,000 in 1910 the number of farmers had shrunk to less than 6,000,000 by 1940. Then another great change came to a climax: an increase in the urban middle class, especially salaried employees, that in its rate of gain outstripped the rise in wage workers. While small independent businessmen declined in relative economic importance, their numbers grew until 1910; since then they have made only a slight advance. But the new middle class of salaried employees and professionals has multiplied sixteen times since 1870, compared with an increase of only five times for wage workers and two times for farmers.

These changes—workers outnumbering farmers, a large middle class that keeps on growing as industry becomes more automatic and personal and professional services multiply—are of great significance for social policy and action today. Farmer-labor cooperation needs to broaden and deepen to include cooperation with all progressive groups in the community.

5.　THE SHEEP SHEARERS UNION

Through its Sheep Shearers Division, which has collective agreements with many sheep raisers, big and small, the Amalgamated Meat Cutters and Butcher Workmen concretely expresses its policy of fighting employers who fight the union and of loyal cooperation with employers who accept unionism. The Sheep Shearers Union, an AFL craft organization of skilled workers organized in 1903, became a division of the Amalgamated in the late 1930's.

Cooperation is, however, a two-way street and cannot depend upon unions alone. The sheep shearers, in their struggles for secure unionism and collective bargaining, have had an experience of bitter opposition that closely parallels the general anti-union attitudes of the American packing industry from the 1870's on. These shearers began in the tough old West, where sheep barons were not particular about the means they chose to stop union organization. Even gunplay was not rare. While methods have changed, the anti-union policy of many sheepmen has not. An Amalgamated organizer wrote in 1946:

The National Association of Wool Growers and nearly all state wool-growers' associations are definitely unfair to organized labor. They either ignore or bitterly oppose any recognition of our Sheep Shearers Division. Wool-grower organizations have a very powerful and highly organized lobby in Washington. With the help of the American Federation of Labor they have received substantial assistance from the government. The high tariff on imported fine wools of 34 cents a pound is over-adequate protection against foreign wools. . . . Few if any of the large or small wool growers desire to employ union shearers. It is plainly antagonism to union labor.

This Amalgamated organizer produced a photostatic copy of a letter sent to its membership by a state wool growers association in Montana, which shows use of an old anti-union tactic: to pay a bit higher wages when there is danger of union organization or to forestall union wage demands. I quote from the letter:

At a meeting last night with the plant men we decided to pay the shearers 23½ cents per head of sheep. This is 1 cent above the union scale, but we felt that the shearers had stuck by the sheepmen and because of this should receive some reward. We have furthermore made this pay retroactive, so if you have had your sheep shorn for 20 cents kindly mail me your check for 3½ cents and I will see that the shearers get this increase.[15]

Not all sheep raisers are antagonistic to union labor; many of them have collective agreements with the union. Nor are all affiliates of the National Wool Growers Association anti-union; one of its officers expressed approval of the right of shearers to organize. In its May 1947 issue *The Butcher Workman* published this statement:

"Our people are not opposed to organized labor," explains J. M. Jones, secretary-treasurer of the National Wool Growers Association. "Ours is a service organization only, with no power to compel state associations of wool growers to sign union contracts. . . . If we believe that only through organization can our members obtain best results, what kind of sincerity would we show if we stated that sheep shearers employed by our members ought not also be privileged to have their own organization. I will cooperate with your union in the sheep-shearing industry in every manner possible, consistent with the rules under which our Association is governed."

The work typically consists of mobile sheep-shearing units which move from one place to another, the shearing being completed within several days. An Amalgamated organizer began work in 1941. Three years later he reported: "I made an extended trip through most of the Western states. My first contacts met with some opposition, but repeated calls brought results; a majority of the wool growers are now helpful and cooperative. . . . In 1941 the Shearers membership totalled a little less than 400. Now it numbers

[15] Editorial article, *The Butcher Workman,* September 1946, p. 3.

approximately 1250, and this year we expect another increase."
The membership has grown to over 2000.[16]

While the Sheep Shearers are aggressive in their struggle for
union recognition, they practice cooperation with their employers
as a part of collective bargaining. This cooperation includes efforts
to improve the industry's work in conjunction with wool growers'
associations and agricultural extension offices. This kind of working
together can help the industry to thrive and economic democracy
to flourish.

[16] Amalgamated Meat Cutters, *Reports of Officers . . . 16th General Convention*, 1944, pp. 60-61.

CHAPTER VIII

SELLING MEATS:
THE REVOLUTION IN RETAIL TRADE

1. CHANGES IN MAJOR FOODS

Figures on the output of food industries from 1899 to 1937 show that meats have declined in their proportional contribution to the American diet; another expression of this fact is the lower per capita consumption of meat. Flour scored the largest decrease, while canned fruits and vegetables and dairy products made substantial gains.

The output of meat products has, of course, grown larger. But it has not grown as fast as population or as fast as most other foodstuffs. This can be seen, from one angle, in the output figures from 1899 to 1937. In those years, the total output of meats rose by 66 per cent. The rate of increase, however, declined steadily. It declined from an increase of 28 per cent in 1899–1909 and of 29 per cent in 1909–19 to an increase of only 7 per cent in 1919–29. It became a decrease of 6 per cent in 1929–37.[1]

The decrease in 1937 was due to depression and has since been overcome. But the increase in meat output during World War II was not as large as that in a number of other foods, and it cannot be maintained. The trend toward a declining percentage of increase in meat products, moving toward a stationary output, is a factor with which packing management and unions have to reckon.

[1] Solomon Fabricant, *The Output of Manufacturing Industries, 1899–1937* (1940), p. 124.

CHANGES IN MANUFACTURED FOOD OUTPUT, U.S.A., 1899–1937

	Per Cent of Total Output		Per Cent of Value Added	
Industry	1899	1937	1899	1937
Meat Products	28.0	13.1	24.6	14.9
Flour	17.8	4.6	17.5	4.9
Rice	0.2	0.3	0.3	0.3
Canned Fish	1.8	1.0	1.7	1.1
Fruits, Vegetables (canned)	5.0	12.5	6.8	10.7
Ice	2.0	4.4	2.5	4.1
Dairy Products	3.8	6.0	5.2	5.2
Beet Sugar	0.4	1.9	0.6	1.4
Cane Sugar	4.5	2.4	4.4	2.6
All Other Products	36.5	53.8	36.4	54.8

"Dairy Products" includes butter, cheese, and canned milk; "all other products" includes cereals, confectionery, shortenings, flavorings, baking powders, and ice cream.

Source: Arranged from Solomon Fabricant, *The Output of Manufacturing Industries, 1899–1937* (1940), pp. 146-48.

The output of poultry has scored more gains than meat has. According to preliminary reports of the Census of Manufactures for 1947, shipments of chickens and turkeys by wholesale dressers amounted to 973,000,000 pounds, an increase of 80 per cent over 1939. For the same years the number of production workers in the poultry-dressing industry rose from 13,954 to 19,187, an increase of 37 per cent.

Another significant development is the upward trend in consumption of fresh and frozen fish (especially marked in the 1930's and 1940's), accompanied by a decline in the use of canned fish.[2] A 1948 study by the United States Bureau of Agricultural Economics, in cooperation with the Fish and Wildlife Service of the Interior Department, and the Tariff Commission, drew three conclusions:

1. Increased use of fresh and frozen fillets, notably during the war as a result of reduction of civilian supplies of canned fish.

[2] The output of fresh and frozen packaged fish rose from 77,829,000 pounds in 1930 to 184,480,000 pounds in 1946. Total fish output in 1900 was around 2,000,000,000 pounds; it went up to 3,286,000,000 pounds in 1930 and 4,400,-000,000 pounds in 1946. U.S. Department of Commerce, *Statistical Abstract of the United States, 1948*, pp. 732-35, 738.

2. Increased inland consumption of fish fillets, due to improved refrigeration methods.

3. Marked advance in fish prices, as sharp as the rise in other food prices, although the price of fish was still low in comparison with that of meat, poultry, and dairy products.

The significance of food changes over the past fifty years appears most clearly from the figures on per capita consumption. Meat's declining contribution to American diets is offset by gains in the consumption of other protein foods, although around 60 per cent of the protein in diets still comes from meat, fish, and dairy products. One undesirable development, from the nutritional standpoint, is the increase in the use of sugars. Encouraging, however, is the increased consumption of fresh vegetables and fruit and fluid milk. These trends continue. For example, the per capita consumption of dairy products (exclusive of fluid milk) rose to a new high of 768 pounds in 1948.

In the packing industry, consumer preference for fresh food meant a substantial shift of meat output away from preserved products. The proportion of fresh meat rose from 58 per cent in 1899 to 73 per cent in 1937, while preserved meats dropped from 42 per cent to 27 per cent with no change in their physical volume.[3] This trend appears likely to continue, despite a 400 per cent increase of canned meats (Army orders) in World War II and substantial improvements in the canning of meat and fish products.

This shift to fresh meat reflects not only consumer preferences but the improved refrigeration that makes their satisfaction possible. The newest manifestation of this trend is the growth of production of frozen foods, including frozen meat products.

The sale of packaged fresh-cut meats, sold on a self-service basis, has been growing steadily.[4] It began with the cutting and

---

[3] Fabricant, *Output of Manufacturing Industries*, p. 128.

[4] Dehydration, which made considerable progress during the war in vegetables, fruits, and soups, does not appear practicable for meats, with the possible exception of hamburger; yet it may have a potential. The Birds Eye Company is trying out "anhydrated" foods, produced by a new quick-drying method for fruits, vegetables, and grains. Dehydration flourished as a war necessity. The output of dried eggs, for example, rose from 392,000 pounds in 1940 to a war peak of 311,369,000 pounds in 1944, then fell to 80,037 pounds in 1947. U.S. Department of Commerce, *Statistical Abstract of the United States, 1948*, p. 707.

TRENDS IN PER CAPITA CONSUMPTION OF FOODS, 1909–1939

LOSSES   GAINS

FLOUR 37%

POTATOES 30%

BEANS 37%

VEGETABLES

COFFEE 26% 26%

FRUIT 23%

DAIRY 19%

SUGARS 15%

MEAT 12%

EGGS 3%

FATS 1%

Food Group	1909–16	1923–29	1935–39
Meat, Poultry, Fish	112	106	100
Fats, Oils, Butter	101	106	100
Dairy Products	81	99	100
Eggs	103	112	100
Potatoes, Sweet Potatoes	130	112	100
Beans, Peas, Nuts	63	91	100
Fruit	77	88	100
Other Vegetables	74	84	100
Flour and Grain Products	137	115	100
Sugars, Sirups	85	108	100
Coffee, Tea, Cocoa, Spices	74	88	100

Index numbers (1935–39 = 100) are averages for the different year groups.

Source: U.S. Department of Agriculture, *The National Food Situation,* July 1944.

packaging of meats in the store, and broadened to include pre-freezing. One disadvantage—a tendency of packaged meats to develop discoloration—was overcome by improving the wrapping materials.

Frozen foods are in the field to stay. They started with a few items and, despite opposition, their sound expansion met interruption only during World War II. In 1948, frozen foods, including a substantial amount of meat, poultry, and fish, attained a volume of 1,125,000,000 pounds—120,000,000 pounds more than in the previous year. There were almost 75,000 dealers in 1948 compared with 45,000 in 1940. At the 1949 convention of the National Association of Frozen Food Packers its president, F. J. Becker, reported that the previous year's production of frozen foods included 25,000,000 pounds of meats, 135,000,000 pounds of poultry, 160,000,000 pounds of sea-foods.[5]

Two developments increased the popularity of frozen foods: quick adoption by consumers of home freezers and modern refrigerators with large frozen-food compartments, and the decentralization of the industry away from its former concentration in California, Washington, and Oregon. But while sales of frozen foods increased, the products were still generally considered a luxury in 1948, according to a survey of the National Industrial Conference Board; 90 per cent of families with yearly incomes of $7500 up bought frozen foods, while only 5 per cent of families with incomes below $2000 did so. Agreement was general that price constituted the biggest obstacle, with industry spokesmen urging reduction of production costs and prices to compete with fresh and canned products.

At the 1948 convention of the National Association of Retail Grocers, Jack W. Dickie, a meat industry consultant, predicted that electrolysis, high-voltage treatment, pre-cooking, and freezing will all play their part in increasing distribution and consumption of meats. Self-service packaged meats at lower prices will be delivered to market for resale in much the same manner that bread is delivered today. Pre-packaging plants can be set up right in the cattle-raising areas, where cattle will be slaughtered and processed to assure standardized products at lower prices. Millions of pounds of bone and gristle, which have heretofore been shipped all over

[5] News story, *New York Times*, March 7, 1949.

the United States, will be removed at central plants to be processed, as they now are to a limited extent, into bone meal for chicken feeds, fertilizer, and cat and dog foods.[6]

Frozen foods are more than a convenience. The process by which they are prepared can improve their nutritional quality and their flavor. Foods retain more of their value when properly frozen, packed, and kept. Low-temperature freezing is a much more effective method of food preservation than cold storage because it stops the growth of molds and bacteria; in general, the lower the temperature at which frozen foods are stored the more slowly they deteriorate. In the case of pork, low-temperature freezing destroys the *Trichinella spiralis* organisms and so protects public health and the consumer. In 1947 a food technologist, Dr. L. J. Bratzler, Professor of Animal Husbandry at Michigan State College, reported that research had proved that the removal of bones from meat prior to freezing and cooking does not lessen its quality and flavor.[7] New research may reveal other advantages in frozen meats.

At the same time there may also be health dangers. It is again the old story of new developments proving harmful where there is insufficient protection for the consumer. Laws to force frozen-food packers to keep the temperature of their products at a proper low may be needed to get frozen foods to the consumer with all their nutritive value. However, there is almost general use of Department of Agriculture certification of frozen food packs, which distributors demand as evidence of quality. Reputable firms insist that nothing shall be frozen which cannot result in a better pack than other preservation methods can provide. The industry in 1948 called upon the Food and Drug Administration to establish quality standards for frozen foods.

One significant development is the preparation and sale of complete pre-cooked meals, including meats, all quick-frozen, ready to pick up before dinnertime in a large number of variations. Much improved and cheaper plastic plates to use with such meals are becoming available.

The packing industry did not pioneer in the development of frozen meats; at first opinions varied and some packers were nega-

[6] News story, *New York Times*, June 23, 1948.
[7] Article, "Technologist Reports Frozen or Cooked Meat Flavor Not Impaired by Prior Bone Removal," *The National Provisioner*, March 17, 1947, p. 17.

tive in their attitude. But a quick change came about as packers discovered these advantages of frozen meat: (1) Lower costs from greater offal recovery in the plant and from shipping savings on reduced weight; (2) simplification of existing costly branch-house structure with, in addition, production of a greater variety of choice meats which can be stocked at strategic warehouse points.

One speaker at the first postwar convention of the American Meat Institute said:

The trend in food handling has been toward the use of packaging to display as well as protect the contents. Why are there not possibilities for the use of quick-freezing and cellophane for the distribution of accurately graded and labeled cuts of meat, attractively packaged? Effective cooperation between packers and the trade may lead to much improvement in meeting consumer requirements. Standardization and quality are important to consumers but so is price. . . . Attention needs to be given to cutting costs as well as to means of providing more and better service. Quick freezing, packaging, and speedy transportation may open up a wide range of specialty outlets which enterprising packers and meat handlers will want to develop and service.[8]

A number of problems confronted the producers of frozen meats. "Those interested in developing the marketing of frozen meat and establishing brand names on these items," said a speaker at the 1945 AMI convention, "should face and solve the following marketing hurdles":

Development of a package that will prevent surface discoloration but still allow the consumer to see what she buys and maintain a constant quality; teaching the trade and housewives the proper methods of handling, displaying, and cooking quick-frozen meats; marketing through channels where the savings on retail costs are passed on to the consumer; teaching consumers to compare the price per pound of the frozen trimmed product with the price of the bone-in untrimmed fresh cut; reduce the costs of cutting, packaging, and handling under constant refrigeration down to a point where quick-frozen meat cuts can compete successfully with precut fresh meats merchandised on a self-service packaged basis.[9]

[8] Proceedings, 40th National Convention, American Meat Institute, *The National Provisioner*, November 10, 1945, p. 136.
[9] Proceedings, American Meat Institute, *The National Provisioner*, November 10, 1945, pp. 179-80.

All these changes, in addition to a quadrupling of food output since 1899 (a larger increase than in population), mean more and better foods for the American consumer. They give him a greater variety from which to choose and combine foods for a balanced diet. Variety in food is as necessary as quantity, a conclusion that is emphasized by the newer nutritional understanding of where proteins, vitamins, and other nutrients fit into dietary balance needed for good health. These changes have made Americans a well-fed people.

Yet, while Americans are largely well fed, they still need more food and better foods. A number of harmful practices persist. Polished rice has its anti-neuritic factor destroyed. Some meats are harmfully "cured" with gelatin, fat, brine, chemicals, and "smoke solutions" to "improve" stringy or tough meat from poor animals. Milling breaks up the whole wheat grain to make white flour, which destroys many of the cereal's nutrients; it is ironical that white bread is "enriched" with synthetic nutrients after milling destroys the natural ones. The refining of sugar extracts all vitamins and minerals from the cane and beet juices. More nutritional understanding is needed to get rid of these harmful practices and educate consumers to choose their foods wisely and well for balanced meals.

AVERAGE NUTRITIVE VALUE OF DAILY DIETS BY INCOME GROUPS, 1942

Annual Net Money Income Class	Food Energy (Calories)	Protein (Grams)	Calcium (Grams)	Iron (Grams)	Vitamin A (Int'l Unit)	Ascorbic Acid (Milligrams)	Thiamine (Milligrams)	Riboflavin (Milligrams)	Niacin (Milligrams)
All urban classes	3,200	95	0.8	16	8,700	155	2.3	2.7	22
Less than $500	2,900	80	.7	15	7,400	120	2.2	2.1	16
$500–$999	3,000	85	.8	15	8,600	130	1.9	2.4	18
$1,000–$1,499	3,200	95	.8	16	7,900	140	2.2	2.6	20
$1,500–$1,999	3,200	95	.9	15	7,900	140	2.2	2.7	20
$2,000–$2,499	3,300	100	.9	16	9,100	160	2.4	2.8	23
$2,500–$2,999	3,300	105	.9	17	9,500	180	2.5	3.0	25
$3,000–$4,999	3,200	100	.9	16	8,700	165	2.4	2.7	23
$5,000 and up	3,100	100	.9	16	9,900	180	2.3	2.8	24

"Value of diets" is calculated on the basis of a "nutrition unit," a moderately active man being considered one unit and other persons expressed in equivalents of the man.

Source: U.S. Department of Agriculture, *Food Consumption in the United States*, Miscellaneous Publication No. 555 (1942).

Moreover, there is a serious, although diminishing, inequality in the amount of nutritional value in the diets of people in different income groups. While no serious differences exist in the intake of caloric food energy, they do in the case of other nutrients, especially of calcium, vitamin A, ascorbic acid, riboflavin, and niacin; these are among the nutrients most essential for health-giving diets.

While income differentials play their part in dietary inequality, they are not the only factors. "The dietary deficiencies of the American people appear to be due just as much to lack of information about adequate diets as to lack of income. . . . The kinds and qualities of various foodstuffs required to provide an adequate balanced diet for various age and sex groups . . . would involve radical dietary changes, not only for the low-income groups but for most of those at higher income levels as well." [10]

That there still is a problem of health in America, despite all nutritional advances, was startlingly proven when, in World War II, nearly a third of the young men examined for the armed forces were found unfit for active service.

Today, with all the evidence in hand and corrections duly entered, there is every reason to accept General Hershey's temperate but realistic judgment: "Whether we are worse off physically than we were in 1917–18 is undoubtedly controversial. That our physical standards are higher now, let us admit. The fact remains that while we may be no worse off than twenty-four years ago, we seem certainly to be no better. Better or worse, or the same, we are physically in a condition of which we nationally should be thoroughly ashamed." . . . Four major deficiencies of the American diet—calcium, riboflavin, ascorbic acid and thiamine—appear to be closely related to the major causes of draft rejections.[11]

We need varying additions to our supply of foods. Authorities agree that, in general, requirements for full national health demand the following increases over 1940: up to 8 per cent more meat, poultry, and fish; up to 25 per cent more eggs; up to 40 per cent more citrus fruits and tomatoes; up to 75 per cent more milk; and over 100 per cent more leafy vegetables.

Those are the over-all food needs. In specific nutritional terms,

[10] J. F. Dewhurst and Associates, *America's Needs and Resources* (1947), pp. 356-57.

[11] James Rorty and N. Philip Norman, *Tomorrow's Food* (1947), pp. 40-41.

FOOD NEEDS, 1960

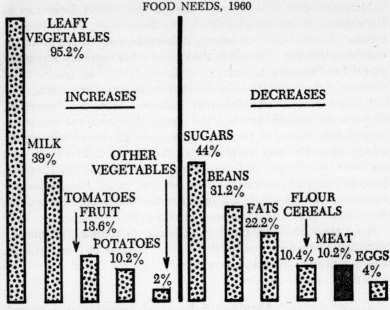

ANNUAL PER CAPITA NEED FOR SPECIFIED FOODS, 1940, 1950, 1960
(Milk in quarts, eggs in dozens, other foods in pounds)

Food Group	Actual Consumption	Needs		
	1940	1940	1950	1960
Meat, Poultry, Fish	147	131	131	132
Fats, Oils, Butter	72	57	56	56
Milk (all forms)	213	300	297	296
Tomatoes, Citrus Fruit	88	100	100	100
Leafy, Green, Yellow Vegetables	83	160	160	162
Potatoes, Sweet Potatoes	137	155	153	151
Dry Beans, Peas, Nuts	16	12	11	11
Other Vegetables and Fruit	197	205	203	201
Eggs	25	25	24	24
Baked Flour Goods, Cereals	201	186	183	180
Sugars, Sirups (household)	100	57	56	56

"Milk" includes fluid milk and its equivalent in condensed, evaporated and dried forms, cheese, cream and ice cream; "meat, poultry, fish" excludes bacon and salt side, which are included under "fats, oils, butter"; sugar in commercial bakery products and canned and preserved foods is excluded from "sugars, sirups."

Source: J. F. Dewhurst and Associates, *America's Needs and Resources* (1947), p. 117. Based upon U.S. Department of Agriculture, Bureau of Home Economics, "Family Food Plans for Good Nutrition," June 1945.

the requirements for balanced diets call for reduced per capita consumption of certain foods—fats and oils, cereals, and especially sugars. A small decline in per capita consumption of meat, poultry, and fish products is indicated, with only unimportant additions required in their total supply.

As for the needed food additions—provisional, but indicative—they offer no problem; American agriculture can produce them. One authoritative analysis gives "this very rough approximation: with the national income at the 1944 level and with farm prices at 90 per cent of parity (very high incomes and relatively low farm prices), *not more than 10 per cent more food would be needed as a supplement to what consumers would buy to meet the nutritional standards.* The 10 per cent figure is on the large and safe side; it very likely would be somewhat less than that." [12]

It is a question of more nutritional education as well as of money, since the worst dietary deficiencies are in the low-income groups and in backward regions.

2. CHANGES IN MEAT OUTLETS

The multiplication of outlets in retail trade is not completely chaotic, although competition adds to the complexity. The situation expresses one aspect of the revolution going on in the variety, production, and distribution of foodstuffs. Today, for example, meat products are bought not only in butcher shops, but in combination grocery-and-meat stores and supermarkets, across the counter from a butcher, and in self-service stores, in packaged and frozen forms.

Changes in retail outlets began a century ago. These outlets multiplied with the growth of city populations and with the rise in living standards. Nearly 1,800,000 stores, according to the 1939 Census, operated in the United States to sell an increasing variety of merchandise. Active proprietors totalled 1,613,000 in 1,770,000 stores, an increase of 12.4 per cent since 1929; they employed 4,600,000 persons who received a total compensation of $4,529,000,000. And the number of stores grows.

Food stores alone numbered 560,550, an increase of 14 per cent since 1929. Of these 42,360 were exclusive meat-and-fish stores, a

[12] Theodore W. Schultz, *Agriculture in an Unstable Economy* (1945), p. 74.

decline of 3.5 per cent; the trend is away from the old butcher shop toward the sale of meat products in general food outlets. It will be noted that meat-and-fish stores are overwhelmingly individual enterprises: there were, in the 42,360 such stores, 42,794 active proprietors, which in many cases means stress on personal service to buyers.

At the same time, competitive pressures multiply. Since 1900 the number of stores, including those that sell both groceries and meats, has grown considerably out of proportion to the increase of population and consumer need. Part of this growth was temporary: during the depression of the 1930's many of the unemployed opened small, often hole-in-the-wall stores, to make some kind of living; most of them disappeared in the post-depression years. Nevertheless, it still remains true that there are more stores, by and large, than are needed to serve consumers or than can provide an adequate living for their owners.

Another influence on retail trade was the rise of great food corporations after World War I. Among the causes, in addition to the drive to catch up with the monopoly parade, were the development of new kinds of foods and of new manufacturing processes. In most cases the processes required large capital equipment and plant facilities, and they were patented. Hence the need for large capital resources and plant equipment gave big corporations an advantage, as did their large-scale distribution facilities.

But here again the will to monopoly played its part. Two of the food giants were General Foods and Standard Brands, whose combined sales rose from $53,000,000 in 1929 to $255,000,000 in 1937 and to over $700,000,000 in 1948. They grew by merging and combining smaller corporations. Income from licensing patents is a substantial part of their earnings. General Foods and Standard Brands manufacture and distribute a varied assortment of "family foods"—breakfast cereals, coffee, tea, flour, mayonnaise, baking powder, yeast products, salt, tapioca, chocolate, and sirup. General Foods pioneered in frozen products, and controls some of the more important patents for quick freezing.[13]

[13] TNEC Monograph No. 35, *Concentration of Economic Power*, pp. 56-57. "All lines of food manufacturing and distribution will show at least some evidence of the trend toward large-scale organization which has been described for the major food groups. As a matter of fact, it is undoubtedly correct to say that concentration of control has proceeded much further in some of the minor

Another phase of competitive pressures is the tendency to an increase of "general stores," where a large variety of goods is sold. Drugstores, in addition to selling almost everything else, are beginning to sell foods, while grocery stores have begun to add lines of greeting cards, kitchen utensils, toilet articles, cosmetics, bakery goods, and candy. This can be done efficiently, on a service basis, by department stores, but not by smaller stores. The retail situation became worse when, as in the case of some of the big packers, tie-in sales forced the storekeeper to stock many unwanted items. This policy may result in an increase of the number of storekeepers who fail or merely "get by."

Store operation has also changed in the direction of giving more service to consumers. On the management side there is much less of the old attitude, "Let the buyer beware!" Better sanitary conditions of all kinds prevail, with less waste in perishable food products and from spoilage. Saving on costs of selling the product and on supervisory and managerial personnel is emphasized, which means saving on employees.

In the distribution of goods (as in their production) the trend is toward distributing a constantly greater amount handled by a diminishing number of workers. This tendency toward reduction of labor costs in merchandising is strikingly manifest in the sale of packaged foods on a self-service basis—among them a growing amount of meat products, including frozen meats. As of early 1949, according to an Armour & Company study, *Prepackaged Self-Service Meats*, approximately 7750 stores operated on *partial* self-service basis, one-fourth of them owned by chains and the balance by independents; they did 6 per cent of all food business. Eight hundred seventy-eight meat markets operated on a *complete* self-service basis, with new markets being opened at the rate of seventy-five a month. Complete self-service stores were large-volume operators; 94.4 per cent of them did a meat business of from $1000 weekly up to $10,000 and over.

These merchandising changes, together with shifts in the con-

---

food lines than in the major ones. This commonly escapes attention because the companies involved are not as large as some of those described in the course of this chapter. Their control over prices and margins in their particular line of enterprise, however, may be just as great and may warrant just as much attention from regulatory agencies as has been given to some of the major food corporations."

sumption of foods, create many problems for the retail trade. The
need for more merchandising education is recognized. For example,
at a meeting with faculty members to discuss operation of a training
center for the food industry, which opened in the fall of 1948 at
the College of the City of New York, Paul Willis, president of the
Grocery Manufacturers of America, said: "Any food concern operating today on the basis of order-taking will soon give way to aggressive
merchandisers. Sound training for staffs in the distributive field will
benefit the whole industry and the public as well."

The training center was backed by food manufacturers, wholesalers, and retailers. The courses were divided into separate programs for wholesale and retail personnel; the wholesale program
included education in buying, transportation, price setting, market
analysis, and salesmanship; the retail course included study of merchandise control, organization, record keeping, and advertising, as
well as some wholesale problems from the retailer's angle. All this
highly specialized education, speakers emphasized, was made necessary by outstanding advances in the growing, processing, and
distribution of foods.[14]

The revolution in retail trade has resulted in an increase of distribution costs. In the years 1913-17 the farmer got 55 cents of the
food consumer's dollar; by 1938 that share was down to 40 cents,
although it went up again temporarily. The argument that prices
will come down if distribution profits are eliminated is, however,
much too simple despite its element of truth. Let me quote from
one analysis:

For most food products probably not over 5 per cent of the retail
selling price is represented by the combined earnings to capital at all
stages in the marketing process. Again, there is no evidence that distribution is becoming less efficient—rather the contrary. Distribution costs
might be reduced considerably by decreasing the numerous services
consumers now receive, but on the other hand these services presumably
add to consumer satisfaction. It can be argued that sizable reductions in
distribution costs might be made by reducing wage rates paid by distributors; but a heavy cut in wage rates would affect the farmer adversely by reducing the purchasing power of large groups of consumers;
and it would be difficult to justify from the standpoint of the general
public interest, of which agricultural interests are only a part. Thus

[14] News story, *New York Times,* July 23, 1948.

there is little reason to believe that food distribution costs can be greatly reduced within the framework of the present marketing system. This is not to say, however, that even small reductions are not worth while, because they are. Farmers' marketing cooperatives, for example, save money for many farmers though these savings represent only a small part of the total costs of food distribution. Reorganization of terminal and wholesale markets can mean real savings, especially in the case of fresh fruits and vegetables. Savings at the retail end of marketing are particularly important, since the retailer commonly gets from twenty to thirty-five cents of the consumer's food dollar. In this field the development of chain stores, chains of independents, supermarkets, and milk depots is especially significant. Labor is the largest item in distribution costs, but there is an alternative to reducing wage rates—namely, to reduce the amount of labor used in food distribution as a whole; and not only the amount of labor but the amount of equipment and of capital to which profits must be paid.[15]

Self-service is one way of bringing down selling costs, but it raises a number of questions. How much does it actually lower costs? And how far are consumers willing to go with self-service? Finally, if self-service is most economical and profitable with large-scale operation, how will it affect the smaller independent dealers?

The most recent development of this kind is the growing use of automatic vending machines to sell packaged foods, including meat products. This form of merchandising is a retail expression of the automatic principle in the production and distribution of goods. As vending machines move from mechanical to electronic devices their efficiency and potential for use will broaden in scope. The Food-O-Mats of the Grand Union Chain, operating on the coin-slot principle, introduced the most automatic kind of selling available, including "self-service meats, frozen foods, toiletries, candies, produce, ice cream, magazines, fruits and vegetables, and household needs." [16]

All these changes should mean, in final analysis, more efficient and

[15] *Yearbook of Agriculture: Farmers in a Changing World* (1940), pp. 53-54.
[16] Article, "Grand Union Features 'Tailor Made' Meats," *Super Market Merchandiser*, May 1948, pp. 91-92. Behind the Food-O-Mat fixtures clerks in a three-foot space move about with new stock. This, the inventor claimed, "eliminates the factor of irritation in clerk-shopper contacts." But what about the clerk, a human being, cooped up in a three-foot space?

serviceable distribution. They can also mean higher wages and shorter working hours. *But in between promise and performance many problems of employment and wages will arise,* problems of the progressive use of changes in retail trade. One conclusion may be drawn: Any substantial reduction in distribution costs seems unlikely. The most likely prospect for lower prices of foods is for technological efficiency to cut their production costs.

3. CHAIN STORES AND INDEPENDENTS

A major expression of the changes in retail trade has been the growth of chain stores, whose greatest importance is in grocery and meat distribution. These chain giants are comparable with the Big Four in meat packing. But it is significant that neither the producing nor selling giants have driven out the independents.

Chain stores began in a small way around the 1860's. The Great Atlantic and Pacific Tea Company (A & P) was organized in 1859, and six years later it had twenty-five stores in operation. The chains' great development came in the 1920's. They made their influence felt in all kinds of retail outlets, but truly giant chains appeared only in the grocery trade, and by 1929 they did about two-fifths of the business. However, the big chains were unable, as the big meat packers were unable, to increase their share of the business in the 1930's and 1940's.

The grocery chains soon opened meat departments and by 1935 were selling around one-tenth of the meat products bought by consumers. These mammoth chains clashed with the big packers on distribution methods. According to one research study:

An interesting sidelight relative to meat distribution at the present time is the friction which has developed between the big packers and the grocery chains over the question of how retail units of the chains shall be served with meats. Since the big packers have their own branch warehouses for this purpose, they have sought to handle chain-store meats through these warehouses. But the chains have wholesale warehouses of their own, and they have insisted that the packers ship meats direct to these warehouses from the central packing plants. In buying their meats this way, the chains of course insist that the packers give them price discounts in line with the lower costs of making direct meat shipment. The larger chains have held rigidly to the policy of handling meat through their own warehouses, but the smaller systems still permit the packers to perform this service for them.[17]

RETAIL OUTLETS FOR MEAT, U.S.A., 1935
(*percentages*)

Outlet	Beef	Veal	Pork
Meat markets and grocers	67	78	74
Corporate grocery chains	11	7	7
Cooperative and voluntary chains	6	4	2
Wholesalers and jobbers	8	5	6
Other outlets	8	6	11

Source: Arranged from material in Federal Trade Commission, *Agricultural Income Inquiry* (1937), Part I, "Principal Farm Products," p. 1018.

Despite opposition from independent storekeepers and friction with the packers, the chains grew. By 1929 the Big Five among them—A & P, Kroger Grocery & Baking Company, American Stores, Safeway Stores, and First National—operated a combined total of 28,252 store units. More than half of these (or 15,418) were operated by A & P. Combined chain sales amounted to $1,804,000,000, or two-fifths of all grocery business. In the ensuing depression years, however, the chains' proportion of sales went down. They went up during World War II and after, but did not exceed their earlier proportion.

All through the 1920's and the early 1930's the giant chain stores made higher rates of profit on their capitalization (or net worth) than other corporations in the food business. The profit rates for the five dominant grocery chains were:

25.7% for 1926
25.2% for 1927
23.9% for 1928
21.4% for 1929

Chain-store profit rates held up fairly well in the early depression years—19.4 per cent for 1930, 18.7 per cent for 1931, 14.7 per cent

[17] TNEC Monograph No. 35, p. 20.

for 1932, and 14.3 per cent for 1933. Then the rate of profit dropped to around 11 per cent for 1934–36 and to 6.9 per cent for 1937, after which it again went up.[18] Expansion of the great chains came primarily from reinvestment of part of their great profits, as in the case of the big meat packers. In the 1920's their rapid expansion led to some sale of securities to the general public to raise additional capital, but ownership still remained close.

Part of the need for additional capital arose because the big chains had multiplied their manufacturing activities. These activities included the production of bread, canned foods (including meats and fish), condensed and evaporated milk, butter and cheese, packaged cereals, mayonnaise, jellies, and beverages. Several of the big chains had also opened meat-packing plants.

The supermarket, including meat departments, was introduced by independents and cooperatives, and came as a competitive challenge to the chain stores, who were forced to adopt the new merchandising outlets. These supermarkets were the retail manifestation of the growing trend toward packaged foods, including meats, sold on a self-service basis.

Prophecies made in the early 1920's that independent grocery and meat stores were doomed to disappear never came true. The chains' share of grocery sales remained pretty much of a constant at around 38 per cent from 1929 to 1947, while competition from regional chains whittled down the Big Three's dominance. The sales of these giants—A & P, Safeway, and Kroger—dropped from 22.4 per cent of all grocery and combination store sales in 1941 to 17.4 per cent in 1947. Combined sales of regional chains increased 155 per cent, with a gain of only 25 per cent in total chain sales.[19]

It must be emphasized that despite all changes in retail outlets the independents survive and offer vigorous competition to chain stores. Another form of competition comes from consumer cooperatives (among which are a number of supermarkets), with their emphasis on group action, no-profit policy, and high nutritional standards.

Among the reasons for survival of independents are the limits to

[18] TNEC Monograph No. 35, p. 96.
[19] Article, "Local Supermarkets' Business Is Growing," *Business Week,* July 17, 1948, p. 61. Figures compiled from U.S. Department of Commerce reports.

bigness determined by organization and efficiency; these are particularly evident in retail trade. Also there is an area where new ideas and the service angle can always offset competition. In addition, independent grocers, through voluntary chains sponsored by wholesalers, and cooperative chains, get the benefits of mass buying (including buying of meat products), with discounts and lower prices, as well as merchandising ideas and aids, and other managerial services. These voluntary and cooperative chains vary greatly in their setups; however, they all secure the benefits of large-scale operation, yet the members remain independent. Around one-third of all grocery stores were included in 1949, and their number is constantly growing.

Among independent stores there is, however, a marked inequality in proportion of sales. In 1947, out of 375,000 food stores, the top 28,800 stores did one-fifth of the total business, while the lower 202,000 (nearly one-half of all food stores) did only 13 per cent of the business. Not all of the inequality comes from the competition of chain stores. At least some of it results from more stores doing business than are needed and from too many people going into retail trade who might do better in other occupational lines. Today retailing calls for at least a minimum of capital and knowledge that many storekeepers do not have. Nevertheless, the place of the independent who can provide nutritional understanding and service for consumers seems secure in the food-distribution field.

4. THE AMALGAMATED RETAIL UNION

The union's constructive part in solving the problems created by retail changes begins, of course, with the problem of what effect those changes will have on employment and wages. It also includes the larger social aspects of nutrition and consumer welfare. Neither management nor society can afford to disregard the interplay of food and merchandising changes with the union's response and policy.

The problems of employment and wages are not limited to retail butcher members of the Amalgamated. They concern over 5,000,000 people engaged in retail distribution. And the significance of the problems is broader still: as employment in the industrial occupations declined in its rate of increase, the slack was taken up by expansion in the service trades, including retail distribution, where the number of employees kept on growing. Employment becomes more and more dependent on the expansion of service occupations. If, therefore, the number of retail employees begins to shrink, a serious danger of general unemployment arises. This is the problem that confronts the Amalgamated retail butchers.

The retail meat business is organized in a network of trade associations. Among these are the National Association of Retail Meat Dealers, many associations on a state or regional basis, and specialized groups such as the Appetizers Association, which represents delicatessen stores. The retail business is organized as far as the employers are concerned. It needs to include organizations of employees as well.

Trade associations and unions are formed to promote their members' interests. But these interests should broaden—and they do—to include consumer welfare, which can be promoted most fully if there is cooperation between the organized storekeeper-employers and their employees' union.

The retail butcher division of the Amalgamated is as old as the union itself. When, in 1897, the American Federation of Labor granted the Amalgamated a charter, its jurisdiction covered "every wage-earner, from the man that takes the bullock on the hoof until it goes into the hands of the consumer as meat, including meat cutters or meat salesmen, no matter where employed, whether in department stores, grocery stores or exclusively meat markets." [20]

[20] Amalgamated Meat Cutters and Butcher Workmen of North America, *Report of Proceedings, 2nd Convention*, 1899, p. 22. From the first jurisdictional disputes began with the Retail Clerks International Association, AFL. While these disputes never degenerated into knockdown affairs, they dragged on annoyingly for years. In 1938 President William Green of the AFL gave a decision as the basis for settlement: "Those employed in butcher shops, those who are engaged in handling and selling meats and who may sell other food products in combination with their regular duties in meat departments, shall be affiliated with the Amalgamated." Finally, in 1942, what seemed to be a satisfactory adjustment was made. (*The Butcher Workman*, November 1942, p. 3.) But the settlement proved inconclusive. Jurisdictional disputes continued. The Amalgamated argues that it should include all selling employees in food stores: "We shall never stop contending that it is an unprogressive policy for the AFL to draw its jurisdictional lines among salespeople in the food field in a manner that permits the Retail Clerks to remain in it. The Clerks have a

The Amalgamated encountered as many difficulties in organizing retail butchers as it did with the packinghouse workers. It was the same uphill struggle, although not as riddled with filth and violence as the conflict with the packers. Among production workers in meat plants, employer-employee relations were impersonal at best; among retail butchers the problem was just the opposite. A delegate to the Amalgamated's 1917 convention explained this: "One serious obstacle was among the retailers, especially the master butcher, who worked so close to his employer that his personal influence largely influenced the butcher's acts, but as time went on we made a little progress until we finally succeeded in getting a foothold in the larger centers." [21]

Here, too, as in packing, retail owners and managements organized into all kinds of associations, yet fought stubbornly to prevent union organization among their employees.

In the 1920's, when few retail butchers were organized, the Amalgamated met and solved a new problem in rational fashion. The chain stores were growing rapidly. Most liberals and labor people opposed them as a manifestation of monopoly. The Amalgamated, which for twenty years or more had fought the packer monopoly, did not join in the fight against chain stores as such. It made a distinction between monopoly abuse of a new distribution method, and the method itself. Patrick E. Gorman, the president, expressed the Amalgamated policy on chain stores at the 1926 convention:

The chains have made vast inroads and seriously endangered the business of the kindly white-frocked gentleman we know as the corner or "neighborhood grocer." It is not the business of this convention to give consideration to the merits of arguments advanced by either of these opposite interests. Our purpose is to organize all meat cutters and butcher workmen no matter where they may be employed. . . . I feel that where these chain systems do business in more than one state, or where they

---

potential membership of about five million, exclusive of retail food. . . . If the entire retail food field in the matter of sales were granted to the Meat Cutters . . . the employers, the workers and the public would be more satisfied." (Editorial, *The Butcher Workman*, March 1949, p. 10.) A 1949 settlement gave the Amalgamated control of all handling of meat, poultry, and fish.

[21] Amalgamated Meat Cutters, *Proceedings, 9th General Convention*, 1917, p. 33.

operate from coast to coast, that interstate and national agreements should be negotiated with them under the guidance of the International Union.[22]

This policy was not acceptable to everyone concerned, whether Amalgamated members or independent grocery and meat dealers. At the 1930 convention, Gorman reported:

In an Iowa city one association of meat men issued an ultimatum to our organization that if it furnished union men to the chain systems they would no longer employ Amalgamated members. This same attitude is prevalent in many other cities. There is but one position that our organization can take in the matter. Our purpose is to organize meat cutters no matter by whom employed and, by mutual agreement with the employer, to improve wages and working conditions.[23]

And, despite some local union opposition, the Amalgamated affirmed its rejection of the kind of anti-chain legislation represented by the Patman Act. The union's attitude constitutes a constructive combination of progressive economic and social policy.

Wages were one important question. By and large, average wages for chain-store workers were a bit higher than among independents. The average chain wage, as it appears in the table, exaggerates the difference, because it includes salaries on the payroll; however, there is a difference. Union policy has been to erase the difference and to secure wage scales that provide equal pay for equal work regardless of whether it is performed in chain or independent stores.

The Amalgamated campaign to organize the chain stores met with stiff opposition. At its 1930 convention, the union declared the A & P "unfair" for its refusal to negotiate with the union. Other chains joined in the opposition; many strikes were called, and some were successful. By the 1940's the Amalgamated had contracts with all the chain giants, including A & P. According to a "progress report" at its 1940 convention the Amalgamated had improved upon its agreement with Safeway Stores; organized, under strictly union conditions, 6000 of the 9200 meat-cutter employees of A & P in sixty-four cities; improved relations with the Kroger Company—80 per cent of its employees eligible for membership were in the union.

[22] Amalgamated Meat Cutters, *Proceedings, 12th General Convention*, 1926, pp. 9-10.
[23] Amalgamated Meat Cutters, *Proceedings, 13th General Convention*, 1930, p. 9.

WAGES IN COMBINATION GROCERY AND MEAT STORES, 1935

	Independents	Chains
Number of stores	139,990	25,600
Number of employees	206,740	151,660
Total payroll	$157,635,000	$145,130,000
Average wage	$762	$957

Source: U.S. Census of Business, Retail Distribution, vol. IV, p. 13. Payroll and average wage items for chain stores include store managers' salaries; similar independent items include only wages. "Independents" includes businesses with two or three store units; "chains" includes those with four or more units.

Progress continued. In 1944 the Amalgamated signed a national agreement with the A & P management, covering local store units where the Amalgamated had become collective bargaining agent. This agreement secured for union members a two-week vacation after one year's employment; the earlier provision provided such a vacation only after three years' employment.[24]

These agreements did not cover all A & P's local units by any means, nor did the struggle for union organization and recognition end. As late as the spring of 1948 four Amalgamated locals in Los Angeles carried on a twenty-two-week strike against twenty-eight A & P stores with meat departments. As part of the struggle the A & P filed suit under the Taft-Hartley law for $150,000 damages from the union, asked for an injunction against the union, and charged it with unfair labor practices. All these actions were withdrawn as a condition of the victorious settlement won by the union.[25]

Conditions of labor-management warfare are not, however, the exclusive pattern. Increasingly chain-store management (and management in general) has come to accept unionism and collective bargaining as an institutional element of democratic, efficient, and peaceful economic activity. An illustration of this attitude appears in an address made by Joseph B. Hall, president of the Kroger Company (which at the time had sixty-eight contracts with local retail unions) at a 1947 conference of Amalgamated organizers:

Your International Union issued a Friendly Chat a few weeks ago en-

[24] "The New A & P Agreement," The Butcher Workman, July 1944, p. 6.
[25] Article, "Agreement Ends Long Strike Against the A & P," The Butcher Workman, May 1948, p. 6.

titled "Five Fingers." Fair play was the theme of that Chat and it concluded with these words: "Fair play—that's all the world has ever needed." We are much better off where we are and what we are—you as representatives of labor and I as a representative of management—meeting together, talking together, working together in the interest of an even better, closer, friendlier cooperation between your organization and our company.[26]

Regional food chains have been included in the establishments brought under the Amalgamated retail union. One example may be cited from the New England area: the 1947 "master agreement" signed with First National Stores, second largest regional food chain, marked ten years of collective bargaining with the company.

Another example: in 1948 the union's Pittsburgh Retail Joint Council, which represented more than 2700 members in Pennsylvania, New Jersey, and Delaware, signed contracts with three regional chains—Food Fair Stores, American Stores, and Baltimore Markets—and with one national chain, the A & P. In addition to an across-the-board raise of five dollars weekly, the contracts included minimum wage rates and a new schedule of rates for all classifications, making a new range of $52 to $73 a week, as well as rewritten clauses on hours, overtime pay (which begins after 43 hours weekly are worked), and holidays to eliminate disputes on interpretation of these provisions. These agreements covered all employees, whether working on meat or not, and became the pattern for independent stores.

One aspect of these negotiations reveals the progressive Amalgamated policy: *The union gave pledges of cooperation with the storekeepers to protect the consumer.* Leon B. Shachter, president of the Retail Joint Council, said: "No unionist desires benefits to be paid by the buying public in the form of increased food prices. To avoid any possibility of the increases in the new contract necessitating price increases, our members will cooperate 100 per cent with the companies in promoting store efficiency, economical store practices, elimination of waste, and maintenance of low sales costs." [27]

The Amalgamated retail butchers made progress among independents too. One substantial achievement was the negotiation of

[26] News story, *The Butcher Workman*, October 1947, p. 1.

[27] Article, "Retail Chains Sign Pact for Eastern Butchers," *The Butcher Workman*, March 1948, p. 5.

a national understanding and agreement in 1938 with the National Association of Retail Meat Dealers, an organization of 25,000 members. After renewal of this agreement in 1942, *The Butcher Workman* said: "It is significant that there was not one dissenting vote in opposition to renewal of the agreement among Association members. Since the agreement has been entered into, strikes in the retail field have been minimized to such an extent that at present they are almost nil." [28]

As evidence of the friendly cooperation between union and retailers, the Amalgamated president, Earl W. Jimerson, spoke at the Association convention in 1940, and three Association officers spoke at the Amalgamated convention. George Steindl, president of the Association, struck the keynote when he said to the union audience:

We want to understand our employees and we want you to understand the employers' end of it. . . . I hope the time will never come when we will have to throw that national agreement into the wastebasket. . . . The union must be given credit for one thing. When I first got into this business I worked from early morning to late at night, Sunday and every other day. If the union did nothing else they did that one thing, they put the men on a par with other organizations.[29]

Whatever technical-economic changes come in production and distribution, there will always be room for the sense of workmanship and the pride of craftsmanship, especially in the service of selling. These may assume new forms, but they will persist. The Amalgamated retail butchers recognize the need for craftsmanship, and, in addition, they are aware of the newer objectives and values that are revolutionizing the food industry. Here is one illustration of this.

For a number of years Amalgamated Local 88, of St. Louis, has sponsored a ten-week course on "Selling Meat and Nutrition in a Rational Economy," attended by union butchers, store managers, and store owners. "The course, designed to meet today's challenge for informative service selling, comes under the St. Louis Board of Education. Men in the trade are learning the nutritional values of little known but more abundant cuts of meats, how to cook them

[28] Article, "International Renews Pact with National Association of Meat Dealers," *The Butcher Workman*, October 1942, p. 3.
[29] Amalgamated Meat Cutters, *Synopsis of Proceedings, 15th General Convention*, 1940, pp. 102-103.

properly and how to guide the taste of the consumer into the channels of available meat cuts and specialties, and the preparation of companion foods." [30]

Both self-service and frozen meats were a serious problem for the union. Packaged meats are prepared by meat cutters on the store premises, but frozen meats may come from outside packing plants, and so dispense with the need for retail meat cutters. At first the Amalgamated stipulated, in a 1930 convention resolution, that "all members of the Union refrain from handling packaged fresh or frozen meats." [31] The union later modified its position but did not wholly abandon it. In a 1946 statement of policy for local retail unions, Amalgamated President Jimerson said:

We realize we cannot stand in the way of progress. A fast developing self-service might to a great extent, however, eliminate the necessity for employment of meat cutters. . . . We ought to be able to prevent meat packers expanding the quick-freeze and self-service counter to a degree that would make the art of meat cutting impotent. Your local union should immediately make an effort to supplement your present existing agreements with a clause . . . that all fish and meat products, fresh or frozen, will be sold under union jurisdiction and cut, prepared and fabricated on the premises or immediately adjacent thereto.[32]

An expression of this policy appeared in Los Angeles, where an Amalgamated official, George Swan, worked for the adoption of a municipal measure to "regulate" self-service on meats. This measure provided for the following requirements for packaging meats to sell on self-service counters:

1. Each piece of meat must be wrapped in cellophane that will permit air passage to prevent condensation, which sours meat.

2. A refrigerator temperature not higher than 40 degrees Fahrenheit must be maintained.

3. An attendant must always be in charge of the counter to watch for and replace broken packages.

[30] Article, "Meat Cutters' Educational Program," *The Butcher Workman*, June 1943, p. 3.
[31] Amalgamated Meat Cutters, *Synopsis of Proceedings, 13th General Convention*, 1930, p. 53.
[32] Article, "Meat Cutters Have to Guard Their Employment," *The Butcher Workman*, July 1946, p. 1.

4. A label must be inside each package stating the grade, weight, and price of the contents.

5. Each retail market must package its own meat on its own premises.[33]

Measures to protect the consumers are necessary. It is doubtful, however, whether a provision which requires that each retail market must package its own meat on its own premises can (or should) be maintained for any considerable period of time. Restrictive measures against self-service have been adopted in a number of cities, under pressure of meat dealers and, in some cases, the union. But there are many objections to this policy.

Restrictive practices should be considered as a problem in economic policy, not as an opportunity for partisan belaboring of a particular group. Such practices include the restrictive policies of monopoly corporations and trade associations, and of producers of butter, who, for several generations, have used legislation to restrict the production and consumption of oleomargarine. And we may also cite the misuse of milk inspection laws in some cases, to keep out milk from other areas by refusing milk inspection to farms more than a certain distance away or by charging prohibitive inspection fees. Many other examples will quickly come to mind. They are all results of bad economic policy.

Yet it remains true that frozen foods and self-service present the union with the problem of protecting employment for its members. Restrictive practices will not work, but something must be done.

Self-service and other forms of low-cost selling can be used to bring higher wages and shorter hours to employees, as well as benefit to consumers. Loss of retail employment from the sale of frozen meats prepared outside the store can be offset by union employment in the frozen-meat plants. Many forms of low-cost selling, however, tend to replace the skilled craft butcher with low-wage wrappers, clerks, etc. It is not constructive technical-economic progress if lower labor costs come from the use of low-paid workers, not from greater efficiency. The real point is to maintain high wages.

[33] Article, "Los Angeles Controls Self-Service," *The Butcher Workman*, May 1947, p. 1.

The union alone cannot solve the problem, nor can retailers ignore it. The need is for an industry policy to introduce changes without injury to workers. This means union-management cooperation for joint action to make adjustments in the interest of all factors in the situation—retailers, consumers, employees.

CHAPTER IX

THE PACKING INDUSTRY TODAY: MONOPOLY, COMPETITION, AND POLICY

1. THE PACKING INDUSTRY AS A WHOLE

IN ITS economic and corporate setup the meat-packing industry in 1949 is much what it was in the early 1920's with two important exceptions: (1) independent packers have grown in number and size; and (2) the trend toward absolute monopoly has stopped, although the Big Four are still dominant.

The packing industry's diversification of products has become greater. More than one-sixth of its total value-output consists of products other than meat; there are more than 150 of these, mostly from livestock parts formerly wasted. Only about 70 per cent of hogs, 55 per cent of cattle, and 47 per cent of lambs will make meat. Sales of by-products from cattle and sheep often bring enough to equal the cost of processing those animals for meat.[1]

As many as seventy-five different foods other than meat are produced in whole or in part from livestock. Packing, in addition, has become a dairy industry in itself. By the 1930's ten packers produced nearly one-half of this country's total cheese output (about as much as the combined output of eleven big dairy companies), nearly one-fifth of our butter, and one-tenth of our condensed and evaporated milk. The industry also produces approximately one-third of the country's oleomargarine and shortenings.[2]

[1] American Meat Institute, *Meat—Reference Book of the Industry* (1945), p. 60.
[2] Federal Trade Commission, *Agricultural Income Inquiry* (1938), p. 228.

179

The number of inedible by-products constantly increases. They range from sporting goods (of which a Wilson subsidiary is one of the largest producers) to materials for footwear, upholstery, and insulation, to chemical products and pharmaceuticals.

Recent scientific research has tremendously augmented the importance of pharmaceuticals, the newest of which is the hormone ACTH, made from the pituitary gland of hogs, for the control of arthritis. Other pharmaceuticals include insulin for diabetes, prepared from the pancreatic glands of hogs, cattle, and calves; pancreatin, made from hog pancreas and three enzymes, for alleviation of some digestive disorders; thyroid extract to treat goiter and cretinism; epinephrine, used to relieve asthma, hay fever, and hives, prepared from the suprarenal glands of livestock, which are also used to make adrenal cortex extract for treating Addison's disease; liver extract, whose use to treat pernicious anemia has saved tens of thousands of human lives. More pharmaceuticals are made from the glands, enzymes, and bile of livestock to relieve some forms of paralysis, convulsions, intestinal disorders, and to remove tissue from unhealthy wounds.

Corporate organization dominates the packing industry. Only a small fraction of its workers are employed by individual and partnership establishments. The same corporate domination prevails in the poultry and sausage industries, and in wholesale food distribution.

The meat-packing industry has a good productive achievement to its credit, but not an outstanding one. A study of the "social performance" of American business ranks packing ninth among twenty-two industries and third among four food industries. The study concludes:

In the slaughtering and meat-packing industry employment in recent years [1919–38] has run well ahead of production due possibly to the decreased length of the working day. The amount of consumer effort commanded has likewise run ahead of production. The industry is one, therefore, *which is requiring more goods from the public in return for what it gives.* In 1937 the industry produced 10 per cent less product and commanded 8.7 per cent more consumer effort than it did in 1927. But it also employed 7 per cent more laborers. Despite the fact that production was 10 per cent lower in 1937 than in 1927, the number of consumer dollars absorbed was 2.2 per cent higher. But payrolls were

SOCIAL PERFORMANCE OF PACKING

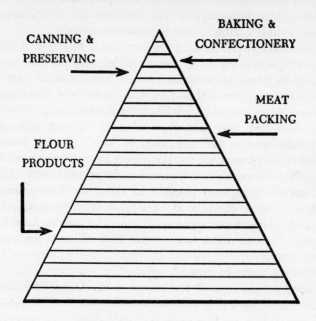

COMPARATIVE RATINGS, 1919–38

Industry	Rating
Baking and Confectionery	3
Canning and Preserving	4
Slaughtering and Meat Packing	9
Flour and Other Grain Products	17

Source: T. J. Kreps, *Measurement of the Social Performance of Business,* pp. 44-45.

also higher by 5.5 per cent. Most unstable of the income streams has been that going to stockholders. During the depression the slaughtering and meat-packing industry decreased most of all the payments going to stockholders and maintained a relatively steady volume of payrolls and of employment.[3]

[3] Theodore J. Kreps, *Measurement of the Social Performance of Business,* TNEC Monograph No. 7 (1940), p. 20. The study's measurement of per-

Among food industries the study on "social performance" gives the highest rating to baking and confectionery, the lowest to flour and other grain-mill industries. These ratings did not evaluate the nutritional value of output, only its economic aspects.

In World War II the packing industry did a good job of increasing production. While most of the more than 100-per-cent increase in meat sales came from higher prices, a substantial part of it represented greater physical output, which rose from 19,000,000,000 pounds in 1940 to around 25,000,000,000 pounds in 1945.

Meat prices rose more than the average of all commodity prices —the opposite of this had happened in World War I. Livestock producers received most of the price increases, but a part of them went to the packers, especially in the early postwar years. Rationing and control kept meat prices from rising too high during the war; this is apparent from the average profit of 1.2 per cent on sales in the years 1940–45, not too much above the prewar return. The return more than doubled, however, in 1946–47 after the removal of price control.[4]

The packers were, in general, opposed to wartime price regulations.[5] They fought against the policy of the Office of Price Ad-

---

formance is based on whether production, employment, and payrolls were increasing or decreasing; total production in comparison with "consumer effort" commanded by that production, that is, increasing value to consumers in terms of lower prices; the ratio of payrolls to consumer purchases, whether payrolls were a smaller or larger proportion of the money spent on buying the industry's product; and the ratio of payrolls to interest and dividend payments.

[4] Article, "Sales, Earnings and Net Worth of 863 Packers Up Sharply in 1946," *The National Provisioner*, September 27, 1947, p. 10.

[5] Opposition to price control began early and included most businessmen. One "spokesman" for an unidentified "major packing company" (*Chicago Tribune*, September 9, 1942) attacked OPA licensing, introduced to unify price regulations and which carried penalties for violation of ceilings, "because it makes it possible for men who may be inexperienced in the meat-packing field, to close down or seriously interfere with our business." Livestock producers opposed price ceilings on meat animals; at a meeting called by the National Livestock Marketing Association (*The Butcher Workman*, October 1942, p. 3), attended by representatives of the National Grange, Farmers Union Livestock Commission, Central Cooperative Association, Texas and Southwestern Cattle Raisers Association, and the National Swine Growers, it was argued that livestock price ceilings "would inevitably curtail seriously future production. . . . Difficulties already experienced in the attempt to control meat prices would be multiplied tremendously by moving to extend the ceilings to live animals." Cooperators and private enterprisers joined to oppose wartime price control.

ministration (OPA), which was to keep profits down to a "reasonable" prewar average. This could be done, OPA decided, by a return of .7 per cent on packing sales, which "represents the average base period [1936–39] return to the industry measured in terms of a percentage of net worth." As we have seen, the actual return on sales averaged 1.2 per cent for 1942–45.

The big packers were aggressively against OPA's "over-all industry earning test." They wanted the industry to be considered as a group with respect to meat processing only, separating by-products from meats, on which, they said, they were not making a "fair profit."

Armour & Company made a legal challenge of the OPA test in 1945, but the Emergency Court of Appeals ruled against them. Smaller packers opposed the "industry earning test" because if an individual firm made no profits it had to apply for an adjustment under OPA's "secondary products test" which permitted recovery of "out of pocket costs"—direct labor and materials costs, not including general overhead such as administrative and selling expenses. Finally a demand was made and enacted into law by Congress that the three kinds of livestock processed (cattle, sheep, and hogs) should be considered separately in determining a "reasonable margin of profit" for meat packers.

The OPA policy of keeping down profits made allowance for 17 per cent of the packing industry's sales volume being in a loss position, the prewar average. When this rose to 28 per cent, OPA decided, for 1945, to increase the returns on sales to 1.5 per cent in order to reduce the loss position by means of additional subsidy payments, which amounted to over $16,000,000.[6]

Meanwhile black-market operations flourished, in disregard of OPA's ceiling prices. And the packing industry, as an argument against price control, exaggerated the extent of black-market activity.

Upon the war's end the packers, together with the Amalgamated Meat Cutters, called for an immediate end of price control, which had kept price rises within reasonable limits compared with the experience in World War I. OPA was scrapped early in 1946, after which prices zoomed in an inflationary rise greater than that of

[6] U.S. Senate Subcommittee, *Barkley-Bates Amendment and Other Factors Affecting Operation of Meat Packing Industry* (1946), pp. 1, 2, 20-23.

1919–20. The sharp rise for the year from June 1946 to June 1947 was distributed as follows, according to the United States Bureau of Labor Statistics: Livestock prices went up 47 per cent; wholesale meat prices went up 89 per cent; retail meat prices went up 61 per cent.

MEAT PRICES COMPARED WITH OTHER PRICES (WHOLESALE)

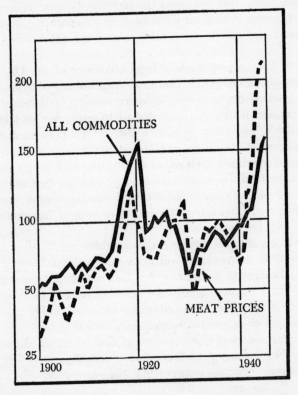

Inflationary prices clearly favored the packers, and their higher postwar profits showed it. Livestock producers made the smallest gains. Part of the increases were absorbed by the retailers, since the prices at which they sold rose less than the prices they paid to the packers. Within one year after the scrapping of OPA an average of $80 yearly was added to the meat bill of a family with income below $3000.

In 1948, two years after price decontrol, the Amalgamated Meat Cutters announced "a national campaign to bring meat within consumer buying range. If prices don't come down, the government must restore controls on meat." The industry split on the issue of restoring controls. While, for example, the National Industry Meat Council, representing 25,000 stores in eight states, favored a resumption of price control, the American Meat Institute opposed it. In between these two extremes stood the National Association of Retail Grocers, which urged buyer resistance as a protest against high meat prices.

The packers were complacent, on the whole, about high meat prices. Their national organ admitted that prices might be lowered: "Consumers could break and hold meat prices at a considerably lower level—but it is improbable that they will do so." The "low return" on sales and "supply and demand" were used to explain away high prices.

R. J. Eggert, associate director of marketing of the American Meat Institute, said: "Meat prices are established by all consumers, as a group, and by what they are able to pay for the available supply. A larger supply results in a lower price, if there is no change in consumers' desires and ability to pay. The more all consumers, as a group, are willing and able to pay, the higher the price if there is no change in the meat supply." [7]

There is an element of truth, of course, in the "supply and demand" influence on prices. But it is far-fetched to use the argument to mean that consumers are to blame for price rises. There is the economic aspect of an unequal distribution of income that permits some people to pay more, while many people cannot buy because of low incomes. And there is the question of individual and social justice, which does not sanction a widespread inequality in the distribution of the necessities of life. Finally, OPA controls *did keep* wartime prices at a reasonable level—around a 30 per cent rise compared with a rise of 60 per cent in World War I. The unreasonable rise came after the controls were scrapped.

Although prices were held down to substantially low levels during the war, the food industries, meat packing included, had the most profitable business they had had since the 1920's. This appears not only from the jump in net income and a higher rate of profit

[7] Article, "People Like Meat," *The National Provisioner,* August 7, 1948, p. 12.

on net worth, but from the decline of 75 per cent in the number of companies which ended the business year with a deficit.

FINANCIAL CONDITION OF FOOD CORPORATIONS, 1937–44

Year	Companies	Net Income	Companies	Deficit
1937	5,300	$286,098,000	6,940	$63,804,000
1940	5,315	444,317,000	4,934	36,523,000
1942	7,086	942,299,000	2,394	14,173,000
1944	6,958	1,124,592,000	1,816	13,398,000

Source: U.S. Department of Commerce, Statistical Abstract of the United States, 1948, p. 342.

In its campaign against OPA the American Meat Institute argued (as did other trade associations) that the end of controls would bring lower prices to consumers. But for two years after OPA's death all prices, including those paid for meat products, kept on rising. The AMI insisted that the only way to secure lower prices was by higher production. This was obviously true for the long run, since what is basic in an inflationary situation is the excess of the demand for goods over the supply. But for the short run it was also true that inflationary pressures would force up prices unless some controls were used to keep them down, since a number of years were needed for production to catch up with demand.

One speaker at the 1945 AMI convention gave the packers some plain talk about their "unfavorable references" to OPA:

There was a time, of course, you could blame the professors for what happened in the OPA; then you filled it with businessmen and you are still avoiding it. It is easy to chafe under controls and to imagine a state of bliss if they were ended. It is unrealistic to believe that we could have gone through a war without serious inflation had there been no price control. Because we controlled prices, we had to employ rationing to attain some equity in the distribution of inadequate supply. No one argues against the point that full production is the best check on inflation, but adequate production of both war and civilian goods is an impossibility in an all-out war.[8]

Not all businessmen were united in favor of the immediate re-

[8] Proceedings, 40th Annual Convention, American Meat Institute, The National Provisioner, November 10, 1945, p. 138.

moval of price controls. While the American Meat Institute and the National Association of Manufacturers demanded total abolition of OPA at once, the National Independent Meat Packers Association (NIMPA) and the Committee for Economic Development (CED) urged gradual decontrol. The CED suggested renewal on a temporary basis of OPA's authority, which expired in June 1946, with the "profit standard" raised by one-third to stimulate maximum production.[9]

The meat-packing industry's war profits, while high, were not so high as those in many other industries, including other food industries. For the more than 600 slaughtering meat packers (among them the Big Four and major independents) reporting under the Packers and Stockyards Act, average earnings on net worth for 1939–45 amounted to 7.5 per cent, with a war peak (1942–44) of 8.5 per cent. "Compared with all manufacturing industries, meat packing has shown a prewar as well as a wartime tendency to have somewhat less variation in earnings and a consistently lower average. Also meat packing has been found to be among the least profitable of the food industries." [10]

Another lag appeared in the meat industry's capital growth compared with that of other corporations. According to the Securities and Exchange Commission, the increase of working capital during the war years for 827 manufacturing corporations was 57 per cent, but only 37 per cent in meat packing. Expansion was relatively less than in other manufacturing industries.

These developments indicate a slowing down of expansion in the meat industry, tending toward a stationary condition in saturated markets. That packing's wartime expansion was relatively less than that of other industries was partly due to an increase of small

[9] Article, "What Price Price Control," *Fortune*, May 1946, p. 100. This article favored gradual decontrol—as quickly as possible, one might say. "The cure for the danger of inflation," said *Fortune*, "is (1) more civilian production and (2) an aggressive Treasury policy, which through taxes and restriction of credit gets at the source of excess demand." *Fortune* argued that competition would keep prices down: "It is time for OPA to wake up to the fact that there is competition. The chance of Chevrolet and Ford boosting prices sky-high is slim. And if Ford were so foolish as to raise his price to say $2000, why not let him?" Well, Ford did boost his price to $2000; so did Chevrolet and others.

[10] Article, "Meat Industry Financial and Economic Trends," *The National Provisioner*, June 28, 1947, p. 14. The article is based on a study by the research department of the Federal Reserve Bank of Chicago.

packers, some of them fly-by-night concerns that made big profits in black-market operations. But part of the reason was also the fact that the rise in the output of meat products was smaller than the increase in most other industries manufacturing perishable consumer goods.

There is little doubt that packing is becoming a mature, stationary industry. More demand for meat products from increasing population will be offset by lower per capita consumption. And as meat packing becomes a stationary industry, problems of price and profit, of the relation of independents to the big packers, and of general economic organization and policy will assume more pressing importance.

2. THE BIG FOUR PACKERS

When in 1920 the big packers, in order to escape trial of the anti-trust suit against them, agreed to accept a "consent decree" they gave up their interests in stockyards, railroad terminals, and market newspapers, their manufacture and distribution of "unrelated lines" of groceries and various other commodities, and their use of public cold-storage warehouses for other products than meats. In addition, they agreed to give up their retail meat stores. The packers were permitted to keep their refrigerator cars, cold-storage plants, and branch warehouses, and to continue the production and sale of dairy and poultry products, cottonseed oil and oleomargarine, in which lines they have since multiplied output. Today Swift owns no refrigerator cars; other packers use both their own and leased cars.

The Big Four abandoned their retail meat outlets reluctantly and grudgingly. They fought bitterly and kept up their fight to "relax" the decree. The Federal Trade Commission repeatedly charged that they were failing to comply with its provisions. In one form or another the packers tried to get back their retail business. With the development of motor truck transportation in the 1920's, they began to use trucks for direct distribution to consumers.

Meanwhile the Big Four expanded their output and sales of dairy products (other than fluid milk), of which they became large distributors to retailers and to institutions. Their volume in this field began to exceed that of a number of dairy companies. By 1940 Swift, Armour, and Wilson were among the six companies that sold

80 per cent of all cheese and among the six companies that sold one-half of all canned milk.

One threat to the Big Four packers' dominance appeared in the 1920's with a considerable growth of interior plants owned by small independent packers. This development began in World War I. The plants were located primarily in cities throughout the Corn Belt. A technological factor, the motor truck, made it feasible to slaughter hogs nearer to the producing areas and thus save on transportation costs, as well as to avoid marketing and yardage costs for livestock shipped to the stockyards of St. Louis, Chicago, and other cities. The new interior plants made a steady advance in their business up to 1929. As a result, the big packers' proportion of all livestock slaughter dropped from 70.5 per cent in 1916 (including Morris & Company) to 58.7 per cent in 1929. They met this threat by buying up interior plants and building plants of their own, after which their proportion of livestock slaughter moved up again to the old levels.[11] In the years 1927–47 the Big Four, according to the government's 1948 anti-trust complaint, absorbed a total of sixty-five small independent companies, as follows: Swift 33, Armour 21, Wilson 7, Cudahy 4.

These four packers control somewhat over one-half of the total output of the packing industry. They control only up to 40 per cent of the meat supply, however, since so large a part of their sales comes from non-meat operations, or by-products. Armour's meat business, for example, accounted for 61 per cent of sales in 1946 and 69 per cent in 1947. Pharmaceuticals made from the membranes and glands of livestock are of increasing importance among the by-products of the big packers, who carry on extensive research on pharmaceuticals and own numerous patents covering their production.

Monopoly dominance looms greatest in relation to the fifty-two companies which are the industry's more important factors. In 1947 the Big Four, on this comparative basis, did 74 per cent of the business and secured 80 per cent of the earnings, with their net worth three and a half times greater than the total of the fifty-two companies. The rest of the industry is fragmentized among more than 600 very small packing enterprises.

[11] TNEC Monograph No. 35, *Concentration of Economic Power* (1940), pp. 16-17.

COMPARISON OF BIG FOUR AND INDEPENDENTS, 1947

	Big Four	52 Companies
Sales	$5,516,200,000	$1,945,500,000
Earnings	87,856,000	21,388,000
Working capital	454,100,000	102,100,000
Net worth	597,647,000	176,150,000

"Earnings" are after taxes and before dividends. Big Four are Armour, Swift, Wilson, and Cudahy.

Source: Arranged from statistics in Research Department, Federal Reserve Bank of Chicago, *Financial and Economic Survey of the Meat Packing Industry, 1948 Supplement*, pp. 9, 11.

The combined Big Four net worth in 1947 was nearly $600,000,-000; their surplus nearly $300,000,000. Swift, Armour, and Wilson belong to the aristocracy of the 250 largest non-financial corporations.[12] In 1947 the first two concerns were among the fifteen corporations with sales of over $1,000,000,000.

The war did not significantly change the relative power of the Big Four. They maintained the policies and activities that were calculated not to outgrow their positions in the industry in relation to one another. This appears clearly from an almost identical increase in their sales, which, using 1939 as base year, were, in 1946, 73 per cent higher for Swift, 66 per cent higher for Armour, 62 per cent higher for Wilson, 73 per cent higher for Cudahy.

As a result of war profits the four companies more than doubled their surplus from profits kept in the business. It rose, according to reports of the Securities and Exchange Commission, from $100,779,000 in 1939 to $235,255,000 in 1946. The Big Four's rate of profit on net worth for the war period averaged around 7 per cent; it rose to 15 per cent in the early postwar years.

Swift and Armour are still the industry's two giants. Their sales in 1947 were three times as great as those of Wilson and Cudahy; similar disproportions prevailed in other comparative financial aspects.

[12] Adolf A. Berle and Gardiner Means, *The Modern Corporation and Private Property* (1933), pp. 20-21. Other food corporations among the aristocratic 250 were Borden, National Dairy Products, National Biscuit, American Sugar Refining, Cuban Cane Products, and the Great Atlantic and Pacific Tea Company.

FINANCIAL COMPARISON OF BIG FOUR PACKERS, 1947

(*in millions of dollars*)

	Swift	Armour	Wilson	Cudahy
Sales	$2,243	$1,956	$738	$573
Net earnings	36	31	15	7
Working capital	206	153	53	40
Surplus	131	70	80	18

Source: Compiled and arranged from the respective financial reports of the corporations.

Three of the Big Four earned smaller profits in 1948, and one sustained losses, because of lower prices and a strike; but aggregate profits were still substantially higher than in most prewar years. Swift's net earnings were $27,889,000, Wilson's $6,702,000, and Cudahy's $1,102,000. Armour's net loss was $1,965,000, although its sales were $1,991,400,000. An economist of the Amalgamated Meat Cutters explained the Armour loss as follows:

Much of it is attributed to the CIO strike. The eleven-week work stoppage by that union did affect the financial condition of the Big Four packers; but that alone is not responsible for the loss reported by Armour & Company. The real reason is probably due to the high costs of managerial functions, and poor business judgment on the part of those who make the policy for that company. It is known that immediately after the strike in March 1948 the Armour company, unlike the others, disposed of all their inventory, cleaned out their freezers and warehouses. When the strike ended they were compelled to buy heavily in the open market to replenish their lost stockpile and they were obliged to sell their products in an unfavorable market. It is perhaps not unfair to say that too much management centralization is another contributory factor to the poor showing of the Armour company.[13]

Unsound financial practices were another factor. They go back to the years after World War I. J. Ogden Armour, who had taken over control of the company when his father, Philip, died, reasoned that postwar Europe would be starving and need food. So he tied up scores of millions of dollars in inventory. When prices collapsed

[13] David Dolnick, "Packinghouse Workers Need Economic Relief," *The Butcher Workman*, April 1949, p. 6.

in 1920–21, Armour was caught owing $56,000,000 to his company, which itself was $38,000,000 in debt.[14] Armour resigned as part of a reorganization. The company has been weighed down with a top-heavy capital structure in the form of long-term funded obligations and their interest charges. This is true of the packing industry in general, but especially of Armour. The company paid no dividends on common stock for eleven years—until early in 1948, when they were resumed but suspended again later in the year; in 1947 Armour paid accrued dividends of $13,324,000 ($25 per share) on the $6 preferred stock and $2,065,000 ($61.25 per share) on the $7 preferred.[15] Wilson and Cudahy also have omitted dividends, Swift alone making regular payments.

While the relative power of the Big Four is much what it was in the 1920's, important changes have appeared in their ownership. The old packer families are no longer dominant. In the case of Wilson & Company, of which, in 1948, Thomas Wilson was chairman of the board of directors and his son, Edward F. Wilson, president, stock ownership is dispersed and bankers are in control. The Swift family, although three of its members were in top administrative positions, in the 1930's owned only around 5 per cent of the company's stock. The Armour family is no longer dominant or active in the enterprise that Philip Armour founded; it owned, in 1937, about 1 per cent of the company's common stock and a much smaller proportion of preferred.[16]

---

[14] J. Ogden Armour was not as clever as his father, who, on the eve of Union victory in the Civil War, sold pork short and made a big profit.

[15] Article, "Armour Annual Report," *The National Provisioner*, January 10, 1948, p. 15. Big Four funded debt in 1946 was as follows: Armour $95,000,000; Swift $18,750,000; Wilson $15,726,000; and Cudahy $14,000,000. Swift had no preferred stock, Wilson 250,000 shares of $4.25 cumulative preferred, and Cudahy 100,000 shares of $4.50 cumulative preferred. Armour, however, had 532,996 shares of $6 cumulative preferred and 33,715 shares of $7 cumulative preferred. Swift dividends on common stock have ranged from a low of $1.20 yearly to a high of $2 in 1929, when, in addition, a four-to-one stock split took place. In 1948 Swift paid $1.20 on the common with a special dividend of $1, or a total of $2.20, equal to $8.60 on a pre-1929 share of stock.

[16] TNEC Monograph No. 29, *Distribution of Stock Ownership in 200 Largest Non-Financial Corporations* (1940), pp. 1500-10. According to this report, F. H. Prince was probably the largest Armour stockholder, with direct and indirect holdings of around 3 per cent; at the same time he owned 40 per cent of stock in the Chicago Stockyards Company, which controls the Union Stockyards and Transit Company.

In all these companies there exists a substantial amount of security ownership and control by banks, insurance companies, and investment houses. Through this, and through interlocking directorships in other corporations by their top officers and directors, the Big Four are interlocked in the "community of interest" of monopoly capitalism today—as they were in the 1900's.

A dispersion of stock ownership, characteristic of large-scale corporate industry, has multiplied the number of stockholders. Functional ownership has been replaced by absentee ownership. The Armours and Swifts and their "friendly competitors" developed industrial packing in this country. These men were owner-capitalists; they managed and directed the enterprises which they built up; they did a constructive job despite the incidental piracy. Today there is a separation of ownership from management. The owners now are tens of thousands of absentee stockholders who own the big corporations but do not manage them, while management is a hired functional skill of employees who manage but do not own.

Big Four organizational power is based on industrial concentration. Mechanization of production and diversification of products make for bigger plants, a characteristic of large-scale production. The Big Four packers together own over a hundred plants, with complex distributing systems which include branch warehouses to supply the needs of large city populations and car routes to serve smaller communities. According to the government's 1948 anti-trust complaint, Swift owns 280 branch houses, Armour 240, Wilson 83, and Cudahy 63. These houses comprise large coolers for storage of meats, dairy and poultry products, and other perishable items, storerooms for non-perishable products and supplies, and sales offices.

A mixture of constructive and destructive elements is evident in the big packers' organizational setup. Some of their mergers and consolidations had as one purpose a reduction of the costs of slaughter and distribution, elimination of unnecessary duplication of facilities for the production and distribution of products. This undoubtedly reduced costs and, in particular, unit overhead costs, which is also true of diversification of products. One study makes that point and concludes:

All this is not to imply that there may not have been a considerable element of financial manipulation and extortive gain involved in the development of large-scale organization in the packing industry. It would be a mistake, however, to look at this development only from this standpoint. Many of the principles of mass distribution and functional integration which the packers were criticized for trying to effectuate thirty or forty years ago are now being applied by the corporate grocery chains and are generally accepted as being in the interest of more efficient food distribution.[17]

The point is a legitimate one, often overlooked, but it is only part of the truth. The big packers went beyond a bigness whose sole objective was economic efficiency. There is no evidence that the financial overlords of packing were concerned exclusively with efficiency. Technical managements were so concerned, in large measure and as they were allowed to be so; but the overlords wanted bigness for monopoly domination, profit, and power. When bigness goes beyond the point of greatest efficiency, it does not matter from the financial profit angle, providing monopoly prices and profits can be extorted. An inefficient monopoly may make more profit than efficient competitive enterprises if it controls the market, competition, and prices.

A distinction must be drawn, moreover, between vertical and horizontal combination. The integration of an enterprise to perform all phases of production, from raw material to finished product, which is vertical combination, is usually a force for efficiency. This does not require, however, bigness in an exclusive dominating sense, as the efficiency of the larger independent packers proves. But horizontal combination, which is what the packing monopolists were primarily concerned with, spreads outward to absorb competing enterprises or kill them, to destroy competition and dominate the market, to fix prices. Of horizontal combination an outstanding American economist has said:

Evidently, horizontal combination is not a guarantee of savings. It is at best an opportunity none too easy to seize and exploit. Both in practice and principle it is hard to disentangle its effects from those of partial monopoly. Eliot Jones, in his recent book, *The Trust Problem* (1920), states that of all successful trusts examined there is not one whose success cannot be explained on other grounds than those of the efficiency resulting from combination. It is fair to conclude that the chief forces

[17] TNEC Monograph No. 35, p. 23.

making for horizontal combination are not the economies that result but rather *the natural urge to cease competing and combine.*[18]

A Federal Trade Commission study in the 1930's gave ample proof that corporate bigness is not necessarily and always equal to efficiency measured in terms of low costs, profitability of operations, and pioneering initiative. The most efficient enterprises, by and large, were found by the FTC to be among the medium enterprises, only rarely among the bigger corporations.[19] Evidence tends to show that in the packing industry, too, bigness is not always outstandingly efficient. During the years 1939–45, for example, the average earnings of medium packers were higher than Big Four earnings. In addition, the earnings of medium packers showed greater stability within a narrow range of about 9 per cent to 11 per cent.

The monopoly packers have a predominant position because of their economic and financial power, not because of their efficiency. The government's 1948 suit against the Big Four charged them with inducing independents to conform to the policies of the Big Four; combining to bid aggressive independents out of the livestock purchasing market; agreeing to allow any one of themselves to keep the buying position of any packing plant that is purchased whether or not the plant is kept operating. Yet the Big Four succeed only in maintaining their power, not in expanding it. The drive toward absolute monopoly has petered out; the four giants merely hold on to what they have. One reason, especially true in the case of pork, is the widespread supply of livestock and the savings on freight and marketing costs of production near supply areas, which make it possible for local independent packers to exist and compete within those areas. Another reason is that, while anti-trust action has not broken up the Big Four, it has prevented their consolidation into one dominant corporate giant and has helped to stop their business from growing at the expense of smaller packers.

Still more important, the Big Four enterprises are not as profitable as they were from 1890 to 1910. The packer rate of profit began to decline after World War I; in 1928, for example, the Big Four made a rate of profit of 5.5 per cent on capitalization, compared with 7.2 per cent for four big dairy companies and 23.9 per cent

[18] John M. Clark, *Studies in the Economics of Overhead Costs* (1923), p. 147.
[19] Federal Trade Commission, *Relative Efficiency of Large, Medium-Sized and Small Business* (1940), p. 129.

for five grocery chains. In the years 1928–45 the packers' earnings were consistently lower than those of other food corporations and of nearly all manufacturing enterprises.[20]

This trend toward comparative unprofitability continued up to 1945. The big packers made a smaller rate of profit in World War II than they did in 1915–19. Their profit increase was considerably less than that of other industrial corporations. Big packer net income was 51.7 per cent greater in 1945 than in 1935, compared with 95.4 per cent for four dairy companies and 75.6 per cent for 380 industrial companies.

COMPARISON OF INCREASE IN NET INCOME, 1935–45

	1935	1939	1940	1941	1942	1943	1944	1945
6 packers	100.0	103.5	121.3	206.8	200.5	204.5	198.7	151.7
4 dairy	100.0	154.2	140.2	154.8	154.6	163.4	168.6	195.4
380 industrials	100.0	134.3	161.3	187.8	154.0	162.8	175.0	175.6

Net income is after taxes and reserves. The six packers are Armour, Swift, Wilson, Cudahy, Morrell, and Hormel; the four dairy companies are Beatrice Foods, Borden, National Dairy, and Carnation Milk.

Source: Standard and Poor's Industry Surveys, *Meats and Dairy Products,* March 21, 1947, p. 113.

In all years except the first three war years, 1941–44, the Big Four profits lagged behind those of most other corporations. The figures show, however, that the packers still did well in the war (as did the independents). Their profits fell in 1945 to rise again in 1946–47.

With the exception of the dairy industry, the bigger packers did better, from the profit angle, than other food concerns, during the war years. But they did not do as well as the independents: "All sizes of meat-packing firms greatly improved their financial positions during the war years. The very small packers (with 1941 assets under $1,000,000) experienced the greatest, *and the large packers the least*—though still substantial—wartime earnings and financial gains." [21]

In 1940 the Big Four rate of profit was smaller than that of other food corporations. And their windfall profits from war needs were

[20] *Yearbook of Agriculture: Farmers in a Changing World* (1940), p. 630.

[21] Article, "Meat Industry Financial and Economic Trends," *The National Provisioner,* June 28, 1947, p. 14. The study was made by the research department of the Federal Reserve Bank of Chicago.

not maintained. In one postwar year, for example, the profits of thirteen packing companies dropped from $76,846,000 in 1947 to $44,070,000 in 1948, while the profits of eleven general food companies experienced a much smaller loss—from $62,690,000 to $50,885,000.[22]

Most significant are the indications that the profit position of the Big Four is poorer than that of independent packers. The independent rate of profit was consistently higher in the years 1940–47. The big packer rate is lowered by their greater burden of long-term debt ($176,841,000 in 1947) and its interest payments, compared with a much lower absolute and proportional debt among independents ($22,297,000 for fifty-two companies). But this fact does not materially change the situation.

EARNINGS AS PER CENT OF NET WORTH, 1940–47

	Big Four	604 Packers
1940	5.0	5.9
1941	8.4	8.7
1942	7.8	8.6
1943	8.0	9.2
1944	7.1	8.9
1945	5.4	5.6
1946	11.0	15.2
1947	14.8	15.9

The 604 corporations (including the Big Four) are those subject to the Packers and Stockyards Act; they dominate the industry.

Source: Research Department, Federal Reserve Bank of Chicago, *Financial and Economic Survey of the Meat Packing Industry, 1949 Supplement*, p. 8.

None of the Big Four rates of profit in World War II and after compare with what they earned in 1916 and 1917: 18.5 per cent and 26.5 per cent respectively.

The Big Four have used monopoly practices (including some tie-in sales, of which OPA complained during the war) to boost profits all they can. It is significant, therefore, that the efforts have not been successful in recent years. Charges of excessive profits made against

[22] *New York Times*, May 8, 1949. The decline in packing and general food profits was against the trend; 815 companies in 70 manufacturing industries showed average profits almost twice as great in 1948 as in the previous year.

DOWNWARD TREND OF BIG FOUR PROFITS

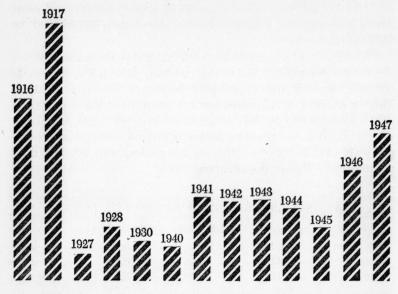

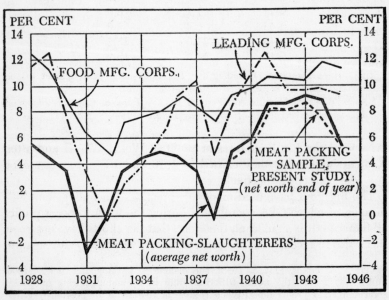

the packers are not altogether convincing. Their wartime profits, as already noted, were lower than for most other industries. And in 1946–47 the packers scored an average gain of 20 per cent compared with a gain of 50 per cent for all other manufacturing enterprises.[23]

Nor are the charges true that packer profits raise the prices of meat products for consumers. The industry is caught between the demands of farmers for higher livestock prices and consumer demands for lower meat prices. On the average the Big Four rate of profit on sales seldom has exceeded 1.4 cents on the dollar. It rose to over 2 cents in the early postwar years and then fell again. And it is true, as the packers claim in their advertising, that they make "a profit of less than 7 cents on a family's weekly meat consumption."[24]

Hence lower profits, as such, would not materially lower the prices of meat products. (Incidentally, the Amalgamated union makes this same point.) But the big packers clumsily overdo it; they never speak of their much larger profits on sales of by-products. Moreover, prices may be too high, as they were in the postwar inflationary period, regardless of whether packing profits are high or low. And packer emphasis on the small profit from sales disregards the point that it is the philosophy of capitalist production to lower unit profits with the increase of volume, which is compensated for with greater volume and larger total profit. It is this total profit, and its rate of return on capital investment or net worth, that is important. On this point the Federal Trade Commission said in 1920:

The packers make use of the word "cent," "fraction of a cent" and "only a few cents" because they know that the public regards a "cent" as a very small element of value. . . . This practice obscures the real facts as to profits [because] a profit of a cent per unit, far from being a

[23] Research Department, Federal Reserve Bank of Chicago, *Financial and Economic Survey of the Meat Packing Industry, 1948, Supplement,* p. 4.

[24] From an advertisement of Swift & Company, *Ohio Farm Bureau News,* February 1947, p. 17: "All these costs [75 cents for livestock and other agricultural products, 12.6 cents for employees, 6.8 cents for transportation, fuel, and other supplies, 3.3 cents for interest, depreciation and miscellaneous business costs, 1 cent for taxes] taken out of the sales dollar left 1.3 cents. This was Swift & Company's net profit in 1946—a profit of only one-fourth of one cent on each pound of the millions of products and by-products handled."

small profit, may be an exorbitant profit. . . . The sound method of deciding whether profits are "reasonable" or not is by aggregating such profit and comparing it with the capital invested in the enterprise. [And this is especially important in the packing industry, which] does a large volume of business on a small investment.[25]

When the FTC made its indictment the big packers' rate of profit was high and had been higher. Their rates of profit since, however, have not been as high as they were in the 1890's and 1900's. It is important to understand the reasons for this change since they are crucial for consideration of economic policy in the meat-packing industry.

Profits in any industry, as a rate on investment, are always larger in the earlier period of expansion than they are later. The development of every industry proves this. As expansion slows down or comes to a standstill the rate of profit moves downward; the situation for profits becomes worse if a decline sets in. Only absolute monopoly could change the trend—providing, however, that monopoly dominated a number of industries, not all. Monopoly profits are made primarily at the expense of "free" or non-monopoly industries. If monopoly dominated everywhere, the "earning" of superprofits would bring economic disaster in one of two ways, or a combination of both: profits would become too high in terms of the need for new capital investment, and effective demand in the market, as consumer purchasing power shrank, would be insufficient to absorb all the goods and services produced.

This tendency toward a lower rate of profit is especially important in an industry where, as in meat packing, the profit depends so much on the volume of output because the unit profit margin is small.

In the 1920's and '30's the Big Four rate of profit on net worth seldom exceeded 5 per cent, with a low of 2.2 per cent in 1927 and deficits in 1931–32 and 1938. The rate rose in World War II and in the early postwar years, only to fall again to the prewar level. This, despite what W. H. Nicholls, a professorial economist, has described as "imperfectly competitive conditions in the packing industry, presumably with ill effects on prices to farmer and consumer"; and despite the limited nature of competition, which has been frankly admitted by Big Four representatives. A Swift economist, for exam-

[25] Federal Trade Commission, *Report on the Meat Packing Industry*, Part V, "Profits of the Packers" (1920), pp. 12-13.

ple, testified before the Temporary National Economic Committee of the United States Senate: "If we try to exceed our customary percentages in any market . . . Armour and Wilson would meet our prices and there would be cutthroat competition." [26]

In addition, the profits of packing enterprises are markedly unstable, including those of the Big Four. This instability is another aspect of the industry's need for volume, and involves the close relation between consumers' disposable income and meat sales. When that income shrinks the consumers substitute other and cheaper products for meat, which brings unusually sharp up-and-down swings in production and consumption. The figures on net income as percentage of sales reveals not only the instability in profits of the Big Four but also substantial variations among them.

BIG FOUR NET INCOME AS PER CENT OF SALES, 1929–46

	Armour	Cudahy	Swift	Wilson
1929	0.6	0.9	1.3	0.7
1939	0.5	0.4	1.3	1.2
1940	0.6	1.0	1.5	1.3
1941	1.2	1.4	1.7	1.9
1942	0.8	0.9	1.2	1.4
1943	0.8	0.8	1.2	1.4
1944	0.8	0.8	1.0	1.4
1945	0.8	0.7	1.0	1.1
1946	1.8	1.9	1.3	1.9

Source: Standard and Poor's Industry Surveys, Meat and Dairy Products, March 21, 1947, pp. 13-14. Some of the variations in profit on sales result from differences in interest payments on long-term debt.

Another factor operating to lower the packers' rate of profit is the growing cost of doing business, including the provision of greater service to consumers. This has resulted in a marked growth in the proportion that wages and salaries are of the industry's value output.

Finally, and to emphasize the points already made, the Big Four monopoly power is not strong enough to offset the downward pressure on profits exerted by the slowdown of the industry's expan-

[26] TNEC Monograph No. 21, Competition and Monopoly in American Industry (1940), pp. 182-84.

sion and the instability of production and consumption. Only a very limited success marks efforts to control livestock supply and prices and the prices of meat products. And Big Four monopoly power, in addition to being limited, is connected with a bureaucratic centralization of managerial control that hampers efficiency and may breed costly mistakes (e.g., the mistakes of Armour & Company in 1948, which helped to bring a large deficit).

But while the monopoly drive for greater profits largely fails, it results nevertheless in a distortion of economic policy. The Big Four continuously strive to make greater profits, and the results are damaging. Restrictive practices, whether or not they achieve bigger profits, set up barriers to economic progress. Packer (and general corporate) opposition to wartime price control came from the urge to make more profit, which eventually led to an early postwar scrapping of OPA and an inflationary rise in profits; the fact that the profits later came down did not offset the evils of inflation. And the Big Four drive for profit brings practices which make miserable the life of many independent packers.

Industry needs and can absorb only a certain amount of profit for expansion; if this amount is exceeded the wheels of industry slow down and grind into depression. The drive for bigger profits, although not altogether successful, periodically brings a condition of imbalance between profit and investment, production and consumption. These factors get out of gear with one another, resulting in cyclical depression. And they get out of gear as profits (however "reasonable" and "small") rise more than wages, salaries, and consumer purchasing power: as profits rise more than the investment needs of industry.

As the packing industry becomes comparatively unprofitable, the profit drive may do greater harm. It can do most harm if the industry tries, through advertising and other pressures, to sell more meat products regardless of whether or not the consumers should eat more meat. Hence the need to consider the industry's profits in relation to economic organization and policy.

*　*　*

The export of meat products has always been a considerable factor in the American packing industry since Colonial times. Yet by 1860 the value of the exports of animal products was only

$15,000,000. The introduction of refrigerator cars and ships brought an increase of exports, especially beef; their value rose to $116,000,000 in 1880 and over $179,000,000 in 1900.[27] Most of the foreign business was done by the monopoly packers—a big element of their growth and power.

One major factor in the development of world trade in meat products was the economic policy of Great Britain as a buyer of imported meats, not as producer. Britain has been, and still is, the largest national buyer of meat from the Americas. As growth of the factory system transformed Britain into an industrial nation it neglected agriculture and livestock and became increasingly dependent on food imports for its growing industrial population.

To provide meat products for their markets the British capitalists invested in a Latin American packing industry. They began in Argentina, the first country outside the United States to become a large meat exporter. This competition from British packers led Armour, Swift, Morris, and Sulzberger (later Wilson & Company) in 1908 to invade Argentina, where they opened their own packing plants and became a dominant factor in the export trade.

For a time the rival British-American packers waged competitive war upon one another. They decided to end this "ruinous" competition by concluding agreements to divide Latin-American exports, with the American packers receiving from one-half to two-thirds of the business. The first "pool" they formed in 1911 broke up two years later; it was resumed, broken up, and resumed again (with one particularly disastrous price war in the 1920's). Of these operations the Federal Trade Commission wrote in 1918:

The Armour, Swift, Morris and Wilson interests, either separately or jointly, own or control more than half of the export-meat production of the Argentine, Brazil and Uruguay, and have large investments in other surplus meat-producing countries, including Australia. . . . [These] interests have entered into a combination with certain foreign corporations by which export shipments of beef, mutton and other meats from the principal South American producing countries are apportioned among the several countries on the basis of agreed percentages. In connection with this conspiracy, meetings are held for the purpose of securing

[27] *Yearbook of Agriculture: Farmers in Changing World* (1940), p. 240. F. A. Shannon, *The Farmer's Last Frontier* (1945), writes, p. 193: "The packers had been shipping better meats than they sold at home."

maintenance of the agreement and making such readjustments as from time to time may be desirable.[28]

While the big packers' business from their plants in foreign countries kept on increasing, a rapid, steady decline of American meat exports set in. By 1913 the exports of pork and lard had fallen by about one-third, while those of beef were negligible. Exports mounted in World War I but they dwindled again in the 1920's, with lard alone about holding its position. By 1940 the export of all meat products was small.

EXPORT OF MEAT PRODUCTS, U.S.A., 1900–1940

	Millions of Pounds			Millions of Dollars		
Year	Beef	Pork	Lard	Beef	Pork	Lard
1900	434	876	662	37	70	42
1911	82	446	605	7	53	60
1912	46	430	553	4	52	58
1913	36	445	575	4	59	65
1914	86	368	460	11	51	51
1921	41	738	893	5	130	116
1922	33	699	787	3	118	94
1923	28	928	1,060	3	133	133
1924	26	702	971	3	99	129
1925	26	519	708	3	105	121
1929	16	344	848	2	61	108
1930	19	277	656	2	50	75
1939	15	130	277	2	20	20
1940	17	94	201	2	11	12

Source: U.S. Department of Commerce, Statistical Abstract of the United States. The figures do not include exports to contiguous U.S. possessions, which for 1940 were 422,000,000 pounds.

During World War II exports mounted again, leveling off, however, to prewar levels in 1947–49. Where, in the early twentieth century, the United States contributed around one-third of the

[28] Federal Trade Commission, Summary of the Report . . . on the Meat Industry (1918), pp. 9-10. The Commission reported that Armour had fifteen subsidiaries in foreign countries, Swift fifteen, Wilson three, Morris two (both in Britain), Cudahy two, with one joint Armour-Morris company in Argentina. The countries included Australia, Argentina, Brazil, Uruguay, Paraguay, Canada, Britain, France, Germany, Denmark, and Italy.

meat products entering into world trade, the contribution normally is now small in relation to that of other countries and especially in relation to domestic sales. American exports are important only in wartime.

Most of the meat products in world trade now come from Australia, New Zealand, Uruguay, Brazil, and Canada (where packing is the second most important industry), and from Denmark, whose exports consist almost exclusively of bacon sold to Britain. South Africa's exports are still small, but that country (along with adjacent areas) may develop into a major exporter of beef.

In 1899 the American consumption of meats, including lard, was less than domestic production because the United States exported more meat than it imported. This condition changed, until in 1937 the exports were less than imports, so that domestic consumption exceeded production.[29] Meat imports in 1937 were small, however, only about 170,000,000 pounds, or less than one and a half pounds per capita; they fell to 81,000,000 pounds in 1940. Most of the imports comprised canned meats and sausage casings.

Livestock and packer interests have consistently opposed the import of meat products. They have not always fought clean, as appears from the malicious charges made from time to time that Argentine meats were tainted from hoof-and-mouth disease. Now and then some beef comes in from Canada, but these imports are also opposed.[30]

The Big Four's stake in the world's meat trade, accordingly, is exclusively in the exports from their packing plants in Canada, Latin America, and Australia. These plants produce primarily for the

---

[29] Solomon Fabricant, The Output of Manufacturing Industries, 1899–1937 (1940), p. 132.

[30] On the other hand, American money and know-how were mobilized to end the hoof-and-mouth disease that began to rage in Mexico in 1946. An appeal for aid was answered by Congress with appropriate legislation and funds. Under a joint commission the infected area of 250,000 square miles, running from coast to coast, was quarantined; other measures included disinfection, limited slaughter, general inspection and vaccination of millions of cattle and other animals. By the summer of 1949 around 8,000,000 head of livestock had been immunized after a two-year campaign at a cost of $90,000,000 to the United States, with another two or three years' work ahead and additional expenditures of up to $500,000,000. The disease did not cross the border, whose closing, however, stopped an average yearly export of 500,000 Mexican cattle to the United States.

export markets. They bring substantial, if not staggering, dividends to their Big Four owners. Thus Swift International, which operates seven packing plants in Argentina, six in Australia, five in Brazil, two in New Zealand, and one in Uruguay, paid in 1944–46 a total of $5.90 on 1,500,000 shares outstanding; current assets were upward of $60,000,000. Several independents do a considerable export business, but their earnings are too small to change the general situation.

American packers have played, on the whole, a constructive part in the world meat industry. This is demonstrably true, despite the monopoly practices; and it is neither justice nor good policy to argue that the Big Four have been wholly predatory. American packers through their foreign operations brought more and better meats to more people, primarily in Britain and continental Europe. At the same time these packers have contributed toward the improvement of livestock in those Latin-American nations where they maintain packing plants. In Argentina, for example, the Big Four packers set their prices for cattle to meet certain quality specifications; to get American prices the livestock growers had to improve feeding and breeding methods until their cattle reached the standards set. Moreover, sanitary and working conditions in the American plants are much better than in local enterprises.

On the other hand, packers engaged in cartel manipulations with their competitors to control and divide world markets among themselves for higher prices and profits. And in Argentina the Big Four worked with the feudal cattle barons, the great landholding *haciendados,* implacable reactionaries who opposed industrialization and diversified farming to maintain their economic and political power, and who were instrumental in setting up the Perón dictatorship. However, while world meat prices skyrocketed during World War II and after, neither the cattle barons nor the American packers got much of the extra profit, because Perón fixed prices at the point where they were when he came to power and his government raked in the profit from higher prices of meat exports. The foreign packers, in addition, were prohibited from selling in the local market and a 20-per-cent "commission" was imposed on their exports.

The Big Four secure additional dividends from their packing operations in foreign countries. But these dividends are neither large enough to offset the trend toward unprofitability, nor are they likely to continue. In all undeveloped countries, including those where American packers operate, there is a growing demand for economic independence, and it is only a matter of years before foreign packing plants will become native enterprises, either private or public. Neither monopoly nor capital investment abroad, which for a time retarded the downward movement of the rate of profit, can any longer help the Big Four to make bigger profits.

3. THE INDEPENDENT PACKERS

An important development of the past twenty-five years has been the steady growth of independent packers, despite the opposition and power of the four dominant giants.

This growth has not come about through any absolute decrease in the business of the Big Four, but largely through expansion of the meat industry. The larger and medium independents have become increasingly more efficient, diversified organizations. In many cases their efficiency is greater (in the technical-economic sense) than that of the Big Four. Statistics for fifty-three packing companies show that, during the early war years, while total business rose 83 per cent, the largest percentage gains were scored by nineteen medium packers, whose increase was 95 per cent.

COMPARISON OF INDEPENDENT PACKERS, 1946

	Net Worth	Per Cent Profit on Net Worth
John Morrell	$25,538,000	8.2
Rath Packing	19,181,000	10.8
George A. Hormel	15,328,000	16.6
Oscar Mayer	7,714,000	18.7
Hygrade Food Products	6,143,000	74.7
E. Kahn's Sons	4,433,000	28.7
Miller & Hart	2,322,000	51.7
Stahl-Meyer	2,083,000	9.1
Adolph Gobel	1,824,000	18.0
Mickleberry's Foods	1,228,000	70.0

Source: Arranged from Survey of American Listed Corporations, Data on Profits and Operations, Including Surplus, 1945–46, Part I, Securities and Exchange Commission, September 1946, pp. 155-66.

While Wilson and Cudahy, the smallest of the Big Four, are bigger than any of the ten major independents, the latter are growing in power. The three biggest independents, John Morrell, Rath Packing, and Hormel, are almost in the same class with Cudahy. Sales of the Morrell company, which specializes in pork products, made a large spurt during the war years. In fact, in 1942–43, the gains in Morrell sales outstripped those of the big packers.

Perhaps the most interesting independent advances have been made by Hygrade Food Products Corporation. The war gave Hygrade its opportunity. Sales of its products mounted from $40,000,-000 in 1935 and $50,000,000 in 1941 to more than double in 1945, and they kept on rising in the postwar years.

Hygrade produces a variety of products, just as the big packers do. It sells all kinds of fresh meats and, in addition, it provides a whole array of delicatessen products: bacon, cured tongue and ham, corned beef, and scores of other products including corned beef hash. What is more significant is that Hygrade, although a dwarf compared with the Big Four giants, also manufactures a variety of by-products, including hides, dyeing and tanning materials, dog food, fertilizers, and soap. It produces many dairy products: eggs, butter, cheese, and poultry. The company capitalized on the frozen food trend, freezing beef and pork cuts, chicken, beef stew, and fish, as it prepared to expand in the frozen foods field. All told, Hygrade produces more than a thousand items; and this comparative dwarf is apparently as efficient as its giant competitors.[31]

What are the factors that help the independents? First of all, the food industries, including meat packing, cannot be completely absorbed into a few giant corporations. Their economic nature—the plentiful sources of raw materials and the unusual variety of products—acts as a barrier to monopoly control in the absolute sense.

Moreover, there are limits to the economic efficiency and desirability of larger and larger plants. Even if it were true that the largest *plants* have the lowest costs, this would not prove that the biggest *corporations* have the lowest costs or the greatest efficiency, for big corporations are combinations of a number of plants of varying size. Also, a giant company with too many subsidiary plants may find it difficult for top management to supervise effectively all its far-flung

[31] Article, "One Man's Meat," *Fortune*, May 1946, pp. 97-99. Hygrade had in 1946 a network of plants with 7000 employees.

operations. There comes a point where bigness gets tangled in over-centralization, with its dead-weight pressures on efficiency, risk-taking, and initiative; Armour & Company is one convincing illustration of this development.

Management in smaller packing plants is normally more flexible, freer to make quick adjustments to changing market conditions. Fixed overhead costs are lower. In addition, small plants have another advantage in being able to operate at fuller average use of productive capacity than their bigger rivals. In the period 1925-29, for example, the packing industry as a whole operated at about 86 per cent of capacity. But "evidence tends to confirm the view somewhat widely held that *the smaller packers have in recent years been able to utilize their capacity more fully than the large packers.*" [32]

Technological developments in the early part of this century favored the big packers against the smaller ones. But the newer technology makes it increasingly possible, as a general proposition, for smaller plants to be as efficient (if not more efficient) as the larger units. One need only mention, to score the point, the growing number of more efficient machines available for greater automatic production in medium and small packing plants.

The swing toward dry rendering for the production of lard has been especially marked, for example, among independents; continuous fat extraction by means of infra-red heat will help them still more. An increasing variety of low-cost power lifting and moving equipment is being produced for small plants. Especially noteworthy is the development of conveyors for the mechanization of several operations while cuts of meat are on the moving tables, and for the elimination of trucking and hauling. Small plants are using an automatic method to move sealed cans into a continuous cooker in a steady stream and to remove them after thorough processing and cooking. Medium independents are setting the pace for mechanization in many fields; the following is one illustration:

The value of careful planning in the elimination of operating bottle-necks and in providing the maximum utilization of departmental work areas is clearly demonstrated in the efficient ham boning, cooking and

[32] Edwin G. Nourse and Associates, *America's Capacity to Produce* (1933), pp. 179-80. In the period covered, the food industries' highest use of capacity was 95 per cent for dairy products, and the lowest 50 per cent for flour milling (p. 303).

canning setup which has recently been completed at one Kingan & Company plant. This new arrangement permits a fast, orderly movement of product through the various processing stations and employs several time- and labor-saving features. The department contains complete facilities for preparing cooked and canned hams in volume, including a large chill cooler and new cook room in addition to the separate molding and canning lines and equipment. Processing areas are laid out so as to be easily accessible one to the other, facilitating product movement. Average weekly production has gone up.[33]

One smaller plant, unlike most of its type, organized itself for the efficient handling of all classes of livestock, and thus had the additional advantage of slaughtering and dressing beef and hogs, beef and calves, sheep and calves, or sheep and hogs at the same time and on the same floor. The areas used for shackling and bleeding of small stock were elevated about five feet above the main killing floor. This provided for gravity movement to transfer carcasses and animals on rails from these areas to the dressing zones without much manual manipulation. The rail system in the dressing areas was planned to provide ample room and stations for all dressing and flooring operations without interference when handling more than one kind of livestock. Glass walls provided necessary physical separation between operations.[34]

Utilization of by-products, in the meat industry's earlier years, promoted big packer dominance. Now new processes and equipment for the handling of inedible by-products permit smaller plants, which previously sold inedible materials to outside manufacturers, to set up their own rendering departments. More efficient utilization of by-products through almost completely automatic production, made possible by dry rendering, lowers costs, especially unit overhead costs, and brings greater returns for medium and small packers. In addition, the truly efficient utilization of by-products has only begun; new vistas are opening for the independents in this field which was once almost solely the province of the Big Four.

Another disadvantage to the independents that is disappearing is

[33] Article, "Kingan's Processed Ham Department," *The National Provisioner*, May 15, 1948, p. 17.

[34] Article, "Model Plant Handles All Types of Livestock," *The National Provisioner*, July 19, 1947, pp. 16-17.

per cent for the big packers, 44 per cent for the medium packers, 37 per cent for the smaller packers.

What happened was this, according to an objective study:

Without rationing and price control, a noticeable narrowing occurred in the spread of earnings between the large and the other meat packing firms. The former companies acquired a greater proportion of available livestock supplies with resultant higher profits than in the previous year. . . . The large packers increased their tonnage by one-fourth. . . . Many small and very small companies, as well as some of the medium packers, experienced substantial declines in slaughter volume. . . . The large meat packers increased their earnings more than one-third during their 1947 fiscal year, [while] earnings of the small and very small companies fell by over 40 per cent.[38]

Now and then an independent speaks up against Big Four domination of the packing industry. Thus in 1949 Samuel Slotkin, chairman of the board of Hygrade Food Products, resigned as a director of the American Meat Institute, and said:

The Institute has strongly resisted each move of a constructive nature to make its important contribution to an ever-increasing better standard of living for the people of America. . . . It has failed to cooperate with the government in its reasonable efforts to achieve economic stability. . . . It is small wonder, therefore, that our industry is summarily dismissed as hidebound selfseekers, oblivious to the general welfare and concerned only with its own profits. Whatever progressive measures have been enacted affecting our industry have been passed over our last-ditch opposition.

At this time America faces a crucial period in its history. The world food problem is in need of a sound and rational solution if we are to have prosperity in our land and peace everywhere. The American people have a right to expect from the leaders of our industry a program which would:

1. Aid the farmer to obtain a stabilized market, enabling him to produce America's needs at a fair price without the roller-coaster ups and downs to which he is constantly subjected.

2. Enable the consumer to have the assurance that his expenditures for food would remain reasonable in proportion to income and earnings.

3. Permit the processor and distributor to earn a fair profit for the services they render.

[38] Research Department, Federal Reserve Bank of Chicago, *Financial and Economic Survey of the Meat Packing Industry, 1949 Supplement,* pp. 3-4.

No such program has been forthcoming from the American Meat Institute. Instead, it has indulged in superficial and unconvincing campaigns hardly calculated to develop public confidence or help solve the serious issues that confront our nation. Any attempts that I have made within the Institute towards the adoption of a more realistic and liberal outlook have invariably been snowed under by the sheer weight of an intrenched and reactionary controlling group.[39]

The independents also must be more aware of the need for cooperative research. While some efforts in that direction are being made through NIMPA, they are a mere beginning. Cooperative research on where the small packers fit into the technical-scientific revolution going on in the meat industry could enormously strengthen their economic and moral position. The revolution favors the independents, but they need to show greater understanding of it. They are too prone to follow trade association policies.

There is, finally, the trend toward decentralization of industry, which also favors independent packers, particularly the smaller ones.

One of the evils of capitalism has been an excessive geographical concentration of industry. In many cases the cause was a similar concentration in the sources of raw material. This is not true, however, of the meat industry and of other food industries. Most of their raw materials are spread throughout the country. Plants located near sources of supply can cut down on transportation costs of animals to the packinghouses and, at the same time, cut down on distribution costs of the final product to consumers. These factors make it possible for local independent packers to exist and to compete in regional areas.

In the 1920's a general trend toward decentralization of industry began, manifested in meat packing by the growth of interior plants. The Big Four, at first, ignored the trend; when it began to cut seriously into their sales they bought up some of the existing interior plants and built new ones of their own, primarily in the Middle West. This meant a decentralization of plant location but not of corporate control. However, decentralization need not be the exclusive province of large corporations; it provides a technical-economic basis for development of independent enterprise and may

[39] News story, "Hygrade Official on Outs with Big Companies," *The Butcher Workman,* September 1949, p. 8.

serve to free industry, at least in part, from monopoly domination.

Another argument for decentralization of meat packing (which applies to industry in general), is that it will promote a more desirable regional economic balance.[40]

Large areas of the United States are over-agricultural while other areas are over-industrial. According to the 1947 Census, manufacturing plants in ten metropolitan city-areas employ 5,000,000 people, or more than one-third of the total. These areas suffer from human congestion and unnecessarily high social overhead costs, among them the cost of services that smaller communities would not need. The over-agricultural areas suffer from low standards of living, a limitation of education and of cultural and recreational opportunity, which result from insufficient economic diversification; they need more industrialization.

A decentralization of industry for greater regional economic diversification and balance is favored by the newer technological-industrial factors. Hydroelectric power, the multiplying use of farm crops for synthetic products, and, in the meat industry, the newer trends toward locating plants near the sources of animal supply, the great potentials in frozen-food developments, and the growth of farmer livestock-and-packing cooperatives—all favor small plants and enterprises located throughout the producing areas.

This is of special concern for smaller packers. The bigger independents, some ten or fifteen of them, while far from being monopoly giants, are still fairly large corporations. There are, in addition, hundreds of smaller packing enterprises, among them cooperative meat-processing plants. These have a stake in the local communities where they operate. Their importance was emphasized by a spokesman of the Amalgamated Meat Cutters in arguing for a restoration of federal meat inspection with government (not the packers) paying the costs:

Small plants, which have accepted federal inspection in recent years, will be the first to drop such inspection. They will be obliged to seek

[40] The Temporary National Economic Committee (TNEC), set up by the U.S. Senate, unanimously agreed to "submit to all public and private bodies responsible for industry location the desirability of decentralizing industry to the end that the maximum economic benefits can be secured from plants operating at their most efficient size, the depressing aspects of the factory system be prevented, and the American way of life approved." See *Final Report and Recommendations* (1940).

new markets and readjust their entire operations in order to remain in business. . . . The meat-packing industry is passing through a period of decentralization. More and more slaughtering and meat processing companies are being located close to the source of supply. . . . Many towns and cities depend upon these plants as the principal source of economic existence and thousands of persons depend upon them for employment. [The] wage-earner wants his employer to remain in business and earn a reasonable profit so that his employment may be assured.[41]

The Tennessee Valley gives evidence of what can be done for decentralization and regional economic balance. In the valley and in other areas supplied with TVA power, 1448 new manufacturing and processing plants were established from 1940 to 1948. Almost one-quarter of them, or 319, are producers of food and kindred products. They include thirty-four packing plants, which do a substantial frozen-meat business; fourteen plants with an output of over 15,000,000 pounds of frozen fruit and vegetables; and 104 freezer-locker and cold-storage establishments.[42]

These Tennessee Valley plants conform to a definite and significant regional economic pattern:

1. They are virtually all small enterprises, including cooperatives, financed almost exclusively by local capital.

2. They are located mainly in small cities and towns—one-third in cities with population from 5000 to 100,000, and another third in towns and villages with under 5000 population.

3. They provide markets for a widely diversified agricultural production.

4. They give employment to people not needed on the farms, who normally would migrate to the big cities.

5. They utilize a considerable amount of seasonal work, through part-time employment, for workers who might otherwise have no jobs.

This pattern of economic diversification and balance, of a closer correlation between industry and agriculture, is not limited to the Tennessee Valley, where it is encouraged by TVA. The pattern is spreading throughout the country. And it offers growing oppor-

[41] David Dolnick, "Officers of the Amalgamated Support Meat Inspection Bill in Senate," *The Butcher Workman*, May 1948, p. 5.

[42] TVA, *Regional Economic Data No. 2*, June 30, 1948, pp. 1-3.

tunities to independent packers with initiative, imagination, and the will to compete. They can work together, cooperate to utilize the newest technology, distribution ideas, and service, to establish themselves and to strengthen the truly free enterprise of which they are a part.

4. PRICE AND PROFIT POLICY IN PACKING

Whatever future dangers may beset our food supply in the United States, the immediate problem (in addition to spread of nutritional understanding) is one of more equal and rational distribution of food. The need is for the production and distribution of old and new foods in proportional amounts, at prices that allow consumers to buy all the food they need for fully nutritional meals.

Soil and price practices in agriculture are important. For example, if meat prices rise because the production costs of livestock go up due to soil depletion, the American people may be forced to shift to a cereal diet, away from consumption of meat and dairy products.

A lower livestock supply and a shift away from meat products would mean a shrinkage of the packing industry and reduced employment. It is not clear, however, that all factors in the industry would suffer alike. If the Big Four retained their dominance they might secure a larger share of the industry's smaller output at the sacrifice of the independents; and they might work to make higher profits through higher prices from a limited meat supply.

The packing industry, like other food industries, is not altogether or fully concerned with these larger aspects of the food supply. In too many cases the attitude is that sufficient unto the day are the profits thereof. And the issue cuts still deeper.

A considerable amount of scientific research is carried on by the meat industry. Many packers have well-equipped laboratories. The American Meat Institute's Department of Scientific Research supervises the program of its Research Foundation (incorporated in 1944) at the University of Chicago, while the Department of Livestock works with producers in projects for improvement of livestock production and marketing. This research is largely in applied science.

For the food industries as a whole, fifty-five of the leading process-

ors and distributors have contributed $3,400,000 to research through
the Nutrition Foundation since its organization in 1942. The
Foundation's work is in basic science apart from applied science.
In six years it made grants of $1,901,530 to finance nutrition research
projects in sixty-four universities and medical centers in the United
States and Canada. According to Dr. Charles Glen King of Columbia University, scientific director of the Foundation, most of the
funds go toward training selected graduate students who work on
"the best levels of fundamental research or at medical centers where
nutrition and public health can best be developed, which is helping
to produce a pool of basic knowledge and immediate information
of value to applied science." [43]

Yet there are limiting factors which must be considered. For the
packing industry's price-and-profit policy encourages neither lower
prices nor a condition where meat takes its rightful place, but only
its rightful place, in balanced American diets. The driving force is
to sell more meat at prices that will bring the highest profits, regardless of whether or not consumers should eat more meat. I quote
again, because of its significance, what one speaker told the packers
at the 1945 convention of the American Meat Institute: "It would
be a little more subtle and a little more effective if [you] were willing to *put more stress on the optimum diet and on the kind of meals
the American people ought to eat and less stress on your particular
contribution to those meals.*" [44]

The AMI, as the industry's trade association representing more
than 350 companies, promotes "meat education campaigns" whose
exclusive aim is to sell more of its products. They state the "original
objective" thus: "The basic policy of the meat advertising campaign
is to sell meat in general, from a nutritional standpoint, and to illustrate this basic story of meat with specific products at times of the
year when they are available in volume and offer the greatest value
to the consumer." It is interesting to observe that there is not one
word about "optimum diet" or balanced meals, or about the use of
other foods in combination with meat.

[43] News story, *New York Times*, May 6, 1949.
[44] Proceedings, 40th Annual Convention, American Meat Institute, *The National Provisioner*, November 10, 1945, p. 155. For the full quotation see
Chapter I.

The whole industry—not only the big packers—takes part in the competitive scramble to get a larger slice of the consumer's food dollar. The need for this scramble was passionately proclaimed by a high-pressure salesman of advertising at the 1947 convention of the National Independent Meat Packers Association:

It is the function of advertising to make the consumer want *your* products in preference to those of your competitors. . . . You not only compete against the meat and meat products of competitive packers. *You compete for every cent of the housewife's weekly budget with every single item of any nature whatsoever that has a place on the shelves of the food store.* . . . There are only so many dollars in this consumer's budget and where she goes over on one product she must, of necessity, go light on the other.[45]

I reproduce on another page some AMI "educational" advertisements which lusciously appeal to the housewife's eye and taste for meats alone. These began to appear in January 1948 in 395 newspapers with 32,750,000 circulation. Everything said about meat values may be 100 per cent right, but the total impression is wrong, for it emphasizes meat to the exclusion of other necessary foods.

The AMI may answer: We are advertising *our* product just as other industries advertise *their* products; you cannot expect us to boost competitors. Exactly; and that is what is wrong with the competition-for-profit motive in the realm of foods. For to sell more meat at the expense of dairy, cereal, vegetable, and fruit products may unbalance the consumer's diet and thus injure his physical and mental well-being. Such action is a more refined expression of the old attitude: Let the buyer beware!

Let me pursue a bit further this AMI advertising for profit. In 1941 the Institute issued a pamphlet, *Meat—Reference Book of the Meat Industry,* with this slogan on the cover: "Eat More Meat, It Keeps You Fit." On the first inside page are four stanzas of doggerel by Edgar A. Guest. The first stanza ends:

> *But what spells U.S.A. to me*
> *Is "meat upon the table"!*

[45] Proceedings, Convention of National Independent Meat Packers Association, *The National Provisioner,* April 26, 1947, p. 121.

MEAT makes the most of America's Food Resources

THESE RAW MATERIALS...

MEAT SERVES EVERYBODY

Your MEAT will be there!

How to get 3 fresh-cooked meals from one Pork Butt

FRESH PORK SHOULDER BUTTS

AMERICAN MEAT INSTITUTE

Meat as a Source of Protein, B Vitamins and Iron

ALL RATINGS BASED ON COOKED VALUES

KIND OF MEAT	COMPLETE PROTEIN	B VITAMINS			FOOD IRON
		THIAMINE (B₁)	RIBOFLAVIN (B₂)	NIACIN	
PORK	Excellent	Excellent	Fair	Excellent	Excellent
BEEF	Excellent	Fair	Excellent	Excellent	Excellent
LAMB	Excellent	Fair	Good	Excellent	Excellent
VEAL	Excellent	Good	Good	Excellent	Excellent
VARIETY MEATS (LIVER, HEART, KIDNEY)	Excellent				
SAUSAGE (FRANKFURTERS, BOLOGNA)	Excellent			Good	Excellent

Nourishing MEAT for a *Real* Breakfast!

All meats also contain the minerals copper and phosphorus in significant quantities

AMI ADVERTISES MEAT—BUT WHAT ABOUT
BALANCED DIETS?

In all four stanzas there is no mention of any food but meat. The final stanza reads:

> Ours is a land of steaks and chops,
>   Of pork, beef, lamb and veal;
> And thrifty costs when woman shops
>   Puts meat in any meal.
> So if at us should any scoff
>   Just show this patriot label—
> One reason we are better off
>   Is "meat upon the table."

Now the fact that Edgar Guest writes of meat alone may be attributed, perhaps, to poetic frenzy. But the AMI's write-up does the same thing. Only once—and not until you get to page 45—is any other food mentioned: "A well-balanced diet is necessary for health. It should include meat, milk, eggs, green, leafy and other vegetables, fresh fruits and whole-grain cereals." The very next sentence is, "Be sure that your diet contains body-building proteins, minerals, vitamins, fats and carbohydrates," after which the writer proceeds to stress that these nutrients are contained in meat. Later on there are five hundred words on the glories of an all-meat diet, but only fifteen words indicating that this might not be altogether desirable.

And in 1948 the AMI issued "study outlines" and "quiz" material for use in schools. This material exclusively emphasizes the importance of meat and is barefaced one-sided propaganda. One quiz question begins: "One reason people are eating more meat [they are not] is that they are learning of meat's outstanding value as a nourishing food."

It is clear that the objective of the AMI, in addition to selling more meat, is to carry on competition against other food industries for a larger slice of the consumer's food dollar. This is reminiscent of the "new competition" that flourished in the later 1920's (followed by depression in the 1930's).

What the "new competition" meant was this: As industry's capacity to produce goods increased faster than the consumers' purchasing power, every industry (packing included) began to limit competition within its area and to cooperate for competitive war on other industries, to get business away from them. Mayonnaise invaded the butter market: at a convention of the Mayonnaise Manufacturers Association a "butterless banquet" was served to "popularize mayonnaise as a substitute for butter." The advertising of one cigarette company against the injurious effects of eating candy ("Reach for a Lucky instead of a Sweet") provoked the Sugar Institute to spend millions of dollars to advertise the benefits of sugar, although overconsumption of sugar was already a health hazard. Sauerkraut manufacturers united to advertise the health-building qualities of their product (as if it had the magic virtues of Popeye's spinach). Large appropriations for institutional advertising were made by the United States Fisheries Congress, the Ice Cream Manufacturers Association, the Allied Baking Industry, and the American Meat Institute.

This bedlam became economic, cultural, and moral lunacy in a new "economic philosophy" which argued that prosperity must depend upon an increase of luxury and waste. One writer formulated the philosophy thus:

If we are to have increasingly large-scale production there must likewise be increasingly large-scale consumption. . . . *To get more money into the consumers' hands with which to buy is a mere minor stop-gap.* There is, however, a far greater and more powerful lever available. [We need] what I name *progressive obsolescence.* This means simply the more intensive spreading—*among those people who now have the buying surplus*—of the belief in and the practice of buying more goods on the basis of obsolescence in efficiency, economy, style or taste . . . *buying goods not to wear out, but to trade in or discard after a short time when new or more attractive goods or models come out: buying for change, whim or fancy.*[46]

This economic, cultural, and moral lunacy was modified by the depression of the 1930's and by World War II, but it is staging a postwar revival. Its greatest danger, of course, is in the food industries, whose output most directly affects human welfare. Always dangerous, it is now more dangerous still because it may interfere with the dietary changes going on and with our growing nutritional understanding.

Progress in nutritional understanding and the introduction of new types of food are a challenge to the food industries and particularly to the meat packers. At the 1947 convention of the AMI a speaker,

[46] J. George Frederick, President of the Business Bourse, "What Price Super-Selling," *Advertising and Selling,* January 25, 1928, pp. 19-20.

Dr. Gerald N. Wendt, warned the packers that scientific research might replace protein food from animals with protein from other sources, including food yeast and synthetic protein, and said: "Biological sciences will expand and will become far more important to American industry and economics and to the American standard of living. . . . We shall see many new biological industries and professions springing up within the next decade. Your industry, as the unquestioned leader in the field, should not only be fully aware of this major development in science, but should sponsor and promote it."

Dr. Wendt pointed to protein and vitamins secured from the microscopic yeast plant, and added a note about the potentials of synthetic protein:

You use meat animals to manufacture attractive, nutritious foods, comprised primarily of proteins and fats, with necessary vitamins and flavors. . . . Yet it remains true that you depend upon a chemical process which is beyond your control. . . . It is more than probable that we shall learn to duplicate this reaction, how it builds its own body from the elements of plant food. It is no doubt a very complex process, but once understood it can be improved in the animal *and perhaps later duplicated without using the living cell as the unit of our manufacturing process.*[47]

Within a year after Dr. Wendt's address came the discovery that vitamin B_{12}, identified with the animal protein factor (APF) that gives meat its nutritional value, can be made from molds on a low-cost basis. Now this is only one in a series of developments that bring nearer the industrial production of "synthetic" foods. Often, however, premature and sometimes misleading claims are made. In one such case, Allied and German scientists announced from Frankfort that they had produced and were ready to distribute "two food substitutes that are said to taste and have the same nutritious qualities as milk and meat." The American Meat Institute issued a bulletin signed by Wesley Hardenbergh, its director, which said:

This is another of the long series of "discoveries" as to how people can get the nutrition of meat from a pill, a capsule, the end result of some chemical process, minute animal life that swims in the sea, protein

[47] Proceedings, American Meat Institute, *The National Provisioner*, September 13, 1947, p. 109.

derived from sawdust, a combination of powdered vegetables, and so on. For example, the flavor of meat does not come from monosodiumglutamate. This product is supposed to enhance the flavor of various foods. For another example, the statement is made that all protein is alike. This emphatically is not true. There are two kinds of protein—complete and incomplete. Meat is a complete protein food.[48]

The Hardenbergh statements were correct in regard to the German foods; one was simply a sausage made of one-half meat and one-half vegetable protein. But the attack is wrong in spirit: extreme claims are used to pour ridicule on what science is doing to enlarge the food supply from other sources than crops and animals. Yes, it is true that "not all protein is alike," but it is also true that protein is being manufactured on an industrial basis and that technical-scientific developments moved toward synthetic production of the animal protein factor, which gives meat its specific nutritional value.

The question arises: where will the production of these new foods fit into the packing (or any food) industry with the kind of price-and-profit policy it now has?

From the 1860's on, with the rapid industrialization of food production, a great improvement came in American diets. But much harm was also caused by bad foods, the wrong kind of foods, or the overuse of certain foods. The damage was rarely malicious; it came mainly from misunderstanding. When this is said, however, something more must be added; *vested economic interests in particular foods persisted in the manufacture and sale of their products after they were proved harmful.* In addition, they opposed the spread of nutritional understanding and remedial legislation, they used all the tricks of advertising to sell more of the harmful foods, and they perverted scientific understanding to "improve" their products or to make them appear desirable.

I cite two examples. For centuries people considered white bread an aristocratic luxury. When mechanical flour milling cheapened white flour enough to make its use universal, the dangers of denaturing wheat were not known. They have since become known, but the milling industry still denatures wheat while white bread is "enriched" with chemical reintroduction of nutrients destroyed by mill-

[48] American Meat Institute, bulletin, *"Ersatz" Meat Crops up Again; New York Times,* February 18, 1949.

ing.[49] Another example is sugar refining, whose process destroys essential nutrients, while the refiners promote an overuse of sugar (in cooked foods, soft drinks, and candy) which is already a menace to American health.

Nor is this attitude of opposing nutritional advance for consumer welfare in order to make more sales altogether unknown in the meat-packing industry:

A few years ago the U.S. Bureau of Home Economics decided to begin giving dietary education to Americans. The average family, they said, eats too much meat. Leave off some of the meat and substitute fruits and vegetables. You will live cheaper, better and happier. They were perfectly right. Every bit of evidence told that. They were paid to ascertain dietary facts of benefit to the nation and to dispense those facts. . . . The Bureau of Home Economics went blissfully on its way telling the truth, but packinghouse officials happened onto some of the insidious literature. They exploded like overheated frankfurters and went at once to the Right People in Washington, [who] saw the light and agreed that no government bureau could afford to put out information that would cut down on the packing business. The Bureau of Home Economics promptly became mum on the matter of meat in the diet.[50]

The attitude of "more sales regardless of the consumer" becomes more serious because of the trend of scientific-economic progress to lower the demand for foodstuffs, including meat. I quote one authority on this subject:

Increasing efficiency in use of food, resulting from advances in knowl-

[49] A new development is production and sale of a number of injurious "nutritional" chemicals. Of one of these, a chemical ingredient that gives a "pleasing" taste to bread, its producers and sellers say in their advertising literature: "In speaking of higher quality, we mean products that not only look good, but are appealing to the sense of taste as well . . . bakery goods that are not overburdened with fats and other richness to the point where substantially less is eaten. We believe that every person—man, woman or child—eats and drinks only that which appeals to the sense of taste, with little or no thought of nutritious value; so, we emphasize, again, that higher quality bakery goods, in our opinion, are attained by balancing formulas to a point where they are not overburdened with rich substances which, in the end, tend to discourage and decrease consumption." In other words, use these chemicals to make people eat more bread, regardless of their well-being!

[50] C. C. Furnas, *The Next Hundred Years: The Unfinished Business of Science* (1938), pp. 379-80.

edge of nutrition, is likely to reduce the demand for food. Many ways are being disclosed for improving diets at less cost. The special effort to economize on resources during the war offers insight as to what may be expected. . . . Advances in nutrition make apparent how better diets may be obtained at less cost. *As this development takes place it will not, as is commonly supposed, create additional demand for food; on the contrary, by making it possible to substitute cheaper nutrients for more expensive ones (for example, some fats and oils from vegetables for some of those from animal sources)*, advances in nutrition are likely to save on food-producing resources.[51]

A downward trend in food consumption may become especially marked in meat products. Nutritional requirements call for smaller per capita meat consumption. And already the trend has gone beyond mere substitution of "some fats and oils from vegetables for some of those from animal sources" to the use of protein from food yeast and to the prospect of industrial production of meat's essential nutrient, the animal protein factor. Since nutritional findings agree that APF makes the vital difference between an all-vegetable diet and a diet containing animal proteins, unlimited low-cost production of synthetic APF may become a means to supplement low-meat diets or replace meat. And the new synthetic foods will be cheaper.[52]

A probable decrease in the demand for food, including meat products, is not a serious problem for American farmers. It can be offset as more crops go into industry as raw materials for synthetics and plastics. But what can the food-manufacturing industries do to

[51] Theodore W. Schultz, *Agriculture in an Unstable Economy* (1945), p. 74.

[52] In 1938 C. C. Furnas, in *The Next Hundred Years* (pp. 312-15) foresaw what is beginning to happen: "Synthetic food costs should be lower because nature's processes are highly inefficient and man can nearly always improve upon them. Plants as stores of energy are woefully inefficient. The best estimates have it that only ½ to 2 per cent of the radiant energy falling on a plant is utilized in building up chemical compounds. . . . Animals are way down on the efficiency list. . . . Few people realize how much they pay for their nutriment. It is in the production of the present day expensive foods that nature is most inefficient and this is the field wherein man can show the greatest improvement. When the chemists have finished their protein pioneering a manufacturer should be able to make a perfect meat protein, which would sell at 20 cents a pound (dry weight) and be a perfect nutritional substitute for porterhouse steak. Almost every foodstuff on anyone's menu should be synthesized cheaper than it can be grown."

offset lower demand? They are geared to maintain and increase profits, to protect their return on capital investment. Shall this be done regardless of consumer welfare?

Nor is competition the answer. Free enterprise and competition have kept economic progress going, it is true: all kinds of old industries have been destroyed and new industries created by technological progress operating through the market. These changes are still going on, but they may be seriously limited by monopoly restrictions. The dominant corporations in the sugar industry, for example, are not petty enterprises that competitive pressures can control; on the contrary, they shape and control competition while their powerful vested interests fight to prevent a lower consumption of sugar. Nor are the packing giants petty enterprises unable to resist change; already the industry is organized to spend millions to sell more meat regardless of whether or not people should eat more of it.

Price policy aims to maximize profit. Lower prices and higher profits are compatible when lower unit prices bring much larger sales—when there are smaller unit profits but bigger total profits. This depends, however, upon a continuous expansion of output and sales. If an industry becomes stationary or declines, then lower prices will mean lower profits because they will not be offset by larger output and sales. So the drive to maximize profits will mean a drive for higher prices.

Profits can remain high and even go up if, under conditions of stationary or declining output, an increase in technological efficiency lowers unit costs. But if these efficiency gains go to higher profits, little if any benefit will accrue to consumers through lower prices, or to employees through higher wages and salaries. And if wages and salaries do not move upward, consumer purchasing power will diminish. Without increasing purchasing power among workers, low-salaried employees, and farmers, the wheels of industry must slow down with catastrophic results for the economy and community.

A speaker at the 1947 meeting of the American Meat Institute pressed this point upon the packers' attention: "We shall certainly have more and more production with less and less labor. . . . *Our economy can keep the pace only if industry is constantly aware that one of its major products is purchasing power.* . . . The manufacture of products is not enough, and the earning of profit is not enough; it must be accompanied by the conscious objective of creating purchasing power as well." [53]

The crucial point is this: *both management and unionism will be ill advised if they oppose progress, whether technological or nutritional.* The packing industry will lose profits from a decline in meat demand; packing workers will lose employment from that decline and from an increase of productive efficiency within the decline. It will be disastrous if either unionism or management opposes the changes, or if they engage in a fratricidal struggle to shift the burdens onto each other. And they cannot combine to "gang up" on the consumer, for if they try to do so the situation will explode in their faces.

The problem requires the cooperation of management and unionism. But cooperation, in turn, can become truly effective only if a new kind of price-and-profit policy works to release fully the constructive potentials of technical-economic progress in meat packing and other food industries.

5.   FROM MONOPOLY TO TVA'S IN MEAT PACKING

The anti-trust suit filed against the Big Four meat packers in 1948 was part of a new drive against monopoly. The action came when there were 120 anti-trust suits pending in the federal courts against 1250 corporations charged with monopoly practices, with the food industries as special targets.

Defendants in anti-trust suits in the food field ranged from Corn Products Refining Company (which does 50 per cent of its industry's business), to thirty-four candy and confectionery manufacturers, to the Big Four packers. In addition, another 1948 anti-trust suit, charging suppression of competition and price-fixing, was filed against the Big Three in the manufacture of farm equipment—International Harvester Company, Deere & Company, and J. I. Case Company, who control 75 per cent of their industry's output.

The anti-trust drive plans to break concentration of control in the food industries, where, it will be recalled, three or four monopoly corporations dominate in every major area. In addition to three

[53] Proceedings, American Meat Institute, *The National Provisioner*, September 13, 1947, pp. 109-110.

corporations doing 43 per cent of the packing business, three corporations do more than 38 per cent of the business in flour milling; another three bake and sell one-third of the nation's bread. Three corporations do 21 per cent of the business in butter; three do 44 per cent of the business in condensed milk; and three do 63 per cent of the business in cheese. Three corporations do 30 per cent of the business in canned fruits; another three do 13 per cent of the business in canned vegetables. Three grocery-and-meat chain stores do 22 per cent of the business of retailing foods.[54]

These monopoly conditions called forth a series of government anti-trust suits. They point up the issue of economic organization and policy in relation to changes in producing and distributing foods.

The new anti-trust suits were filed after sixty years of action to break monopoly power, which all the while grew stronger. During fifteen of these years, from 1933 to 1948, the drive against monopoly was pressed with more vigor than in all the preceding years. A large number of the 120 anti-trust suits were filed after 1940. In the war

[54] On September 15, 1949, the U.S. Department of Justice filed a civil suit to break up the Atlantic & Pacific Company, whose annual retail sales were $1,900,000,000 or approximately 6.4 per cent of all retail food store business. Three years earlier the A & P had been found guilty of criminal violation of the anti-trust laws, with the decision unanimously affirmed by the U.S. Court of Appeals, Chicago, in February 1949. The new civil action requested a court order requiring A & P to separate its manufacturing and processing activities from its buying and selling business, to convert its seven retail store divisions into seven independent corporate enterprises, with A & P allowed to own only one of them, and to dissolve the Atlantic Commission Company, A & P's purchasing and sales agent in the produce markets. The complaint charged A & P with using its position and power to "impose unreasonable restraints of trade upon competitors at all levels of the food industry," including discriminatory price preferences over retail competitors "by exercising a dual threat permanently to withhold its patronage [from suppliers] or to manufacture for itself." An A & P spokesman said: "This suit is a threat to the welfare and living standards of every American citizen. The basis of the attack is the fact that we sold goods too cheap. . . . If the anti-trust lawyers succeed in destroying A & P, the way will be cleared for the destruction of every other efficient large-scale distributor. . . . It will serve only to put down competition and force prices up. A & P's policy always kept alive the spirit of competition." *The Butcher Workman* (editorial, "Why Pick on the A & P?" October 1949, p. 6) said: "Is there any proof that A & P has used its bigness to raise the price of food? . . . While A & P here and there has not been too friendly with some of our local unions, particularly in the South, our International Union stands solidly on the side of the Tea Company."

PERCENTAGE OF BUSINESS DONE BY THREE CORPORATIONS
IN MAJOR FOOD FIELDS

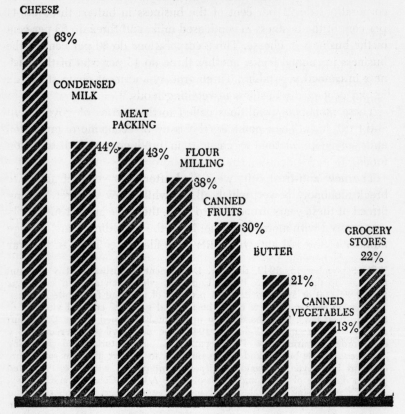

CHEESE
63%

CONDENSED
MILK

MEAT
PACKING

44%   43%   FLOUR
MILLING

38%

CANNED
FRUITS

30%   GROCERY
STORES
22%

BUTTER

21%

CANNED
VEGETABLES

13%

years 1941–45, according to a Federal Trade Commission report,
2450 independent manufacturing concerns merged with other corporations, involving total assets of $5,200,000,000.[55]

This growing concentration of industry must be considered
against the background of legislative action to invigorate the strug-

[55] From 1933 to 1946 nearly three times as many anti-trust suits were filed as
in the thirty-two years from passage of the Sherman Act in 1890 to 1932—
162 cases involving 3034 defendants compared with 64 cases and 1301 defendants. It is interesting to note that, although the Sherman Act was not
directed against labor unions, the courts so interpreted it; 108 union representatives have been sentenced to prison under the act and only seven businessmen.

gle against monopoly. In 1914, Congress enacted the Clayton Act to put teeth into the Sherman anti-trust law of 1890. It set up the Federal Trade Commission to enforce the law. And it prohibited, in Section 7, the acquisition by a corporation of the capital stock of a competitor if this restricted competition and led to monopoly. The teeth were yanked out by three cases which came before the courts in the 1920's. One of them involved Swift & Company.

Swift (the procedure was the same in all three cases) illegally purchased the stock of a competing corporation and so acquired control of its property, or assets. The Federal Trade Commission said "No," and ordered Swift to give up both stock and assets. The lower courts sustained the FTC, but the Supreme Court overruled them. In its 5-4 decision the Court admitted that Swift's *purchase of the stock* of a competitor was illegal; but, the decision went on, Swift had legally secured *control of the assets* of the competitor prior to FTC action, and so the Commission had exceeded its authority in ordering Swift to give up control of the assets. The decision gave aid and comfort to builders of monopoly; acquisition of assets became the usual method of mergers and consolidation.[56]

Then, in 1933-35, came a new twist to trust policy—the National Recovery Administration (NRA)—under which the government made cartelization and monopoly practices compulsory. The NRA approved 874 "codes of fair competition," which were drawn up, administered, and policed by trade associations. These codes legalized monopoly's restrictive practices: direct or indirect limitation of output, including provisions that producers could not add new productive capacity without permission; restriction of competition through establishment of sales quotas and the awarding of zones and markets to specific companies; and provisions for price-fixing (in 560 codes), including the assurance of uniform prices through price-reporting systems, which earlier Supreme Court decisions had declared illegal. The NRA was declared unconstitutional and scrapped. But this "was not sufficient to eliminate the new instruments of collaboration to which business had become accustomed, for which it had worked so assiduously, and which had been temporarily championed and made obligatory by the government. In fact, a frequent defense which anti-trust violators subsequently advanced in Federal Trade Commission cases was that the particu-

[56] David Lynch, *The Concentration of Economic Power* (1946), p. 281.

lar practice with which they were charged had been either required or sanctioned by the NRA." [57]

Industrial concentration and monopoly made gains during World War II. In 1944 the 250 largest manufacturing corporations had 80 per cent of prime war contracts (some of which were subcontracted); they owned 60 per cent of all productive assets in manufacturing, with 75,000 corporations owning only 40 per cent; and they operated, with options to buy, the new plants in which the government invested upward of $15,000,000,000.[58]

Cases of absolute monopoly are rare. This is particularly true of the food industries, because, among other reasons, of the great variety of their products. What prevails in meat packing is a limited monopoly (what economists call "oligopoly"), but it is dominant and permeates the industry with restrictive practices. What shall be done about it?

What has been done so far has not been very effective. From 1930 to 1942, after the failure to secure modification of the Consent Decree, eleven different anti-trust suits were filed against the Big Four packers. The results were as follows: The government moved for dismissal of eight cases; two were dismissed by the court for want of prosecution; and in one the court directed the jury to return a verdict of "not guilty." This kind of policy piles up annoyances for the corporations and fees for the lawyers, but that is all. The record was cited by the Big Four's lawyers in their brief for dismissal of the 1948 indictment:

The defendants have been subjected to burdensome and expensive preparation for trial in many cases, including cases ultimately dismissed by the government. The cases brought to trial resulted in hearings of great length. There were a good many appeals from interlocutors and final orders. The net result was a failure to obtain an adjudication of guilt in any criminal or civil case and the issuance of two injunctions without any evidence or finding that any defendant had violated any law.

The 1948 anti-trust action against the Big Four packers proposes to dissolve them into fourteen "independent" corporations in order

[57] Lynch, *Economic Power*, pp. 150-53. This book provides an excellent summary and analysis of the facts. It may be added that the meat-packing industry never agreed on a "code of fair competition."
[58] Smaller War Plants Corporation, *Eighteenth Bimonthly Report to Congress* (1945), p. 6.

to "free" competition in the industry. This move raises two significant questions of policy which call for concrete answers:

1. Can a dissolution of the Big Four into separate companies restore and insure truly unrestricted competition?

2. Is unrestricted competition altogether desirable and constructive, and can it solve the food problems that press upon industry and consumers?

One successful anti-trust suit after another has failed to free competition and check monopoly. Fourteen separate meat-packing companies, made up from the Big Four, would have a substantial amount of common private ownership; and, as Standard Oil experience has shown, break-up of a monopoly corporation into separate companies neither prevents "community of interest" nor truly frees competition.

Unrestricted competition is not, moreover, altogether desirable, especially in the food industries, whose output so closely affects consumer welfare. Businessmen are not in favor of competition that might get beyond bounds and depress profits to disastrously low levels. Moreover, competition for profit would still be the dominant force and drive toward maximization of profit, not toward consumer welfare. The problems of the food industries, in addition, are so many and so complex because of new developments, that they cannot be solved by competition in constructive fashion.

Although anti-trust policy has prevented greater monopoly and salvaged a measure of economic freedom, it has failed, because it contains a fatal flaw. The flaw is the conception of competition as the primary economic force.

While competition for low prices is desirable, it is not the only or major factor in economic policy. There can be price competition and lower prices, but the situation will not necessarily help industry, agriculture, or society to solve the problems of an adequate food supply and balanced nutritional diets. We need to decide where competition is desirable and where a newer policy of cooperation might better promote economic activity for human welfare.

In recent years anti-trust policy has broadened from an exclusive emphasis on *conspiracy* to suppress competition and fix prices to consideration of monopoly *power* to suppress competition. The United States Supreme Court, in its decision in the tobacco Big Three case, ruled that "no formal agreement is necessary to constitute unlawful conspiracy." The Court went even further: it ruled that monopoly power to exclude competitors is unlawful even if the power is not used. This decision, while it clearly can strengthen anti-trust action, still puts the emphasis on competition.

Nowhere in all the philosophy and practices of regulation is there a glimmer of objectives and values other than those of competition. Competition is important. But it is impossible (as experience shows) to restore competition within the monopoly areas. And even if it could be restored, competition that is limited to price and profit will not necessarily benefit the food industries.

What is needed, it seems to me, is to give the production and distribution of food a public-utility character. American economic and political policy has already recognized the concept of public utilities in one form or another over a growing number of economic areas. In taking the stockyards away from big packer ownership and control (although allowing private ownership), we made the stockyards a public utility under federal regulation and controlled by the United States Department of Agriculture. We also recognized the public-utility character of the food industries (and the drug industry) in the form of pure food and drug laws to protect the consumer against adulteration and other evils. So far, so good. But this regulation has neither broken monopoly nor assured full consumer welfare.

What is needed is larger, more positive action. I suggest that the key areas in the food industries (in this case meat packing) be given a public-utility character, with monopoly corporations converted into public corporations on the model of TVA. The independent concerns should be allowed to operate under free private or cooperative enterprise.

American industry needs a restoration of free enterprise in terms of economic freedom. Free enterprise, for the early liberals who gave it a philosophy, meant economic freedom. They emphasized private ownership as against the mercantilist state in order to break up state economic monopolies and restrictions, to free enterprise and initiative from hampering bureaucratic controls, to release the creative energy of man. The emphasis was on the "free" in "free private enterprise."

But monopoly corporations are destroyers of free enterprise as economic freedom. Competition cannot be altogether destroyed.

The big packers' failure did not come from any deficiency of will; they failed because of public opposition, the economic nature of the industry, and government intervention. Nevertheless, a condition where four corporations produce more than one-half the output of meat packing is not a condition of economic freedom.

The system of free enterprise has jammed into the same barrier the guilds did: restrictive practices on a growing scale. Guilds began as a liberating force; they ended as an obstruction to further economic progress and freedom. The same change has come in free enterprise under monopoly capitalism with its network of restrictive practices carried on through giant corporations, trade associations, and cartels. Downfall of the guilds brought a consolidation of mercantilism and its absolute state. Unless free enterprise *as economic freedom* is invigorated by the destruction of monopoly, it may be replaced by the neo-mercantilism of monopoly corporate statism or communist dictatorship.

To convert monopoly corporations into public enterprises on the TVA model means to restore and strengthen economic freedom. It means to emphasize the *free* in free private enterprise, not the private. It means, in addition, to restore economic freedom for small independent businessmen. For packing TVA's would not strive to get all the business they could, regardless of independent packers, in order to pile up the biggest profits. Since their policy would be to promote the service aspects of meat packing, they would cooperate with the independents for greater and more efficient production, for regional economic balance, and for consumer welfare.

Independent packers complain about "big business" or monopoly pressure. "Along with the tendency toward big government goes the tendency toward bigger and bigger business," said a speaker at the 1947 meeting of the National Independent Meat Packers Association. "The danger to small business from gigantic corporations is a very real danger. Independent meat packing is every day beginning to feel the squeeze of the large packers more and more." All of which is true. But then the speaker concentrated on criticism of "big government" and boasted: "I am glad that NIMPA, in helping to put an end to OPA, was able to reduce the size of a top-heavy government." [59]

[59] Proceedings, 6th Annual Meeting, National Independent Meat Packers Association, *The National Provisioner*, April 26, 1947, p. 42.

But much of "big government" results from regulation and control of big business. The small businessmen demand and approve this regulation, then cry out against "big government"! They fail to realize that only a break-up of monopoly can end the need for government regulation and provide the conditions of survival and progress for independent small business. They do not recognize that truly free private enterprise can survive only as monopoly is destroyed. And monopoly can be destroyed only by its conversion into public enterprises to provide a new kind of economic freedom.

Let me be specific. I suggest that whatever separate corporations are formed from the Big Four be set up as public corporations on the TVA model. In addition, refrigerator cars should either operate as a public enterprise or become the property of railroads to serve all packers (public, private, and cooperative) alike, as freight cars do. Whatever distributive facilities now owned by the Big Four are not needed by the new public corporations should operate as a public service for the industry and the public. The Big Four should not become a "trust" under federal ownership and control, an undesirable state monopoly; but, as public corporations, they would maintain a separate identity and compete with one another on a production-for-service basis. They would be subject to the same taxes that private packers are.

These public corporations in packing should be even more independent of direct government control than TVA now is, and should operate exclusively as economic enterprises but within the framework of a new policy and purposes. While government check on policy is needed, there is no need for political interference with the management of public corporations.

As Big Four stocks and bonds are retired, the present owners might be given, say, 3 per cent bonds of the new public corporations, with provisions for their eventual retirement. The public packing corporations must earn a reasonable (or "yardstick") rate of profit on their prices. They cannot and must not sell on a nonprofit basis, for this would be unfair competition for independent private and cooperative packers. Profits of the public corporations, after whatever portion may be needed for expansion, if any, should go into research work for the whole industry or go to the government in place of taxes.

If small independent packers can earn higher profits *from effi-*

ciency than the "yardstick" rate of the packing TVA's, they may do so. The answer is not arbitrary government interference to lower their profits but greater efficiency from the public corporations. If private or cooperative packers want to lower prices, they can do so, and the others must follow. In both cases, competitive pressures will operate to influence the public packers. Turn about is fair play: if the meat TVA's increase their efficiency, the private and cooperative packers will also have to do so. But since their policy is not to wage destructive competition, the public corporations will make their efficiency know-how available to one another and to the independent packers.

Competition will prevail. It is not ended by public enterprise but raised to new, more constructive levels. Competition is necessary for economic efficiency and new ideas, for consumer freedom of choice, and to prevent bureaucratic centralization of managerial and government power. It is noteworthy that at the 1949 conference of the British Labour party the need for competition in a socialist mixed economy, such as Britain is creating, was defended by Aneurin Bevan. And the Labour Government recognizes that both competition and private independent enterprise are necessary for a liberal socialist economy:

By the provision of scientific research, technical assistance, and where necessary help for small business with equipment and capital, the government proposes to clear away material obstacles [to all-out production]. By central economic planning, through the control of foreign exchange, capital investment, and the location and character of industrial construction, the government will enforce those basic rules of the game which the national interest requires. It will dispense as rapidly as possible with hampering and superfluous controls, and throw the race open to all runners, with the rewards going to the swiftest. In operating its own industries and services, the government will seek to set a good example. Fully aware of the strong tendency in British business to moderate the pace to suit the most laggard firms, it has by the establishment of the Monopolies and Restrictive Practices Commission sought to make sure that competition really does take place. But, in view of American experience, the leaders of Labour feel that "trust-busting" is not enough. They mean to reinforce it with "competitive public enterprise." . . . The remedies prescribed [for high prices, in addition to greater productive efficiency] are a shrewd mixture of free competition and government intervention. All restrictions on opening new shops, whether imposed by law or by collusive agreements, are to be abolished, and private fixing of minimum retail prices is to go. These measures should release a storm of price-cutting competition in Britain's retail shops. Quality will be assured in two ways. First, the government will set up an official body for testing consumers' goods and publicizing its findings. Second, the government will centralize its own purchases, and order standard products on a scale in excess of its own requirements, directing the overspill into private shops.[60]

In a general way, one can project a setup for the meat industry if the dominant Big Four were converted into a number of public corporations:

1. *A Public Meat Authority is appointed by the President of the United States* from a panel of nominations made by independent packers, managements in the public corporations, unions in the meat industry, farmer and consumer organizations, cooperatives, and retailers. The Authority will operate within a framework of policy on the economic objectives and values of the new setup formulated by the Congress in an enacting law. It will make the policy specific for the public corporation in particular and the meat industry in general.[61]

2. *The public enterprises created as the Big Four are broken up operate as independent corporations under supervision of the Public Meat Authority.* Their managements receive powers to manage, subject to no political interference; they are responsible only and directly to the Public Meat Authority. They operate with their own funds as business enterprises in a new economic setup. The managerial job becomes exclusively one of securing most efficient production, in terms of quantity and quality, with profit a limited objective. The separate public corporations are independent as enterprises, but they cooperate with one another and with independent packers on the industry's common interests, while they compete with one and all for maximum service to consumers. Management is held to

---

[60] Mary Saran, "Labour Party Conference," *Socialist Commentary* (London), July 1949, p. 152; David C. Williams, "The Labor Party Convention," *Labor and Nation,* July-August 1949, p. 11.

[61] While the proposed setup calls for representation of functional interests in the Public Meat Authority, an alternative arrangement might consist of an Authority composed of nonpartisan technical-economic and administrative experts, with functional interests represented on advisory councils or an independent consumer board, as Britain is doing in its public corporations.

strict accountability for efficiency and costs, for the promotion of economic progress and welfare.

3. *Since monopoly pursuit of profit is abolished, price-making can become a rational economic process.* The norm of price is costs plus profit. Competition does not fully set prices, it only determines how much profit can be added to costs in the final price, with pressure to maximize profit. Price-fixing under monopoly, with its "administered" prices, works for high prices to make high profits, which is undesirable. But competition is no answer, since it cannot fully work where monopoly exists, nor can it rationally set prices where it does work. In a public-utility setup for the meat industry, the public corporations, independent packers, and cooperatives can get together, legally, to decide on prices by a calculation of costs plus reasonable profit, with the gains of increasing productivity (and its lower costs) shared between higher wage and salary payments for employees and lower prices for consumers.

4. *All rights of labor unions, including collective bargaining and the right to strike, remain, with emphasis on union-management co-operation.* TVA has shown that when the monopoly profit drive is not operating cooperation between management and unions becomes truly feasible and fruitful. In public corporations there are consultative union-management channels on all levels to discuss and act on matters of mutual interest and to assure cooperation for doing the most effective job. While the right to strike remains, as a democratic freedom and a check and balance on arbitrary managerial power, its use would become rare under the new arrangements.

5. *The new setup dispenses with the need for an American Meat Institute as the industry's trade association;* but the Independent Meat Packers Association continues to exist to serve the smaller packers. A new institute replaces the AMI's "educational" campaigns to sell more meat for profit with a policy of research, nutritional education, and promotion of consumer welfare. The new institute can help promote more widespread understanding of balanced nutritious diets and the proper role of meat in them. It can do needed research on more nutritional and cheaper meats, on application of the new technology for greater technical efficiency and more humane working conditions, on the new synthetic foods *regardless of what they may do to the meat industry.* Finally, the new institute's research can

make its contribution to a larger ecological understanding and balance for the unity of agriculture, industry, and science to promote more satisfying living.

The proposed setup for the meat industry might become a pattern for all food industries. Their monopoly corporations should be broken up too, and converted into a number of public corporations operating on the "packing TVA" model, alongside of independent and private cooperative enterprises. Each particular food industry would have its own public authority. A National Food Authority, set up under government initiative and responsible to a Secretary for Food of cabinet rank, but not under exclusive government control, would unite the forces of all food industries through functional representation of farmers, management and unions, retailers and consumers.

Monopoly corporations in farm implement and fertilizer industries also should be converted into public corporations.[62]

It is important to observe that my proposal does not call for public ownership of all enterprises in the packing industry. Nor does it call for centralization of public enterprises in government. Such centralization is, in my opinion, even more undesirable than the present setup, where at least a measure of economic freedom prevails despite monopoly. Exclusive government ownership and control could easily destroy all economic freedom; impose a deadening bureaucratic centralization on enterprise, research, and progress; and bring a despotic statism, as in Soviet Russia.

What is needed is *to increase economic freedom*. Conversion of the Big Four packing companies into public corporations would free their managements from the domination of financial interests and

---

[62] The Amalgamated Meat Cutters has no commitments on this subject. Its official organ may be quoted: "There is something repulsive in the idea that private enterprise should control those basic industries upon which the life of the people depend. [But] we have never quite reconciled ourselves to the idea that the capitalist system need be doomed. . . . The United States and England are engaged in two economic experiments, the success or failure of which might demonstrate whether the capitalist economic system will survive in either of these great nations. The English Labour party is now engaged in socializing all basic industries. [But] private enterprise will remain and individual initiative will not be hampered. . . . More stringent government regulation of large corporations and public service companies should offer the solution of successful capitalism. . . . The success of either the present English or American experiment, or both, can definitely stop the Russian movement." Editorial, "The Russian Movement," *The Butcher Workman*, January 1949, p. 11.

their restrictive practices. Liberation of all the constructive progressive potentials of management will come from liberation from the compulsions of competition-for-profit. Operational management is already doing a great productive job; it can do a greater job in public corporations, where management can use all its talents to promote the most efficient production of the most desirable foods for consumer welfare. It can freely cooperate with workers and their unions for constitutional democracy in industry. Managers, too, can develop more humanity and self-respect as they need no longer conspire to keep the workers down.

The public corporation is the device used by the Labour Government in Britain to transform economic organization and policy. One British authority writes:

Public corporations bring a new factor into play. They make possible a revival of confidence, the creation of a new sense of the value of life, and of a new spirit animating the workers to give of their best. . . . *The unions representing organized labor have a vital role to play.* The most enlightened public corporation will not know where the shoe pinches as much as the man who wears the shoe. . . . *The existence of public corporations is likely to mean greater security for managerial employees.* The possibility of personal enrichment, of earning the kind of salary to which, say, a film star could aspire, will have gone for good. [I may add: How many operational managers get film-star salaries?] In its place there will be, for the many, greater opportunities for advancement to a new range of responsible posts with the prestige and satisfaction which only public service can confer.[63]

Conversion of the monopoly Big Four into public corporations will bring a new freedom to small independent packers. They should recognize, once and for all, that monopoly power grows, it is not destroyed, as government uses anti-trust actions to "restore" competition. What is illegal is not monopoly suppression of competition but a *conspiracy* to suppress it, and conspiracy is hard to prove in the courts. Even if the Supreme Court ruling that monopoly power to exclude competitors is illegal is implemented, anti-trust action can punish violators of the law only after they have built up monopoly and suppressed competition, which is neither a satisfactory procedure nor a solution.

[63] Sir Arthur Street, *The Public Corporation in British Experience* (1947), pp. 27-28.

This point was emphasized by Senator Joseph C. O'Mahoney in an address to a 1948 meeting of the Western States Meat Packers Association: "What chance do you think the little packer has to maintain his own independent existence if he becomes the victim of monopoly and is forced to depend solely upon punitive action by the Department of Justice? Punitive action *after the event* is not an effective method of maintaining free competitive enterprise; for the power of these concentrated giant companies is so great as to enable them to outlast their victims." [64]

Monopoly interests, as a barrier to economic progress, are especially serious, let me repeat, in food. As nutritional emphasis shifts from one food to another, and as new foods develop, the danger arises that monopoly will fetter progressive changes. It might resist certain new food developments because their production would mean the scrapping of old capital equipment. Or monopoly might get control of new foods for its own profit and precipitate a mad competitive scramble for the consumer's dollar regardless of his welfare. There is need for public corporations to prevent these antisocial practices. This public-utility type of organization and policy is all the more necessary because of the interdependence of food problems within the larger framework of ecological balance—from the soil that produces food to the human beings who consume it.

The American people are, I believe, in a mood where they may come to see the desirability of the kind of public enterprise suggested in these pages. For it is significant that neither the public nor labor unions nor small business nor reformers became excited about the 1948 anti-trust suit against the big packers—which, one year later, had not yet come to trial. Compare this with the general excitement when the government cracked down on the monopoly packers in 1917–19. The change expresses public weariness and skepticism about an anti-trust policy that is a petty annoyance to big business but does not achieve substantial results. It may well be that the American people will in time accept a policy of truly effective action against monopoly corporations—their conversion into public enterprise.

[64] Article, "Monopoly Menaces Free Enterprise System Here," *The National Provisioner,* February 21, 1948, p. 42.

CHAPTER X

PACKINGHOUSE LABOR:
HUMAN AND TECHNOLOGICAL
ASPECTS

1. WORKERS AS COMMODITIES AND AS PEOPLE

PACKINGHOUSE workers are people. They are, or ought to be, citizens of industry. These are, perhaps, truisms, but they have been in large measure ignored by management and by economists.

Classical economists began their analyses with three factors of production: land, labor, and capital. But it never appeared, from what they wrote, that there was much difference between labor, which is composed of men and women, and objectified land and capital. Labor is, of course, a factor of production. But labor is also people, with minds and souls and aspirations.

As economic historians pile up statistics on the production of goods and services, on technological advances, corporate enterprise, and profit, on wages, working hours, and strikes, an impressive story emerges of economic progress. There is more to the story, however. Behind much of it are human agony and heartbreak, the inability to provide for one's family, frustration and degradation of men and women for whom industry and employment ought to be one means to finer human living.

Low wages and unwholesome working conditions were bad enough. More degrading for human dignity, however, was the industrial magnates' assumption that they alone knew what was good for the workers, and that they acted for the workers' good—one reason for their opposition to labor unionism. When, in 1902, 140,000 bituminous coal miners went on strike and the operators refused to negotiate or arbitrate, their spokesman, George F. Baer, said: "The rights and interests of the laboring man will be protected and cared for—not by the labor agitators, but by the Christian men to whom God in his infinite wisdom has given control of the property interests of this country."

Most of the corporate magnates were moral men, convinced of their righteousness. It is not necessary to impugn their sincerity to doubt the wisdom of their "moral" opposition to unionism. For, if unions are immoral, the suffering and starvation—even the killing —of union people may be deplorable but justified by the moral purposes that anti-unionism serves. Capitalist magnates opposed the introduction of democracy into industrial government with the same moral fervor with which aristocratic magnates earlier opposed the introduction of democracy into political government.

In few industries were the workers as people more degraded than in the meat industry. And this was true from the beginning of industrial packing.

It began with the shift from hand work to machine work. Mechanization meant breaking down the older craft skills into simple mechanical operations, in a minute subdivision of labor, that could be performed by semi-skilled and unskilled workers. Much of the economy of mechanization came not from efficiency as such, but from the possibility of paying low wages to workers who needed no skills. As already noted, at arbitration hearings on union wage demands in 1918 the advisory superintendent for Swift & Company admitted that the 27½-cent hourly rate paid laborers by his company was lower than the rate in any other industry.

Immigrant workers, notably Poles, Lithuanians, Slovaks, and Bohemians, because of their ignorance and inexperience in a new country, were easily imposed upon, as were Negroes because of their color. The big packers, after using the Negroes to break strikes, fired them. I quote an authoritative study:

When the strike [of 1894] broke out the whole number of Negroes employed in the stockyards was about 500. . . . Few of the Negroes that came into the yards during the trouble of 1894 stayed on after the strike was settled and the number grew but little during the ten years of industrial peace which followed. The colored working force of 1904, ten years after the sympathetic strike, was probably less than 5 per cent of the entire force of the yards. Nearly all of these were unskilled laborers receiving a wage of 18 cents an hour. In the 1904 Amalgamated strike, the packers immediately turned to the well-supplied labor market of which they had boasted and directed their main efforts toward securing strikebreakers. They brought salesmen and employees from their branch houses to take over the skilled positions and for the rougher work they imported large numbers from outside. Most of these were foreigners, many fresh from abroad, and Negroes from the South. . . . Sometimes, when they found out what they were doing, workers refused to continue at their jobs. A colored strikebreaker told of how a whole trainload of Negroes brought up from the South refused to go to work when they learned they were to take the jobs of men on strike. Most of the Negroes, however, and many of the immigrants had no idea as to what a strike or a union was. Estimates placed the number of Negroes employed in the plants as high as 10,000. To prevent violence the strikebreakers were housed in the yards. Sanitary and moral conditions were so bad that Ogden Armour himself is reported to have said after a visit to his plant, "My God! I can't stand that!" . . . Evidently the great majority of Negroes who were brought into the stockyards in 1904 lost their places when the more experienced men, who had walked out, returned to work. Six years after the strike the census of 1910 showed that there were but sixty-seven Negroes in a total of 10,840 semi-skilled and unskilled workers in the Chicago industry.[1]

Not all Negro workers were strikebreakers. Their numbers grew in the packinghouses until today nearly a third of the labor force are Negroes. And they are loyal union members.

In addition to low wages, on which it was almost impossible to live, the economic insecurity of packinghouse workers was aggravated by seasonal unemployment. This was both cause and effect of the use of low-wage unskilled and semi-skilled labor. The layoff of workers began from November to January and continued until the summer months, when employment picked up with the pickup in the run of livestock. A large number of workers was always available for temporary work. Owner-management, instead of making efforts to ease, if not end, seasonal unemployment, used its existence to pressure the workers into accepting low wages and to break strikes.

Within the scourge of seasonal unemployment a condition of

[1] Sterling D. Spero and Abram L. Harris, *Black Worker* (1931), pp. 264-68.

temporary layoffs for hours, days, and weeks tormented the workers. The ten-hour day, sixty-hour week prevailed. However, of eighty-three plants investigated in 1917, only three paid full daily and weekly wages. "All plants have what are presumed to be regular hours of work for employees. But insofar as they apply to killing, cutting, hide, casing and offal departments, and to a lesser extent to other departments, they are more regular in the breach than in the keeping. The hours actually worked by many employees vary from day to day and from week to week." About five-eighths of the plants had, usually for the killing, cutting, and lugging gangs, guaranteed or "gang" time, that is, a guarantee, in most cases, of pay equal to a minimum of forty hours a week. Workers had to report for work every day, do other work in addition to their regular "gang" work if necessary, and often hang around for sixty hours in order to get pay for forty hours.[2] Horeover, as Nelson Morris admitted in 1918, workers were often fired, instead of being given a temporary layoff, to escape paying them the "guaranteed" weekly minimum.

For years the big packers fought union and legislative efforts to make them pay a full day's wage. A letter found in the files of Swift & Company by the Federal Trade Commission in 1918, addressed to Louis F. Swift, told of efforts to prevent the Nebraska legislature from adopting a "full day's pay" bill: "There is a good chance the House will kill the bill, and that if by any chance it shall pass the House, it cannot, in Mr. Selby's opinion, pass the Senate. If necessary he will take such action as will insure its defeat."

Packing managements later made a number of efforts, however, to regularize day and week employment. They took steps to get railroads and shippers to cooperate to make packinghouse livestock receipts more regular, distributed over the week instead of being concentrated in two or three days. The early 1920's found this situation improved, although there were still losses of around 2.7 per cent of nominal weekly hours. But in this respect packing stood among the better industries. Losses in the worst industries ranged from 9.6 per cent in hosiery and knit goods to 18.4 per cent in agricultural implements.[3]

[2] U.S. Bureau of Labor Statistics, Bulletin No. 252, *Wages and Hours of Labor in the Slaughtering and Meat Packing Industry, 1917* (1919), pp. 61-62.

[3] National Bureau of Economic Research, *Recent Economic Changes* (1929), vol. II, p. 466.

Technological displacement of labor made insecurity greater. The packing industry from the very beginning swiftly transformed, and continued to transform, its mechanical equipment with a constant introduction of labor-saving devices. These devices eliminated skills and threw many workers out of a job. True enough, technological improvements in the long run were offset by expansion of the packing industry; but in the short run it meant loss of jobs for many workers.

There is little, if any, evidence that owner-management in packinghouses considered the economic and human interests of the workers when they introduced labor-saving devices. There is little, if any, evidence that owner-management saw the need for a policy to ease the impact of labor-saving, to conserve the job tenure and income of workers, to cooperate with them in their adjustments to new jobs.

And little was done about occupational hazards. Diseases contracted on the job scourged the workers: fever, many types of skin diseases and ulcers, flu, pneumonia, sinus trouble. More frightful was the accident toll—from crushed fingers to broken arms and legs to death. No sick leaves were provided and no compensation. In fact, the monopoly packers opposed adequate laws for compulsory workmen's compensation. Among the letters the Federal Trade Commission found in the packers' files in 1918 was a letter from Swift & Company to a member of the Kansas legislature, which read: "We are perfectly safe in assuming that the compensation bill is going to be more favorable to the workman unless decided opposition is put up or some other means used for getting through legislation that will suit us."

There is something terrible in this opposition to payment of decent compensation to a worker who, alive but injured, may be unable to make a living; or, dead, has been unable to provide, however meagerly, for his widow and children.

Back in 1917 the packing industry's accident rates were among the worst in the country. They were still so more than a quarter of a century later: the worst among consumer industries and second worst among all industries.

In 1944 the War Production Board stated that, for 1943, the slaughtering and meat-packing industry had the highest accident frequency and spent the least money for personal safety equipment of any of twelve major consumer industries reporting to the Board. For the same period the Bureau of Labor Statistics, United States Department of Labor, made a survey covering about 50 per cent of the slaughtering and meat-packing establishments, which employed about 55 per cent of the industry's workers. I quote:

Available information shows that insofar as industrial accidents and health are concerned, *the slaughtering and meat-packing industry has not kept pace with others of equal importance. . . .* This industry's employees suffered some 16,480 serious injuries, employers paid out approximately $3,000,000 in direct compensation costs, exclusive of medical costs and administrative overhead, and over 1,500,000 man-hours were lost by the injured workers alone. These figures indicate an accident frequency of 50 injuries per million man-hours worked for an industry which is certainly no more hazardous than the aircraft industry with a frequency of 11, the iron and steel industry with a frequency of 10, or the electrical machinery industry with a frequency of 11. *The accident frequency rate of 50 for the slaughtering and meat packing industry is the second highest in the United States.* On an average, one out of each ten employees in the meat-packing industry suffered a disabling accident last year [1943]. While this figure may seem high, it is lower than other evidence indicates. Information from the unpublished files of various companies indicated a lack of proper reporting of the complete accident experience in the industry. Some large plants, with the most modern equipment insofar as mechanical and building construction are concerned, show frequency rates as high as 200.

It need not be, this maiming and killing of human beings. The report of the Department of Labor said:

There are some establishments in the packing industry that have a very good accident record; one plant having 100 employees now averages only one serious accident a year, or a frequency of only 5, another establishment having several thousand employees maintains a frequency of 10, while one of the largest West Coast plants has completed 5,000,000 hours without any serious injuries. This performance shows accidents can be prevented.

These packing plants with low accident rates prove what can be done when the professional competence and pride of management swing into action. Model plants bring imitation. And the packing industry is coming to grips, finally, with the accident problem. In a book issued by the Institute of Meat Packing of the University of Chicago, plant superintendents are told:

Safe operation is just as essential in the meat-packing plant as is efficient control of labor output and satisfactory supervision of the quality of product. . . . In order to operate a plant safely, definite safety programs must be adopted and actively sponsored and supported by top management. The direction of the program should be assigned to some ranking executive working directly under top management. It should be his duty to obtain the wholehearted cooperation of all classes of employees in an effort to eliminate accidents and to develop and energize the safety program. If possible he should have available the service of a medical director and the facilities of a hospital or first-aid room. . . . It should be emphasized again that top management must take a direct interest in the progress being made in safe plant operation if any safety program is to reach its full effectiveness.[4]

A number of illustrations will show what the packers are doing to promote safety. And, also, what can be done.

After starting a new program, all plants of Armour & Company reduced the accident severity rate in 1947 by 48 per cent. Two of this company's units, in Baltimore and Pittsburgh, each worked 1,000,000 man-hours without an accident. In the Kansas City plant the accident frequency rate was decreased to a low of 5.3 lost-time accidents per 1,000,000 man-hours of work—far below the packing industry's average. The safety work for Swift & Company had good results; its accident rate in 1948 was lower than that of the packing industry as a whole. At a celebration of the safety achievement, John Holmes, Swift's president, declared the goal was abolition of accidents.

Independent packers also made substantial progress in their safety work. One of them, Kingan & Company, had in 1946 the industry's lowest accident frequency rate and the third lowest in severity. This company's safety program starts the moment a worker is hired and follows through systematically and continuously.

[4] The Committee on Textbooks of the American Meat Institute, *Meat Packing Plant Superintendency* (1948), pp. 229-30, 245. According to the National Safety Council, *Accident Facts* (1949), p. 23, the meat-packing industry in 1948 had 17.84 disabling injuries per 1,000,000 man-hours' exposure, compared with a rate of 11.49 for all industries. The severity rating for packing—.63 days lost per 1000 man-hours worked—was lower than the average for all industries —1.12 days lost.

"Although our methods may appear unorthodox," said Alex Spink, Kingan's safety director, "the results justify their continuance." [5]

Another director, Richard Winkler of Wilson & Company, stressed the human element:

> You will note in the title of my talk the words "labor and management." . . . The first is "labor"—your employees, the men and women on the firing line, who are *just plain human beings*. Now let us look at the second word, "management"—the people who run the plants, supervisors, foremen, the men and women responsible for operations, production, sales and distribution of the finished products. They are *just plain human beings*, too. . . . Eliminate the accident cost consideration in dealing with your workers, reserving the cost data for statistical purposes in the files of your company comptroller. . . . Preach the elimination of human suffering; for example, a wife's agony due to her husband's injuries which may result in impediments on future earnings, or due to industrial fatalities which leave widows, minor children and broken homes. It is an unpleasant task to have to advise a wife that her husband was injured or killed in an industrial accident, no matter how diplomatic you try to be.[6]

Finally, the housing conditions under which workers lived in Packingtown were abominable. The packers did nothing about it, but their attorney in the 1918 wage arbitration hearings said: "The only remedy is absolute destruction of the district. You should tear down the district, burn all of the houses. The landlords who accept rent for such disgraceful hovels are more to blame than the packers. The average woman, the frugal housewife can keep a good home, in a respectable condition, on the wages paid the stockyards workers." [7]

Of course, these degrading life-distorting conditions among packinghouse workers were not peculiar to this industry. They were characteristic of workers' housing in most mass-production industries during the years from 1890 to 1918; corrupt municipal politics and greedy landlords were also to blame. But this is no sufficient alibi for owner-management in packing, where conditions were among the worst. Nor is it convincing to argue that housing conditions elsewhere were as bad or that they were part of the American

[5] Articles, *The National Provisioner*, October 18, 1947, p. 11; February 7, 1948, p. 17; February 14, 1948, p. 24.

[6] Richard C. Winkler, "A Positive Approach to Safety," *The National Provisioner*, October 18, 1947, p. 18.

[7] News story, *Chicago Daily Tribune*, March 6, 1918.

civilization of the times. Pontius Pilate, washing his hands of a crime to which he was an accessory, did not wash away his guilt.

Substantial improvements have been made in housing, wages, and working conditions. Welfare work—lockers, rest rooms and nurseries, emergency hospitals, and meals at reasonable prices—has been introduced. Much more still needs to be done. The greatest change came with the establishment of permanent unionism, which made workers citizens of industry.

2. MECHANIZATION: I—THE IMPACT ON LABOR

Mechanization is general in large-scale industry. But there are few industries where it developed as early and as highly as in meat packing. The packing industry has a large capital investment per plant and per worker. This results in a constantly greater amount of raw material worked up into finished products by smaller amounts of human labor.

Already by the early twentieth century most packinghouse operations were mechanized, particularly in the "chain" (or "disassembly" line), which set the speed of operations and so determined the speed of workers under the chain's control. Labor, moreover, became increasingly unskilled or semi-skilled. Craftsmen butchers largely disappeared from meat packing; the "butchers" who were employed in packinghouses were skilled men but of a different character. Each of the operations was minutely subdivided with separate tasks performed by a separate worker, whose "skill" was, in most cases, comparatively slight and easily learned in a brief time.

Mechanization kept increasing in the 1920's and after. In addition to improved mechanical equipment, new and more efficient plant layouts resulted in reducing the amount of time and motion used to transfer products being processed from one part of the plant to another. Workers' waste of time and motion was also reduced by combinations of a number of jobs into one job to cut down on labor. Skills were also reduced: as of 1946–47 common labor represented 30 per cent of the workers; from 30 per cent to 40 per cent were semi-skilled.

Productive efficiency went up. For slaughtering and meat packing the productivity increase, measured in terms of output per worker, from 1914 to 1925 was 27 per cent. The increases kept on. By 1930, for example, 2070 workers did the work 2585 workers had performed in 1914. Specific increases in man-hour productivity from 1914 to 1931 in various divisions of the packing industry were, according to a 1932 study of the United States Bureau of Labor Statistics: 5.7 per cent in cattle killing, 33.2 per cent in hog killing, 21.1 per cent in hog cutting, 41.6 per cent in calf killing, 61 per cent in sheep killing. Corresponding increases in productive efficiency took place in other areas of the industry.

Although meat packing's productivity gains were considerable, they were smaller than those in most other industries. In 1937 it took 17 per cent fewer man-hours to produce a unit of meat output than it did in 1909; for the food industries as a whole the productivity gains averaged around one-third.

CHANGES IN LABOR PER UNIT OF PRODUCT, U.S.A., 1909–1937

	Percentage Changes		Average Yearly Change	
Industry	Wage Earners	Wage-Earner Hours	Wage Earners	Wage-Earner Hours
All food products	− 20	°	− 0.8	°
Meat packing	− 11	− 17	0.4	− 0.6
Canned products	− 41	− 60	− 1.9	− 3.2
Dairy products	− 48	°	2.3	°
Flour milling	− 20	− 37	− 0.8	− 1.6
Beet sugar	− 51	− 65	− 2.5	− 3.7
Cane sugar	− 8.2	− 42	− 0.3	− 2.0
Corn products	− 18	°	− 0.7	°
All manufactures	− 42	− 58	− 1.9	− 3.0

° No data.

Source: Arranged from Solomon Fabricant, *Labor Saving in American Industry, 1899–1937* (1945), pp. 12-15; Occasional Paper No. 23 of the National Bureau of Economic Research.

Labor saving from mechanization is also evident from the figures of the percentage of "value added by manufacture" accounted for by wages. These percentages, according to Census reports, dropped from 54.5 per cent in 1869 to 39.6 per cent in 1931. The low point was 29.5 per cent in 1914; thereafter the proportion of wages to "value added" rose up to 1931, indicating a higher wage level in the packing industry.

WAGE WORKERS IN PACKING, 1899–1947

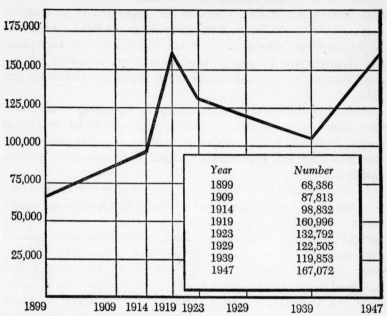

Year	Number
1899	68,386
1909	87,813
1914	98,832
1919	160,996
1923	132,792
1929	122,505
1939	119,853
1947	167,072

Source: U.S. Department of Commerce, Census of Manufactures for the respective years.

Up until 1920 the number of packinghouse workers grew steadily, in spite of increasing productivity per worker, because of the industry's tremendous expansion. In the 1920's, however, an absolute displacement of workers began. Discounting the drop from 1919 to 1923 (the 1919 employment was a war condition), the number of wage workers decreased from 132,792 in 1923 to 122,505 in 1929 and 119,853 in 1939, despite a considerable increase in output. This means 12,939 workers were displaced from the packing industry because the rate of productivity increase was greater than the industry's expansion rate. If we measure the employment and output trend from 1923 to 1939, we find that output in the slaughtering and meat-packing industry went up by 17.7 per cent. The number of man-hours worked went down by 14.3 per cent.[8]

[8] John J. Dunlop, "Productivity and the Wage Structure," in *Income, Employment and Public Policy* (1940), p. 352.

The significant point about this trend toward an absolute displacement of workers because of increasing technological efficiency and productivity is this: wherever the expansion of an industry begins to slow down while productivity keeps on rising, an absolute displacement of labor within that industry is bound to take place. The meat-packing industry is in this condition. Although employment rose in the 1940's, the trend of the 1920's and 1930's still prevails.

Productivity, by and large, is constantly increasing in all industries. Whether or not this brings a displacement of labor depends upon whether or not the particular industry, or all industry, experiences a sufficient expansion of output to absorb the displaced workers.

In the 1920's up to 1929 the total number of industrial workers—in mining and manufactures and on the railroads—shrank because productivity increased more than output. The story differed with specific industries, of course. For example, the automobile industry registered a large increase in employment because this industry went through its greatest development during the 1920's; output increased more than productivity. This was not true of some other industries, including packing and another food industry, flour milling, which experienced an absolute decrease in the number of their workers.

There is another important aspect of the situation, moreover. While the number of wage workers in packing decreased in the 1920's the number of salaried employees grew. By 1929 salaried employees in the packing industry numbered 23,349; of these, 1484 were officers and executives, the other 21,865 were technical-managerial, supervisory and sales personnel and office workers. For all manufacturing industries the number of salaried employees rose from 274,120 in 1899 to 1,358,775 in 1929, and kept growing; in the same period the number of wage workers rose from 4,712,763 to 8,838,743. In other words, while salaried employees increased four times, the number of wage workers increased only twice. The same story is told by the years after 1929.

This development in meat packing, as in all industry, comes from greater mechanization, more complicated technical-chemical processes, and more insistence on quality. All these advances call for relatively smaller numbers of manual workers and more technical-managerial and other salaried personnel. More chemists, engineers, and technicians of all kinds are needed; the increasing amount of paper work for planning, direction, and control of operations, and the sale of output, require more salaried employees in the plants, in the offices, and on sales forces.

Another aspect of these changes is the shift from production workers to service workers. For American industry as a whole the proportion of workers employed in the production of physical goods dropped from 75 per cent in 1870 to 50 per cent in 1940. The number of people engaged in distribution and in personal and professional service rose from 25 per cent to 50 per cent. This is a result of increasing technological efficiency and, in addition, of rising living standards.

The American people have so increased their incomes that they have had, over the years, a constantly larger amount of money to spend on services, while the output of physical goods increased because of the tremendous rise in productivity both in industry and in agriculture. Another aspect of the situation is shorter working hours, which decreased from around seventy a week in 1870 to forty (and in some cases thirty-five) in 1940. As leisure grows, because productivity makes it possible to shorten hours by increasing total output with a smaller amount of labor working fewer hours, the workers have more time to use recreational and other personal and professional services, which multiply.

But higher wages and shorter hours are not automatic results of increasing productivity. There is a lag period in which many workers lose from increasing productive efficiency; they may be fired or they may have to take lower-wage jobs. Managements have made some efforts to solve the problem of what to do with workers who are displaced from jobs by technological improvements; they have not solved it.

The problem may become acute in meat packing. Although this industry has not made any basic changes in its technology for years, it has piled up labor-saving improvements. Today a typical packing plant is an intricate and integrated electrical machine, highly mechanized and increasingly automatic, with the emphasis on labor saving.

Innumerable mechanical devices are used to perform particular operations. The trend is toward faster, more automatic units for greater production and quality control and lower labor costs. What is claimed for one machine is typical: "Its great speed means higher output per man-hour and higher product yield; both together mean a higher profit margin." [9]

Savings are made on equipment using new materials (e.g., stainless steel), which means improved quality, lower maintenance costs, fewer man-hours for production. Hams and other meats are branded by automatic machines; also sprinkled and rubbed with salt and packed in the same automatic fashion. A new small dehairer for hogs, using hydraulic cylinders for operating throw-in and throw-out cradles, furnishes high capacity in relatively small space because of the new unit's elimination of gearing, etc., and its general construction.

One significant operating development of the later 1940's was a hydromatic bacon slicer, operated at the rate of 650 slices a minute, or 3000 pounds an hour; this slicer, used with a high-speed conveyor and a finger-and-paper dispensing arrangement, made grouping and paper placing automatic. More efficient handling of inedible by-products (especially dry rendering) is making the process completely mechanical, from raw material to finished product. Power-driven saws, used widely in beef splitting, are invading other operations:

Hog splitting, one of the most skilled jobs on the killing floor, generally is a hand operation performed with a cleaver by a highly skilled butcher. In recent years, however, mechanical equipment has been developed which improves and speeds up accurate splitting; and, in the last year, a new power saw has been brought out which is designed to further mechanize the operation. The first piece of equipment developed to aid in hog splitting was the B & D backbone marking saw, which is a great aid to accuracy and reduces the degree of skill required in the hand splitter. It likewise permits rapid splitting by less skilled butchers and, with its aid, semi-skilled splitters are reported to handle 250 to 300 hogs per hour without impairment of loin quality. A more recent development is a hog-splitting saw made of stainless steel, and one user reports it can be cleaned easily with a steam hose. . . . One of the most interesting attributes of this saw is its ability to split hog carcasses at high speed— in six to eight seconds. . . . The saw can be used in connection with a conveyor. Current users, for the most part, are convinced that a good

[9] Advertisement, Townsend Engineering Company, *The National Provisioner*, June 5, 1948, p. 51.

operator with the saw should be able almost to equal the output of two hand splitters. All packers employing the saw report it is relatively easy to train workmen in its use, and this is probably one of the greatest advantages of the unit.[10]

More progress is being made on mechanization of handling methods, with substantial time and labor savings. Case studies have shown that in some industries as much as 80 per cent of indirect labor can be "saved" through modernization of equipment for handling and moving materials.

In many plants the live animals, a carload at a time, are hoisted from the ground floor to an upper story by means of electrical elevators. More use of conveyors, especially in small plants, allows a further satisfactory combination of several operations being made while cuts of meat are on moving tables.

The new equipment, moreover, eliminates trucking and handling for more consolidation of operations in a more integrated plant layout, with savings in product, labor, and time. Mechanization of handling work constantly spreads into new areas. Here is a typical example:

Many plants have been able to mechanize one or more product handling steps in connection with curing operations. Thus, at the John Morrell & Company plant at Sioux Falls, S.D., fork trucks are not only used for moving meat in tierces to and from the curing cellar, but are also employed in combination with a vat dumper in performing the overhauling operation. In a Chicago establishment one fork truck is employed in moving 200,000 pounds of cured meat per man-day from the pickle pumping room to the curing cellar and from the curing cellar to an elevator serving the washing room.[11]

A significant development is the spread of mechanized handling methods to smaller plants, because of improved, lower-cost equipment. The superintendent of one small plant, in Texas, proposed the use of power equipment for all intraplant transport, and said: "After we have had a few months to use the power movers I believe it will be possible to save 1000 man-hours per week at the present

[10] Article, "First Report on Results With New Hog Splitting Saw," *The National Provisioner*, May 15, 1948, p. 19.

[11] Report on new technical developments, *The National Provisioner*, April 12, 1947, p. 89.

rate of production. If we save only 25 per cent of this estimate, the equipment would pay for itself in about one year." [12]

The trend toward mechanical consolidation and integration of operations, which means greater automatic production, is accelerated by the growing use of instruments. One important postwar development is the increasing use in industry, including the food industries, of complete instrument installations, with substantial cost reductions from labor-saving automatic operation.

This modernization of equipment is accompanied by the modernization of factory buildings for better external appearance and greater internal efficiency. Improvement of packing plants, long noted for their drabness, filth, and odors, is calculated to make packers into "good neighbors." The multi-story plant is preferred to the one-story unit because it is more compact and adaptable, utilizes more fully the expensive pieces of land, and promotes sanitary conditions. Within modern plants the emphasis is on improved lighting, ventilation, and sanitation, on speedier, more accurate work and better quality. More use is made of glass areas in the walls and ceilings, of glazed tile for better appearance and sanitation, of efficient artificial lighting (including fluorescent lights) and exhaust fans. One packer gives the following reasons for the obsolescence of many plants:

1. The nature of the materials from which they are constructed makes it very difficult and expensive to keep them clean.

2. Obsolete equipment and antiquated design make mandatory the use of expensive materials and handling methods, such as small elevators and hand trucking. Varying levels and the weakness of floors prohibit the use of modern industrial trucks.

3. Lack of integration between buildings and departments makes it difficult to employ modern processing techniques with economy. Too many handling operations may be required, for example, in smoking, chilling, pressing and slicing bacon. Many older plants were designed as fresh and cured meat establishments with no thought that they might some day house complicated fabricating and processing operations.[13]

Plant modernization, as with improved plant equipment, betters

[12] Article, "Superintendent Reports on Labor Savings Through Use of Power Movers," *The National Provisioner*, July 24, 1948, p. 19.

[13] Article, "Industry Expanding and Modernizing," *The National Provisioner*, April 12, 1947, p. 40.

the quality of product and reduces production costs. It also, however, reduces the relative number of man-hours required for a particular volume of output. This problem will become more acute as technological progress results in still more labor saving. And this ties in with the problem of production costs and wages and their relation to prices.

3. WAGES, COSTS, AND PRICES

As the result of growing technical-managerial efficiency and union pressure in the meat industry, together with general economic progress, the packinghouse worker's wages have moved upward since the beginning of the century and brought a considerable improvement in his standard of living. Packing is no longer among the lowest-wage industries.

By 1923 the average yearly earnings of meat workers were $1260, compared with only $650 in 1914. They rose to $1360 in 1929 and fell slightly to $1350 in 1939 (in which year average earnings for all manufactures were $1152).

WAGES, EMPLOYMENT, AND OUTPUT, MEAT PACKING, 1914–47

	Output	Wage Workers	Wages	Per Cent Wages of Output
1914	$1,652,000,000	98,832	$62,100,000	3.7
1919	4,246,000,000	160,996	209,500,000	4.9
1923	2,585,000,000	132,792	167,600,000	6.5
1925	3,050,000,000	120,422	159,300,000	5.2
1929	3,434,000,000	122,505	165,900,000	4.8
1933	1,080,000,000	113,193	112,266,000	10.4
1935	2,362,000,000	116,620	136,400,000	5.8
1939	2,649,000,000	119,853	161,524,000	6.1
1947	*	167,072	468,700,000	*

* Not available.

Source: U.S. Department of Commerce, Census of Manufactures for the respective years. The table does not include figures for poultry dressing and packing and for sausages, prepared meats, and other meat products not prepared in slaughtering and packing plants.

It will be noted that total wages in 1939 were smaller by $6,076,000 than in 1923. The increase in the average yearly earnings of packinghouse workers had a measurable connection with the shrinkage in the number employed, which dropped from 160,996 in 1919 to 132,792 in 1923 to 119,853 in 1939. The drop in 1919–23 came from the decline from war-swollen employment, but in later years the major cause was increasing productivity. In the six-year period 1923–29 the average hourly earnings rose little, from 49.9 cents to 52.5 cents.

The Amalgamated used World War I to force meat packing out of its low-wage condition, assisted by government arbitration and wage policy. Employers reduced wages in the postwar depression of 1920–21, but prices fell more than wages so that many of the workers' war gains were kept. For packing workers this development meant that they kept their yearly earnings at $1260, only slightly below 1919; but since prices had fallen, it brought a considerable rise in real wages. By 1929 average earnings were up by another $100, largely because of increasing productivity; compensated for management, however, by a reduction in the employment of workers.

Yearly earnings went down to a low of $990 in 1933 during the depression of the 1930's. They moved up to $1350 in 1939, only slightly below 1929, as a result of economic recovery and, especially, of an upsurge of union organization in the packing industry.

The influence of unionism is important. It was largely its influence that brought packinghouse yearly earnings by 1923 to twice what they had been in 1914. It is significant to note that, although the meat workers' wages rose slightly from 1923 to 1929, the proportion that wages are of total value output declined from 6.5 per cent to 4.8 per cent; and during these six years the Amalgamated was only a remnant-union with little influence on wages. Finally, the recovery of yearly earnings in 1939 was, in large measure, a result of collective bargaining.[14]

Although the workers from 1923 on received only small gains from increasing productivity, the increase of technical-managerial efficiency

[14] Arthur M. Ross, *Trade Union Wage Policy* (1948), p. 132, shows that real average hourly earnings in meat packing from 1890 to 1926, when it was predominantly non-union, rose only 23 per cent compared with rises in unionized industries of from 44 per cent to 87 per cent. He concludes: "Unionization was a decided source of wage advantage and a real influence on relative earning movements in the 1890–1926 period. . . . Real hourly earnings have advanced more sharply in highly organized industries than in less unionized industries, in periods of stable or declining union membership as well as periods of active organization. No reason has been found to believe that the relationship is coincidental."

provided the foundation for higher wages. The influence of unionism may be seen in the fact that efficiency went up from 1900 to 1910 as much, if not more than in later years, yet packing was a dismal low-wage industry. We may summarize developments thus:

Packing wages went up around 100 per cent from 1914 to 1939, with a somewhat larger increase in the real wages that augment buying power and improve living standards. Salaries rose more than wages because of the multiplication of salaried employees, whose number, for example, rose to 23,349 in 1929 and their compensation to $54,734,000; a decline to 17,156 salaried employees in 1939 (exclusive of around 18,000 salesmen and 6000 employees in central offices of companies with several plants), with compensation of $40,000,000, was reversed in later years. For 1947, according to the Census of Manufactures, there were 41,317 salaried employees who received $154,027,000 in salaries.[15]

Wages went up again during World War II and after. Average weekly earnings, according to the United States Bureau of Labor Statistics, rose from $27.85 in 1939 to around $46 in 1945 and $65 in 1948, with average hourly earnings rising from 68 cents in 1939 to $1.40 in 1948.

One reservation is important: weekly earnings are not necessarily indicative of the worker's yearly income. Weekly earnings fluctuate up and down with the number of working hours. In addition, the turnover rate in meat packing is still among the highest in American industry; in 1947 the separation rate ranged from a low of 6.1 per cent in July to a high of 10.9 per cent in February, with about three-eighths of the separations coming from layoffs and five-eighths from voluntary quits. Since union seniority operates in most plants, many of the workers laid off are on the payroll and off it several times a year, thus considerably curtailing their yearly earnings.

For some years now packing has been among the better-wage industries. Its average weekly earnings of $67.66 and average hourly earnings of $1.42 in May 1948 were higher than the $51.76 and $1.30 average for manufacturing as a whole. Packing also compared favor-

[15] The rise in the proportion that wages are of the packing industry's value output from 3.7 per cent in 1914 to 6.1 per cent in 1939 (and around 8 per cent in 1948) indicates that the workers are receiving a larger share of the industry's proceeds. This appears also in the proportion that wages are of value added by manufacture, which rose from 29.5 per cent in 1914 to 40.9 per cent in 1923, fell to 36 per cent in 1929 and rose to 39.6 per cent in 1939.

ably with other food industries, whose average weekly earnings were only $50.95 and hourly earnings $1.21.

COMPARATIVE WAGE EARNINGS, FOOD INDUSTRIES, 1948

	Average Weekly	Average Hourly
Meat packing	$67.66	$1.42
Flour milling	55.64	1.20
Cereal preparations	55.59	1.37
Condensed milk	55.36	1.16
Sugar refining, cane	52.07	1.23
Baking products	49.30	1.15
Butter	46.59	1.02
Canning, preserving	41.33	1.13
Confectionery	39.23	1.04

The figures are for May 1948. Weekly earnings fluctuate considerably with the number of working hours; they were $56.62 in packing for March 1948, when working hours were 43.6 weekly compared with 46.7 in May 1948. The other industries experience similar fluctuations.

Source: U.S. Bureau of Labor Statistics, *Hours and Earnings, Industry Report,* October 4, 1948, p. 6. ("Condensed milk" includes evaporated milk.)

World War II ended with a considerable increase in the real wages of packinghouse workers, since money earnings rose more than living costs. In the early postwar years—from 1946 to 1948—real wages suffered a decline, however, despite additional money increases in rates, because of the sharp inflationary rise of prices and profits. All the indications are that real earnings will rise again as prices fall and unionism maintains or increases hourly rates while productivity mounts.

Despite the substantial improvements in packing wages over the past forty years, conditions are still bad in the industry. In 1944 a report of the War Manpower Commission said:

Although January employment in meat-packing plants totaled 183,000 —an 8 per cent increase over the 169,000 employed two months earlier— an additional 9000 workers will be needed by March. The separation rate in December averaged 12 per 100 employees, with voluntary quits accounting for the bulk of all separations. *Inability of the industry to retain its workers and expand employment more rapidly is primarily due to low wages and disagreeable working conditions.* In Chicago and in the South Atlantic and East South Central States the wage scales of the packing industry are at a level which makes competition for labor with war plants and shipyards impossible.[16]

The backward aspects of labor's situation in the packing industry were thus described by the Amalgamated's economist in 1949:

In spite of progress, however, the present economic position of our members employed in the packinghouses is not good, and for the following reasons:

1. The work week of the packinghouse worker is steadily declining [with consequent reduction in take-home pay]. The high average weekly hours for April, May and June 1948 are attributable to the strike during those months and the high average weekly earnings reported by the BLS takes into account only those plants which were not on strike. . . . Actually, a large proportion of the packinghouse workers today work only an average of thirty-six hours a week which they are guaranteed by contract.

2. The real wages of packinghouse workers have likewise decreased. In spite of the fact that the workers have received substantial wage increases since 1941, their real wages today are less than they were in 1944 and 1945. An analysis of real wages from 1939 to November 1948 shows that the packinghouse worker earned an average of $27.85 a week in 1939, and that, based on 1935–39, the real average weekly wage in that year was $28.02 weekly. For the month of November 1948 he earned an average of $61.07 a week, but his real wages were $33.82, or only $5.80 more than in 1939.

3. It is my opinion that the average weekly earnings of packinghouse workers employed by the Big Four companies is less than the industry average. My assumptions are based primarily on reports which we have received from our local unions throughout the country, but it is also substantiated by data which we have for the first eight months of 1948. This information discloses that unlike previous years the average weekly earnings of employees of Swift & Company are, on the whole, below the average of the industry for the same period. What is true of this company is also true of the other three.

4. Because of the reduced work week, reduced take-home pay and substantial layoffs, the average annual income of the packinghouse worker will be less than $2500. That maximum will only represent the income of those employed in the skilled job classifications. A large number of unskilled and semi-skilled workers will earn an average of less than $2000 a year. This is far below the amount required by an average family.

[16] War Manpower Commission, *The Labor Market*, April 1944, p. 3.

5. Another important factor, which cannot be ignored when real wages and economic conditions are discussed, is that so large a number of packinghouse workers are unskilled and semi-skilled. Approximately 28 per cent of the workers are on common labor rates, which today, for

PRODUCTIVITY IN PACKING, 1939–46

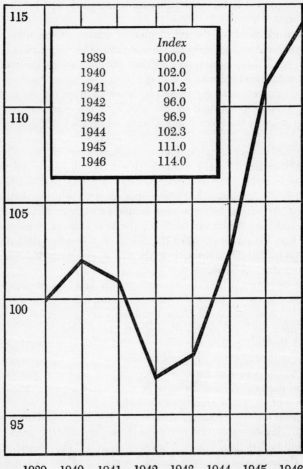

	Index
1939	100.0
1940	102.0
1941	101.2
1942	96.0
1943	96.9
1944	102.3
1945	111.0
1946	114.0

Source: U.S. Bureau of Labor Statistics. Index based on output per man-hour.

males, range from 97.5 cents an hour to $1.23, depending upon the area where they are employed. The female rates are far below those. About 70 per cent of all packinghouse workers are in semi-skilled and unskilled job classifications. This large group must have immediate economic relief.[17]

Unit labor costs in World War II moved in a confusing, contradictory fashion. Startling productivity gains were made in the war industries. But this was not true in the civilian goods industries; in many cases efficiency declined, primarily because they were unable to get new equipment, but also because they lost many experienced workers, who were replaced by less efficient personnel. In meat packing, productivity, measured in terms of output per man-hour, went up more than 40 per cent from 1919 to 1939, decreased about 4 per cent in 1942–43, but was up by 14 per cent in 1946. And in the postwar years productivity in meat packing, as in other industries, resumed its upward climb.

Nor were higher wages and salaries a factor in the inflationary movement of meat prices, especially in the early postwar years. For, as a proportion of the sales dollar, wages and salaries dropped almost one-third—from 14.1 per cent in 1939 to 12 per cent in 1945–46 to 9.4 per cent in 1947.[18]

If we take 12 cents of the sales dollar for wages and salaries as typical, labor costs, which are around two-thirds of the total, will amount to 8 cents. Obviously, wage rises contribute only a small amount to any increase in price. With unit labor costs at 8 cents on the dollar, a 25 per cent increase in wages would mean only an additional 2 cents added to the selling price (providing the increase was not offset by higher productivity). To make the illustration concrete,

[17] David Dolnick, "Packinghouse Workers Need Economic Relief," *The Butcher Workman,* April 1949, pp. 5-6.

[18] Research Department, Federal Reserve Bank of Chicago, *A Financial and Economic Survey of the Meat Packing Industry, 1948 Supplement* (1948), p. 7. The costs of livestock and other farm products as a proportion of the meat sales dollar went up from 72.3 cents in 1939 to 75.1 cents in 1945 and 79.4 cents in 1947; the proportion of net earnings to the sales dollar was 1.2 cents in 1939, 0.9 cents in 1945, 2.3 cents in 1946, and 1.5 cents in 1947. It may be noted that the proportion that wages and salaries are of the sales dollar varies from enterprise to enterprise. It was 10.1 cents for Armour, 9.7 cents for Swift, 9.3 cents for Wilson, and 7.6 cents for Cudahy. One independent, Kingan & Company, spent only 8.6 cents of the sales dollar on wages and salaries.

straight-time average hourly earnings in meat plants went up 65 per cent from 1939 to 1947, while wholesale meat prices advanced 185 per cent. With wage costs at 8 cents, the 65 per cent wage increase should have meant a price rise of only 5.2 per cent instead of the actual rise of 85 per cent.

Apparently, from 1939 to 1947, wages rose from 6 per cent to 8 per cent as a proportion of packing sales, or output. If this larger proportion is maintained it will mean another substantial advance in labor's share of the meat industry's proceeds. The rise of two percentage points, it must be emphasized, adds very little to the prices of meat products, only 2 cents on the dollar.

Just as with wages in packing, so with profits; they are too small to have any material influence on prices. With net profits at around 2 cents of the sales dollar, even if they were completely abolished (an impossibility) it would decrease prices by an almost insignificant amount.

This whole problem of pricing is complicated by the magnitude of "joint costs" in the packing industry, since the output is greatly varied. Included are not only overhead costs but the cost of materials and of much of the labor. How shall the costs of a steer and of plant labor be divided among the various cuts of meat and the by-products? The joint costs can be so allocated that it may seem that the profit on meat sales is "only a fraction of a penny" and justify the complaint that "there's no profit in meat; the profit is in the by-products." It may be, however, that meat products are assigned too heavy a load of joint costs. At the same time, the pressure of joint costs drives toward "agreements" or "understandings" to regulate prices. For if "competitive" prices prevail on every one of the multitude of products, joint costs might be so distributed (to "justify" competitive prices) that, in the end, total revenue from sales might be lower than total costs. Neither the apologists for nor the critics of the packing industry fully recognize the complexity and pitfalls of the joint-cost problem.

Any hope for a downward movement of real prices for meat products must come from a substantial increase in productive efficiency. This means packing efficiency, for it is unlikely that the livestock industry can do it. But the prospects for greater productivity in packing are limited. In final analysis, lower meat costs for the consumer can come not from any considerable lowering of real prices but from an increase of the consumers' income, so that the costs of meat in their diets will shrink in proportion to income. And that calls for constant productivity advances in the majority of industries where they are possible, and probable, because of a new technology that becomes infinitely more productive than the old.

4. MECHANIZATION: II–THE NEW TECHNOLOGY

The packing industry's problems of costs, wages, and employment have not been as acute as they will become. For despite its mechanization the industry has lagged in technological progress; it has become, in contrast to its outstanding position in the early part of the century, comparatively backward. One recent study bluntly told the packers so: "Technological developments in this industry, since the perfection of mechanical refrigeration, have been of minor significance. Most observers agree that the technological level of manufacturing in the packing industry is relatively low, but no far-reaching changes are now generally foreseen, with the possible exception of packaging and quick-freezing of final products." [19]

Within two years it became evident that the study's conclusions were on the conservative side. Far-reaching changes began to appear, indicating that meat packing is now being engulfed by the new technological revolution at work in American industry.

The revolution has already begun in the chemical areas of meat packing. The industry, since it produces food products and uses complex chemical processes, has always employed a considerable number of chemists, bacteriologists, and nutritionists to control operations and carry on research. Their number is increasing as one scientific discovery piles on another and reveals the industry's existing technical-scientific shortcomings and the possibilities of new products from research.

Meat packing is noted for its by-products, yet one scientist told the packers:

We sometimes think we have reached the zenith to which we can go on using by-products. But evidence shows we have only begun. . . . I

[19] Article, "Meat Industry Financial and Economic Trends," *The National Provisioner*, June 28, 1947, p. 15. The study was made by W. E. Hoardley, E. Baughman, and W. P. Mors of the research department of the Federal Reserve Bank of Chicago.

might mention the waste in fats, oils and greases which are sold by certain packers to soap manufacturers, who separate out the fatty acids, have glycerine left and make soap. This is a very crude way to handle the fatty acids that are left over in the meat business because those acids contain stearic, oleic, palmitic and linoric acids which are very important in industry. They can be used as flotation agents to separate low phosphate ores, as wetting agents and detergents in a great variety of chemical compounds. . . . The serum derived from animal blood contains globulin and albumin, and the globulin in turn contains antibodies to infection. The idea of getting these antibodies out and utilizing them for the saving of human and animal life has become very important, which might produce one of the most important projects ever developed for suffering mankind. Other pharmaceuticals derived from animal tissues and glands include insulin, thyro protein, thiorucil, thyroxin and the twenty amino acids. All of these products should be investigated and exploited for the benefit of humanity and the packers and consumers. The need for insulin has become so great in relation to supply that men of science predict that some day it may be necessary to require every slaughterer to salvage all pancreas.[20]

Production of pharmaceuticals provides increasing scope for packing by-products. ACTH, the newest development, is an illustration. In 1948 scientists of the Mayo Clinic announced they had secured remarkable success in the treatment of rheumatoid arthritis through the use of two new hormones—one, ACTH, derived from the pituitary glands at the base of hogs' brains; the other, cortisone, a newly synthesized hormone of the cortex of the adrenal gland. These hormones may also prove useful in the treatment of other chronic diseases, including possibly mental illnesses. ACTH was extracted from hogs by a process developed at the laboratories of Armour & Company. The glands of hogs are the only ones from which ACTH can be extracted in practical amounts; yet it takes 400,000 hogs to yield one pound of the hormone. The Armour company began production at the rate of sixty pounds a year, requiring the total output of glands from 24,000,000 hogs. The product was not for sale—sixty pounds would supply the needs of only 3600 patients, each of whom requires 7500 milligrams of ACTH a year—but for distribution to institutions for experimental purposes. However, plant sources are opening up to

[20] George E. Hart, "By-Product Utilization Has Barely Been Touched," *The National Provisioner*, February 21, 1948, pp. 31-32.

supply substitutes for cattle bile, which should lower production costs of cortisone.

The packing industry carries on intensive scientific research, specific but useful, to develop more satisfactory operating conditions in packinghouses. For example: lethal violet rays are proving valuable in some walk-in coolers to help disinfect the air and reduce surface contamination; salts of proponic acid are reducing the mold flora on containers and wrapping papers; DDT is a potent new weapon against the millions of flies which infest packinghouses and stockyards. At the Meat Institute Foundation of the University of Chicago the research projects include work on lard improvement, the use of corn sugar to cure bacon, and the prevention of greenish discoloration on the surface of cured sausages (wieners). The Armour Research Foundation in June 1949 warned that technical progress in rendering had been slow compared with other industries and declared that a continuous rendering unit can be designed to shorten production time and insure better control through automatic operation.

New vistas open: infra-red heat may bring continuous fat extraction; some beef and lard shortening is already being produced by extraction rather than by rendering. Solvent extraction would increase the yield of fat (fat salvage becomes animal feed, lard, fertilizer, shortening, oleomargarine, and soap) and reduce manpower requirements.

Electronics offers new possibilities in processing meats, both for preservation and for immediate consumption. Radiation by high-speed electrons, used to preserve foods in their fresh, raw state, can be applied to meat products.

Research has proved that electrons are hundreds of times more effective than X rays in sterilization of foods. They provide new weapons against spoilage from bacteria and enzymes. The new electronic devices, not yet available for commercial production, will be able to sterilize meats and augment their capacity for preservation, while not destroying any of their nutrients. At the same time the use of electronics will make it possible to discard more or less harmful drugs, such as formaldehyde and boric, salicylic, and sulphurous acids.

All these changes, significant as they are, are of minor importance in comparison with the revolution that is potential in the growing scientific understanding of the nature of food and its sources. Said

Dr. Wendt at the 1947 convention of the American Meat Institute:

The meat animal is not the only one that can successfully make high-quality protein and vitamins out of crude feedstuffs. . . . The animal is of interest to you primarily as a converter of feedstuffs, most of which are not suitable for human food, into highly nutritious and palatable proteins and fats—a process which is not yet commercially possible in any other manner. Yet it remains true that you depend on a chemical process which is beyond your control and your knowledge. You make use of natural products which were not primarily intended by nature to benefit you. . . . Glance for a moment at another industry: cotton fiber was not developed by the cotton plant for man's sake but for its own reproduction. Fortuitously it served man's purposes well for thousands of years. But it was not ideal, and in recent years superior fibers have been made synthetically in enormous quantities. Rayon and nylon are made by the chemical industry exclusively for man's specific purposes, and it is no wonder they improve upon nature. . . . Shall we also duplicate the animal reaction some day? . . . It is no doubt a very complex process, but once understood it can be improved in the animal and perhaps later duplicated without using the living cell as the unit of our manufacturing process.[21]

The production of synthetic protein would transform the technology and economics of meat packing. Food-yeast, of a meatlike quality, is already being manufactured from molasses, lumber wastes, and wastes of the brewery industry. Vitamin B_{12}, connected with the animal protein factor, is produced from molds like penicillin. Scientists are making increasing discoveries in photosynthesis, with the object of creating synthetic chlorophyll, which would open unlimited possibilities for the factory production of foodstuffs.

Another transformation, more immediate, looms in the industry's technology for production. This involves new machines—more complex, productive, and labor-saving. They are different from the machines of the steam-power age, which mechanized simple manual operations. Our electrical technology and its newer electronic control instruments *mechanize all human senses:* sight, speech, smell, hearing, and touch. They mechanize memory and certain functions of the human intelligence itself. These electronic devices sort, count, inspect, reject, order, control; and they do it all with greater speed, accuracy,

[21] Proceedings, 42nd Annual Convention, American Meat Institute, *The National Provisioner,* September 13, 1947, pp. 108-109.

and judgment than the human senses can, tirelessly and endlessly. They move toward the final perfection of automatic production.

The "electric brain" of the new technology is most amazing in those calculating machines which open vast fields in mathematical work by speeding it up 100,000 times or more, performing in one hour problems a human being would need months or years to solve. These electronic calculators have arithmetical, memory, and control organs which function much like the human brain (without, of course, its initiative).

Their industrial use is growing. Electronic calculators, which ingest large numbers of variable factors and compound their net result, are used in airplane flying to figure out a plan of action ahead and to control signals to meet any situation—all in automatic fashion. Automatic telephone accounting machines, one of which will record all "bookkeeping" data for 25,000 calls on a single roll of paper, are in use. The United States Departments of Agriculture and Commerce have developed a rapid selector; it uses microfilms, properly coded, which are scanned by photoelectric eyes, and it will, in fifteen minutes, scan and select what is wanted by the research worker from, say, thirty years' issues of *Chemical Abstracts*. This selector can be coded for 10,000,000 subjects.[22]

Electronic devices increase automatic production. For example, one of the biggest manufacturing jobs is to inspect and reject defective products. Today practically all inspection, counting, and rejection is done by photoelectric cells—the "electric eye." Back in 1930, of 8,000,000 workers employed in manufactures, 1,000,000 were engaged in these monotonous, repetitive jobs.[23] Now electronic devices do the work more efficiently, accurately, and swiftly: the electric eye and the mechanical finger are superior to the human eye and finger. In

[22] A digression, but interesting: Prof. W. Leontief, of Harvard University, and the U.S. Navy are constructing an "electric brain" to calculate all the economic effects of any particular Navy procurement program. The possibilities of this idea are immense. It will make possible infinitely more and speedier calculations, make them available in hours or days, before economic conditions have changed. If and when the Leontief idea comes into general use, it will call for a new kind of mathematical economists—not the escapists that so many of them are today, playing abstract logical games instead of facing economic reality— but economists who will use mathematics to interpret the findings of "electric brains" and feed them problems, in order to understand the real economic world for purposes of policy and planning.

[23] C. C. Furnas, *The Next Hundred Years* (1938), pp. 207-210.

one plant of the American Can Company a machine introduced in 1949 checks 15,000 cans an hour and automatically discards those that are defective.[24] The Production and Marketing Administration of the Department of Agriculture perfected in 1949 an electronic scale that weighs livestock at public markets with high accuracy and speed; it automatically prints the weight, number, type of animal, name of the weigher and selling agency, and date and time of weighing. The scale was accurate to within five pounds on loads up to 32,000 pounds.

The technicians propose an automatic factory with few, if any, manual workers. While hardly any solid-material plants are as yet automatic, chemical plants are. In a modern sugar mill, for example, the sugar cane is dumped from trucks into grinders. Beyond that point, until the sugar appears in bags at the farther end of the plant, no worker touches any part of the process. The pulp from the ground cane moves on a conveyor to the basement, where automatically it feeds the fire that produces steam for the engine that operates the dynamo which generates the electric power to run the mill (with perhaps surplus electricity to sell). The juice moves from one vat to another and finally appears as sugar. A handful of technicians alone are needed to direct the automatic mechanism, with a sprinkling of manual workers.

What is emerging is a technology with which industries working on solid materials can also manufacture their products in a series of wholly automatic operations.

Electronic devices not only perform specific jobs but can make the whole production more automatic. The assembly line, or conveyor, may be used as an illustration. Despite intensive development of automatic machines, it is still necessary to use human workers for assembly. But electronic devices on a new type of line can do the work that human workers now do. For the workers' operations are all reducible to simple arm-and-hand motions, which can be performed by mechanical devices set in action at the appropriate time by an "electric eye" as the product (say, an automobile) moves on:

	1st	2nd	3rd	4th	Other	
Beginning	Stop	Stop	Stop	Stop	Stops	Completion
Chassis - - - - - - x - - - - - - x - - - - - x - - - - - - x - - - - - x x x - - - - - - Car

24 News story, *New York Times*, May 29, 1949.

At each stop the car will hit a beam of light which automatically stops it and sets a device in motion to perform an operation; another automatic operation happens with the next stop, and so on until the assembled car emerges. The assembly-line and fabricating units can be interconnected by electronic devices to make a wholly automatic plant, with virtually no need for manual workers (except maintenance workers). The theory and devices are available.

All manufacturing operations are reducible to a few basic functions. Standard machines, made to perform each function, can be connected with electronic control units which will all have standard connections. A machine for manufacturing a single part will be made up of many interconnected small units. The finished parts will move through an inspection unit, equipped with photoelectric cells or other detector devices, and defective parts will be rejected. Control systems transmit and direct the sequence and duration of operations. Hand-arm devices, which may be built for different purposes, have electric controls to move them with great speed and accuracy to do their particular work. The whole sequence of fabricating operations endlessly repeats itself as long as the plant managers want it to do so. An automatic factory where complete products are manufactured will be made up of a number of such units fabricating single parts, which flow on conveyors to subassembly units and from there to the final assembly machine. The heart of this machine is an endless belt of assembly jigs, fed and manipulated by hand-arm machines, with master controls to make everything happen in sequence. And the completed product drops on a conveyor belt to go through final inspection.[25]

The new technology, as it makes production completely automatic, will abolish the need for most of the manual workers now employed in industry. This tendency is not altogether new. From 1920 to 1940, for example, the number of industrial workers rose from 15,100,000 to 16,100,000, while the number of salaried employees rose from 8,300,000 to 12,770,000. More significant, the number of technical-managerial employees rose from 129,000 in 1870 to 2,000,000 in 1940: an increase of fifteen times compared with an increase of only five times in the number of industrial workers.[26]

[25] Article, "The Manless Factory," *Fortune*, December 1946, pp. 110-11.
[26] Lewis Corey, "The Middle Class," *Antioch Review*, Spring 1945, pp. 69, 76-77.

What will be left of the manual labor force in industry, as the automatic principle becomes wholly dominant, will be handfuls of highly skilled workers (e.g., electricians). These have been called "junior technicians" by Marion H. Hedges, former research director for the International Brotherhood of Electrical Workers.[27]

There is nothing in the suggestions for automatic plants that is not applicable to the meat industry, where a great many conveyors are used with human workers to operate them. Already an increasing number of new machines for packing plants combine several operations for automatic interconnected performance. The new technology, as it adapts itself to packing, will make operations even more automatic. So, too, will the use of new chemical processes and new types of products, among them frozen foods.

The new technological revolution will leave no industry and no process untouched. It will bring new foods with greater nutritional value and will promote human welfare. It can also bring displacement of labor and unemployment on a larger, more disastrous scale than the old technology did. This situation calls for union-management cooperation within the larger framework of progressive social policy.

[27] Every union ought to have a committee on technological change—including outside experts to guide it—to keep in touch with what the laboratories and industry are doing. Where new technical devices are introduced suddenly, without union awareness, they can create serious problems for union and workers. One union, the Brotherhood of Electrical Workers, foresaw early in World War II the tremendous use of electronics in industry; it realized that an electrician who knew nothing about electronics might be unable to get a job. The union started to teach its members enough about electronics so they could qualify for jobs on electronic equipment.

CHAPTER XI

PACKINGHOUSE UNIONISM: CONFLICT OR COOPERATION?

1. OPPOSITION TO UNIONISM

WHILE businessmen in general opposed unionism at its inception, the monopoly oligarchs in mass-production industries spearheaded the anti-union drive. The meat packers differed not one jot in their opposition to unions from other oligarchs, except that they were a bit worse than many of them. Let me give a few illustrations of the packers' bitter anti-union attitude.

In May 1886, a strike in the Chicago stockyards for the eight-hour day was successful. At the first chance, however, which came six months later, the packers repudiated the agreement.

Already the packers were using yellow-dog contracts, degrading devices which provided that workers, as one condition of employment, must sign an agreement not to join a union. Packers used the blacklist too, and all the well-known anti-union methods, including espionage and corruption, to prevent their workers from joining unions.

In the 1890's the big packers agreed among themselves not to recognize the meat workers' union. An early official of the Amalgamated Meat Cutters and Butcher Workmen tells the story: "While your secretary-treasurer desired an agreement from the company signed by them making the house a strictly union house, we were met with this objection—that an agreement existed among the big packers which made it impossible for them to sign an agreement of this kind.

275

We had to accept a verbal agreement. . . . Soon after the [verbal] settlement the company began to weed out union men." [1]

When the Federal Trade Commission investigated the packers in 1918–19 it found evidence in their files that proved they had undertaken organized anti-union activities. A letter from Swift & Company, Chicago, to its Denver plant reads as follows:

Answering: Want you to work closely with Hanson to prevent your house becoming organized, handling so as not to force a strike. Advise find cause other than being members of labor unions for dropping two men mentioned or other active members, and dispense with services as soon as practicable. Keep us fully posted.

Another letter to prove the anti-union attitude: On August 17, 1917, Louis F. Swift wrote to Edward Swift:

If it looks as though our Sioux City men are going out on strike, what would you think of telling them just before they go out the plant will be closed down permanently? This, to a certain extent, is a threat, something we have never done; but sometimes I'd like to try a thing once to see whether or not it will work.

Yet in 1918, while testifying in wage arbitration hearings, Louis Swift and Nelson Morris declared they were indifferent to labor unions. Morris and the packing workers' attorney, Frank P. Walsh, had this little exchange:

WALSH: You are aware that a number of your men joined the union? MORRIS: I don't know. I am not interested whether they are members of the union or not.

Yet the Morris company cooperated with other big packers in a common anti-labor policy. One letter found in the Swift files by the Federal Trade Commission, written by Wilson & Company's local manager in Topeka, Kansas (February 28, 1917), stated: "Copies to F. O. Cunningham, Armour; J. M. Rich, Swift; Mr. Hale, Cudahy; Mr. Charles, Morris." The letter reported: "Female Labor Bill very desirable not to have any limit in hours per day or per week. If you have to compromise, offer nine hours a day, total fifty hours per week, but do not permit fixed time for beginning or ending day. Defeat whole measure if possible."

[1] Amalgamated Meat Cutters, *Report of Proceedings, 2nd Convention,* 1899, p. 27.

This cooperation in opposing labor legislation broadened to include opposition to unionism. A letter from "Mr. Charles, Morris" (December 5, 1917) said:

Armour's people called up today and stated they understood that there was some trouble with the branch house employees, that you had a meeting with Kennedy [an Amalgamated official], and they felt we would get better results if we all worked together. We are working with the other packers here on labor matters, and I think it would be better for us to work with them in the East and not try to arrive at any individual settlement.

The coercive methods used to fight the Amalgamated union are revealed in a letter written by W. B. Traynor, "Swift's right hand confidential man in Chicago," to Louis F. Swift (August 2, 1917):

Armour & Company and ourselves have been in the same position in this matter and have worked together. We got word on July 13 that the butchers of the Denver plant were being organized and that they would make a demand for guaranteed eight-hour day at the ten-hour wages. It was agreed by both firms [Armour and Swift] that on Monday morning, July 16th, we would reduce the killing gang 25 per cent. This was done, and in making the cut we were careful to drop not only the most active agitators, but also some men who are not identified with the union movement.

Another letter, from South Omaha, tells an interesting story. It quotes a representative of the Employers Association who told the letter writer that they had the biggest newspaper in Kansas City, Missouri, on their side, for they had threatened to withdraw all their advertising if the paper did not publish things "their way." In addition, they had "put up" $12,000 with the city's chief of police, so if there was any trouble the police "would know what to do."

Still another Swift company letter (copies to E. F. Swift and C. H. Swift), November 14, 1917, tells of the writer's visit in Pueblo, Colorado, to officers of the Armour company with "J. P. Murphy of the Coffin Packing Company accompanying." They discussed a local packing plant, 100 per cent union, whose workers were asking an eight-hour day. To head off the demand they called upon the Fuel Administrator of Colorado, John Stearns (who had been at the head of the local business groups which "covered up" the Ludlow massacre where striking miners, evicted from company homes and living in a tent colony, were fired upon with machine guns and muskets and their tents set afire; eleven women and children were killed). Administrator Stearns, acting upon the behest of his packer friends, commandeered twenty-five workers as "food conservators" and ordered them into the union plant to "conserve" the meat. "That act had a sobering effect on the union officials." The letter writer suggested it might be "a good idea" to commandeer all workers and so end strikes. But Henry Veeder, confidential attorney for the Swift company, did not agree. He wrote to Louis F. Swift: "In reference to the employment of food conservators under the Colorado State Food law . . . it is my opinion that the employment of state officials should be held in reserve as a last resort and that we should not be in a hurry to place either state or federal officials in our plants." [2]

When in 1920–21 postwar reaction and factional disputes undermined the Amalgamated, the Big Five (Swift, Armour, Morris, Wilson, and Cudahy) seized the opportunity to set up company unions called "Employee Conference Boards." They were composed of twelve "employee representatives" *approved by management,* and twelve company representatives. All decisions required a unanimous vote; it meant nothing if all twelve "employee representatives" were agreed. Moreover, all decisions needed final approval by the plant manager, and there was no appeal to outside arbitration. The boards were used to engineer the wage reductions that provoked the 1921 strike.

The Amalgamated said the Employee Conference Boards set up by the Big Five were "bogus," the result of a "despotic paternalism of unfair, reactionary and greedy employers." Nor were these merely partisan sentiments of the union. "The fact that 'company unions' are owned and controlled by the packers," said the National Catholic Welfare Council, "is shown by the acceptance of wage reductions when the employees were not making a decent living." [3]

In their struggle against unionism the monopoly packers went in for all the tricks of the "welfare capitalism" which flourished in the 1920's. They kept company unions going until enactment of the Na-

[2] All letters are from the proceedings of the FTC investigation of the packing industry. They were used by the union's attorney in the 1918 arbitration proceedings. See *Over the Top at the Yards, The Arguments of Frank P. Walsh in the Stockyards Arbitration Hearing and the Award of U.S. Administrator Samuel Alschuler* (published in 1918 by the Chicago Labor News), pp. 63-74.
[3] Amalgamated Meat Cutters, *Report of Proceedings, 12th General Convention,* 1926, pp. 58-59.

tional Labor Relations Act in 1935. Efforts were made to keep them going after the NLRB began to operate; four plants of Wilson & Company, for example, were found guilty by the NLRB of trying to force company unions on the workers, and, on appeal, the courts in all cases decided against Wilson.

This ruthless opposition by the packers has not stopped unionism, but it has created a mood of warfare within which union-management cooperation cannot effectively work. On the difficulties of the Amalgamated Meat Cutters and Butcher Workmen, one scholarly writer had this to say in 1932:

> Sporadic strikes gave evidence of workers' resistance but these yielded only unimportant gains, especially in job security. Not even the notable evidences of solidarity in the bitter strikes of 1886, 1894, 1904, and 1921 brought significant results. . . . Union organization has made little headway, save temporarily in periods of strike agitation. The large packer employers have steadily refused to recognize or deal with the unions directly.[4]

Since 1933 unionism has grown in the packing industry. But the packers are not entirely reconciled. They still refuse to accept unionism unreservedly as a part of the democratic way of life and as an organizational economic necessity of industry. The opposition is not absolute, however, and unionism makes its way. A wider acceptance of collective bargaining and of union-management cooperation is evident in American industry, in meat packing as elsewhere. There are still managements, and elements within otherwise friendly managements, however, that either refuse to accept unions or whose acceptance is conditional until the first opportunity arises to destroy them.

Armour, Swift, Wilson, and Cudahy, as late as 1945, gave illustrations of how management, compelled to recognize the union and to bargain collectively with it, nevertheless does so grudgingly. For a long time the Amalgamated made efforts to get from the packers, for local unions certified as bargaining agents by the NLRB, complete lists of job specifications, descriptions, and rates. The union wanted the lists in order to bargain intelligently, particularly on wage inequities in plants. Existing wage structures in Big Four plants are arbitrary, argued the Amalgamated; job requirements never are made

---

[4] Myron W. Watkins, "Meat Packing and Slaughtering—Social Aspects," *Encyclopedia of the Social Sciences* (1933), vol. X, p. 261.

known either to workers or to their union; wage rates are fixed without regard to skills and the kind of work done; the entire wage policy, set without consultation with the union, multiplies intra-plant inequities in earnings.

The managements refused this constructive request for cooperation on a matter of mutual interest.[5] Only compulsion worked. In December 1944 the National War Labor Board decided for the Amalgamated and ordered each of the four companies to furnish the union, within fifteen days of the order, "a copy of the existing wage rate schedules in each plant, department by department, including job classifications, job descriptions, and existing job requirements, wage rates and incentive provisions." [6]

For a hundred years employers have met unions with the argument that they were un-American or that their demands would wreck American industry. American industry has not been wrecked; on the contrary, it has grown beyond all imagining. And one important element in the tremendous growth of American industry has been the high wages paid to American labor; by increasing mass consumer purchasing power, these wages provided the needed mass markets for mass production, while compelling management to speed up introduction of labor-saving devices for more productive efficiency and lower costs. For these developments, the American people owe a debt of gratitude to workers and their unions. The high level of American wages, in comparison with those of all other nations, is one major support of the economic might of the United States, whose industrial producing power is as great as that of all the world's other nations put together.

In the 1830's American wage levels were higher than were those in Europe—and they had been since Colonial times. These comparatively high wages forced American industrial capitalists to promote labor-saving devices in order to lower unit labor costs. By the 1870's the United States was ahead of all nations in labor-saving work, with a resulting greater output of goods and services at lower costs and lower prices for the consumer.

In the final analysis, of course, higher wages and shorter hours

---

[5] Another approach to collective bargaining is that illustrated in 1947 by the United States Steel Corporation and the United Steelworkers of America, CIO, in which management and union cooperated on making up job classifications.

[6] News story, *The Butcher Workman*, January 1945, p. 1.

have come from increasing technical-managerial efficiency and productivity. But higher wages and shorter working hours have not come without opposition from employers, and this has been especially true in the packing industry. They have not come without workers and their unions being forced to fight for a legitimate share of economic progress.

Unions, moreover, have been a major force in broadening and deepening American democracy. It is not economic motivations alone that animate workers when they join unions. As important, and perhaps more important, are the human-psychological motives. Workers want human dignity on the job, the right to speak up and to confer through collective bargaining on the conditions under which they are to work. A worker wants the right to bring up grievances without being answered by some burly foreman, perhaps, spitting tobacco juice in his eye and telling him: "If you don't like it, get your time and get the hell out of here!" The workers want a sense of human dignity as workers and as citizens of industry.

2. THE AMALGAMATED: I—A BIT OF HISTORY

After the Amalgamated Meat Cutters and Butcher Workmen of North America began operations in 1897, chartered by the American Federation of Labor, it met with many severe setbacks and reverses, worse than any experienced by most American unions. Nevertheless, the Amalgamated finally emerged as a truly effective organization.

Since the 1930's it has become a body of nearly 200,000 members. Within it are not only packinghouse workers but retail butchers, sheep shearers, and fish workers; workers in canneries, creameries, butter-and-egg and poultry plants; and workers in sausage factories. In its own economic framework, the Amalgamated is an industrial union which organizes workers in the production of meat products from the stages of slaughtering and processing up to their distribution in retail stores.

A measure of craft organization among cattle, sheep, and hog butchers, sausage makers and meat cutters preceded organization of the Amalgamated. Some of these craft unions existed as early as 1870, and later they joined the Knights of Labor. Their efforts at first were intended primarily to preserve their skills and jobs as butcher craftsmen against industrialization; this had been the policy

of earlier union workers in the 1830's. But industrialization swept onward, and butcher workers quickly gave up their primitive objectives.

On May 1, 1886, a national strike of 400,000 workers broke out for
an eight-hour day in answer to a call issued by the Federation of
Organized Trades and Labor Unions (later the American Federation of Labor). The Knights of Labor meat unions in Kansas City
joined the strike, which quickly spread to the Chicago stockyard
workers. The packinghouse unions won their strike, got an eight-
hour day without a pay reduction. Then, in the summer, Armour
and Swift reneged on their agreement and reintroduced the ten-
hour day; in November the workers went on strike, but the effort
collapsed when Terence Powderly, Grand Master Workman of the
Knights, ordered it called off.

But the unions came up again in 1894, this time in a sympathetic
strike that also involved the issue of union recognition in packing.
The Pullman workers' strike, led by Eugene V. Debs and the National Railway Union, was being broken by use of the injunction
and federal troops. Debs issued a call for sympathetic strikes. The
packinghouse workers answered the call with an impressive demon-
stration of solidarity—but again they met with defeat.

Butcher unions in the Knights of Labor formed four separate
organizations: cattle and sheep butchers, hog butchers, sausage
makers, and meat cutters. As a result of the 1894 experience they decided to amalgamate into a national organization. In July 1896
eleven representatives of these unions from seven cities (including
New York City, Chicago, and Kansas City, Missouri) met in Nash-
ville, Tennessee, to form a new organization. One year later, in 1897,
they were granted a charter by the AFL as the Amalgamated Meat
Cutters and Butcher Workmen of North America, an industrial
union with jurisdiction over all meat workers from laborers in packinghouses to butchers in retail stores.

The new organization's problems were immense. Already by 1897
meat packing was a highly industrial activity dominated by five
giant corporations—the same corporations that kept on being dominant through the first half of the next century. Like other monopoly barons of the age, the big packers brooked no independence
from labor. They threw everything in the anti-union book at their
workers to prevent formation of unions.

MICHAEL DONNELLY
President, 1898–1905

DENNIS LANE
Secretary-Treasurer, 1917–42

EARL W. JIMERSON
President

PATRICK E. GORMAN
Secretary-Treasurer

SOME AMALGAMATED OFFICERS, PAST AND PRESENT

PHILIP D. ARMOUR

GUSTAVUS F. SWIFT

MICHAEL CUDAHY

NELSON MORRIS

THOMAS E. WILSON

BIG PACKERS IN THE 1900's

As great a difficulty, if not greater, lay in the composition of the labor force in packinghouses; there were masses of unskilled workers, most of them immigrants. These immigrants came from the old countries with national and religious animosities bred of generations of hatred and war, which the packers deliberately exploited to keep the workers disunited and away from unions. Finally, another difficulty for union organization presented itself in the packing industry's tremendous labor turnover.

Under these conditions the work of organization could not proceed in a methodical manner with enduring results. It was hard to arouse workers to take an interest in the union except when indignation flared up against particular abuses of managerial power. As defeat came the Amalgamated dwindled in membership and power, but not in spirit.

Organizational difficulties appeared clearly in the 1904 strike, an uprising that ended in defeat, after which the union broke apart. Wages remained stationary, as has been noted, until pressure of wartime living costs in 1916 compelled the big packers, in self-defense, to grant small increases.

The First World War gave workers and the Amalgamated an opportunity for organization; the government's policy encouraged formation of unions. Moreover, the war, as a struggle against tyranny to make the world safe for democracy, aroused a liberal crusading spirit in the country and helped labor organization. Unions grew rapidly.

The 1917 convention of the Amalgamated convened in July, after American entry into the war. Many reports of progress were heard by the delegates. A voluntary assessment of 25 cents per month for four months had been levied in the fall of 1916. The beginnings of a shop steward movement were reported. Organization, actively aided by the AFL, which supplied six or seven organizers, had brought increasing results. Wages had gone up. A "district council" plan of organization had proved successful in several cities. The national office of the Amalgamated was out of debt. Against this background the factional disputes ended in a determination to use existing favorable conditions to build the union.

One dispute involved an independent union in New York City, the Brotherhood of Butcher Workmen, which had seceded from the

Amalgamated but sent delegates to the convention to ask for re-admission. Representatives of the Brotherhood and the Amalgamated president, John F. Hart, had been brought together for unity nego-tiations by Samuel Gompers and the AFL Executive Council. But some delegates were suspicious of the move. Only after a protracted, often bitter debate—Hart was accused of "underhanded negotiations" —was the Brotherhood admitted. A number of delegates opposed admission because they felt the Brotherhood's president, John Ken-nedy, had come to the convention only in an effort to become Amal-gamated president, but he surprised them by nominating the in-cumbent, Hart, who was elected.[7]

Another factional dispute that ended in harmony concerned Homer D. Call, secretary-treasurer since 1897. The story is thus told by John J. Walsh, who was at the convention (he later became an Amalgamated vice-president):

Secretary Call had made quite a name for himself, not only in the labor movement but in the political field as well. He was very close to most of the Executive Council of the American Federation of Labor, including President Gompers. In politics, he climbed the ladder of success until he was made Treasurer of the Empire State of New York. There were many delegates who felt that politics and the International Union did not mix. Some even felt that Secretary Call was satisfied with the International Union at its then numerical strength. This feeling was engendered out of the belief that with new members coming in by the thousands, Homer Call's position as International secretary-treasurer would be none too secure. The desire of all delegates, however, was that no one should be allowed to stop the progress of the organization. Call was now sixty-seven; many felt that he should step out and let a younger man in. Call, however, was sincere, and seeming to sense what was in the making, he sent a telegram to the International Convention that because of ill-ness he would be unable to attend.

The convention, upon motion of Earl W. Jimerson and several other delegates, elected Dennis Lane as secretary-treasurer.[8]

By early 1919 the Amalgamated had 100,000 members, largely a result of benefits gained for workers by its successful fight in 1918

[7] Amalgamated Meat Cutters, *Report of Proceedings, 9th General Convention,* 1917, pp. 13-16, 123.

[8] Amalgamated Meat Cutters, *Proceedings, 9th General Convention,* p. 131. A motion to increase the secretary-treasurer's salary was withdrawn because of Lane's opposition.

for higher wages and better working conditions. When the big packers refused the union demands, the issue went to arbitration before
Federal Judge Samuel Alschuler, whom President Woodrow Wilson
had appointed Administrator for the meat industry to settle disputes. He granted the packinghouse workers a basic eight-hour day
to replace the ten-hour day, substantial raises in wage rates, including time-and-a-half for overtime, and equal pay for men and women
doing the same class of work. Independent packers followed this
pattern in agreements with their workers. Of the results of this
arbitration *The Butcher Workman* said: "The Amalgamated has
gained every weighty point in the recent struggle for urgent relief
from intolerable conditions for the welfare of 100,000 packinghouse
workers." [9]

After the 1918 arbitration victory another raise of $3.20 a week
came in 1919; but the union felt that this raise was not commen-
surate with the sharp inflationary rise in living costs.

Meanwhile the Amalgamated membership grew beyond 100,000.
This was a dramatic comeback after fifteen years of what amounted
to no organization. For after the 1904 defeat union members had
been discriminated against and blacklisted, it will be recalled, and
the union was virtually forced underground.

Within the Amalgamated's new upsurge, however, forces were at
work that brought it down again. The union's quick growth over-
whelmed the handful of old seasoned members. Dissension began
to grow. Organized factional groups became clamorous, among
them "radical" politicians who attempted to use the Amalgamated
for outside doctrinaire purposes.

The Stockyards Labor Council, set up by the Chicago Federation
of Labor, AFL, which in 1917–18 had helped organization among
the packinghouse workers, became a source of intrigue, factionalism, and disruption. For a time its secretary was William Z. Foster,
who several years later became a Communist. Small but well-
organized and vocal "radical" elements in the Council tried to use
it to shunt aside the Amalgamated, which fought back. The Amalgamated set up a council of its own to concentrate on trade-union
organization. This move called forth vicious attacks from factional
elements in the Stockyards Labor Council, now becoming a rump
organization. One leaflet issued in its name said:

[9] Editorial, *The Butcher Workman*, April 1918, p. 1.

Beware of the dual Council organized for the purpose of breaking up your organization. Dennis Lane, International Secretary-Treasurer of the Amalgamated Meat Cutters and Butcher Workmen and others has [sic] notified Judge Alschuler not to recognize your demands for an increase in wages. President John Hart [of the Amalgamated] and Dennis Lane helped to organize the Stockyards Labor Council, now they want to break it up. They will do the same with their new Council, if it does not suit them. Do not be fooled by them, they never did anything for the stockyards workers and they never will.

Signs of factionalism appeared at the 1920 convention. Among the 208 resolutions, was one which demanded that the Amalgamated favor organization of a farmer-labor party, for, said its sponsor, "unless labor in this country immediately gets control of the public offices, economic organization will be practically worthless." A "very large" majority defeated the resolution. Another delegate made a general attack upon the national organizers and their work. "I have information in my possession," he said, "to show that certain organizers have been paid to disorganize some of our local unions." Answered President Hart: "Let me say to the delegate from New York City that he is the last man who ought to try to accuse anybody of disorganizing. There is a difference in being a disorganizer by mistake and a disorganizer by design, and I am prepared to show, if necessary, that there was work of disorganization in our ranks by design."

A demand was raised for the retirement on half pay of President Hart, who said in his report: "I am not a candidate for any office." Whereupon a delegate, Patrick E. Gorman, spoke up: "I believe there was a cold chill, a shudder running over each and every delegate when he heard the words, 'I am not a candidate.' I want to say to you that John Hart is really the father of this movement. I want to say to you that as he was drafted at the 1910 convention, so he will be drafted at the 1920 convention." Hart was re-elected president without a dissenting vote; Gorman became general vice-president.[10] But, aware of the terrific factional struggle ahead, Hart resigned from the presidency in September 1920.

[10] Amalgamated Meat Cutters, *Proceedings . . . 9th Convention*, pp. 91, 97, 134-35. President Hart, in a mood of premonition, saw disaster ahead; he said in his report (p. 89): "At times I see the same handwriting [the union's collapse in 1904] on the wall. I see the same rock ahead of us that wrecked us at that time. Let us in this convention try and avoid a recurrence of the past."

Intrigues, inexperience and incompetence, a bit of dishonesty here and there—all these wracked the union and fed the flames of factional struggle. The big packers used undercover agents to keep these flames burning. Factionalism broke out into secession and the Amalgamated split into several competing groups.

A weakened union (financial resources reported to the 1920 convention were $4112 in cash) had to meet a deliberate offensive of the packers, who used the 1920–21 depression to smash the union. All evidence indicates that the big packers wanted a fight. On their own initiative, in March 1919, the Big Five had asked the United States Secretary of Labor to continue for another year the wartime arbitration agreement. They gave as their reason "a desire for peace in the industry during the reconstruction period." The Amalgamated accepted. But early in 1920 the packers tried to withdraw from the agreement; only with difficulty were they persuaded by the Secretary of Labor to abide by it until its expiration on September 15, 1921. As a condition of this, however, the packers made their employees accept a 12½ per cent reduction in wages. In July 1921 the Big Five asked the arbitrator, Judge Alschuler, to grant another wage cut of 5 cents an hour. He refused.

Upon expiration of the arbitration agreement the Amalgamated asked for negotiation of its demands for continuation of prevailing wage scales and working conditions, with no changes to be made except by mutual agreement or arbitration. The Big Five refused to negotiate or arbitrate; and, on November 19, 1921, they announced another wage reduction, to take effect within a week, in the hourly rates of unskilled workers (a large number of the industry's employees) from 45 cents to 37½ cents. Semi-skilled workers' hourly rates were cut 5 cents and skilled workers' 3 cents. Again the Amalgamated asked for a conference to negotiate, and again it met with refusal.

Meanwhile the company unions, the "Employee Conference Boards," approved the wage reductions. Upon referendum the Amalgamated had decided, by 93 per cent, to strike if the packers refused to negotiate, and in December the plants were shut down by striking workers.

The Amalgamated made just two demands: abrogation of wage reductions and submission of the dispute to arbitration. At no point during the strike did the packers make any move to settle the dispute by accepting the union's wage proposal or offering to arbitrate. Trade unions supported the strike on the issue, as expressed in a letter to its affiliates by the Illinois State Federation of Labor, of "preventing a reduction in wages and of asserting the right to organize and maintain trade unions."

Despite factionalism and turmoil within the union, and the prevailing unemployment, workers responded to the strike call in overwhelming numbers. More than 100,000 men and women went on strike in Chicago and other packing centers. They remained on strike for over two months. They picketed in the midst of freezing weather; they held demonstrations despite police efforts to deprive them of this constitutional right. Violence came; eight Amalgamated officials were killed. The suffering of most of the workers was extreme, since the earnings of most of them were too small for savings. Hence soup kitchens were established to provide some warm food for the strikers. Many of them were evicted from their homes, and in some towns the evictions were so great that tent colonies were set up.

Again the packers imported Negroes as strikebreakers. The leader of an organization known as the American Negro Protective League (who, according to President Fitzpatrick of the Chicago Federation of Labor, was an agent of the Big Five, and was later alleged in an investigation of authorities of the State of Illinois to have had "close relations" with the packers) carried on a disruptive campaign, issuing leaflets which screamed, "Beware of the Stockyards Union! All colored men—do not join the Union, save your jobs."

But this campaign was not altogether successful. "The use of the Negro as a strikebreaker seems to have led the white unionists to forget that the Negro also played his part in the conflict as a striker. 'Our union workmen,' said the *Chicago Defender*, the largest Negro paper in the country, 'obeyed the dictum of their superior union officials and did exactly what their white brothers did—struck.' " [11]

Race riots, in which one Negro was killed, flared up, and Packingtown became an armed camp occupied by 2000 policemen. Although the union had a short time earlier made successful efforts to prevent race riots, the situation finally got beyond its control; when riots came they were blamed upon the union. So, after two months, the strike ended in complete defeat. Torn apart by the strike's failure,

[11] Sterling D. Spero and Abram L. Harris, *The Black Worker*, pp. 276-81.

by renewed, more bitter factionalism, and by secession, the Amalgamated now shrank to its prewar stature of a remnant-union.[12]

It is instructive to recall the violent fluctuations in Amalgamated membership. They were startling: from a membership of 75,000 in 1904 down to 7500 members in 1916 and up to 100,000 or more in 1919; after the 1921 strike a drop in membership to 5000. It is true that the anti-union offensive of employers in 1920–21 brought many other unions down; the AFL lost several million members, virtually all the new members it had gained in the war. But there were

[12] Caught within the factional disputes was Dennis Lane, secretary-treasurer, who served until his death in 1942. All men make mistakes, and Lane made them too. But he clung to the union with indomitable spirit; when he died the Amalgamated paid tribute to his "continuous, most useful and constructive service for twenty-five years in rebuilding of the weakened structure of the Amalgamated." It is suggestive of the character of certain types of people in the labor movement that Stanley Nowak wrote the following about Lane and the Amalgamated ("Early Unionism in Meat Packing," *The Packinghouse Worker*, organ of United Packinghouse Workers of America, CIO, October 3, 1947, p. 7): ". . . the sabotage of the progressive movement by officials of the old craft union, especially Dennis Lane of the Amalgamated. Lane resented new blood in the organization. He, and other officials of the union, did nothing to organize the remaining potential membership of the industry. [In the 1921 strike] the corrupt leadership threw in a sponge and called the strike off against the desires of the strikers. The Amalgamated Meat Cutters and Butcher Workmen became again a half-dead craft union. The old leaders saved their own jobs at the expense of the workers." This is the sort of adverse made-to-pattern criticism by "radical" intellectuals which has been a demoralizing factor in American labor. Nowak's ideological animus appears in the way he drags in praise of William Z. Foster and Jack Johnstone, who, a year or two after the 1921 strike, became active Communists. And Foster himself spewed venom, especially in his book, *Misleaders of Labor* (1927), where he vigorously attacked the Amalgamated officials (as he did many outstanding labor leaders): "The great armies of workers in the packing industry have paid a high price for the treason and venality of their leaders. . . . The half-dead Amalgamated Meat Cutters and Butcher Workmen did nothing for them. Led by such Gompersites as Dennis Lane, who is reputed to be heavily interested financially in the packing business, [it] is incapable as well as unwilling to tackle the great packing industry" (pp. 159–60). That was in the 1920's and early 1930's, the period of "revolutionary" dual unionism. Then, from 1933 to 1945, the "popular front" and war period, when Russia pursued a conciliatory policy, Foster and his Communists cultivated and praised, often nauseatingly, the men he had called "misleaders" (including John L. Lewis). After 1945, the Soviet Union abandoned conciliation and ordered its Communist agents in all countries to "make trouble" in order to weaken the world's opposition to Russia's forcible expansion. Foster and his comrades obeyed the orders, and all union leaders, except those who were Communists or willing to play their conspiratorial game, were again denounced as misleaders.

specific factors in the Amalgamated case, of which I want to emphasize three:

1. *The economic and racial composition of packinghouse workers made it heartbreakingly difficult to organize them.* I have already mentioned these conditions, but they call for emphasis. Seasonal unemployment and an immense labor turnover meant continuous change in the plant workers and in union membership. And the large number of immigrants and Negroes gave anti-union managements a chance to stir up racial and national prejudices to keep the workers divided.

2. *While five (later four) monopoly giants dominated half of the packing industry, the other half was composed of small establishments, owned mainly by single proprietors employing only a few workers.* These were difficult to organize because of their large numbers and because, in addition, the small enterprisers were afraid to go against the big packers' anti-unionism. This situation changed with the appearance of larger independents.

3. *There were not enough skilled workers in packing to form powerful craft unions, while the Amalgamated's industrial unionism came a bit too early.* Only industrial unionism, which ignores distinctions of skills and crafts, met the needs of organization among packinghouse workers, with their large numbers of unskilled laborers. But the industrial union idea (it was tried by one or two other unions) did not take hold in the early twentieth century; only craft unions, by and large, flourished.

An industry comparable with meat packing, in the difficulties it offered for union organization, is the steel industry. Steel also experienced great and bitter labor-management struggles, from the Homestead strike of 1893 to the general strike of 1919, all of them defeats. It was not until the organization of the United Steelworkers, CIO, after 1935, that unionism established itself in steel. The Amalgamated in meat packing did somewhat better; at least it survived from 1897 on.

The 1920's began, for the Amalgamated, with a broken union and the packers on the offensive, with internal rancors, demoralization, and despair for the remnant-union to overcome. Moreover, with the upsurge of prosperity, "welfare capitalism" and a postwar mood of "Let us alone, the gin is cooking in the bathtub," labor's militant spirit drooped. Most unions went in for "business unionism." But only big, entrenched unions with large memberships and treasuries could practice that kind of unionism. The Amalgamated had neither the membership nor the money.

Yet the union overcame its worst disaster, slowly recovered from factional disputes, and knit the organization together again. It did this with little money, a debt that piled up, and, for a time, no payment of members' death benefits. The Amalgamated revived, with its officers underpaid, or, in many local unions, not paid at all.

After the 1921 collapse Lane and Gorman began a comeback drive sparked by a three-point program:

1. Revival of the Amalgamated's determination to increase its membership and improve the union's standing.

2. Rigorous enforcement of the Amalgamated's union principles, and uncompromising work to achieve them.

3. Cultivation of satisfactory employer-employee relations, which implied a friendly, not belligerent, approach to employers:

It must be said, in fairness to many employers, that they favored the working out of some plan with our union that would eventually stimulate peace in the industry and lessen the danger of strikes. There had been a series of strikes not approved by the International Union. . . . The idea of friendly contacts was pounded into the Executive Board by Lane and Gorman. Bad feeling had to be eliminated. Confidence had to be restored. No strike sanction was to be granted where there was the slightest possibility of settling the dispute, and strikers engaged in "outlaw" work stoppages would have to be penalized. Much time was consumed arranging dinner dates with employers in all sections of the country; the whole idea being that if an organizer could sell himself to the employer, he could at the same time sell the organization. Promises had to be made that any agreement entered into would be carried out in good faith both in letter and in spirit. Arbitration or conciliation was promised in the event a controversy became acute. . . . To some of us it seemed asinine that a bad employer could, with proper diplomacy, be made overnight into a good and friendly employer. Nevertheless, the program of contact continued. . . . When depression came in 1929–30 letters were written to employers, and particularly to those who had agreements with our organization, that the Amalgamated had "a deep interest in the successful operation of their business and wanted to contribute every aid possible." In some places our members took a reduction in pay in order to salvage the business of a friendly employer. That it was appreciated will be realized because, during the worst of it all, few Amalgamated members were locked out and few engaged in strikes.[13]

One major task was to bring seceding local unions back into the Amalgamated. The spirit of secession had been fed by factionalism, misunderstanding, and defeat. To get these unions back would give the Amalgamated needed strength to forge ahead.

At the 1926 convention Earl W. Jimerson, vice-president, reported on his efforts in a local union to raise dues so that the overworked secretary could get two assistants to carry on the local's work. The report of Dennis Lane, secretary-treasurer, showed a total balance on hand of only $8730.23. International officers, among them two vice-presidents, for long periods were compelled to work only two days a week for a salary of $20; not a single vice-president had drawn a full week's salary in over four years. The General Executive Board recommended raising "the per capita tax to the International to at least $1 per month" to provide money for organizing work.

"To go among the unorganized of our trade and preach the gospel of trade unionism," said the Board, "requires men to do the talking and money to provide for the men appointed to the task." The Amalgamated looked ahead, planning for organizational drives and, in addition, a union pension fund.[14]

In his report to the same 1926 convention Patrick E. Gorman, who had become the union's president, said:

We meet with prospects brighter for a better organization than in any other convention I have attended. No longer are we menaced by established secession which retards the real progress of a labor union, perhaps more than the combined opposition of unfair employers. Secession in our organization now belongs to the past. It has been eliminated by reasoning rather than by force; by fair play rather than by deception. . . . We, in this convention, must be the sculptors of our own existence. The goal we set is the model by which we work. We cannot remodel the past; but the future is ours to anticipate."

As the Amalgamated in the 1920's rebuilt the union it carried on activities on a larger front, too. When the Kansas legislature enacted

[13] T. J. Lloyd, "Fourth Golden Decade," *The Butcher Workman*, October 1948, pp. 3-4.
[14] Amalgamated Meat Cutters, *Report of Proceedings, 12th General Convention*, 1926, pp. 7, 35, 38, 70.

a compulsory arbitration no-strike law, the Amalgamated carried the issue to the Supreme Court, which declared the law unconstitutional. The Amalgamated was active in the campaign to secure freedom for Tom Mooney, who had been convicted in a mood of war hysteria; it adopted a resolution at the 1926 convention that called for granting a new trial to Bartolomeo Vanzetti and Nicola Sacco, two Massachusetts anarchists convicted of a murder they did not commit and later executed despite world protests.

As it reorganized, the Amalgamated responded increasingly to issues of progressive social policy.

Yet by 1930, according to Dennis Lane's report to that year's convention, the Amalgamated membership was only 13,000. The union entered the depression of the 1930's still hardly a union in membership, but with factional wounds all healed and a new spirit of cooperative action. After calling attention to the depression, whose worst economic disasters were still to come, President Gorman told the 1930 convention:

> For four years there has been no discontent manifested with the conduct of International Union affairs, and because of this harmony we have, so to speak, no independent or seceding unions. The Butte, Montana, organization, for so many years an independent association, is now an integral unit of the International Union; the California State Federation of Butcher Workmen is now solidified from one end of the "Golden State" to the other, and this unity is reflecting itself in Southern California where, for the past year, there has been as much accomplished as in the preceding three years. . . . This unity and cooperation makes it possible to meet under strikingly different circumstances than those under which we met in 1926. We are now out of debt, death claims are now being paid, the International can give full time and support to organizers in the field.[15]

As the depression slowdown of industry ground out its increasing millions of unemployed, the unions everywhere were weakened; their members were out of jobs and their revenues became driblets. The Amalgamated was among the unions worst hit. Its income from a small membership became still smaller, and again it had to borrow money to carry on.

Then came the New Deal, a joint product of depression and of

[15] Amalgamated Meat Cutters, *Synopsis of Proceedings, 13th General Convention*, 1930, p. 6.

cooperation for liberal politics among progressive workers, farmers, and middle class. Millions of unorganized workers came into unions, old and new. The Amalgamated, along with other labor organizations, profited by the prohibition of unfair labor practices, of employer refusal to bargain collectively, and of company unions, incorporated in Section 7A of the National Industrial Recovery Act (NIRA); and by the representation it gave union labor in the National Recovery Administration (NRA). The union took advantage of the same provisions in the National Labor Relations Act, which set up the NLRB after NIRA was declared unconstitutional.

The 1940 Amalgamated convention heard substantial progress reports: organizations among the Big Four and, especially, among independent packers. Kingan & Company, for example, employing approximately 6000 workers, had become 100 per cent organized. Progress, too, was made among retail butchers. It was clear that unionism had come to stay in the meat industry.

For the first time at an Amalgamated convention there were no complaints of insufficient finances to carry on organization work. On one new problem the Committee on the Shorter Work Day reported:

The Fair Labor Standards Act [Wage and Hour Law] of 1938 is, we believe, one of the greatest boons to the progress of that part of our industry engaged in interstate commerce. All members of our International Union should regard as their special business combating of all efforts to destroy or weaken in any way the safeguards provided by this law. . . . While we hail this advent of the 40-hour week [which in the packing industry went into effect in October 1940], we wish to point out that inasmuch as most of our workers in the packinghouse industry are paid by the hour, it is important that we battle to prevent this from becoming a cut in weekly earnings. . . . Unfortunately the Wage and Hour Law does not affect our retail members, as they are not engaged in interstate commerce. We urge our locals to work for State labor standards acts, to redouble efforts to shorten store hours, and to discourage the stagger system.[16]

Amalgamated gains were not, however, an NLRB handout, useful as were the mechanisms of elections for certification as bargaining agent and the prohibition, as illegal, of employers' using the old

[16] Amalgamated Meat Cutters, *Synopsis of Proceedings, 15th General Convention,* 1940, pp. 176-77.

ruthless means to prevent union organization. It took working and thinking, on the local and international levels, and the sacrifices of going on strike in a number of cases.

Among the struggles was a two-year strike in the Sioux Falls, South Dakota, plant of John Morrell & Company, an independent packer. The Amalgamated had organized the plant in 1934 and a number of disputes followed, culminating in 1935 when the workers made a protest against the layoff of 108 employees. This protest took the form of a sitdown strike, that is, the workers stayed in the plant but without working. Within one day the governor sent troops to occupy the plant and proclaim martial law. A local paper reported this interview with Sam Tweedel, the local union's business agent (later an International vice-president):

TWEEDEL: Our plan is to stand pat until the company sees fit to do collective bargaining with us. However, if we're forced out, of course we'll have to leave.

REPORTERS: What will your men do if efforts are made to force them out of the plant?

TWEEDEL: Well, that's pretty hard to say. I don't feel qualified to speak for the other fellows. I can't say until that time comes.[17]

The end of the sitdown came without violence. But the strike itself dragged on for two years, the longest strike in Amalgamated history, accompanied by a national boycott on Morrell products. It ended with recognition of the Amalgamated union in 1937 by the Morrell company.

As in 1917–19, the Amalgamated made substantial membership gains in World War II. The gains were not as spectacular as they had been twenty-five years earlier, but they were sounder. In the first place, the Amalgamated started with a larger membership, not with the 7500 members of 1916. In the second place, a larger, more seasoned membership and more experienced officers absorbed the new union recruits in an effective unifying fashion. And, in the third place, the Amalgamated had already, by 1940, started to work to make its organizational structure more rational, especially by consolidation of small local units into larger units.

The 1944 convention met with a paid-up membership of 113,366.

---

[17] News story, the Sioux Falls *Daily Argus-Leader*, March 9, 1935.

It heard the union's president, Earl W. Jimerson (who became president in 1940, when Gorman was elected secretary-treasurer) report that, in the four years since the 1940 convention, the Amalgamated had won ninety-seven NLRB elections and lost twenty; and that 178 new local unions had been chartered, of which 62 were retail meat cutter unions, 51 were packinghouse unions, 36 were poultry unions, 7 were cannery unions, 22 were unions of miscellaneous groups of food workers.[18]

In addition, four new state branches were formed in 1940–44; master agreements were negotiated with Armour and Swift, covering 19 per cent of their principal plants; the International's assets rose from $905,530 to $2,169,000, and death benefits of $339,000 were paid.[19]

Four years later, at the 1948 convention, President Jimerson reported more gains. Membership had gone up to 175,000 (40,000 in Big Four plants), a gain of around 60,000 members, with 117 new local unions, five district councils, and five state federations chartered. Secretary-Treasurer Gorman reported, as of February 29, 1948, financial resources of $3,741,000, almost twice the 1944 amount ($2,253,300 invested in United States Government bonds); death claims of $518,000 were paid.[20]

On the wage front the Amalgamated secured substantial increases for its members, although in the early postwar years it could not, any more than other unions, score gains that wholly offset the inflationary skyrocketing of living costs. Some provisions of agree-

[18] Among "miscellaneous groups of food workers" were workers in plants that process seafood, who are being increasingly organized by the Amalgamated. One report is typical; it gave the results of twenty-eight NLRB elections in packinghouses, oyster and crab houses, etc., in Crisfield, on the Eastern Shore of Maryland. In all but nine of these elections the workers voted unanimously for the Seafood Union, an Amalgamated affiliate. In eight of the nine houses where the vote was not unanimous only one or two votes were cast against the union, with one house casting seven negative votes. See *The Butcher Workman,* March 1948, p. 7.

[19] Amalgamated Meat Cutters, *Report of Officers . . . 16th General Convention,* 1944, pp. 2-5, 18.

[20] Amalgamated Meat Cutters, *Proceedings, 17th General Convention,* 1948, pp. 9, 21, 28, 41. It is interesting to note that new members initiated in 1940–44 numbered 233,000, nearly four times the net membership increase. This was partly a result of the war. Labor turnover in the meat industry is still, however, among the highest.

ments signed in 1946–48 will illustrate achievements and policy. Early in 1946 a national strike ended with a 16-cent-per-hour general increase across the board. Later in the year came another general increase of 7½ cents an hour. In addition, the Amalgamated secured for its members pay for eight holidays not worked, equivalent to 3 cents more an hour; with an improvement in the vacation plans in all agreements, whereby an employee going on his vacation during a holiday week would receive an additional day off or eight hours' pay upon his return to work. Successful efforts were made to lessen wage differentials: a 4-cent-per-hour increase for members employed in Southern plants, for the purpose of bringing more closely together wages paid in the North and the South; 2½ cents to bring wage rates in the following cities up to the metropolitan rates: Peoria, Illinois; Columbus, Ohio; and Reading, Pennsylvania; and another national adjustment of semi-skilled and skilled female rates in which further increases were obtained in brackets of 2½ cents, 5 cents, 7½ cents, and 10 cents per hour. Finally, the Amalgamated secured inclusion in the Armour Master Agreement of a sick- and non-compensable-accident plan, which the packers estimated would cost 1½ cents per hour. For the first half of 1947 a general increase raised rates 6 cents an hour, including an adjustment of rates in San Francisco to bring them up to those paid by independent packers, which resulted in an additional 3½ cents an hour plus an additional 10 cents an hour for ham boners, beef boners, beef breakers, and sausage makers. The general increase was retroactive to June 16, 1946.[21] Within the first nine months of 1948 two general wage rises, for a total of 13 cents an hour, were secured from the big packers, while the guaranteed work week in Armour and Swift plants was increased from thirty-two to thirty-six hours. As of spring 1948 the lowest Amalgamated packinghouse hourly rate was 97½ cents for male and 89½ cents for female labor; "fringe" benefits (eight paid yearly holidays, sick benefits, etc.) added another 9 cents to 11½ cents an hour.[22] Severance pay is being secured.

The Amalgamated Meat Cutters and Butcher Workmen have come

[21] Earl W. Jimerson, "Consummates Pacts with Armour and Swift," *The Butcher Workman*, March 1948, p. 1.

[22] Amalgamated Meat Cutters, *Proceedings, 17th General Convention*, 1948, p. 11.

a long way since 1904 and 1921. They did the job with a combination of uncompromising insistence on the rights of labor and a friendly, cooperative approach to management. And where it was needed the Amalgamated used the strike weapon, but never if it could be avoided. The achievements justify the policy.

Behind these achievements and policy, it should be remembered, are the struggles, the human aspirations and sacrifices that built up the Amalgamated—and that build up all unions. Unions are institutions, but they are made up of people who, although they organize to promote their economic interests, do not live by bread alone. Unionism is an expression of liberal democracy; both provide the freedoms and values that people need. Unionism and liberal democracy depend upon and strengthen each other. They will both wither —the victims of totalitarian reaction—if their supporters forget that it is their job to serve *people*.

3.   UNION RIVALS: THE AMALGAMATED AND UPWA-CIO

Since the upsurge of the Congress of Industrial Organizations (CIO) in the late 1930's, another union has operated in packing— the United Packinghouse Workers of America (UPWA-CIO). It enrolled a substantial membership in the plants of the Big Four, where it competed for power with the Amalgamated, but it achieved little of importance in the plants of independent packers.

The value of UPWA to the workers and to unionism has been limited, however, because of Communist influence—not control—within it. The influence is evident from the twists of union policy in accord with the maneuvers of Russian communism.

Up to June 1941, when Hitler's hordes invaded Russia, the Communists in UPWA whooped it up for "militancy" and strikes against support of the "imperialist" war. Then, from 1941 until the war's end, Stalin's agents in the unions were as gentle as mice and supported a policy of no strikes and cooperation with management to carry on the war. But in the postwar years they became "militant" again and called for strikes on any pretext—or on none—all the while screaming about "plots of American imperialism against peace-loving Soviet Russia." They adopted the world Communist policy—raise all kinds of turmoil everywhere, in all free countries, to weaken resistance to

Russian imperialist expansion by force of arms in Europe and Asia.

The new policy became evident in 1946, when the Communists in UPWA tried to convert a strike for higher wages into a "make trouble" affair. Together the Amalgamated and UPWA called a national strike against the big packers. Splendid cooperation on the local level prevailed among AFL and CIO union workers.

But on the upper levels divergences on tactics were sharp. Where the Amalgamated sought presidential intervention for government seizure of packing plants and arbitration, UPWA opposed this policy with statements that its members would not work for the government if it took over the plants. Some of the Communists said they would, if necessary, fight the government and its soldiers. President Truman seized the plants and appointed as administrator the Secretary of Agriculture, Clinton Anderson, who declared he would put into effect any wage increase recommended by a presidential fact-finding commission. When seizure of the plants came, the Communists and their allies tried to keep the strike going, but succeeded only for a day or so; sober trade-union policy prevailed. The Amalgamated, whose members had gone solidly on strike, returned to work at once. The fact-finding commission granted a 16-cent increase in hourly rates for every packing-plant worker in the United States.

This attempt of the Communists to keep a strike going to make the kind of trouble that Russia wanted was a dress rehearsal. Two years later they succeeded in their militant policy; Communist extremism in UPWA combined with the kind of trade-union extremism (not always dominant) which says, "To hell with management, let's strike to get all we can." The power-seekers and opportunists went along. Result: a disastrous ten-week strike.

The Amalgamated met in conference with officials of the United Packinghouse Workers to discuss wage demands. The UPWA seemed determined upon a strike at all costs and rejected the Amalgamated position that negotiations should begin before they decided on a strike. "Before Ralph Helstein [UPWA president] even discussed with the large packers his demand for a 29-cent increase for his membership," said *The Butcher Workman,* "he wanted the officials of our International Union to agree with him that a strike in the packing industry should be called in June. . . . Helstein was plainly told that the Amalgamated was not going into a strike before it went into negotiations. To do this would be as amateurish as it would be impractical." [23]

The UPWA officials persisted in their "militant" demands and policy. The Amalgamated, on the contrary, negotiated and accepted a 9-cent hourly increase.

From its start the UPWA strike was obviously a lost cause, but it was kept going for over ten weeks. The workers' fighting spirit and sacrifices served non-union objectives. Even when no one could deny the strike's defeat the Communists worked to prolong it—to make trouble, regardless of the workers' interests. After dragging on for ten weeks the strike ended in disaster.

The facts seemed to justify this criticism of UPWA policy made by Patrick Gorman:

It will be admitted that the United Packinghouse Workers made considerable numerical headway. It gave their leaders a very exalted personal ego. They actually felt that the Big Four were pygmy corporations that could be kicked about at will. A casual examination of the big packers' past record in labor disputes would have convinced this exalted leadership otherwise. . . . From the very beginning, the CIO in the meat industry was a trigger organization. The gun its leadership constantly held at the head of the meat packers was strife and strike. It could not be visualized by the UPWA misfits that the Big Four would one day become a trigger corporation. When trigger men meet face to face, someone is bound to bite the dust. . . . Trigger labor leaders and trigger labor organizations have no right to exist in an industry such as meat packing, whose officials are beginning to show an inclination to bargain fairly with their workers. A labor organization always pulling the trigger will sooner or later meet unexpected opposition, just as an employer who constantly pulls the trigger on a labor union will certainly run headlong into a strike. [24]

The defeat of their ten-week strike left the United Packinghouse Workers in a serious financial condition. Strike expenditures by the national office of $235,135 were $112,454 in excess of contributions. UPWA ended 1948 with a deficit of $7111 and outstanding loans

[23] Editorial, "Mr. Helstein," *The Butcher Workman,* March 1948, p. 1. Helstein denied (*New York Times,* February 3, 1948) the accusation about negotiations as "a gross misrepresentation of facts." But subsequent events confirmed the Amalgamated charge.

[24] Patrick E. Gorman, "National Strike of the CIO Has Failed," *The Butcher Workman,* May 1948, pp. 13-14.

(from the United Steelworkers and the Amalgamated Clothing Workers) of $125,000.[25]

In their report to the Packinghouse Workers' convention, one year after the strike, the officers unfolded what they called "a proud record of a union which could not be defeated" and added: "We made no apologies for the strike. . . . The UPWA stands today more solidly united than ever." The officers' report added: "Enormous handicaps, which could have wrecked a less principled union and which in fact did cripple the AFL Amalgamated Meat Cutters after its 1921 strike, have been overcome on all sides." This statement does not say a word about the differences in the circumstances of the two strikes, among them the fact that 1921 was a year of depression and unemployment while 1948 was a prosperity year with full employment.

The strike, however, aroused in UPWA opposition to the leadership and criticism of policy. One observer gave this analysis of the inner union struggle:

Since the first organization of UPWA the Communists have been active in the affairs of the union. In the key Chicago district, a well-known Communist, Herb March, has been District Director since 1943. March is a member of the National Committee of the Communist party. Recently, under pressure from the membership of the union, fearful of the possible inroads which could be made by the Amalgamated Meat Cutters, the International Board of the union decided to comply with the Taft-Hartley provisions regarding the signing of non-Communist affidavits. March and Meyer Stern, the District Director of the New York area, both resigned in protest against the signing of the affidavits. Stern has since changed his mind and was re-elected to his position upon the promise to sign the affidavit.

Strengthened by failure of the strike, the CIO Policy Caucus was organized at the convention to elect a leadership of the union based on friendlier relations with the national leadership of the CIO and that CIO policies should be followed in the United Packinghouse Workers Union.

In the important elections for national officers and district directors, the CIO Policy Caucus polled 527 votes for its candidate for president, Svend Godfredsen, as against 633 votes for the re-election of Ralph Helstein, an attorney for the union who managed, with "left-wing" support, to become its president, although he had never worked in the industry. The CIO group captured six out of ten district directors. On

[25] Report, "Statement of Financial Condition," *The Packinghouse Worker,* May 27, 1949, pp. 7-10.

the International Board the vote will be eight for the Helstein group and six for the CIO Policy group. Undoubtedly it was a victory for the Helstein-Communist alliance. Helstein has never identified himself openly with the so-called left-wing in the CIO, but he has played their game.[26]

While exposing and fighting Communist influence in the UPWA-CIO, the Amalgamated does not make unfair use of that issue. One illustration of this was the rejoinder to Swift & Company when this concern, in a questionnaire to its workers, asked: "Do you think Communists or members of any other party which plans to overthrow the government of the United States by force or violence, should be allowed to represent you?" The Amalgamated replied:

This is an insulting question. The officials of Swift & Company know perhaps better than anyone else that unions are not composed of Communists. They should know also that our Amalgamated has less communism among its members than perhaps any other union in the United States. And as to the United Packinghouse Workers, CIO, while having some Communists as leaders, Swift should know of the terrific fight the good Americans are making to eliminate their bad leadership.[27]

Despite some Amalgamated efforts to get the UPWA-CIO to cooperate, jurisdictional fights kept on. Some moves toward cooperation have been made. Early in 1947, for example, statements were issued by the two organizations' local unions in the Chicago area that presaged a "no-raiding" agreement. The UPWA statement said: "Unity must be realized if the labor movement is to survive," and the Amalgamated added: "This joint action to eliminate jurisdictional disputes is another move in the direction of united action."[28] But unity did not come. In the summer of 1949, however, the rival unions agreed to act jointly in their contract talks with the big packers (except Wilson, which abrogated its contract in August 1948 and against which the CIO union filed charges with the NLRB of unfair labor practices). The results were satisfactory.

One result of Amalgamated and UPWA raids upon one another's jurisdiction is illuminating: The raids are unsuccessful despite the large amounts of money and time spent on them. The workers stick

[26] A. B. Held, "The CIO Packers' Convention," *The New Leader*, July 10, 1948, p. 3.

[27] Editorial, "Swift's Ice Cream," *The Butcher Workman*, June 1949, p. 10.

[28] Report, "District 1, UPWA, Signs 'No Raid' Pact with AFL," *The Packinghouse Worker*, June 1947, p. 5.

to their respective unions. These raids benefit neither the Amalgamated and UPWA nor the good name of labor. The multiplication of jurisdictional disputes and strikes among American unions is one of their graver dangers. Labor cooperation and unity are needed. A cleaning out of the survivals of Communist influence in UPWA will make united action possible with the Amalgamated. But unification waits for CIO-AFL unity.

While fighting to maintain and expand its organization against a rival, the Amalgamated has repeatedly called for AFL-CIO unity, which would also bring unity of the packinghouse unions. It did so again at its 1948 convention:

It is inconceivable that the top leaders of the AFL and CIO should permit a continued division in the house of labor. . . . A continued division makes for inevitable defeat should the time arrive when it might be that the selfish interests of large corporations would make warfare against the trade union movement. . . . It is difficult to understand how in Europe, when conditions affecting the workers' welfare are being discussed, we find the AFL and CIO representatives in perfect accord, whereas in this country there is no unanimity of action among persons high in the councils of both groups or by the two great labor organizations as national groups. Where sincerity of purpose leads the way, the question of multiple jurisdictional problems becomes secondary in an effort to remold the trade union movement into one great fighting organization. We must continue to work for an amalgamation of the AFL and the CIO.[29]

Unity, the end of jurisdictional disputes and of "trigger" tactics in the packing industry are necessary for the welfare of workers, unions, and management. Such a development might build a foundation for the formation of a Confederation of Food Unions.

A confederation must begin, clearly, with one union in the industries connected with meat and related products, to include: (1) producers—workers on cattle and sheep ranches and in fisheries; (2) processors—workers in plants that manufacture animal products, fresh and canned; (3) distributors—workers in stores which sell animal foods, including combination grocery-meat stores. The Amalgamated Meat Cutters and Butcher Workmen constitutes that kind of union in large measure, as its membership has at least some of all these

[29] Amalgamated Meat Cutters, *Proceedings, 17th General Convention,* 1948, pp. 51-52.

different kinds of workers. But the Amalgamated is far from being all-inclusive, although it moves in that direction.

Such a meat union might then combine in a confederation with other food unions, again from production to distribution. It would be a *federal* organization, not one of tight centralization, to promote organizational simplicity and efficiency and to prevent concentration of power (as dangerous in unions as it is in industry and government).

The Confederation of Food Unions whose formation I am suggesting would work not only to further its members' economic interests but in the broad field of food policy and nutrition. The importance of this field for human well-being demands the cooperation of all who work within it—from management and unionism in the food industries to scientists, colleges, and government, to the United Nations. The perspectives are immense, unlimited, and inspiring, for they encompass the whole of humanity and its future.

4. THE AMALGAMATED: II—ACHIEVEMENTS AND POLICY

The achievements and policy of a union—of any institution—should be judged by what is done for *people*. A union should not pursue power for its own sake but for the sake of promoting life, liberty, and the pursuit of happiness.

Power-seekers are everywhere. For a Harry Bridges in unionism there is in management a Sewell Avery, whose vigorous opposition to unionism is matched by similar intransigence toward his colleagues, many of whom resigned because of it. There are no power-seekers among the Amalgamated's top officials. Their urge is not to "make history" but to serve the economic and human interests of their people, to make their everyday lives more secure and free, meaningful and happy. But this, after all, is the true meaning of history as man's struggle in pursuit of his human ends.

One expression of Amalgamated attitudes is its friendly, cooperative approach to management. The union, whose history contains a series of bitter, often bloody struggles, is nevertheless friendly and cooperative. It rejects, in the words of Secretary-Treasurer Gorman, the policy of being "a trigger organization which constantly holds the gun of strife and strike at the heads of the meat packers." And a vice-president, T. J. Lloyd, wrote in 1948:

No employer becomes extremely wicked all at once. In the apparent bitterness that underlies the opposition of some employers toward our organization there may be found a reason for such opposition. Perhaps opposition was created by a breach of faith on the part of someone who represented labor years ago. A strike called too hastily could have done it. Then again the forcing of members into employment who were not fitted for their jobs may have left its scars. Or perhaps it was a lie that left its sting. There might always be a wide gulf separating the interest of capital and the interest of labor. We have bridged that gulf as far as is humanly possible, but when we have trouble brewing in the pot, we should lower our fires and cook more slowly. It is not good to stir rice when some of the grains are sticking to the pot.[30]

This policy has been an effective approach to organization for the betterment of workers' conditions. And they are better. Higher wage rates, including overtime, have been secured, with paid holidays and vacations. Seniority rights protect the meat worker's stake in his job. As of 1948 the master agreements of the Amalgamated provided eight hours pay for each of eight non-work holidays. The Amalgamated was the first international union to negotiate and secure fringe benefits, among them time for changing into and out of work clothes, payment in lieu of work clothes, the furnishing of tools, and pay for time spent in sharpening them.

A system of effective procedures for the settlement of grievances not only works to right wrongs but gives workers the freedom to speak up against injustice. There is no individual dignity without this freedom. One of the oldest Amalgamated union songs, sung to the music of "Auld Lang Syne," goes in part as follows:

> Shall true men starve, while thieves and rings
> Reap where they have not sown?
> No! By our cause eternal, No!
> It shall not forever be;
> And union men will ere long show
> How the workers can be free.[31]

The Amalgamated is still working for regularization of employment in the packinghouses. Back in World War I the federal administrator of the industry awarded the workers a guaranteed thirty-six-hour

[30] T. J. Lloyd, "Fourth Golden Decade," *The Butcher Workman,* October 1948, p. 3.

[31] Earl W. Jimerson, "The Singingest Union in the World," *The Butcher Workman,* June 1949, p. 3.

work week, but this was lost after the disastrous strike defeat of 1921. The guarantee means that a worker who starts at the beginning of a week must be given work or pay for the total of the guaranteed weekly hours of work. In 1934 the Amalgamated signed agreements for a twenty-eight-hour week, with the guarantee rising to a thirty-six-hour week as of 1948.

While recognizing the value of the guaranteed annual wage idea, the Amalgamated appreciates the difficulties raised by it. One study gives a summary of the union's attitude:

In the meat-packing industry, the caution respecting more extensive coverage under the guaranteed annual wage arises from problems of union status. It was brought out that a guaranteed annual wage would require a shift of workers from one department to another. Seniority rights would be disturbed; eligibility for preferred status under employment guarantees would tend to be on a general plant seniority rather than a department seniority basis. Wage differentials between types of skills would thereupon have to be reduced, and some of the craft lines erased. Hence, the Amalgamated leaders were not prepared to rush into a disturbance of the union structure, even where they recognized the ultimate value of annual-wage guarantees when they can be made to stick.[32]

Still, in 1947, the Amalgamated, in negotiations with the Big Four, asked for a guaranteed annual wage and, in addition, for severance pay for employees separated from their jobs, based upon their length of service with the company. These demands were still pending in 1949.

At its 1948 convention the Amalgamated decided to consider and work for a thirty-five-hour week—a seven-hour day for five days a week. The Executive Board was instructed to study the issue and prepare to raise it in future negotiations, with the understanding that a shorter work week should not reduce take-home pay.[33]

The Amalgamated's policy on collective bargaining is to work for agreements on a national basis or at least to follow a national pattern, both in packinghouses and in retail trade. This does not mean, however, that all local or regional agreements must be negotiated through the International Union. The master agreements provide uniformity

[32] A. D. H. Kaplan, *The Guarantee of Annual Wages* (1947), p. 31.
[33] Amalgamated Meat Cutters, *Proceedings, 17th General Convention,* 1948, p. 310.

on major issues to set a pattern for local negotiations. This policy parallels that of management.

While friendly and cooperative, the Amalgamated is unyielding where its members' interests and rights are concerned. One illustration of this policy was its fight to make merit wage increases a subject for collective bargaining. It was sustained in this battle by the United States Supreme Court.

In May 1945 a company in Tennessee gave wage increases to 31 of its 105 employees. An Amalgamated officer asked the company for the names of employees affected and the amount of the increase. The company officials refused the union's request, declaring that merit increases were not subject to collective bargaining but were managerial functions. The case went to the National Labor Relations Board, whose examiner heard the union's complaint and reported that the company had violated its agreement by refusing to bargain on the wage rates. This report became a decision of the NLRB. The Board's investigation also disclosed that a year after the violation took place, during collective negotiations, the company turned down the union's request that merit increases be included in the agreement. Following a cease and desist order of the Board that the contract be lived up to, the case was taken to the United States Circuit Court of Appeals. The court found that the company had violated the National Labor Relations Act with respect to collective bargaining. When the case came before the Supreme Court, the Court concurred with the first decision by denying the company's petition for appeal on the ground that employers cannot ignore union agreements when changing wage rates.[34]

The Amalgamated has never opposed the increase of productive efficiency in packinghouses, for it recognizes that higher productivity is the only real basis for higher wages. But it insists that efficiency shall be a two-way cooperative street. The Amalgamated attitude was expressed in three demands it made on the big packers during the 1946 negotiations:

1. All production standards now in effect shall be made available to the union.

2. The employer to train a minimum of one and a maximum of three employees to be designated by the union in the incentive plan and par-

[34] Editorial, " 'Merit' Pay Raises," *The Butcher Workman*, December 1948, p. 10.

ticularly in the time study. The union shall have the right to question the work standards of any job presently in operation or any job change in the future.

3. All grievances concerning work standards, piece-work rates and incentive plans, if not satisfactorily settled, shall be processed through grievance procedure.[35]

The Amalgamated has worked continuously to eliminate discriminatory wage differentials based on sex, color, or region. In its report to the 1948 convention the International Executive Board urged support of legislation pending in Congress to equalize the wages of women with those paid to men for the same work. The report added: "There is no justifiable reason why women, who perform the same work as men, and have acquired the same skills, should be discriminated against when it comes to paying wages. Although we have provisions in most of our collective bargaining agreements which require equal pay for equal work, regardless of sex, the enactment of this law will eliminate a great many presently existing inequalities."

And at the same convention President Jimerson reported that wages of Amalgamated members in the South had almost doubled in the four years 1944–48; special increases were negotiated to reduce the regional differentials.[36]

The most flagrant discrimination in industry has been practiced against Negro workers. Many unions have been, and still are, guilty of anti-Negro prejudice. But never the Amalgamated, which from its formation in 1897 has provided among its laws for every new member, upon initiation, to undertake the following obligation, which he repeats after the chairman: "I solemnly promise, upon my honor as a man, never knowingly to wrong a brother or see him wronged if it is within my power to prevent it. I further promise that I will never knowingly discriminate against a fellow worker on account of creed, color, or nationality."

This obligation has never been changed. And the Amalgamated insists upon insertion in its master agreements of the following pro-

[35] Report, "Nation-Wide Negotiations Begin July 27," *The Butcher Workman*, August 1946, p. 1. The Amalgamated did not press the demand for training of union-designated employees in time study. Its real grievance is the habit of some companies of changing production standards during a contract term without consulting the union.

[36] Amalgamated Meat Cutters, *Proceedings, 17th General Convention*, 1948, pp. 11, 48.

vision: "The Company agrees that it will not discriminate against any employee or applicant because of race, sex, color, creed, nationality or because of membership in the Union."

The Amalgamated, like nearly all unions, has always been concerned about the welfare of its members. At the 1930 convention the Executive Board reported:

In years past our outstanding problems were the organization of the unorganized, recognition of the Union, the establishment of wage standards and hours of labor. In recent years we have added to these problems a serious discrimination because of age. The employers of today want young people in their employ and discriminate against the worker when reaching middle age. This has become very serious to the middle-aged man who finds himself out of employment when seeking a job. During the past four years it was cause for a turnover in the membership of our International Union of some 10,423 members. And, therefore, we are submitting to the convention, with our recommendation, a plan to . . . provide a Union Home for old or disabled members and a Pension Fund for those who would prefer a pension to being a resident at the Home.

This plan offers to the membership a degree of security, when security is most needed, that can be obtained by no other means. It would stabilize our membership and be cause for a lesser turnover. The employers in recent years have adopted systems of granting sick benefits, insurance, vacations and pensions, but this offer by the employers is guaranteed only so long as the worker remains with a particular concern. In soliciting membership to the Union we are forced to meet this competition and in the past it has been a tough problem to overcome. The Union must meet this problem by establishing securities for its membership that would be of greater value than those offered by the employer, which, in most cases, are used to offset trade union activities.[37]

The beneficial provisions of unions cannot go very far for lack of financial resources. Earlier union welfare plans supported by employer contributions, at first strictly limited, have now become a major objective of organized labor, including the Amalgamated. At the 1948 convention President Jimerson reported that one of the union's most pressing problems was the negotiation of health and welfare plans, with considerable progress made for members employed in packing and meat processing as well as in the retail field. Master agreements signed with the Big Four packing companies after

[37] Amalgamated Meat Cutters, *Synopsis of Proceedings . . . 13th General Convention,* 1930, pp. 42, 53.

November 1946 all contained a non-compensable accident and sick-leave plan under which employees received two weeks of sick leave pay at one-half their wages for every year of service with the company. The benefits start from the eighth day of illness for those employees with less than ten years of service, and from the first day of illness for those with ten years or more of service. In the past only Swift & Company paid such benefits. A great many independent packing companies also accepted the plan. "We are not altogether satisfied with the benefits presently paid," said Jimerson, "but we have only begun." An agreement with the Packers Association of Chicago provided for a complete medical care plan rather than the sick leave benefits contained in most packinghouse contracts. In the contract finally concluded, a health and welfare fund was established and a board of trustees (three representatives of the Association and three representatives of the union) was selected to administer the program. The agreement provided that each employer should pay into the welfare fund 80 cents weekly for every employee on the payroll during that week, regardless of the number of hours worked. It called for a medical center in the stockyards area with a medical director, a staff of competent physicians, surgeons and medical specialists, and a clinic equipped with X-ray machines, electrocardiographs, basal metabolism, diathermy, and other equipment, including a laboratory necessary for complete and thorough examinations. Every member of the union working in the plants under contract would receive free medical care at the clinic, or at home if confined to bed, and all medical and surgical care necessary when confined in a hospital. Arrangements were later made to include members of the workers' families at a small cost. The undertaking required an initial expenditure of about $15,000, and an over-all yearly budget of about $35,000. These payments were provided for in the contract.

In New York City many local retail and packinghouse unions had earlier health and welfare benefit plans, with employer payments, providing sick leave pay, life insurance, accident insurance benefits, medical care, dental care, the furnishing of eyeglasses, and payment of specific amounts for medical or surgical care while in the hospital. The Amalgamated local in Philadelphia had a welfare plan, two-thirds of whose costs were paid by the employer and one-third by the union members.

"Many other plans are in negotiation," reported Jimerson, "and there are some that are in practice which we have not mentioned. It is important that more and more of our local unions try to negotiate and establish such health and welfare plans." [38]

The Amalgamated has a positive strike policy: it strikes only when peaceful bargaining gets nowhere. It will not make impossible demands in order to provoke a strike, and it always considers the industry's capacity to pay. When in 1948 the United Packinghouse Workers union asked for a 29-cent hourly increase, the Amalgamated insisted this demand was "leading up a blind alley" because the big packers could not pay it. "In the last fiscal year Swift & Company earned slightly more than $34,000,000 in net profits. If this company with its more than 50,000 employees granted a 29-cent increase, it would cost $36,000,000, or $2,000,000 more than the entire profit Swift & Company made the past year." [39]

What the Amalgamated strike policy is was clearly stated in the report of its Executive Board to the 1948 convention:

Perhaps there will never be a time when industry will be entirely free of strikes. Strikes, therefore, occasionally are inevitable. But as long as employers within our industry meet with our representatives with an open mind on matters affecting the welfare of our membership, we feel that a solution to our problems can always be found. Occasionally, however, some employers assume a position with relation to our organization that we could never permit to pass unchallenged. In all such cases where indications point to a desire on the part of any employer or group of employers to destroy any of our local unions, *we must be prepared to strike with all of the economic strength we possess.*[40]

The Amalgamated will conciliate before it will fight, but then it fights with all its energy. Its conciliatory policy flows from its attitude toward management, which is thus expressed as a provision in

[38] Amalgamated Meat Cutters, *Proceedings, 17th General Convention,* 1948, pp. 15-16. Secretary-Treasurer Gorman reported there was a combined total of $2,496,680 in the Death Fund and the Retirement Fund. In the two years after this convention the Amalgamated negotiated a number of additional health and welfare plans with packers, among them Hunter Packing Company, St. Louis Independent Packers Association, Oscar Mayer Company, and Kingan & Company, while New York and Philadelphia improved and extended their plans. The plans mentioned in this footnote covered approximately 35,000 employees.

[39] Editorial, "Mr. Helstein," *The Butcher Workman,* March 1948, p. 1.

[40] Amalgamated Meat Cutters, *Proceedings, 17th General Convention,* p. 41.

the master agreements it signs with the big packers (Item 13 of the 1948–49 agreement with Armour & Company):

The management of the plants and the direction of the working forces, including the right to hire, promote, suspend or discharge for proper cause, or transfer, and the right to relieve employees because of lack of work, or because of other legitimate reasons, to determine the products to be handled, produced, or manufactured, the schedules and standards of production and methods, processes and the means of production or handling, schedule of working hours, and operations to be contracted or subcontracted, is vested exclusively in the Company, subject only to such restrictions governing the exercise of these rights as are expressly provided in this agreement.

These Amalgamated attitudes on management and strikes provide a truly acceptable basis for union-management cooperation. But it takes two sides to cooperate, in the packing industry as elsewhere.

5.   FOR UNION-MANAGEMENT COOPERATION

Unions and management today are dominant institutional elements in economic activity. They may still act as antagonists, but they are in essence complementary and need to cooperate for industrial peace and progress to serve human welfare.

Recognition of the need for union-management cooperation has become increasingly evident among the packers. Let me recall what Patrick Gorman of the Amalgamated said: "Trigger labor leaders and trigger labor organizations have no right to exist in an industry like meat packing, *whose officials are beginning to show an inclination to bargain fairly with their workers.*" And in a publication celebrating the Golden Jubilee of the Amalgamated one of its vice-presidents, Milton S. Maxwell, wrote:

We have made tremendous strides. With respect to the employers, it seems fair to point out that the men who now represent them in their labor relations apparently belong to a new age. Gone are the days when these employer representatives enter a conference with an overbearing attitude, obviously intended to browbeat or intimidate the men who represent their workers. There has developed, with the passing years, what appears to us to be a genuine attempt by these men to negotiate in good faith. This is true of representatives of the independent packers, as well as those who speak for the large meat-packing companies. We are convinced that our improved relations with the employers have paid valuable dividends to our membership.

A similar cooperative attitude is developing in packing management, of which I have given some evidence in an earlier chapter. There is a considerable amount of additional evidence. For example, early in 1949 the trade publication *Food Industries* published a story about Meat Cannery Workers Local 56 of the Amalgamated, with headquarters in Camden, New Jersey, and P. J. Ritter Company of Bridgeton, New Jersey. The question asked: Why has this company been free of labor difficulties when they have been so general? The answer given: division of responsibility; that is, the Ritter company gave the union some of the responsibilities which employers generally have considered functions (prerogatives) they should not share with employees. With the coming of the Amalgamated union came improved labor relations and a material increase in production per man-hour. President W. H. Ritter, Jr., of the company was quoted by *Food Industries* as saying:

Our continual effort to reach the best possible relationship between management and employee is just good business. During the eight years our employees have belonged to the union, we have learned that the building of workable arrangements between management, union and its membership is not easy, but certainly not impossible. We have learned it is not as simple as merely signing a contract once a year. It must be worked for 24 hours every day.

What is it we all seek? It seems to me as simple as this—mutual trust. And that's something you can never take for granted.

Of course, establishing a satisfactory working arrangement between management, union and membership requires mutual effort. It's never one-sided. However, mutual effort is only possible if management takes the lead. Management has taken the lead here at our plant, and both the union and its membership have cooperated. Management-labor relations have progressed more rapidly and profitably since the AFL unionized our plant in 1940 than before.[41]

These cooperative relations are not universal in the meat industry, but they exist and are growing, if slowly and unevenly, among

[41] Article, "This Company Is Proud of Its Employee Relations," *The Butcher Workman,* March 1949, p. 6.

small and big packers. And the change offers a challenge to management to recognize and accept unionism as a legitimate institutional factor in industry.

Management arose out of the growing complexity of economic activity, and, in particular, out of the separation of ownership from management and control in large-scale corporate enterprise. Unionism arose out of the same general developments, expressed in the conversion of independent craftsmen into dependent wage workers, which began in the later guilds and was completed by the Industrial Revolution of the eighteenth century and its aftermath. Under the conditions of impersonal wage relations the workers needed an organized power to protect and promote their interests. Labor is as much a "factor" of production as are capital and management.

All factors of economic activity today are organized. This is true not only in large-scale corporate industry, but also in those areas where small-scale enterprise exists. Although agriculture is made up of millions of small enterprisers, large numbers of farmers are organized in a network of cooperatives and of other farm organizations. Among small businessmen organization prevails in the form of trade associations, cooperative and voluntary chains, and other groups.

It is in large-scale industry that organization is greatest. From the small plants of a hundred and fifty years ago, with their limited, largely local markets, industry has become a complex network of organizations engaged in the production and distribution of goods and services in large enterprises operating in far-flung markets.

Under these conditions, one can no longer talk of "natural" economic laws or of a free market where economic forces automatically operate. The organization and regulation of economic activity are dominant.

Within this organizational complex are two major elements: professional management and labor unionism. Both of them express the conversion of economic activity from small-scale individual enterprise to large-scale corporate enterprise. They both affect the free play of economic forces in the market: competition, prices, wages, profit. Their relations, whether antagonistic or cooperative, are of major importance for economic and social progress.

In their struggles to form unions the workers, among them the meat cutters and butchers, were trying to do only what their "masters" had already done. That is, to organize themselves as an element of production, as employers and management were increasingly organizing their enterprise and activity.

One conclusion is inescapable: *labor organization parallels the organization of industry and its management.* If unions "interfere with the free play of economic laws," so do organized corporate industry and management.

Moreover, "economic laws" worked differently for employers and for their workers. For example, price competition was beneficial: as prices were lowered the consumers were enabled to buy more and so improved their living standards. But when wage competition lowered wages to the levels they reached in packing (the lowest wage rates of any industry in the early 1900's, let us remember), it meant a disastrous lowering of living standards for workers—not for "labor" as an economic abstraction, but for particular human beings.

There never was a wholly free play of economic forces; there never can be. Always, in varying degrees, organization of economic activity has existed among employers. In an earlier competitive capitalism, with no large corporations and no trade associations, employers were organized by the simple fact of being employers in possession of economic enterprises and in control of jobs. Moreover, they were organized, if loosely so, because they knew one another and they acted together. It was Adam Smith who wrote:

The masters [employers] have the advantage. These masters, being fewer in numbers, can combine much more easily; and the law, besides, authorizes, or at least does not prohibit their combinations, while it prohibits those of workmen. . . . We rarely hear, it has been said, of the combinations of masters, though frequently of those of workmen. But whoever imagines, upon this account, that masters rarely combine, is as ignorant of the world as of the subject. Masters are always and everywhere in a sort of tacit, but constant and uniform combination, not to raise the wages of labor above their actual rate. To violate this combination is everywhere a most unpopular action. . . . Masters, too, sometimes enter into particular combinations to sink the wages of labor even below this rate. These are always conducted with the utmost silence and secrecy, till the moment of execution, and when the workmen yield, as they sometimes do, without resistance, though severely felt by them, they are never heard of by other people. . . . But workmen's combinations, be they offensive or defensive, are always abundantly heard of.[42]

[42] Adam Smith, *The Wealth of Nations* (Modern Library edition), pp. 66-67.

Management, as a specialized group of people in industry performing definite functional tasks, grew up with modern industry. In the earlier small-scale industry of petty capitalists the owner was himself the manager of his enterprise. Not only were enterprises small and capable of being managed by owner-capitalists, but the technology of production was simple. It did not require engineers and technicians of all kinds with specialized knowledge to organize and carry on plant operations. As industry became increasingly large-scale, however, and its organization (in production and distribution) became more complex, more and more specialized people were necessary to carry on constantly multiplying technical and managerial functions. Finally, as large-scale industry grew into corporate industry with its tens of thousands of absentee owner-stockholders who owned the corporate enterprises but did not manage them, the managerial functions were wholly absorbed by a professional managerial group.

I distinguish between management and administration. Although they overlap, the distinction is meaningful. Management comprises the technical-professional forces in industry which carry out and control economic operations within the policy laid down by administration. Corporate administration has been largely a part of ownership, dominated by the profit motive; these administrators, or what is sometimes called "top management," are essentially institutional capitalists. Technical management, wholly constructive in the sense that its job is to organize and carry on operations in the most efficient manner, is imbued with a sense of workmanship in terms of keeping a plant operating all the time in order that all its capacity is fully used to produce goods and services.

These constructive functional attitudes of management, however, were distorted because management grew up under the domination of captains of industry and financiers of the years 1870–1920, within the framework of monopoly capitalism. These men, although they accomplished much constructive work, were economic and financial robber barons—the Rockefellers and Carnegies, the Swifts and Armours, the Morgans. Management had to take orders from these men, who were dominated by an anti-social insistence on piling up profits regardless of the welfare of workers and consumers. Hence, management grew up in a largely predatory rough-and-tumble school, under conditions of administrative-financial domination which distorted some of the constructive managerial attitudes and warped much of their service to human values.

Owner-management bitterly fought, and in some cases still fights, the efforts of workers to use their right of freedom of association—a right accorded them in a liberal democratic society—to organize unions for a collective bargaining which, in its legislative, judicial, and executive aspects, is the foundation of democracy in industry.

On an acceptance of the methods of democracy unions and management can get together for cooperation. Nor does cooperation necessarily exclude differences and conflict, providing there is the will to settle them by peaceful means for mutual advantage. The areas of cooperation are broad—from mutual efforts for an increase of productivity to the cultivation of public understanding. One Amalgamated union in a small town placed an advertisement in the Labor Day edition of the local labor paper, which mentioned the union's achievements in securing better wages and conditions, and added:

> In view of the fact that it takes two parties to make a contract, let us in fairness also congratulate and credit all employers of organized labor—who not only met our negotiating committees half-way, with courtesy and conscientiousness, during the past year, but also volunteered worthwhile concessions of their own during such negotiations. In this respect our hats are off to the management of the Dubuque Packing Company; its president, Mr. H. W. Wahlert, and to the remarkable strides the company has made in its contributions to the harmony and welfare of its employees and in the substantial upbuilding of this community and its adjacent trade areas.[43]

A more general illustration of cooperation for industrial welfare was the work of the Amalgamated's Research Division in Washington during World War II. According to the Division's report, its two directors worked on their own and in cooperation with others to bring about a more equitable ceiling on pork products, cut down the bonus payment for Army, Navy, and Lend-Lease meat supplies, modify the federal inspection laws, which resulted in an increased federal inspection and more war contracts for smaller packinghouses. They also protested, with many others, to put an end to the unfair trading practices of upgrading meat products; presented and argued for an over-all plan of regulation for the meat industry to include

[43] Report, "A Union Thanks an Employer," *The Butcher Workman*, October 1948, p. 9.

ceilings on livestock and equitable rationing and allocation programs —and the plan was accepted. The Division further worked to institute a subsidy program to take care of non-processing slaughterers who were unfairly squeezed by inequitable ceilings, and to make sure, in cooperation with the more progressive farm representatives, that the over-all program was to the best interests of the war effort and of all workers in allied industries and in agriculture.[44]

It is important, from the standpoint of an objective understanding of economic history and of the larger issues of social change and social policy, to remember that management is a constructive function, animated with a sense of workmanship which is potential of great social-economic and cultural progress. One student of management has expressed its potential in these words:

As those who practice the profession of management in all its branches come to appreciate the social purpose of their work—the vital service to the community which both the exalted and the humble in their ranks are rendering; as this conception of their work as a social service comes to be accepted as a professional objective; and as one and all come to feel their common unity in that service and a common pride in the good exercise of their profession, so will the standard of that service be raised to the level which its vast responsibilities demand.[45]

One area for progressive union-management cooperation in packing is the introduction and regulation of technical changes. This problem has always been important in the meat industry, but its importance will become greater as the new technological revolution sweeps on. Neither unions nor management have done much about it. After a study of fifty companies (among them one meat-packing and three packaged-food companies), the director of the Bureau of Industrial Relations of the University of Michigan called for "an adequate managerial organization to supervise technological change; a practice of recognizing and dealing frankly with employee fears

[44] Amalgamated Meat Cutters, *Report of Officers . . . 16th General Convention,* 1944, p. 18. The Amalgamated went along, during the war, with the packers in their demand for an immediate postwar end of price control, which was a mistaken form of union-management cooperation and might have led consumers to believe it was directed against them. When, however, prices zoomed sky-high after the removal of controls, the Amalgamated disagreed with the industry's position and called for controls if increases continued.

[45] Oliver Sheldon, "Management," *Encyclopedia of the Social Sciences,* vol. X (1933), p. 79.

regarding it; and a set of policies intended to safeguard employee tenure, earnings and status when processes are improved." One packing plant's policy was "to give workers on a job first chance to operate new equipment." The study had this to say about union policy:

Union attempts to prevent technological changes are rare. The common union policy is to regulate them in the interests of the unionists, as far as that is feasible. Two phases of policy may be distinguished in recent collective agreements: (1) to gain joint control over the introduction of technological changes, and (2) to impose obligations on employers who retain their initiative in introducing technological changes. The joint control of the introduction of innovations is intended to minimize worker displacement and to equalize competitive conditions. Some agreements provide that any deadlock in the joint control shall be broken by arbitration, the arrangements for which are clearly specified.[46]

The problem of technological change is a crucial one, for its constructive potentials may be distorted into destruction. And management has a direct responsibility for what happens with the advance of technology. Management's action will be decisive for mankind.

No social class, however, realizes its potentialities through itself alone. It depends upon the cooperation of other class-economic forces. The potentialities of management as a constructive force for social progress cannot be realized as long as management pursues, or is compelled to pursue, anti-democratic policies antagonistic to the workers and to their unions. The most destructive force in management's history, the one that did most to distort its constructive functions and to warp its humanity, was the policy of suppressing workers to prevent organization of unions or to destroy them.

In our generation looms the barbaric menace of totalitarianism. This menace feeds on social conflict and turmoil. If management and unionism engage in a knockdown fight, they will make impossible, or at least hamper, American participation in the struggle for world cooperation and peace. And if the knockdown fight becomes bad enough it will bring the economic breakdown and social chaos out of which communism or fascism arises.

Union-management cooperation is one means to insure complete realization of all that technology, industry, and democracy can mean for the welfare of mankind.

[46] John W. Riegel, *Management, Labor and Technological Change* (1942), pp. 3, 47, 113, 154.

CHAPTER XII

WORLD POLICY:
PEOPLE CAN BE FED

1. POPULATION AND FOOD RESOURCES

THE food crisis after World War II served to emphasize that chronic malnutrition is still a major world problem and that in many regions growing populations still press upon relatively diminishing food resources. Periodic famines are the frightful interludes in a persistent condition of semi-starvation.

Europe's postwar food supply lagged behind its needs; there was a deficiency in meat products as well as in other things. Except, however, for East-Central Europe, where Communist dictatorship and collectivization made the food situation worse, Europe staged a substantial recovery to prewar levels, although these levels were below what they should have been.

Asia's recovery in food production did not bring diets up to pre-war standards because of an increase in population and because of economic difficulties aggravated by, among other factors, civil war. This situation is the more serious because a permanent menace of famine has tormented Asia. According to general estimates, more than 26,000,000 human beings died in India from famines in the twenty-five years from 1875 to 1900. And famines have been more deadly in China.

Even restoration of food output to 1936–39 levels means varying degrees of starvation and malnutrition for most of the world's people. An adequate minimum diet for all people, according to the United

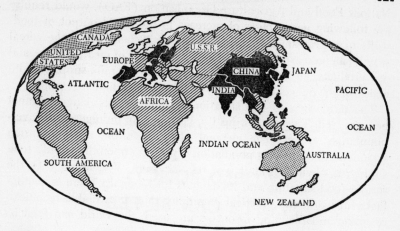

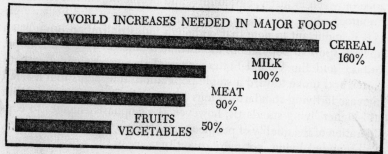

WELL FED	ADEQUATELY FED	POORLY FED	CRITICAL
United States	United Kingdom	France	China
Canada	Netherlands	Czechoslovakia	Malaya
Australia	Norway	Bulgaria	Italy
New Zealand	Switzerland	Belgium	Austria
Denmark	Luxembourg	Yugoslavia	Germany
Sweden		Rumania	Korea
		Finland	India
		Hungary	Burma
		U.S.S.R.	Java
		Indo-China	Philippines
MOST OF THE WORLD'S		Siam	Japan
PEOPLE ARE UNDERFED		Greece	Spain
(Partly adapted from a *Fortune* chart)		Latin America	Poland
		Africa	Portugal

THE WORLD'S HUNGER AND FOOD NEEDS

Nations Food and Agriculture Organization (FAO), would require the following percentages of increase in the world output of food-stuffs over prewar levels: an increase of 50 per cent in the cereal supply; an increase of 90 per cent in the supply of meat, poultry, and fish products; an increase of 100 per cent in the milk supply; an increase of 160 per cent in the supply of fresh fruits and vegetables.

The seriousness of this situation is universal. Its dangers cannot be dismissed. They do not justify, however, an indulgence in "over-population" scares. The element of truth in the neo-Malthusian argument, that growing population is pressing upon the world's food supply, is obvious. But it is a *relative* truth. For, along with the serious food situation and its dangers for humanity there is another factor at work: the practical possibility that, if available technical-scientific and planning resources are used, the world can feed its people.

Yet there is a problem of population pressure on the food supply. Most of the world's peoples have grown faster in numbers than in their capacity to produce foodstuffs. Population grows, but economic progress lags. From the settled areas of Africa and most Latin American nations to all Asia, East-Central Europe, Italy, and Spain, a backward agriculture operates on largely depleted soils, whose diminishing returns are unable to feed the people that live on them.

The general development for the past hundred and fifty years has been this: enough economic, medical, and social progress to reduce the death rate and let more people live, but not enough progress to permit them to live well-nourished, satisfying lives. The answer is agricultural modernization and more industrialization, together with a rational population policy that recognizes the necessity for a balance between industry, agriculture, and people in relation to natural resources.

It is important to note that, although industrialization brought an upward spurt in population, there came a time—in Western Europe, Britain, and the United States—when the upward trend began to flatten and move toward a stable population. It appears that a small increase in living standards brings a large population increase. With still higher living standards, however, the emphasis changes to consideration of the quality of people and their opportunities for creative, well-rounded living, not mere quantity.

In some countries (notably England), however, the population has begun to level off under conditions where national agricultural output is not enough to feed the people. And the situation is worse in undeveloped countries with primitive farming and little industry, where population keeps growing while the food supply lags.

There is no problem of nature's inability to provide enough food. The problem is primarily one of policy—of some countries that are backward in their social-economic and cultural development; of other countries, under one pressure or another, that have adopted injurious policies in the past and have not yet found the answers. There is nothing that cannot be undone or done better.

The danger is not that nature may revolt against man because of his abuse of it, and so destroy him. The danger is that man may not use the technical-scientific resources at his disposal effectively to solve the food problems that press upon the world. For the problems can be solved, since man now has the means to solve them. The only limiting factor is man himself.

2. NEW SOURCES OF FOOD

The world can feed its people by a combination of means. Man already has it within his power to make old sources of food yield more and to open up new sources of food. The means include not only improved farming but, at least as important, the use of scientific-technical developments to produce new foods.

At the one hundred and fourteenth annual meeting of the American Chemical Society, in 1948, one report dealt with the use of "growth-regulating" chemicals in agriculture that "bring higher yields or a greater certainty of yields." The Society considered the report so important that it issued a statement which said: "Development of growth-regulating compounds or hormones is the key to victory in the struggle to overcome the 'suicidal' waste of natural wealth and the depredations of natural forces which, it is held by some authorities, threaten to make the earth ultimately uninhabitable."

This discovery highlights the mistake the neo-Malthusians make—which Malthus himself made. The mistake is the projection of past or present trends into the future without making sufficient allowance for new technical-scientific and cultural forces.

Malthus overlooked the Industrial Revolution, and particularly its agricultural aspect. That revolution enormously increased the productive capacity of industry and farming, making it possible for more people to get more food and the higher wages with which to buy. True, much of the food to sustain Europe's growing population came from new lands overseas; nevertheless European agriculture also produced larger amounts of food from the same amount of land.

Today's neo-Malthusians either overlook or minimize the new technological revolution now going on. There has been a constant improvement of chemical and electrical technology from the 1880's onward, climaxed by the development of electronics and atomic energy. The revolution has been going on in the realm of agriculture and foods, too. One of its aspects is the production of more food from land. Some of the outstanding developments are:

1. *Greater understanding of soils and their classification* in terms of what particular soils will grow the largest amount of a particular crop; plus the understanding of soil deficiencies and how to overcome them for more and better crops.

2. *Constantly improved breeding of plants* more fully adapted to local environment for greater yields and more resistance to disease and pests. The growing use of hybrid seed brings higher yields of corn, oats, soybeans, and certain kinds of wheat from the same amount of land. Rust-resistant wheat revolutionized American prairie farming. And hybrid plants with higher resistance are multiplying. One 1948 development is typical: the creation, by Canadian scientists after fifteen years of work with more than 160,000 seedlings, of a potato resistant to blight, which yearly ruined at least 25 per cent— in some cases 50 per cent—of the world's crop. Commercial distribution of seedlings began in 1949.

3. *Constant multiplication and improvement of fertilizers,* with emphasis on the concentrated variety and on minerals, to increase their plant-food content, for correction of soil deficiencies and greater acre-crop yields. Among the more important developments is the use of phosphate to improve soil fertility and livestock and the nutritional quality of their food products. Chemical and production research is moving toward a revolution in the fertilizer industry that will bring still more abundant and efficient low-cost fertilizers. The newest perspectives are opened up by radioactivity research; for example, there exists a joint project by the United States Department of Agriculture and the Atomic Energy Commission to study the way

radioactive fertilizer works on plant growth and to determine the most favorable cycles of fertilizer application.

4. *Research on the chemistry of soils, plants, and foods;* the end product will be a greater food supply. One development is typical: Two scientists of the United States Army Chemical Corps, Dr. R. J. Weintraub and Dr. A. G. Norman, reported at the September 1948 meeting of the American Chemical Society, on the use of chemicals to control growing plants. They predicted that growth-regulating compounds will be increasingly used to govern the yield and quality of crops. The chemical substances they described either speed, delay, or wholly check the development of a part or parts of a plant. One of them—the weed-killer "2,4-D"—can inhibit the growth of weeds and also speed the ripening of bananas in storage. These scientists used growth-regulating chemicals to produce bigger and heavier fruit, to control the flowering time of pineapples to meet seasonal requirements, and to induce the sprouting of dormant buds in potatoes designed for planting as seed. They foresaw great benefits ahead: "In an early spring the bud development and flower opening in fruit crops might be delayed to obviate frost injury. In a late season the flowering of some plants might be advanced in order to secure maturity before the frost of autumn. The dependence upon insects and other natural pollinating agencies may be reduced so that insecticides may be more effectively used." The final conclusion of the chemists was: "This may result in higher yields or a greater certainty of yields." Another potential use of growth chemicals is to create new varieties of food plants, more of which will grow on an acre of land and with more nutritional value.[1]

[1] Report, *Journal of the American Chemical Society,* October 1948, pp. 121-24. Creation of new varieties of food plants will undoubtedly be speeded up by the use in scientific research of more potent tools such as isotopes and our growing knowledge of genetics. Meanwhile the need for new plants is being urged from another angle. Charles Morrow Wilson, *New Crops for the New World* (1945), pp. 1-2, writes: "In a great part of our hemisphere the existing list of cultivated crops is distressingly small. . . . As an over-all proposition [its] fields, ranges and woodlands can use new crops to advantage—dozens or scores and perhaps thousands of them. [We should] substitute the planned migration of benefiting plants and livestock for the repetitious migration of distressed people. . . . Patently, more proved crops can mean fewer sick or underfed Americans, better lands, better homes and better lives." He adds (p. 5): "The prevailing migration of crops clearly implies that valid crops, regardless of how procured or developed, must be made freely available to all men of goodwill who would grow them. [There can be no] arbitrary

5. *Substantial improvements in livestock breeding and production.* These include better breeding and care of animals, changes in cropping systems and feed crops for meat and milk animals that provide farmers with a better and increased output of feeds, and development of earlier maturity in animals. Improvements are constantly being made. Two reports to the 1948 meeting of the American Chemical Society are indicative. One research scientist reported that cattle fed on diets deficient in copper develop severe bone malformations, despite plenty of sunlight and adequate phosphorus and calcium in their feeds. Another report described a new synthetic process to increase the supply and lower the cost of bone-nourishing vitamin D_3 (the human vitamin D); among other benefits, this should lower the cost of poultry feed. American breeders have developed the cross-bred Brahman cattle that thrive in hot climates and, at the same time, are finer and heavier animals which yield more and better beef. And Canadians have cross-bred a new hardy strain of beef cattle, the Cattalo, that thrive in rigorous northern winters. In livestock breeding, moreover, there have been increasing savings on the use of land to supply animals with food. Good protein-rich feeds are being made from wastes of the lumber and brewery industries. Another development that may save on land for livestock foods: artificial ammonia and its derivatives, manufactured from atmospheric nitrogen and hydrogen, can be fed to farm animals as substitutes for part of their protein needs.

6. *New technical-scientific possibilities for more effective control of the bacteria that cause plant-foods and meats to spoil.* Atomic research is speeding up advances in this field. According to Professor N. R. Brewer of the University of Chicago: "If meat can be kept indefinitely, large quantities of grains stored permanently, and delicate products like fats, eggs, and butter protected, then stores of food can be tided over from plentiful to lean seasons and the long hauls to remote famine regions made practicable. And it will no longer be necessary to reduce the food value of some products to keep them, such as extraction of the wheat germ."

---

monopoly of valid crops or planting material for the exclusive benefit of vested groups or privileged individuals . . . no quinine monopolies, or spice monopoly, or fiber monopoly, or any other collusive establishment that would arbitrarily anchor the decisive production of a given crop to a particular area for the exclusive benefit of a favored few."

All these developments, directly and indirectly, add up to more food from the same amount of land. They offer man-made means to offset the "limiting factors on biotic potential."

We may conclude this part of the discussion with a reference to food from the oceans which make up three-quarters of the earth's surface.

The minerals and food that man needs for an expanding civilization are not only in the land. Oceans are fabulously rich in minerals, and science is beginning to show us how to recover them. For many years the Dow Chemical Company has been recovering chlorine and magnesium from waters of the Atlantic Ocean and the Gulf of Mexico; in addition, the company rearranges and combines elements from these ocean minerals into more than five hundred trade preparations. And within the watery deeps are immense food possibilities.

Fish, an excellent protein food, can contribute much more to human energy than it now does. What has held back its larger consumption has been the inability to supply quantities of fresh fish over large areas. But with the development of low-temperature freezing for warehouses, railroad cars, and ships, and the use of quick-freezing, the conditions exist for a substantial increase in the world consumption of fish. Fish foods make up around 5 per cent of the Japanese diet, but, in terms of protein, they supply 20 per cent of the people's energy.

One illustration of what can be done: Venezuela has abundant sources of fish, but in the past its people consumed little of it, and much of that was in a spoiled condition because of lack of refrigeration. American enterprise supplied the fishermen with iceboxes, while refrigerated trucks and airplanes were used for transportation. So Venezuelans began to consume more fish.

The seas, lakes, and ponds can yield a more bountiful supply of fish foods, especially if it becomes known that many varieties of fish now thrown away by fishermen can provide palatable, nutritious meals. New fisheries in the Central and South Pacific are being developed by the United States through its Navy. One FAO project is the development of information on little-known fishing resources. The United States Fish and Wildlife Service is making a scientific study of fish as a food resource.

Supplies of many fish have begun to decline. In 1932, for example, the United States and Canada had to set up regulations for control of halibut-fishing off their western coasts. The British government later warned that the rich North Sea fishing grounds are seriously overfished and called for an international agreement to remedy the situation. Meanwhile the Ministry of Agriculture and Fisheries in Britain carries on research in breeding greater supplies of fish life.

Water plants, including seaweed, can yield considerable amounts of food. Ocean farming, encouraged in Japan, Ireland, and Britain, offers considerable possibilities.[2] Another possible source of food from the ocean waters is plankton, the microscopic life on which fish feed; American scientists are continuing the plankton research begun by the Germans before World War II. And according to Dr. F. N. Woodward, director of the Scottish Seaweed Research Institute, much laboratory research is being done on tiny aqueous animals which can be cultivated in fresh or sea water to make organic matter out of elemental substances; by further processing some of these substances can be converted into edible materials and some can be used for industrial purposes, thus saving on the use of limited land areas.

Newer food potentials, moreover, are being opened up as multiplying scientific research piles one discovery upon another. Life is, from the chemical angle, an exchange of energy and matter among

[2] Ferdinand C. Lane, *The Mysterious Sea* (1947), pp. 162-64, writes: "Man's failure to utilize that rich and varied vegetation produced by the sea has been indefensible. . . . That seaweed possesses considerable food value has long been known. While some European nations have far outstripped us in the use of seaweed as food, only the Orient has shown any adequate appreciation of this vast food source. In native Philippine markets one may observe piles of seaweed resembling masses of maple sugar. Throughout the East Indies and along the coast of China edible seaweeds are popular, but Japan, of all nations, has been the most successful in farming the seas. More than thirty types of marine vegetation are staple food products. . . . The Japanese use agar-agar, prepared from a red seaweed, not only for scientific research but as an article of food. In fact they transform such marine growths into soup stock, vegetables, and even candy. The annual value of sea vegetation for fertilizer, chemicals and food mounted high into the millions. . . . To plant or cultivate marine vegetation seems impossible, yet it is not. Along the Irish coast, where the bottom is firm and level, flat stones are laid down to catch the floating spores of marine vegetation. This is harvested the second year and the stones turned over for a new crop. In Japan thousands of acres of similar bottom have been devoted to the propagation of nori, a red alga known to us as laver. Instead of stones, bushes were placed so as to catch the spores and the resultant crop was harvested from January to March."

the proteins in living cells. And chemistry is not only providing means to step up plant and animal yields from the soil, but also the means to manufacture food, especially proteins, from non-soil sources in the factory on a mass production basis. This is the great new frontier whose wonders we are just beginning to glimpse. It is the final assurance that man need not hunger.

Farm wastes are utilized to create foods, and so save on plants grown on millions of acres. Simple sugars, fermentable into industrial alcohol and other products, can be made from cellulose in corncobs, oat hulls, sugar-cane bagasse, straw and other wastes, to produce a low-cost protein feed that fattens hogs, cattle, and poultry as well as other feeds do; this adds up to a saving of cereal grains.

Plant breeders have produced a variety of sugar cane which can be made to yield enough fermentable sugar, from one acre of land, to produce about 25,000 pounds of edible yeast, which in turn contains about 12,000 pounds of protein good for animals or humans.

This production of yeast is particularly important in areas where diets have a high protein deficiency. In Jamaica several factories manufacture food-yeast from crude molasses; it is an improved strain of Torula yeast, which, in the form of a light brown powder, is around 40 per cent protein—more protein than in good steaks—made palatable as food with appropriate seasoning. It sold in 1948 at 10 cents to 15 cents a pound. The protein-starved Jamaicans mix the "yeast meat" in their porridges, flapjacks, and fishcakes. Its use as protein-enrichment for canned soups and meats is growing in England. This new food-yeast industry is spreading to Mexico and South America, to Asia and Africa, where protein deficiencies are appalling. British scientists in Trinidad are studying to perfect processes for the manufacture of protein direct from sugar cane.

Food yeast for humans can also be derived from wastes of the pulp industries and from brewers' wastes. In 1948 twelve Wisconsin pulp makers started a $500,000 experimental plant to transform spent sulphite liquor into dried yeast as a powder rich in vitamin B complex. Brewers' dried yeast is already being used for various human food purposes and as a highly nutritional addition to feed for livestock. In 1948 there were 59 breweries (out of 450 in the United States) that collected 18,625,000 pounds of yeast; this indicates existence of a large potential supply.[3]

[3] News story, *New York Times*, May 5, 1949.

Food yeast made from wood is rich in meat-like proteins. Many tons of this food were used in Germany during World War II, but it was not wholly satisfactory; American chemists have substantially improved it. According to Dr. Farrington Daniels of the University of Wisconsin, in an early 1949 report to the American Association for the Advancement of Science:

From 65 per cent to 70 per cent of most woods now can be converted into sugars by heating with dilute sulphuric acid under special conditions developed at the U.S. forest products laboratory in Wisconsin. This sugar can be used for growing yeast and producing alcohol which can be used for liquid fuel. These yeasts are cheap and they possess splendid nutritive value. With intensive research on improving the flavor, this source of protein should be a great help in solving a food shortage, particularly in the tropics where large-scale production of meat is difficult. Nitrogen compounds must be supplied to growing yeast in order to produce proteins. Possibly this fixed nitrogen can be supplied directly from the nitrogen of the air by a new process in which the air is heated to a high temperature. In any event the wheat and meat of the limited, rich farming lands cannot be used indefinitely to feed the world. Trees and quick-growing bushes and grass can be grown on poorer soil and it now is perfectly practical to eat wood products.

Wood has become a resource that constantly develops new uses—for paper and plastics, as a structural material with the durability of metals, for explosives and motor fuel, and now for food. Egon Glesinger, who works with the FAO, writes that "utilization of the forest . . . could eliminate want." Up to 75 per cent of wood used as lumber is thrown away as slash and shaping losses; other losses up to 85 per cent occur in the manufacture of products from wood. All these wastes can be utilized to produce sugars, alcohols, and proteins; thus saving on use of land for foods. Trees can be made to grow almost anywhere. Dr. Glesinger proposes the reforestation of millions of depleted or destroyed acres as self-perpetuating forest reserves, with "great tree factories over the world to feed cellulose, lignin and raw wood into an integrated industry," producing meat-like protein among a variety of other products.[4]

Another source of protein looms in algae, in a microscopic plant known as Chlorella. This green single-celled plant needs only water, sunlight, and mineral salts for its growth. Two scientists of the

[4] Egon Glesinger, *The Coming Age of Wood* (1949), pp. 21-24.

Carnegie Institution, H. A. Spoeler and H. W. Milner, have discovered that, with manipulation of its environment and mineral supply, Chlorella can produce as much as half its dry weight as protein and up to three-fourths of its weight as fat. They calculated that a maximum of 1390 pounds of fat might be produced by Chlorella in a growing season on an acre of water surface, as against 227 pounds of soybean oil or 360 pounds of peanut oil from one acre of land. Suggestions are being made for the industrial manufacture of Chlorella with tanks, pipes, and pumps to produce proteins, fats, and oils. (This has no relation to "hydroponic" foods, whose costs are prohibitive.) Chlorella might be used as food for yeast in place of molasses or sugar cane, and so again save on food-crop land.

The sources of foodstuffs spread from organic materials to inorganic. A new chemical compound, manufactured in the Netherlands, is 4000 times as sweet as cane sugar (saccharine is only 200 to 700 times as sweet); it is a benzene derivative, with large potentialities for industrial use. Moreover, "We do not," in the words of Carl S. Miner, "eat soil." In an address at the dinner in his honor on receiving the 1949 Perkin Medal of the Society of Chemical Industry (American section) Dr. Miner said:

The foods we eat are composed in largest percentage of carbon, hydrogen, oxygen and nitrogen, all of which elements are available in what appear to be ample quantities from air and water. The additional essential food elements of the inorganic class do not appear likely to be exhausted at such a rate as to affect importantly the starvation problem. . . . Recently it has been found that artificial ammonia (manufactured from atmospheric nitrogen and hydrogen) and its derivatives can be fed to farm animals as substitutes for part of their normal protein requirements. Thus it should be possible to increase the amount of protein available for human consumption without decreasing supplies of meat, poultry or eggs. When we realize that one of the most serious food shortages is in protein, which in this manner can be made from air and water, the tremendous potentialities become apparent.[5]

[5] The increasing use of chemicals in agriculture and of synthetics in foods, potential of so much good for humanity, creates some immediate dangers for consumers. Again ignorance or malicious indifference raises a health hazard for the American people. The U.S. Department of Agriculture issued a warning in 1948 to farmers that if dairy cows are fed silage bearing DDT, if they are sprayed with it, or even if it is used in dairy barns the milk will contain DDT, which is injurious and against regulations of the Food and Drug Administration. The greatest danger is in the indiscriminate use of chemical

Finally, research in photosynthesis, if and when it succeeds in producing synthetic chlorophyll, will move toward factory production of foodstuffs without the use of soil. Dr. Gerald N. Wendt, in an address to the 1947 meeting of the American Meat Institute, told the packers about it:

All plant industries depend on a chemical reaction which man cannot effect: the production of carbohydrates from the carbon dioxide and water of the atmosphere under the action of sunlight. How the plant does it has always been a mystery. No man can do it—yet. But within the past few months a very vital clue has come to light by the use of a radioactive form of carbon. Working with Carbon-14 Professor Calvin of the University of California and his assistants have found that carbon dioxide itself plays no part in the light reaction. Instead exposure of the green leaf to light builds in it a reservoir of reducing power, which afterwards, in the dark, is able to reduce carbon dioxide and to cause it to combine to form the materials of the plant. It is only the first step in a long series of researches, but already it has greatly simplified the problem. It offers increased hope that before long man can eliminate the green plant and can make carbohydrates—including perhaps both foods and fibers—direct from the carbon dioxide of the air and from sunshine. In-

---

preparations to "enrich" foods. For many months in 1948–49 the Food and Drug Administration held hearings to prepare a new "standard of identity" for white bread. The hearings revealed that more and more chemicals, some of which may be injurious to health, are being added to bread while its nourishment value decreases. Among the chemicals is a "shortening extender" added to the mix. Of these extenders Dr. William J. Darby of Vanderbilt University, testifying on behalf of the Council on Foods and Nutrition of the American Medical Association, said: "Their use allows the production of a smooth-textured product, often of superior sales appeal, which contains less fat than one made without the extender. In some instances the addition of the agent also permits lowering of the proportions of other important food ingredients in the product—for example, their use in bread imparts 'freshness' as does the use of non-fat milk solids. . . . Unless complete harmlessness of these [chemical] agents can be demonstrated beyond reasonable doubt they should not, in the Council's opinion, be employed in basic foods." Two bills were introduced, early in 1949, in the House of Representatives, to put "more teeth" into the Food and Drug Act. One bill called for a committee to investigate the extent to which chemicals are used and their effect on foods. The other bill would make it law that all new chemicals to be used as insecticides and pesticides or in foods must first be tested for their toxic effects before they can be sold commercially, a policy already in effect for drugs. Dr. Paul B. Dunbar, commissioner of the Food and Drug Administration, gave his approval to the measure. See news story, *New York Times*, May 16, 1949.

deed, with the potent radiations from atomic power now also available, we may even dispense with sunlight, once the reaction is mastered.[6]

Within not much more than a year after this address came substantial progress in photosynthesis research. In March 1949 Professor Hans Gaffron of the University of Chicago reported discovery, from research involving the exposure of single-celled algae to light in an atmosphere of radioactive carbon dioxide, of an intermediate key substance that may provide a most significant clue to the mystery of photosynthesis. Another important discovery was the isolation, in pure form, of protochlorophyll, the "mother" of chlorophyll. Finally (again in 1949), Dr. Martin Kamen, in collaboration with Howard Gest of Washington University, St. Louis, reported the first experimental evidence that sunlight can liberate hydrogen as a photosynthetic product. Dr. Kamen also reported they were on the trail of another vital process—a system until now unsuspected by scientists for incorporating nitrogen in building up the plant's essential protein elements. The experimenters used a purple bacterium, one of a group of photosynthesizing bacteria that has the same ability as green plants to utilize the energy of sunlight for growth.[7]

These discoveries provide new approaches to the solution of the mystery of photosynthesis, which will make possible the artificial production of food from simple substances. An almost unlimited food supply will open up—along with the means for more direct use of the sun's energy and for the production of synthetic materials of all kinds.

Some of these developments toward obtaining new sources of food are actual; others are potential. The most important aspect is the growing understanding of proteins, which build body structure with the necessary tissue, muscle, and fat.

Diets with a protein deficiency produce the scrawny, anemic, and deformed humans who abound in slums and in the world's backward nations. Some vegetables (peas, soybeans), cereals, fruits, and nuts are rich in proteins, but deficient in the amino-acids, the real builders of tissue which are found abundantly only in meat and dairy products. (Plant protein foods provide, however, needed vita-

[6] Proceedings, 42nd Annual Convention, American Meat Institute, *The National Provisioner*, September 13, 1947, p. 108.

[7] Howard Gest and Martin D. Kamen, "Photoproduction of a Molecular Hydrogen," *Science*, June 3, 1949, pp. 558-59.

mins, carbohydrates, and fats.) Research is being carried on for a fuller understanding of amino-acids, those building stones of the protein mass. The industrial production of low-cost protein will mean a revolution in the food supply and in nutrition.

One series of developments is of the greatest significance. Scientists isolated vitamin B_{12} as the active principle in liver. This saved the lives of tens of thousands of pernicious anemia victims in the years after 1922. This precious nutrient has been rare, since one ton of whole liver yields only about twenty milligrams of B_{12}. Then, in December 1948, came the announcement that Merck & Company's laboratory scientists had produced B_{12} from molds (like penicillin). The company's president said: "The next step is to produce this vitamin in quantities adequate for medical and nutritional use." In addition to its medical use for anemia, the vitamin is usable for fighting infantile paralysis, digestive disturbances such as tropical shrue, and perhaps other diseases that result from a B_{12} deficiency.

Vitamin B_{12} and APF, the nutrient which gives meat its particular nutritional value, are not identical. Associated with animal proteins is an unidentified factor (or factors), not present in yeast or in the major plant proteins, which is essential for normal growth.[8] Experiments with chickens and pigs have shown that B_{12} is two to ten times as effective when combined with APF, the animal protein factor. Other experiments with chickens, rats, and mice indicate that APF is necessary for the maintenance of life itself.[9]

A disastrous deficiency of animal protein constitutes the world's gravest nutritional problem. Animal food in total diets ranges from 3 per cent in Asia and 4 per cent in Africa to 16 per cent in South America, 17 per cent in Europe, and 26 per cent in North America. This inequality in the consumption of protein is a major factor in producing other forms of inequality.

The world's meat supply is not enough to provide the needed animal proteins. The supply will go up, of course. Canada has grass-

---

[8] APF is necessary where livestock is fed a strictly vegetable diet. With the use of synthetic APF as a feed supplement to plant diets, a twofold economy arises: a saving of crop foods (or land) and of dairy, meat, and fish products now mixed with livestock feeds. This means a net addition to the amount of food available for human consumption.

[9] Article, "Assay of 'Animal Protein Factors' Using Mice," *Nutritional Reviews,* June 1949, pp. 167-68.

lands where livestock production can multiply. This is particularly true of its northern regions, as well as of those of northern Russia and Siberia; and production of the hardy Cattalo breed of beef cattle will extend the use of northern regions for livestock breeding. Australia and New Zealand, some parts of Latin America and Africa, also can increase their livestock output, especially now with development of Brahman cattle and the discovery of a specific for sleeping sickness. India can become a substantial consumer of meat if the Hindus end their religious ban on killing cattle for food; it has more cattle than any country in the world (including the United States). And China has great range lands in its southwestern areas where cattle and sheep breeding might flourish.

In addition, as long-term projects, grasslands for animal grazing can be increased by means of irrigation and atomic-power projects to reclaim areas like the Sahara and Gobi Deserts and the run-down lands of the Middle East.

Any substantial increase in the meat supply must come, however, from modernization of agriculture. The great open spaces are limited; it might be more desirable to use land, wherever possible, for diversified farming. As modernization of farming throughout the world takes place it will be identified with livestock breeding on a scientific basis, which alone can supply large quantities of meat. Beef production is closely identified with general farming. Hog breeding can grow as dairy farming broadens in scope, in certain areas of Southeastern Europe, in Latin America, Africa and Asia, and Oceania. The meat supply will also increase as more efficient livestock is bred in terms of greater poundage, earlier maturity, and better nutritional quality.

Yet there will be severe limitations on supplies of meat for at least many years to come and for many of the world's regions. Japan, China, and India, most European areas, and some areas in Latin America are overcrowded; little of their relatively scarce agricultural land can be spared for pasture. Hence these regions may find it necessary to limit meat-animal production in favor of cereals, vegetables, and fruits, with livestock used primarily for dairy products. This was done in a number of European nations as a postwar emergency measure, and it has some aspects of permanency as part of a long-range program of efficient land use.

Direct consumption of crops means more food, since it requires

up to eight pounds of plant food for the production of one pound
of meat. Where land is scarce its use for livestock may adversely
affect the supply of grains and other required plant foods. It will be
necessary to offset the scarcity of meat, and to balance diets, by the
use of proteins from other sources. Foods from non-land sources
are needed to supplement the crop foods.

Industrial production of proteins, especially APF, can become an
almost magic gift to mankind. The addition of low-cost APF to all-
vegetable diets will give them the nutritional value of meals with
meat. It will, at the same time, constitute a permanent addition to
the world's food supply produced from the soils and oceans.

3. WHAT THE WORLD IS DOING

While the world land-and-food problem has major elements in
common, important national and regional differences exist.

For Eastern Europe the problem is essentially the same as in Asia,
Latin America, and Africa, although not so acute—the pressure of
population on low-yield agricultural (and industrial) production.
But for Central and Northwestern Europe, with its high level of
industrialization, the problem is this: *an inability to grow enough
food under any conditions to feed people,* because industry has been
overdeveloped at the expense of agriculture, with not enough land
left available for farming.

What Europe did after the Industrial Revolution (from the 1820's
to the 1930's) was to develop industry and neglect, where it did not
sacrifice, agriculture. An increasingly industrial Europe, with its
growing population, depended upon the import of cheap crop foods
and meats from new lands overseas. Meanwhile, soils were depleted
in many nations. The situation was aggravated, from Spain and Italy
to Eastern Europe and Turkey, by the persistence of feudal conditions in agriculture, with a consequent economic and social backwardness. Density of population grew and pressed upon relatively
diminishing land resources. Meat, especially, suffered, not only from
an insufficiency of livestock but from the inefficiency of small-scale
operations in municipal packinghouses and meat markets, and low
purchasing power among the people.

The imbalance between growing industrialization and urbanization and the shrinking of agricultural resources developed most

dangerously in Great Britain. Since 1891 alone, according to Sir John Russell, president of the British Association for the Advancement of Science, population has increased 14,000,000 while 4,000,-000 acres of land have gone out of cultivation. Of these, 1,000,000 acres have been used for larger cities, highways, and airfields, with 3,000,000 acres abandoned because of soil depletion.

In pre-1939 years Britain produced only one-third of its food requirements. In addition, British farming itself was unbalanced between food crops and livestock. Arable farming had sunk to 12,000,-000 acres, the lowest in British history; the number of dairy cattle, sheep, pigs, and poultry, however, was the highest on record; Britain was forced to import yearly between 7,000,000 and 8,000,000 tons of animal feeds, one out of every three tons needed to feed this livestock.

When World War II came the British concentrated on producing more of the food they consume. Through education on better farming methods, substantial advances in the development and use of farm machinery (two-thirds of it of domestic manufacture), land improvement through drainage, and greater use of fertilizers, Britain produced 70 per cent of its wartime rations. The British ended the most agonizing years in their history with a permanent increase in food production, but still not enough for economic balance and security.

The Labour government made a twofold attack on problems of the food supply: (1) development of food production in colonial areas, and (2) stepping up of agricultural production at home to lessen Britain's dependence on food imports. In its program the government combined the technical approach with larger social-economic policy. In 1947 Parliament adopted a comprehensive agricultural act, which brought farm lands under national planning with emphasis on three aspects: 1) Assured markets and guaranteed prices for farm products; prices for cereals, potatoes, and sugar beets are set eighteen months before the harvest; prices are set two to four years in advance for meat, milk, and eggs. 2) Guaranteed minimum wages for agricultural workers, who were miserably underpaid; protection of tenants against landlords who may want to exploit both land and tenants. 3) Compulsory powers, to be used as a last resort, to insure that the land is properly farmed. Land belongs to the nation and to future generations, not merely to present owners. The indifferent farmer or owner may be given twelve months' notice to improve his farming; if no satisfactory improvement is made, the Minister of Agriculture has power to dispossess him, although the farmer is allowed to appeal to the courts if he wants to. Cooperation is the rule, however. During the first year's operation of the act, 1947–48, only forty farmers (among 370,000) were dispossessed for non-cooperation with national policy. A State Land Commission will take over land from dispossessed farmers or from voluntary sale.

An Agricultural Advisory Service operates in eight regional centers in Britain; its staff of advisers works directly with farmers for more efficient production. In addition to work for greater efficiency in farming, the policy envisages "provision for a satisfactory career on the land" through better wages, housing, and social-cultural opportunities. It includes providing an "agricultural ladder" for farm laborers and tenants up which they can climb, with experience and capacity, to become free owner-farmers. The new policy recognizes that the advancement of farming cannot be separated from an advancement of *people* in farming.

Land is not nationalized under the new policy, which has nothing in common with the despotic "collective farm" system of Soviet Russia and its satellites. On the contrary, one British objective is to promote free farmer-ownership by the abolition of landlordism. Speculation in farm lands is made impossible, however; land prices are frozen as of 1947, and if a sale is made at a higher price the difference is taxed 100 per cent by the government. Free farmers operate within a flexible planning policy for most efficient land-use, which combines the farmer's individual interests with the social stake in food. Agricultural cooperatives are encouraged by the Labour government, although it is criticized for not doing enough about them and urged to do more. In addition to buying and marketing, cooperatives exist for processing eggs, poultry, and meat products— there are several large farmers' bacon plants—for joint use of machinery, and for artificial insemination of livestock.[10]

As part of its participation in the Marshall Plan the British government worked out a four-year program for agricultural improvement and expansion. It provided for an expenditure of $1,800,000,000 on capital investment, over one-half in machinery, including labor-

[10] Margaret Higby, "Cooperation and the Farmers," *Socialist Commentary*, June 1949, pp. 124-25.

saving and crop-saving machines such as combined harvester-threshers and grass-driers. The program aimed to increase, by 1952, Britain's agricultural output by 50 per cent.[11] This will not, of course, make Britain self-sufficient in food supply, but it will lessen dependence upon imports.

In addition, the British are carrying on experimental work to supplement the land supply with more food from ocean farming and from supplementary industrial foods (e.g., food-yeast from molasses used to enrich soups). Measures to promote fishing include subsidies and loans for acquisition of boats and equipment, and experimental research and pilot-plants to increase by-products from fish and for quicker processing.

On meat and dairy products the four-year program called for the following percentages of the average yearly output for 1936–39: mutton and lamb, 83 per cent; pork, 92 per cent; beef and veal, 110 per cent; milk, 123 per cent; eggs, 131 per cent.

This program reversed the Coalition government's decision (to switch British agriculture from cereals to livestock) in favor of more cereals, the output of which is planned to increase 100 per cent. Growing more grains will reduce grazing for cattle and sheep, thus limiting, at least for a temporary period, the output of home-produced meats. But some increases in beef and milk were provided for, although below the 1947 estimate of Britain's need for 25 per cent more beef and 65 per cent more milk. The 1948–49 targets aimed at increases of 35 per cent in bread grains, 87 per cent in corn grains, and 9 per cent in milk, with meat and bacon output two-thirds of the prewar average.[12]

The government also proposed to nationalize cold-storage facilities, with inspection of all warehouses and plants used for storage or processing of foods and the grading of these foods for quality, as well as a Consumers Advice Center to test goods and issue buying grades for the public.

A new Ministry for Food was set up (in addition to the existing agricultural ministry) to correlate the food work. Its chief, John

[11] Article, "Capital Investment in Britain," *Labor and Industry in Britain,* March 1949, p. 17.

[12] Livestock is not neglected, however. In its first year of office the Labour government enacted the Artificial Insemination Act, which provided for state expenditure on research and financial assistance to centers during the initial development of this method of livestock breeding.

Strachey, declared that the new office "will be responsible for ensuring that adequate supplies of food necessary to health are available to all members of the public at reasonable prices." [13]

The continental nations of Europe, too, began work to develop their domestic food supply. For at least many years to come the Europeans will depend upon overseas food imports; some of them, especially Britain and France, are using their technological and scientific resources to promote agricultural production in the world's backward regions. But Europe must use all its ability to produce more food within its own areas.

National efforts at "self-sufficiency" make the situation worse. There is need for economic unity, as the basis for a United States of Europe, to encourage *continental* agriculture through *continental* agricultural planning, markets, and consumption.

American experts are working with the French to modernize agriculture, and especially to transform North Africa from a "nomadic economy" to a dry farming system with large-scale mechanized farming. Israel is refertilizing the Negev desert to make it bloom again. Italy is going through an agricultural revolution. And Germany, in the highly industrialized western areas, is concentrating on research for the production of industrial foods.

One project under the Marshall Plan provides for modernization of agriculture in southern Italy, which is unbelievably backward. The project includes measures to transform feudal land ownership into democratic ownership, to make free farmers of subjugated peasants. Less than 1 per cent of the landholders own up to 25 per cent of Italy's arable land. These Italian absentee landlords are unbelievably crude, avaricious, and backward. One of them, who collects rents from seven hundred peasants on his 24,700 acres, which are infested with malaria, whose eroded soils yield four bushels to an American forty-five, says: "We aren't concerned with production. We collect rents. Anyway, the peasants are retrograde. If we built clean, good homes they'd only dirty them." [14]

Five major plans are relied upon for the modernization of Italian

[13] Labour Publications Department, *Labour's First Year: the Facts* (1947), pp. 16-17.

[14] Article, "The Underprivileged and Unreformed," *Time*, May 30, 1949, pp. 21-22.

agriculture, according to the chief of the Food and Agricultural Division of the Economic Cooperation Administration (ECA): 1) reclamation of 2,500,000 acres of land within three years, with improved productivity to yield 30 per cent more output; 2) irrigation for 1,250,000 acres, with a twofold increase of persons employed in those fields; 3) direct assistance to individual farmers for improvement of their farms and buildings, with experimental services made available to them; 4) training centers to provide practical instruction in farming; and 5) provision of funds to permit specialists chosen by the Italian government to go to the United States for intensive training in new agricultural practices.

Another contribution to solving Italy's food problem was the introduction of American hybrid corn seed supplied under the Marshall Plan. Plantings made during the season 1947–48 stepped up acre yields by as much as 128 per cent. Greater corn crops will increase livestock production. It is calculated that Italian farm income will increase by $5,000,000 for every 1000 tons of hybrid seed used. Italy may also develop mass production of vegetables and citrus fruits for the use of its own low-income groups and for export to northwestern Europe.[15] There will still be need, however, for a rational Italian population policy to balance land resources and people.

Communism has made the food problem worse in Soviet Russia and its East-European satellites. Russian food consumption will not rise to the prewar levels of the 1930's until after 1950, and those levels were lower than in earlier years. Collectivization, the Communist quack-magic for solving all agrarian problems, has produced more fantastic propaganda claims than food for the Russian people. Statistical manipulation has grown infinitely faster than agricultural output. An agrarian bureaucracy of up to 2,000,000 state employees, composed of directors, office workers and other "managerial" employees, and police, whose primary job is to keep the peasants under state-Communist control, get larger incomes than do the "collective" workers. The peasants have little left for themselves after meeting the state's demands, and urban consumers who are not members of the new ruling class have had continually less food to eat. According to an outstanding authority, only in 1937 was collective farm

15 News stories, *New York Times,* December 21, 1948; June 6, 1949.

output slightly higher than in earlier years, and it has since declined.[16]

What happened to livestock in Russia is characteristic of the general agricultural situation. The collectivization drive of the early 1930's, carried on with machine guns and the accompaniment of a famine in the Ukraine which killed 5,000,000 people, resulted in losses of two-fifths of the cattle, two-thirds of the sheep, and over one-half of the hogs. These losses were not yet fully made up (except in hogs) when the Nazi attack came and brought further destruction of livestock, although on a smaller scale than in the collectivization drive. By 1948, while the wartime losses were largely made up, livestock herds were still generally smaller than in 1928. A three-year "livestock plan" was intended to increase deliveries to the state for urban consumers, not to increase the supply of livestock.[17]

Despite all the "reforms" and the claims made by the Soviet government, the level of per capita production and consumption of foodstuffs is below that which prevailed in the years preceding the Communist Revolution of 1917. And this was also true of industrial productivity in 1948, of which Colin Clark, outstanding Australian economist, said: "Economic progress in Russia has been uncertain and slow, and the most recent figures indicate that productivity is only at about [its] 1900 level."

In the fall of 1948 Soviet Russia announced a fifteen-year land-use plan to conserve and promote its land resources. The plan proposed, by 1965, to plant "eight basic systems of forest belts in four basic defense lines" to break the winds; total length of the belts will be more than 3000 miles; to build a "forest defense" on their big collective farms by planting 15,000,000 acres of forests; to put in 45,000 reservoirs and ponds on collective farms for irrigation, production of electric power, and to help keep up a high ground water level; to place 80,000 collective farms on an improved grass and

[16] Naum Jasny, *Socialized Agriculture in the U.S.S.R.* (1948), the most exhaustive and objective study available. Soviet collectivization has proved a terrible failure, according to Jasny. He shows that farm labor in the United States is four and one-half times more productive than in Russia.

[17] A. Bergson, J. H. Blockman and A. Erlich, "Postwar Economic Reconstruction and Development in the USSR," *Annals of the American Academy of Political and Social Science,* May 1949, p. 63.

crop rotation system in the next six years; the government did not say how many acres this involves.[18]

The Communist dictatorships in East Europe have also begun to introduce collectivization. This has helped to keep the people down and strengthen dictatorship, but it has meant a smaller production of food. The satellites are moving slowly toward collectivization, while Moscow prods them to go faster. One important difference is that the amount of land per person dependent on agriculture is three times as great in Russia as the average for the satellites. This means that while in Russia persons displaced from the land by collectivization could be put to work on new farms, it cannot be done among the more densely populated satellites because there is not enough land, and industrialization would have to move at tremendous speed to absorb persons displaced from the land. Collectivization in the Communist nations of East Europe will prove more disastrous than in Russia. It may end, according to the Royal Institute of International Affairs, in forcing 10,000,000 dispossessed, unemployed peasants into slave-labor camps.

Israel's scientific research on reclaiming the desert has a number of outstanding achievements to its credit. One is successful desalting of water, which provides means for irrigation to rehabilitate desert areas where fresh water is lacking; this de-salting process is being marketed in other parts of the world by an American corporation. And plans are completed for a Jordan Valley Authority which, in addition to a large supply of low-cost hydroelectric power, will increase by seven times the 100,000 irrigated acres of Palestine. The Israeli have also developed use of the indigenous castor oil bean for plastics and of citrus wastes in the fermentation process for producing acetone and butyl alcohol.

These achievements point the way to reclamation of eroded and desert lands not only in Israel and the Middle East but in similar

[18] News story, *New York Times*, October 31, 1948. With their usual hysteria—a mixture of doctrinaire fanaticism, propaganda, and ignorance—the Russians proclaimed that what they planned to do was not only bigger than anything a capitalist nation is doing, but that *no capitalist nation could do it*. A *Pravda* editorial said: "Nothing like it exists or can exist under the conditions of capitalism." But, in fact, what the Russians merely plan to do they have mostly learned from American doing, and the United States has done more in the past fifteen years than the Soviet plans to do. For figures on what has been done see Chapter VI, p. 119.

regions elsewhere, with millions of acres made to produce food again. In Egypt, for example, whose agriculture is unbelievably backward and where overpopulation problems are severe, the government plans to harness the Nile River for a multiple program of land and industry development. Included in the program is aid for irrigating farmlands and producing fertilizer.

While the French plan to transform North Africa from a "nomadic economy" to a dry farming system, the British work to advance agriculture in tropical Africa. They have started a significant number of projects for African production and export of vegetable oils, coffee, beans, and meats. Liberal socialist cooperation for mutual gains and self-government in place of colonial exploitation is the Labour government's policy. Its economic plans are carried out by a mixture of public and private enterprise (including American enterprise).

Much of Britain's work of agricultural development in backward areas is under direction of the Overseas Food Corporation, which operates throughout the world, but with special concentration on Africa. This public corporation has at its disposal one-third of a $600,000,000 appropriation (two-thirds are at the disposal of another public corporation, the Colonial Development Company) to finance a four-year plan for economic advance.

One of the Food Corporation's plans is the "ground-nuts" project, launched in 1947, to clear up to 3,500,000 acres in and around Tanganyika for the production of peanuts to provide fats, edible oils, and margarine. This project includes extermination of the tsetse fly, which makes large areas of these tropical regions uninhabitable, and building of railroads and ports. In addition, according to the plan, "A high proportion of investment must be concentrated on basic services, on health and education, on irrigation, water supply and research. . . . If investment is pushed too far too fast, it would give rise to conditions that have the gravest consequences to social welfare and stability." As of 1949 the "ground nuts" project had cost more than anticipated and produced smaller results.

The discovery in 1948 of a drug, antrycide, that cures sleeping sickness carried by the tsetse fly, will not only help the ground-nuts project but advance the transformation of tropical Africa into one of the world's great cattle regions. Successful experiments are being made on the immunization of cattle.

These plans envisage the economic development of 4,500,000 square miles of desolate, largely uninhabitable African hinterland, mainly in the Sudan, Kenya, Uganda, and West Africa. As a tie-in, the American ECA in March 1949 added a colonial division to work with other nations to "unlock" colonial resources in line with President Truman's call for American technical know-how and private capital to help promote the economic development of undeveloped regions. In addition, the Dominion of South Africa, upward of three-quarters of whose land is good only for pasture, may become one of the world's great producers of meat and dairy products.

Brazilian farmers are worried about the British plans for African agricultural development, since many of the products—e.g., coffee, vegetable oils, beans—produced by the two tropical regions are the same and compete in the world markets. One Brazilian spokesman said: "We are faced with great competition and a severe commercial struggle." It is highly doubtful that this is so, considering the world's need for food. The only consequence may be to force more agricultural diversification and industrialization on Brazil, which is highly desirable. This is what a Joint Brazil-United States Technical Commission has urged—"a balanced development of Brazil's resources: mining, manufactures, transportation and electric utilities, farming." [19]

In Latin America, too, substantial work for agricultural modernization is going on. Mexico is pressing land reform along with measures for greater agricultural efficiency. These measures to grow more food include a program to stop erosion, which threatens to convert more farm acres into dust bowls and deserts, and plans for greater instruction in fertilization, contour tillage, and reforestation. The government of Venezuela has made considerable appropriations for agricultural improvement, including purchase of farm equipment. Puerto Rico is constructing a $25,000,000 hydroelectric project along TVA lines that will serve to irrigate 25,000 semi-arid acres in the Lajas Valley. Without any crop increase, Guatemala has made a gain of 25 per cent in its usable grain through reduction of wastage in storage. Although good land is comparatively scarce in Chile, the arable potential is twice the amount of land now under cultivation, while large areas in the south can provide excellent grazing for sheep. Since 1920 many large feudal estates have been broken up

[19] News story, *New York Times*, March 11, 1949.

into small farms, while the government has started a conservation program to tackle Chile's serious problem of soil erosion. The country has a high per capita meat consumption but not enough milk; the government plans to overcome this situation. Bolivia is working to make mountain slopes available for livestock grazing with a new type of grass, while improving transportation to bring all its fertile soils into cultivation. Brazil begins to recognize the need for agricultural diversification, plans to open up vast undeveloped regions, and prepares to expand cattle breeding with the use of Brahman cattle cross-bred for tropical climes. In Cuba, too, Brahman crossbreeds are being used to expand cattle production, with nearly a hundred ranches (as of 1948) doing so.

The world's most serious food situation is in Asia. Growing population presses upon the food supply. Cultivated lands are the smallest in relation to people, and little new land is available for cultivation. China is characteristic: the average farm household consists of six persons who cultivate four acres, compared with the American average of four persons on 155 acres. Acre-crop yields are good, but they come from an intensive farming which involves a wasteful, back-breaking use of manpower. Asia's manpower requirements for one acre of crops are from ten to more than twenty times higher than in the United States.

From two-thirds to three-quarters of Asia's people live off the land, which makes surplus population, poverty, and hunger inevitable. Grains provide up to 90 per cent of the diet, with rice a staple food; little fruit, nuts, and meat are eaten. China and Japan have hardly any livestock. India has large numbers of cattle, malnourished and scrawny, which are used primarily as draft animals and not for meat. A disastrous protein deficiency prevails among the 1,000,000,000 Asiatics; the Japanese total protein consumption, the highest in Asia, is 10 per cent compared with 45 per cent in the United States.

Chinese farm output can probably be increased 50 per cent, experts agree, if the following is done: 1) uniform enforcement of an equitable land law; 2) wider credit facilities with suppression of money and landlord sharks; 3) consolidation of separate farm fragments into larger units; 4) extension of transportation to improve access to markets; and 5) marketing cooperatives, an increase in mechanization, and better farming techniques covering seed, fertilizer, and irrigation. The needs, in addition, include conservation to check erosion and floods, and reclamation projects to bring unused lands into cultivation. A Chinese network of TVA's is feasible; one proposed project alone, a Yangtze dam, would irrigate 10,000,-000 acres and supply immense quantities of electricity.

South of the Yangtze River are great sloping grasslands where dairy cows would thrive to provide milk, fresh and dried, for the Chinese people, who now virtually never drink milk. What can be done is illustrated by one development: three or four agricultural experiment stations have spread, among hundreds of thousands of peasants, knowledge of how to eliminate poultry diseases; many peasants have walked miles, carrying chickens on their backs, to learn the treatments. In 1949, however, these plans were all upset by the Communist invasion.

Population pressure on an inadequate food supply is perhaps most severe in India. Agricultural yields are low, fodder crops scarce and of poor quality, and cows give only 10 per cent as much milk as American cows do.

The new Indian government tackled the problem with a "Grow More Food" campaign. It proposed that all reclaimed lands, cultivable fallow land, and 10 per cent of the sugar-cane acres be put into production of food crops. Feudal estates are being abolished and measures taken to reduce rural peasant indebtedness. Land reclamation projects, using heavy reclamation tractors and standard tractors, are planned to add, within five years, 6,000,000 acres to India's farmlands for the production of 2,000,000 tons of food. Irrigation projects, a number of them combined with the generation of hydroelectric power, are being promoted; one such project in the Central Provinces will irrigate 1,350,000 acres, while another in Hyderabad will irrigate 227,000 acres of arable lands and 30,000 acres of pasture and forests.

Other modernization measures include more extensive use of commercial fertilizers, increasing the production of milk, training technicians to operate tractors, and research institutes for agricultural and animal husbandry. Local manufacture of agricultural implements is being developed. Research is also encouraged on deep-sea fishing, with measures to promote the catching and consumption of more fish.

Indian scientists and food experts began work on the cultivation and use of food yeast to fortify vegetarian diets deficient in protein foods such as meat, dairy products, and fish. India has an abundance of molasses and sugar from which yeast can be made. Indian scientists engaged in plant and food research have succeeded in growing a giant jute plant (two to three times as large as older varieties); it was done by treating the seeds with X rays. This new plant will save on land use. The Indian Institute of Science at Bangalore, using American equipment, set up a pilot plant for experiments on the fortification of rice with vitamins; it developed a process, superior to those in use elsewhere, of impregnating raw rice with a vitamin solution which has a very low loss in cooking. Finally, nine countries in 1949 accepted India's invitation to join an international organization on irrigation and canals with headquarters in India. The countries were Brazil, Canada, Ceylon, Egypt, Indonesia, Pakistan, Siam, Switzerland, and Turkey.[20]

Japan's food situation is better than that of other Asiatic nations, but it is still bad. The Japanese population—now 80,000,000—keeps on growing. Although one-half the people work on farms and intensive farming—one-third of the farm lands are made to yield two crops a year—is highly developed, only four-fifths of the people's food needs (on not too high a level) are met. Japan's acre-crop yields, the highest in Asia, result not only from farming skill but from an excessive use of human labor. Rice, which is deficient in protein, is still the basic food. Pressure of population on scarce land for food, together with a small amount of pasture, poor indigenous grasses, and long hot summers, result in underdevelopment of livestock. Cattle are used primarily as draft animals; there is little breeding of pigs and sheep. A land reform and agricultural rehabilitation program is being pressed, with the aid of American experts, to break up large landed estates to create a class of free farmers, greater agricultural diversification, and higher yields with smaller use of labor. In addition to research to get more food from ocean farming and fishing, scientists are working on new processes for production of industrial foods.

Reports to the United Nations Scientific Conference on the Conservation and Utilization of Resources have urged fish-farming as one

[20] Reports, *Government of India Information Services*, April 25, 1949, pp. 4-5; April 28, 1949, p. 7; July 14, 1949, p. 4; *New York Times*, April 12, 1949.

means to combat Asia's food shortage. Scientific-technical study of fish yields in the tropical waters off Bengal and Madras is needed. In warm-water ponds annual yields of fish as high as 2000 to 4000 pounds per acre have been reported in certain parts of China and Malaya, while in Bengal the yield ranges from 700 to 2000 pounds a year. Much unused land is usable for fish-farming. In the Philippines over 1,000,000 acres of low swamps and mud flats can become productive fish farms. In Japan carp-rearing rice paddies were increased to 7400 acres in 1946; although their area represents only 1 per cent of the total area of rice paddies, it produced 3,895,000 pounds of carp in 1946. Throughout Asia there are many unused lands where fish-farming might flourish.

A final example of what the world is doing to increase its food supply: In May 1949, in the winter sunshine of Central Queensland, Australia, the first crop of grain sorghum—1,000,000 bushels—was harvested on 30,000 acres of land formerly used as sheep runs and considered useless for crop-raising. The sorghum is being grown to provide pork and bacon for Britain. The 1,000,000 bushels of sorghum should produce 10,000,000 pounds of pork from 60,000 pigs. Intensive mechanization and mass-production methods are used to plant and harvest the sorghum. More than 500,000 acres of former sheep runs are available for the project, which is part of the activities of the British Food Corporation. Plans envisage 200 pig farms to surround the sorghum granary.[21]

One aspect of the plans for agricultural modernization and development requires a brief mention: the need for industrialization. The program of consolidating fragmentary small farms into larger farms and mechanizing them will displace, for example, millions of people from the land in highly populated regions as increasing productivity grows more crops with smaller amounts of manpower. The absorption of these displaced people into industrial work will be necessary to avoid unemployment. This will mean rapid, intensive industrialization: building factories and communications, developing service industries. On the other hand, in sparsely populated regions like Australia, agricultural expansion will not raise the danger of unemployment, but it will raise another one unless industrialization develops at the same time: the danger of economic

[21] News story, *New York Times*, May 24, 1949.

unbalance, of an overdevelopment of agriculture in relation to industry. These problems will confront all undeveloped countries as they
modernize and expand their agriculture.

The twofold task of agricultural modernization and industrialization, in all its dimensions, involves aspects of larger social-economic
policy. Greater production will need more equal distribution of its
proceeds to increase the people's purchasing power. A 1948 FAO
report insisted that, in low-income lands (the world excluding
northwestern Europe, the United States, Canada, and Oceania),
*"the overwhelming problem is to raise the productivity and income
of the entire community,"* in addition to work to check soil erosion
and promote higher crop yields through use of fertilizers, farm machinery, and pesticides.

The world's food problems are a unity. The logic of accumulating
scientific knowledge, in its ecological aspect, makes imperative a
synthesis of agriculture, animal husbandry, and fisheries with industry and nutrition in one design for living. It compels international
planning and action for the production and distribution of enough
food to provide all human beings with satisfactory diets.

The United Nations early began to develop a comprehensive program for increasing the world's food supply. FAO arranged conferences on regional problems in agriculture, forestry, fisheries, and
nutrition, in cooperation with United Nations regional economic
commissions. The 1949 program included plans for control of animal
diseases and food infestation; development of information on little-
known fishery resources; aid to governments in fostering practical
nutrition projects and the encouragement of extension work in
agriculture.

One major project, to end the world's fertilizer shortage, indicates
the importance of FAO work. Twenty countries alone, from Egypt
to Asia, need 900,000 tons of fertilizer yearly. Yet, according to a
1949 report of FAO, up to 800,000 tons of fixed nitrogen can be produced yearly from natural gas now burned as waste in the oilfields
of Saudi Arabia. And this natural gas supply can be counted on for
at least forty years to come. The FAO report suggests a $50,000,000
investment (perhaps financed by the Bank for International Reconstruction and Development) to build a plant, near Qatif, with the
production of 250,000 tons of ammonium sulphate as a start. This
investment could be amortized in ten years while paying annual

dividends of 15 per cent. Use of this source of available fertilizer would provide a life-giving step-up for Oriental output of crop and animal foods.

So far, FAO's emphasis has been on agriculture. It is doubtful, however, if agricultural modernization alone can bring adequate diets to Asia's people, especially the animal proteins necessary for balanced nutritious diets.

There seems to be need for a gigantic effort to investigate and make usable the new sources of industrial protein foods. Which of them are the most practical, how can they combine with available plant and fish foods for adequate nutrition, how can they be produced and distributed at costs low enough for the world's malnourished people to buy? What is indicated is an international effort on the grand scale to speed up further development of *existing* scientific and economic knowledge in this area. It can be done if money, brains, and work are put in one mighty effort to get quick results—as was done with the A-bomb.

The United Nations through FAO might form a commission of food scientists, engineers, and economists to decide on the most practical discoveries for the production of industrial foods, with the Bank for International Reconstruction and Development financing the building of pilot-plants in strategic parts of the world.

Some steps in that direction have already been taken by FAO, two of whose projects are thus described by N. E. Dodd, its director general:

Food yeast—Carbohydrate material not used for human food can be converted into yeast rich in proteins and B vitamins. Such a food has been produced successfully on a factory basis in Jamaica and Germany. Technical help is needed to determine the possibilities of production and to develop ways of working yeast into the diet.

Developing alternatives for milk—This is greatly needed in many countries of the Orient. The development of easily emulsified powders made from soybeans and other pulses would be of much value.

These are the kind of projects in food technology that FAO has started and hopes to stimulate further.[22]

One change in policy should be toward more equal distribution of income and, consequently, of food. A 1948 report of FAO in-

[22] N. E. Dodd, "Filling Empty Bellies Is World's No. 1 Problem," *Food Industries*, August 1949, p. 39.

cludes the United States among the seven nations (the other six are Australia, New Zealand, Canada, Switzerland, Sweden, and Norway) which "would have had available sufficient food in 1947–48 to provide an adequate calorie level for all their people *if such supplies were distributed in accordance with nutritional needs*." The report adds: "The variation in distribution from this ideal is so great, however, that even these countries are still faced with many food-management and distribution problems."

Many changes in world economic policy will be needed to solve the food problem. The phosphate cartel may be used as an illustration of economic practices that endanger the food supply.

In the early twentieth century the world began to recognize the indispensability of phosphate for soil fertility and human nutrition, and farmers increased their use of it. Then came a cartel to limit output, set sales quotas, and raise prices. The Phosphate Export Association, organized by Florida producers, signed a ten-year agreement in 1933 with North African producers of phosphates to keep them out of the American market. This agreement was broadened to include the apportionment of the Japanese market with the Italian (Kosseir) producers in Egypt, a small share going to the French North African producers. Foreign competition in the American market was completely eliminated in 1934 when the Phosphate Export Association came to an agreement with Dutch producers in Curaçao. Yet phosphate at low cost and in large quantities is needed to fertilize the world's agriculture to feed the people. The nutritional stakes are great: "Liberal use of fertilizer helped Australia to rescue her mineral-starved sheep-raising industry, while New Zealand farmers were enabled to establish a grassland agriculture and supply the British Empire with butter. . . . What this comes down to is that phosphate, like petroleum, uranium and other critical natural resources, must somehow be equitably distributed internationally if the world is to be healed, pacified, and fed." [23]

Cartels impose monopoly restrictions on output to raise prices and profits. Moreover, they distort and unbalance the economy of undeveloped nations as they encourage overdevelopment of one crop (or mineral), with underdevelopment of agriculture and industry as a whole. Sugar in Cuba and Puerto Rico, petroleum in Mexico and

[23] Tennessee Valley Authority, *Food at the Grass Roots,* by James Rorty (1947), pp. 39-40, 46.

Venezuela, tin in Bolivia, coffee in Brazil, rubber in Southeast Asia—these developments are typical of backward regions. The resulting economic imbalance and insecurity bring exploitation and poverty. In most of these regions an insufficient agricultural output compels the importation of foodstuffs at prices that make it impossible for a majority of the people to get enough food. The human expressions of this condition are malformed, undernourished, and diseased men, women, and children.

The problem of what to do with cartels is obviously one of the problems for an expanding world economy. These restrictive economic practices must go. International action is necessary, of the kind which United Nations economic agencies (especially FAO) are developing. But the problem also requires that individual nations conform their economic policies to the needs of an expanding world economy.

In this design for international action the United States plays, and will continue to play, a decisive part. It has dominating productive resources—one-half the world's industrial capacity to produce and the world's biggest, most efficient agricultural plant. Moreover, the interests of the United States and its international leadership are identified with a peaceful democratic world. And world peace and democracy need a foundation of economic welfare for all peoples.

In 1939 Congress gave the United States Department of Agriculture authority to start a "Good Neighbor" program to provide technical economic aid to Central and South American countries. In 1947 Congress authorized the Institute of Inter-American Affairs to continue for three years the programs successfully operating in Latin America, particularly in agriculture, public health, and sanitation. As of 1948 the work covered fifteen of those countries. It included providing technicians and other assistance to set up cooperative agricultural stations throughout the Western Hemisphere. In addition, a number of fruitful Inter-American conferences on the conservation of renewable resources have been held.

In 1940 another act of Congress provided for broadening the program of technical aid on a world scale, with agricultural missions sent to China, the Philippines, Syria, Lebanon, Iraq, Saudi Arabia, Greece, and Egypt.

The world aspects of this part of United States economic foreign policy were correlated and raised to a new level in Point Four of

President Harry Truman's inaugural address to Congress on January 29, 1949. It announced that this country would embark on a co-operative program to extend technical assistance to the world's undeveloped areas. The purpose, said the President, is "to help the free peoples of the world, through their own efforts, to produce more food, more clothing, more materials for housing, and more mechanical power to lighten their burdens," and by so doing to promote peace and enable all men to attain "freedom and dignity and the fullness of life." Particular emphasis will be given to development in the following three fields:

Natural resources: soil conservation and utilization; plant and animal husbandry; forest and fisheries management; water control and use, including water supply, irrigation and reclamation, waterways, and power development; mining and fuels.

Human resources: health and welfare, including sanitation and nutrition; education, particularly fundamental, rural and vocational; manpower training and utilization.

Capital resources: industrial technology, facilities, and equipment; organization of business and finance; housing; transportation; marketing and distribution.

The United States Department of State interpreted some aspects of Point Four as follows:

In many areas, a basic improvement in health and education may be prerequisite to increased production and improved standards of living. It is probable also that among less developed countries, now predominantly agricultural, plans should stress the improvement of techniques in agriculture, local credit facilities, food and fiber processing, rural and small-scale industry, and transportation, power and, where appropriate, mining.

The Point Four program springs from the recognition that desperate poverty and the absence of hope for the future make men easy prey to the promises of totalitarian systems. . . . A struggle for the hearts and minds of men is being waged by profoundly conflicting philosophies. One philosophy promises man material security only at the cost of unconditional surrender of his human dignity and personal freedom. The other philosophy, which is exemplified by Point Four, also seeks material security for all men, but as a means to the greater non-material end of personal fulfillment—and denies that the way to make men free is first to enslave them. . . . In the struggle between progressive democracy and the reactionary systems that pose as revolutionary, the Point Four program introduces the evolutionary element of modern technical knowledge.

WORLD POLICY 355

Finally, the program implies a clear recognition of the power of modern technology as an instrument for good or evil. It recognizes that this force must be consciously directed for the good of mankind.[24]

The Point Four policy involves cooperation with the United Nations Social and Economic Council, through which specific plans will be made. American industry and capital are needed, as they alone can provide the requisite industrial equipment and know-how. This will and can be done only on terms that benefit the people whose economy is being developed. "The old imperialism—exploitation for foreign profit—has no place in the plan," President Truman emphasized. "New economic developments must be devised and controlled to benefit the peoples of the areas in which they are established." This policy should be an inspiration to our food scientists and economists, and similar technicians, who will have an opportunity to devote their talents and faith to unrestricted progressive work for world reconstruction and peace.[25]

[24] U.S. Department of State, Foreign Affairs Outlines, "Building the Peace," *The "Point Four" Program*, No. 21, Spring 1949, pp. 1-2.

[25] On July 26, 1949, a Soviet Russian spokesman in the Social and Economic Council, Dr. Amazasp Arutiunian, denounced Point Four as "just another colonial plan . . . a new kind of imperialism to exploit impoverished colonial peoples." This was just as untrue as when Dr. Arutiunian added that Soviet Russia was prepared to aid the economic development of all nations if they reject cooperation with the United States: "The industrial development of the Soviet Union has reached a point where we can manufacture any kind of machinery or build any kind of plant." The unanswerable facts are clear: Russia does not produce enough machinery for its own needs, much less for export. The Communist nations of Eastern Europe were told they would get Russian economic help (under the Molotov Plan) when Moscow forced them to stay out of the Marshall Plan; but while Western Europe recovers with American cooperation, the Communist nations' economic conditions become worse. There are no colonial or political strings to Point Four policy—it leaves the people who cooperate with it independent and free. Soviet Russia, on the contrary, imposes economic and political bondage on its satellites. Economic agreements with these countries are all one-sidedly in favor of Russia: a Communist colonialism and imperialism more enslaving than the capitalist variety of the nineteenth century. And when a satellite kicks over the traces, as Tito's Yugoslavia did, Russia breaks its "friendship" treaties, imposes economic sanctions on the rebel nation, and uses Soviet agents to work for civil war within it. Russia considers all the agencies and policies of the United States and the United Nations as "imperialistic"—including FAO! In April 1949 the Soviet "trade union" organ, *Trud*, said: "FAO is an agency of American monopolists, the organ of the food dictators of the USA, supplying them with valuable information in their struggle to dominate the world's food, agriculture, forestry, and fishing."

It is crucial for Point Four that it work with the self-help of people in the regions being developed. The problem is not only technical-economic but social-political in scope. Many changes will be necessary in existing institutions and policies. Reactionary interests, in the undeveloped nations and in the United States, may try to distort the program to benefit them, not the people. This danger can be averted only by the cooperative action of all progressive groups, including democratic labor unions. In an address to the 1948 conference of the British Trades Union Congress, Patrick Gorman, Secretary-Treasurer, Amalgamated Meat Cutters, said:

The economy of the world at present is terribly lopsided. Some nations are without sufficient food, while they struggle for economic stabilization. Some nations afford their people an existence close to the borderline of starvation. . . . No labor movement in any nation can long remain substantial and maintain its growth unless it clings to the thought that our world is inhabited by a family of human beings—human beings who require the same nourishment for their existence, who experience the same hardships, the same pains, and occasionally the same moments of happiness which the whole human family experiences or desires to experience. . . . So long as a single nation of people is unhappy because of the inequities of a world economic system, our civilization will still be improperly planned.[26]

Democratic unions that want to promote the people's welfare and not totalitarian tyranny will cooperate with world plans to advance economic progress and living standards in every country where they operate. International action will strengthen the cooperation. Democratic unions have united in a new world federation free from Communist influence. It might be advisable, in addition, for unions engaged in the production and distribution of foodstuffs to form an International of Food Unions (within the new international) to cooperate with all the agencies working to increase the food supply.

Food shortages and malnutrition torment primarily (although not exclusively) the kind of people who become union members. An International of Food Unions would comprise labor organizations in the production and distribution of most kinds of foodstuffs. They

[26] Amalgamated Meat Cutters and Butcher Workmen, AFL, *Address of Patrick E. Gorman . . . Fraternal Delegate of the American Federation of Labor to the British Trades Union Congress Held in Margate, England, September 6 to 10, 1948* (1949), pp. 2, 7.

are in intimate contact with the economic and social problems of food. If these unions, in all countries where they exist, set up councils to cooperate with one another for study and action of their food problems, they can influence national progress in nutrition. If they set up an International of Food Unions, they can mesh in their national activities with world policy.

Such union cooperation fits in with the policy of Point Four (and with FAO). The policy, according to the State Department, "cannot be one solely or even mainly of government action; the United States will seek the cooperation of private institutions and other organizations, of business, finance, agriculture, *labor*, scientific, educational and other groups to complement and reinforce the governmental program." Already representatives of labor unions, American and European, have been in on the formulation of programs and have been helping to carry them out under the Marshall Plan. It will be so with Point Four and its work to develop the means with which to feed the world's people.

4. FOOD AS A LIBERATING FORCE

To feed people is not simply to fill their bellies, although this is important in more than a physical sense.

Cato the Elder said, "The belly . . . has no ears." This is, however, a limited truth. A hungry belly may have no ears for truth, justice, and peace; but a hungry belly may have a millions ears with which to hear demagogues who preach injustice, national and race hatreds, and war. As hungry people are prone to desperate action, so a hungry world is never altogether peaceful and progressive.

Our newer nutritional understanding sees in food, moreover, a means to liberate man from disease, from sloth and servitude, from immorality. In this sense the basic element of policy to consider is where food fits into the creative job of shaping a free world of free peoples.

A new vision has come to inspire men of goodwill—a vision of what food can do for humanity:

The science of nutrition promises to unsettle society as nothing has done since the Industrial Revolution. The effect of an adequate diet on the stupid, the shiftless and the anti-social will be profound. Apathy is one of the common attributes of the underfed, whether in the Orient, in parts of Europe or in our own South. Clinical nutritionists will testify that listlessness, even lack of appetite, is a symptom of lack of nourishment. The mishaps of life begin to mutilate the human creature in the first moments after conception, and none more powerfully than poor nutrition. Given an adequate diet, with the magic it works on dull brains and slacked muscles, and persons all over the world who now "know their places" will be found making new places for themselves.[27]

The elements of backwardness in Africa, Latin America, and Asia are not racial in their origin, but historical and social-economic. The race-superiority mongers are bad scientists and worse human beings. Sloth, inertia, and servility among "backward" people are fundamentally products of malnutrition and disease that flourish in the midst of backward social-economic and cultural conditions. Authorities estimate that nearly half the world's people—1,000,000,000—suffer from disease. More food and better food, and abolition of such degenerating diseases as malaria (it affects 300,000,000 people) can work a revolution among those peoples. They will rise from their knees and stand up as freer men in a freer society.

What starvation and malnutrition can do to degenerate human beings has been the subject of experimental verification. In 1945 scientists of the University of Minnesota carried on a research project on semi-starvation with thirty-six conscientious objectors as the guinea pigs. They were put on a restricted diet of 1700 calories (considerably higher than the Latin American, Asiatic, and postwar European average) for six months. This is a summary of the findings on what semi-starvation does to people:

The tendency toward spontaneous activity, universally present in healthy adults, was notably lacking.

· Men saw the negative side of things more than ever before. Discouragement and lack of confidence often followed in the wake of their encounters with the real world.

One of the more profound changes was the increased unsociability of the men. . . . They lost their sense of humor; did not sing or whistle; music failed to bring its former warmth. They were not interested in the ideas and activities of others, except as related to getting food.

Decisions came very hard to those on starvation diets. On walking, a man could not make up his mind which corner to take. Little matters, on which decisions are usually inconsequential, became matters of delibera-

[27] Arthur Moore, *The Farmer and the Rest of Us* (1945), p. 211.

tion, with all the torment that overtakes a person unable to choose between two alternatives.

Although fasting supposedly quickens one spiritually, none of the men reported significant progress in their religious lives. Most of them felt that the semi-starvation had coarsened rather than refined them. They marveled at how thin their moral and social veneers seemed to be.

These findings emphasize the negative aspect of what food—or rather its lack—can do to human beings. The positive aspect appears in the newer nutritional understanding of how food may be used to build better men, women, and children.

Ill health, malnutrition, and social-economic backwardness work together to distort human progress. They call for unified action. In the fall of 1949 two UN agencies, FAO and the World Health Organization (WHO), held a conference of their Joint Expert Committee on Nutrition. Their objective was to outline "a program to increase food production in areas susceptible to agricultural development and in which ill health, particularly severe endemic malaria, is the primary obstacle to such development." The work will cost $10,000-000 and cover at least 10,000,000 acres of agricultural land now inadequately worked by disease-ridden people in the Eastern Mediterranean area, Southeast Asia, the Western Pacific, and Latin America.[28]

Nutritional science is not much more than twenty-five years old, yet it already provides enough evidence that food can improve human beings. Let me cite some of this evidence; to begin with, the findings that gave nutritional science an initial great advance:

Differences in mineral intake, determined both by soil differences and human dietary habits, undoubtedly are a factor in the extraordinary contrast—as striking as that between the scrubby Indian cattle and the high-bred imported breeds—between the tall and hardy Pathans and Hunzas of North India and the undersized and disease-ridden Bengali and Madrassi of the South. McCarrison, in one of the most famous experiments in nutritional history, fed rats on a diet identical with that of the Hunzas, who live on whole grains, vegetables, sprouted legumes, apricots and goats' milk, and whose irrigated fields are fertilized in some degree by the rock silt carried down from the mountains by ancient aqueducts. Other rats he fed on polished and phosphorus-deficient rice, tapioca, pulses and vegetables, plus a little milk—the diet on which most of the

[28] News story, *New York Times,* October 23, 1949.

southern Indian populations subsist. The rats fed on the Hunza diet grew rapidly, were seldom sick, mated with enthusiasm and had healthy young. When they were killed at an age corresponding to 55 years in man, the autopsies showed almost no evidence of disease. In contrast, the rats fed on the South Indian diet developed a multitude of diseases.[29]

As important was this discovery: rats fed on the Hunza diet were peaceful and cooperative, while rats fed on the South Indian diet were belligerent and vicious, attacking one another and the keepers.

British scientists kept up their work on nutrition. It brought results in World War II, when the British people were better fed and healthier than they were with prewar food consumption. Many basic dietary improvements were made, including abandonment of the inadequate, wasteful bread and flour fortification program and adoption of the National Wholemeal loaf. Nutritional advances were also made in the United States:

In the case of riboflavin, in 1936, three-fourths of all families had diets that fell below the National Research Council's recommendations; in 1942 about one-half were below this mark. In calcium, thiamine and ascorbic acid, where in 1936 only one-half were up to the recommendations of the National Research Council, by 1942 the proportion had risen to two-thirds for calcium, three-fourths for thiamine and nine-tenths for ascorbic acid. There are also marked dietary improvements in vitamin A value, iron and protein.[30]

Scientists and reformers throughout the world respond to the new nutritional understanding. A number of food scientists in Japan, for example, are working on remaking the Japanese people through improved nutrition. They argue that the Japanese diet of rice, fish, and more rice is a monotonous, unhealthy diet, in which, among other things, there are not enough animal proteins and vegetables. Their investigations have shown that life energy and life expectancy are greater in those parts of Japan where little rice is eaten. These scientists (one of whom has developed a substitute for soy sauce)

[29] TVA, *Food at the Grass Roots*, p. 28.

[30] Theodore W. Schultz, *Agriculture in an Unstable Economy* (1945), p. 72. We may recall, from an earlier chapter, Professor Schultz's conclusion that, with the American National income "at the 1944 level and with farm prices at 90 per cent of parity (very high incomes and relatively low farm prices), not more than 10 per cent more food would be needed to be added as a supplement to what consumers would buy to meet the nutritional standards."

propose a campaign of nutrition education for more varied diets, together with a program of research on new foods. Food, the scientists insist, can increase the Japanese people's stature, improve their eyesight and their teeth, to begin with; it can go farther as more progress is made.

A 1948 FAO report gave evidence of what can be done with food on the basis of what is being done in New Zealand:

Before the war the chief deficiencies in the New Zealand diet were iron, iodine, calcium, and thiamine. Iodized salt was introduced and the incidence of goiter among school children fell from 33 per cent to 8 per cent. The use of higher extraction wheat has doubled the intake of thiamine. A free milk scheme, covering 90 per cent of the school children, has been introduced to overcome the deficiency of calcium. These, coupled with a high level of food consumption, have resulted in improved health and progressively lower mortality rates.

Much has been done to postpone death. Children born today in the United States have an average life expectancy of about eighteen years more than their grandparents. This progress has come about largely from learning how to combat infections.

But not nearly as much has been done to make old age healthy as to add to its years. Degenerative diseases of the circulatory system and kidneys will kill probably one-half of the children born in 1940. These diseases, which are particularly deadly among older people, range from heart trouble, cancer, and diabetes to hardening of the arteries, cerebral hemorrhage, and arthritis.

Research in recent years has, at long last, begun to work on diseases of age, and substantial progress already has been made. Cancer is beginning to yield to medicine. Another example: in 1949 a partial cure, or rather "control" for rheumatoid arthritis was discovered in the form of two new hormones: ACTH (Compound E) made from the pituitary glands of hogs, and cortisone from the adrenal glands of cattle. These hormones may prove useful to relieve other degenerative diseases. Already ACTH is proving an effective agent for the treatment of rheumatic fever, asthma, hay fever, drug sensitivity, and other allergy illnesses. Although available only in very small quantities, ACTH and cortisone provide new weapons for the attack on arthritis. As a direct result of their discovery the Federal Security Administration set up a committee of medical scientists to study the new methods as well as advise on a program of research on the basic causes of the various forms of rheumatism and allied degenerative diseases.

As important, if not more so, is growing research and understanding on how to prevent the degenerative diseases of age. Malnutrition is a major factor in the origins of these diseases and in their courses. Hence one preventive is use of the right kind of foods. "Good nutrition," according to Dr. Charles Glen King, Scientific Director of the Nutrition Foundation, "can make a contribution to the added years of our lives, to make them years of vigorous living, not just survival."

It all adds up to this: We have the scientific knowledge to use food as a liberating force. We can end hunger, go on to use food to abolish physical and psychological malformations in human beings. Men and women can become more alive mentally, more independent personally, more moral.

A hungry world cannot be an altogether moral world. I am not arguing that the man with a filled belly is necessarily a moral man. I am arguing that malnourished people, tormented with physical and mental deformations, are not the best material for moral and cultural living. In its nutritional and medical aspects food can be used to build finer human beings.

For consider: With proper nutrition our children can be born without congenital physical or mental defects, and they all can grow into healthy adults. The aging process can be retarded by nutrition and medicine, with a prolongation of the active life-span. Still more desirable, man's final years on earth can be made healthier, more satisfyingly alive as the degenerative diseases of age are prevented, cured, or eased. In between youth and old age the growing understanding of food use can help to conquer physical and mental disease; to modify, if not end, the physical deformity and the psychosomatic ill health that create the neuroses out of which much of the world's evil springs.

Food's liberating potentials can come alive with the combined use of available technical-scientific understanding and social-economic policy. All barriers of misunderstanding or of resistance must be swept aside. No nation can enjoy freedom, independence, and peace unless these are enjoyed by all nations. In the words of FAO's director: "The key to the problem of food and people is international cooperation."

INDEX

366 INDEX

Concentration, industrial, 214, 230-31, 232; see also Mergers

Confederation of Food Unions (proposed), 303-304

Congress of Industrial Organizations, 191, 298-99, 301

Conservation, livestock, 137

Conservation, soil, 6, 103, 145, 354; in Chile, 346; in China, 347; farm and range lands (U.S.), 103-104, 117-26, 129-30; and Point Four program, 354; in Soviet Russia, 342; and unions, 145; in Western Hemisphere, 353; see also Natural resources; Reforestation; Soil depletion; Soil erosion

Consumers, 54; advice center for (Great Britain), 339; cooperatives, 117, 169; frozen meats and, 157; preferences in food, 154; prices and, 185; protection for, 67-73, 174; reaction to The Jungle, 34; welfare of, 170, 177, 225, 226, 235, 241; see also Grading; Purchasing power

Consumption: and advertising, 222; of fish, 152-53; of food and balanced diet, 160, changes in, 5, 153-54, 226, relative per capita, 154, in Soviet Russia, 341; of meat—ancient, 16-17, Colonial (American), 36, early modern, 28, eighteenth century, 30, modern, 13-14, (per capita) 5, 31, 98, 111-113, 346; and prices, 42, 44, 136; and production, 205; see also Supply

Converted foods, 114

Conveyors, 44-45, 209, 257, 272-74

Cooperation, 304; AFL-CIO, 299, 303; farm community, 124; farmer-labor, 141-48; international, 355, 362; socialist, 344; union-management, 11, 12, 148, 150, 174, 178, 228, 239, 274, 279, 291-92, 298, 304, 312-19

Cooperatives: abattoirs 109; and conservation, 121; consumer, 117. 169; farm, 131, 133, 134, 165, 215, (China) 346, (Great Britain) 338; livestock, 116-17; lockers, 135; marketing, 4, 117, 130-31, 134; as meat outlets, 167; poultry, 135; processing, 130-31, 134, (Great Britain) 338; and unions, 143-145

Corey, Lewis, 48 n., 273 n.

Corn, 102-103, 137; hybrid, 119, 341

Corn Products Refining Company, 228

Corporate state, 20, 21, 235

Corporation farming, 133, 134 n.

Corporations: ancient, 21; food, 162; public, see Public corporations; state (ancient) 19-20

Cortisone, 268-69, 362

Costs, 265-67; distribution, 164; labor, 46, 163; livestock, 138, 265 n.; production, 42, 44, 193, 209, 259; "test cost" formulas, 49-50, 93

Cotton, 105-119

Coulton, G. G., 24 n.

Cows, 97, 113

Credit, farm, 131

Cromwell, Oliver, 27, 28

Cross-breeding, 98, 99, 106-107, (Brazil, Cuba) 346; see also Hybrid

Cuba, 107, 346, 352

Cuban Cane Products Company, 190 n.

Cudahy, Michael, 46

Cudahy Packing Company, 48, 49-53, 63, 77, 93, 189-93 passim, 196, 201, 204 n., 208, 265 n., 276-79 passim

Cured meats and curing, 28, 36, 71, 74, 102, 158, 257, 269

Dairy products industry: consumption of products, 153-54; livestock, 107, (Great Britain) 337, see also Cows; monopoly in, 90, 229; packers in, 179, 188, 208; production, 113, 152; productive capacity, 209 n.; productivity, 252; products used as feed, 102, for relief, 137; profits, 195; in undeveloped areas, 335; unionism in, 281; value of products and labor force, 4

Daniels, Dr. Farrington, 330

Darby, Dr. William J., 332 n.

Davies, Godfrey, 28 n.

DDT, 269, 331 n.

Debs, Eugene V., 282

Deere and Company, 228

Deflation, 76

Dehairing, 256

Dehorning, 100

Dehydration, 114; of feed, 100; of food, 7, 153 n.

Delicatessen, 208; stores, 170

Democracy, 319, 353; economic, 150; guild, 22; industrial, 317; Jacksonian, 147; in Puritan revolution, 27; opposition to, 244; unionism and, 281, 298

Denmark, 204 n., 205

Depressions, 9, 11, 136, 137, 168, 202, 260, 287, 293

Devon (cattle), 123

De Voto, Bernard, 105

Dewhurst and Associates, J. F., 159 n., 160

Dickie, Jack W., 155

Diet, 6, 153, 158-60, 217, 218, 224, 225-

National Food Authority (proposed), 240

National Grange, 130, 132-33, 182 n.

National Independent Meat Packers Association, 73, 187, 211, 212, 214, 219, 235

National Industrial Conference Board, 155

National Industrial Recovery Act, 294

National Industry Meat Council, 185

National Labor Relations Act, 278-79, 294, 307

National Labor Relations Board, 279, 294-96, 302, 307

National Livestock Association, 127

National Livestock Marketing Association, 131, 182 n.

National Packing Company, 51-53

National Park Service, 104

National parks, 128

National Public Health Service, 118

National Railway Union, 282

National Recovery Act, 11

National Recovery Administration, 231-232, 294

National Research Council, 360

National Swine Growers, 182 n.

National War Labor Board, 280

National Wool Growers Association, 127-28, 148

Nationalization (Great Britain), 339

Natural resources, 118, 122, 354; see also Conservation; Resources

Negroes, 62, 244-45, 288, 290, 308

Nelson, Dr. D. H., 70

Netherlands, 331

New Deal, 293

New Leicester (sheep), 28

New Mexico Wool Growers Association, 129

New York City, 310; first cold storage warehouse, 39; livestock in (early 19th cent.), 29

New Zealand: diet, 361; food supply, 352; livestock production, 96, 335; meat consumption, 31; meat production, 205; packing industry, 48 n., 206

Nicholls, W. H., 200

Nile River, 344

Norman, Dr. A. G., 325

Norman, N. Philip, 29 n., 115 n., 159 n.

Norris Reservoir, 125

North Africa, 340, 352

North Sea fishing grounds, 328

Norway, 352

Nourse and Associates, Edwin G., 209 n.

Nowak, Stanley, 289 n.

Nutrition, 5-6, 10, 13, 29, 97, 99, 111-117, 122, 156, 158-60, 217-27, 239, 351, 354, 357-62; see also Diet

Nutrition Foundation, 218, 362

Oceania, 335

Office of Price Administration, 92, 182-187, 197, 202, 212

Ohio Farm Bureau, 133, 146

Oils: as by-product, 43; consumption, 154, 160; packers and, 188; production (Africa), 344; rendering, 211; tariffs on, 137

Oleomargarine: adulteration, legislation against, 68; as by-product, 43; from fat, 269; and packers, 179, 188; production (Africa), 344; restrictions on production, 177

O'Mahoney, Sen. Joseph C., 242

Oppenheim, J. H., 97

Organizations, 314-15; see also Farming and farmers; Livestock (organizations in industry); Trade Associations; Unionism

Overseas Food Corporation, 344

Packaged foods, 7, 176-77, 267; meat, 154, 155, 157, 163; see also Vending machines

Packers and Stockyards Act, 87, 107-110, 187

Packers' Consent Decree, 86-92, 107, 188, 232

Packing industry, 36-53, 107-111, 179-242; accident rate, 247-48; chain grocers and, 166-68; chemistry in, 267-69; conditions in, 54-60; cooperatives, 116; as depicted in *The Jungle*, 34; inspection, 68-70; labor in, 243-274; locker plants, 116-17, 135; mechanization, 251-59; modern plants, 257-58; monopoly in, 9, 45-53, 179, 228-42; production, 180-82, 259; productivity, 209, 253, 264, 265; profits, 7-8, 41, 42, 75, 187-88, 189-91, 195-202, 207, 213; public corporation (proposed), 238-42; unionism in, 275-319; value of products and labor force, 3-4, 259; wages, 259-67; see also Independents (packing industry); Livestock; Slaughtering

Pakistan, 348

Pancreatin, 180

Paraguay, 204 n.

Parity prices, 131-45 *passim*

Patents, 39, 162, 189

Patman Act, 172

Patton, James G., 146